School Choice or Best Systems

What Improves Education?

School Choice or Best Systems

What Improves Education?

Edited by

Margaret C. Wang
Temple University Center for Research in Human Development and Education

Herbert J. Walberg
University of Illinois at Chicago

LEA LAWRENCE ERLBAUM ASSOCIATES, PUBLISHERS
2001 Mahwah, New Jersey London

The final camera copy for this volume was prepared by the editors.

Lawrence Erlbaum Associates, Inc., Publishers
10 Industrial Avenue
Mahwah, NJ 07430

Cover design by Kathryn Houghtaling Lacey

Library of Congress Cataloging-in-Publication Data

School choice or best systems: What improves education? / edited by Margaret C. Wang and Herbert J. Walberg.
p. cm.
Includes bibliographical references and indexes.
ISBN 0-8058-3486-9 (cloth : alk. paper) — ISBN 0-8058-3487-7 (pbk. : alk. paper)
1. School choice—United States. 2. Educational change—United States. 3. School improvement programs—United States—Case studies. I. Wang, Margaret C. II. Walberg, Herbert J., 1937–

LB1027.9 .S535 2001
379.1'11'0973—dc21 00-069168
CIP

Books published by Lawrence Erlbaum Associates are printed on acid-free paper, and their bindings are chosen for strength and durability.

Printed in the United States of America
10 9 8 7 6 5 4 3 2 1

Contents

Preface

Margaret C. Wang
Temple University Center for Research In Human Development and Education

Herbert J. Walberg
University of Illinois at Chicago

The chapters in this book provide an overview of research and practical applications of innovative—even radical—school reforms being implemented across the nation. The original versions of the chapters were presented and discussed at an invitational conference co-sponsored by the Johnson Foundation and the National Center on Education in the Inner Cites and the Laboratory for Student Success at Temple University Center for Research in Human Development and Education. On the basis of intensive discussions and debate, the authors revised their papers, which constitute the main body of this book.

We invited to the conference education leaders and scholars known for their differing views. Also represented were parents, teachers' union leaders, principals, superintendents, and state and federal officials. The overall goals were to provide a national forum for examining findings from the latest and most significant research on school reform and to showcase school systems and programs that appear to be effective in achieving student success.

In addition to addressing the key issues framed by the commissioned papers, conference participants devoted much time to participating in small work groups. They discussed what is known from research and practical applications of the various reform strategies and their implications for next-step recommendations to advance schools' capacity for achieving student success.

Despite their differing opinions, the conference participants respectfully heard views sharply different from their own. They made constructive suggestions for improved policies and research that would be more definitive with respect to opposing views.

Many approaches to school reform were discussed. They may be characterized as lying along a continuum of parental choice versus best systems. Near one extreme are publicly and privately funded scholarships that allow parents to choose and even govern schools for their children. Near the other extreme are centralized state or district systems that specify uniform goals, policies, and programs for each school. The chapters in this book describe these alternatives and a range of intermediate forms. These alternatives are referred to as "school choice" and "best systems."

School Choice

Parental choice includes both charter schools and scholarships. Charter schools are paid for by and accountable to the public, but are governed by private boards and are, to varying degrees, independent of state regulations, local boards, and teachers' unions. "Weak" charter laws in some states, however, allow unsympathetic local boards to retain considerable operating control over charter school staff. Private scholarships, now used in several dozen cities, are funded by both firms and wealthy individuals. They enable children and youth, usually from economically and educationally disadvantaged backgrounds, to attend private, that is, parochial and independent schools. Public scholarships or vouchers distribute publicly funded grants to parents, which can be employed in independent and parochial schools.

Best Systems

Experiences in several cities and discussions at the conference suggested a number of best systems that appear promising for increasing students' achievement. Many conferees, both those favoring best systems and those preferring school choice, would agree with a core set of system practices including the following:

- Basing planning on research.

- Aligning curriculum, teaching, and testing to goals.
- Decentralizing operational authority to the school level.
- Employing information systems to monitor progress.
- Holding schools accountable for meeting standards.
- Providing alternatives in cases of failure.

Overview of the Chapters

The chapters in the main body of this book are divided into the two fundamental approaches to contemporary education reform delineated. In the epilogue, we present our view of the consensual conclusions and recommendations that could be drawn from the chapters and conference discussions.

The choice section begins with an analysis of the economic theory of choice, which shows how education can be viewed as an industry like many others. In free-market societies, education may be judged at least in part by its productivity and its appeal to its customers or clients. Thinking about education in this way may seem novel or repugnant to some, but it affords a parsimonious means of analyzing and understanding school problems and identifying ways they can be solved.

The remaining chapters in Part I present findings on the achievement effectiveness and appeal of major forms of school choice now being investigated—charters and public and private scholarships or vouchers.

Part II begins with case studies of how the cities of Chicago; Birmingham, England; Washington, DC; San Antonio; and Houston are employing best systems to transform their school systems. Also included is a chapter on New York State's new Regents examination program that is apparently raising achievement in that state. One chapter is devoted to how school boards might request proposals for schools they believe most appropriate for their communities.

In our epilogue, we share what we learned at the conference. We synthesize what we learned at the conference. We summarize what we took to be the points by most of the conferees as well as those siding with school choice and best systems. Our conclusion offers some ways the two approaches may be reconciled.

This volume could not have come to fruition without much effort from many of our colleagues. To the authors of this volume, we thank you for your commitment to take time out of your busy schedule to discuss your work at the conference and to complete the final submission of your chapter. Finally, but not the least, a special acknowledgment of our deep appreciation to the administrative and editorial staff at Temple University Center for Research in Human Development and Education for their support throughout the preparation of the national conference and this volume. Julia St. George and Marilyn Murphy played critical coordinating roles to ensure a well-managed and productive conference. Stacy Loonstyn, Elena Lahr-Vivaz, and Robert Sullivan provided invaluable editorial support to ensure the timely completion of this publication.

Part I

School Choice

1

Understanding Market-Based School Reform

Herbert J. Walberg
Joseph L. Bast[1]
The Heartland Institute

The debate over the best way to reform public education in the United States has changed dramatically since we first collaborated to address the topic in the late 1980s (Walberg, Bakalis, Bast, & Baer, 1988) and even since our most recent collaborations (Bast & Walberg, 1994; Bast, Walberg, & Genetski, 1996; Walberg & Bast, 1993). Reform proposals considered radical then are now mainstream, whereas many ideas claimed to be best have faded from sight. The purpose of this chapter is to provide an understanding of market-based school reform. This chapter is divided into four sections.

The first section describes some of the events that illustrate the enormous momentum gained by market-based reform ideas during the past decade. It ends by observing that the rapid pace of change has left many reformers unprepared to understand or participate in the new reform debate.

The second section provides an overview of price and public choice theory, the two topics within the discipline of economics most important for understanding the theoretical basis of market-based reform. Most educators confuse the methodology of economics with ideology or bias. In fact, it is a value-neutral language for describing how an important part of the world works that yields testable propositions with predictive power. This section ends with a series of testable propositions about school reform.

The third section explains where various market-based school reform proposals fall in a taxonomy of privatization, or the process of moving a service or asset from the government sector to the market sector of society. The result is a series of tables revealing the choices that communities face once the tyranny of the status quo is overcome. By presenting these choices in an orderly format, we give advocates and critics a common vocabulary to carry the debate beyond its usual broad-stroke claims and denials.

The final section contains a brief summary and closing remarks. The reference section that follows is long because many critics of market-based school reform are unfamiliar with most of the important literature on the subject. A bibliography of specific references on school choice and sources for model legislation and bills follows the reference section.

THE RISE OF THE MARKET-BASED REFORM MOVEMENT

The most dramatic change in the national debate over school reform in the United States has been the rise in influence and sophistication of calls for market-based reforms (Kirkpatrick, 1997; Manno, 1998; Shokraii & Hanks, 1997). Even school choice critics admit that "political will behind tax programs and vouchers for educational and social services has climbed dramatically over the past decade" (Fuller & Elmore, 1996, p. 11).

Pilot voucher programs are operating in Milwaukee and Cleveland. Proposals for statewide voucher plans were introduced in more than 20 states in 1998.[2] The Center for Education Reform reported in August 1997 that 777 charter schools were approved and 750 were expected to be operating later that year, tripling the number from 2 years earlier. Approximately 200,000 students were expected to enroll (Allen, 1997). Significant tuition tax credit legislation was enacted into law in Arizona and Minnesota in 1997 and narrowly missed adoption in Illinois.

In recent years, other market-based reforms have also moved from theory to practice. Private-practice teaching—the idea that teachers can form professional practices similar to those created by lawyers and doctors and offer their services to schools in return for a negotiated fee (Beales, 1994)—has spread across the country and is now represented by a rapidly growing professional association. "Outsourcing" or contracting out for services by state and local governments and government school systems has become more widespread and accepted (Hendrie, 1996; Kittower, 1998; Staley, 1996).[3]

The notion that private-sector initiatives can improve public schools received a boost during the past decade from the private scholarship movement, a loosely organized national effort to test the voucher idea by offering privately funded tuition scholarships to the parents of school-age children (National Scholarship Center, 1994). The number of programs increased from one in 1991 to 41 in 1998 (CEO America, 1998). These programs are distinguished from other private scholarship efforts, many of long standing, by the random selection of recipients among applicants and other devices that allow social scientists to study the effects of choice on student achievement.

Politically, the profile of free-market reform ideas has risen because of Republican advances nationally and in state houses across the country, majority approval of vouchers in opinion polls, and approximately 70% approval among Blacks (Harwood Group, 1995; Phi Delta Kappa/Gallup, 1998).

Since 1996, voucher proponents have won major victories in both federal and state courts. In *Agostino v. Felton*, decided in June 1997, the U.S. Supreme Court ruled that public school teachers funded by federal tax dollars may teach special education classes to parochial school students inside the private institution. The ruling overturned a previous decision, *Aguilar v. Felton*, issued in 1985, that was widely viewed as a barrier to including religious schools in choice plans. On June 10, 1998, the Wisconsin Supreme Court ruled in favor of expanding the Milwaukee Parental Choice Program to include religious schools. School choice cases are pending in Arizona, Maine, Ohio, Pennsylvania, and Vermont.[4] The Wisconsin Supreme Court ruling was appealed to the U.S. Supreme Court, which in November 1998 allowed the program to stand (Institute for Justice, 1997; Landmark Legal Foundation, 1998).

Finally, the resources and sophistication of the organizations devoted to studying, popularizing, and advocating market-based school reform have grown considerably in the past decade. Public interest law organizations are helping to draft and successfully defend tuition tax credit and voucher bills; national think tanks are publishing books and policy studies and hosting conferences (Bast, Harmer, & Dewey, 1997; Judy & D'Amico, 1997; Peterson & Hassel, 1998; Shokraii & Barry,

1998); and state-based think tanks in 35 states are formulating school reform legislation and leading reform coalitions (National Education Association [NEA], 1998). New foundations, such as the Milton and Rose Friedman Foundation, provide funding to think tanks and other organizations that explore or promote market-based school reform.

The sudden emergence of well-organized advocates of market-based school reform surprised many long-time participants in the reform debate. Dismissing the market-based reform movement as being "anti-public education" or a front for the "religious right" has never passed the threshold of honest debate, but this hardly mattered when the market-based reform movement was financially weak and divided. Today, opponents of market-based reform risk being overwhelmed by an idea they barely understand, but that is popular with voters, judges, and elected officials.

To understand market-based school reform, one must first understand markets. The following two sections provide a brief overview of those aspects of economic methodology that are most often misunderstood or misrepresented by opponents of market-based reform.

WHAT ECONOMICS CAN TELL US ABOUT EDUCATION

> There's a saying among teachers: If you think education is expensive, try ignorance. Education is tremendously expensive in the United States, but what we are getting for our money is ignorance.
>
> — Chancellor (1990)

What Is Economics?

Economics is the science of how a particular society solves the problem of allocating scarce resources to fulfill competing needs (Friedman, 1976). Where resources are plentiful, there is no need for allocation, and therefore no economic problem. Where a single objective exists rather than many competing ends, the problem is technological rather than economical.

Positive economics explains how economic problems are solved and then uses this understanding to make reliable predictions. Theories are accepted as true (or unfalsified) if their predictions are validated by empirical evidence (Friedman, 1953/1982) or deduced from a rigorous theory or science of human action (Von Mises, 1949/1966, 1962/1978). Although proponents of empirical testing and proponents of deduction from first principles disagree on methodology, their descriptions of most market processes are similar, and consequently their predictions are too (Buchanan, 1979).[5]

Economic activity occurs in four sectors: government, households, civic (or nonprofit) institutions, and the marketplace. Each sector has its own rules and ends, which the positive economist accepts as given. Economic activity inside government and civic institutions, for example, is voting and giving or receiving commands. Within households, rules commonly resemble a primitive communism. In the marketplace, the primary activities are purchase, sale, savings, and investment.

Based on the discussion so far, delivering education or schooling[6] in the United States clearly fits the description of an economic problem. Most of the known resources that make schooling possible are scarce: teachers, administrators, books, other learning aids, and facilities. All of these resources must be purchased, which means bidding them away from competing uses. More than 80% of schooled children attend government schools, where policy is generally set by voting. The remaining children attend private schools, where policy is most often determined by contract, or are home-schooled, where a parent sets the rules.

Assumptions Versus Implications

Most doubts about the legitimacy of economics arise from assumptions in economic methodology. Economists, it is widely believed, assume such things as perfect competition, perfect information, zero transaction costs, the divisibility of goods and services, and that people act as rational profit maximizers in every part of our lives. It was this caricature of an economist that Bruce Fuller and Richard F. Elmore evidently had in mind when they described school choice proponents as "proponents of idealized markets" who view parents and youths as "blank slates" (Fuller & Elmore, 1996, p. 23).

The actual methodology of economists, called *methodological individualism*, is based on two principles: First, all social phenomena must be explained in terms of actions occurring at the level of individuals, and second, only the most minimal assumption about individual motivation—that people choose rationally among the choices they face—is allowed. The first principle was defended by Abell (1992):

> Things happen in the social world because individuals do and do not do things, and they are the only things that do or do not do things. All statements that attribute "doing" to other things can, in principle if not in practice, be translated without loss into statements about individuals doing things. (p. 191)

The second principle assumes great complexity of human action. Human action has so many determinants that a realistic model is impossible in principle: New variables could always be added to the model (Hayek, 1968). Moreover, a set of truly realistic assumptions would compose a photographic reproduction of the transaction. This reproduction would fail to accomplish the first-order task of any economic theory, namely to make more apparent the processes that lay beneath the surface of the economic phenomenon under study. This would surely be true of education in the United States, "a system with 15,000 districts, 85,000 schools, millions of staff members, and some 42,000,000 students [that] is so varied that almost anything you say is true somewhere" (Kirkpatrick, 1997, p. 34).

Economists solve the problem of complexity by assuming as little as possible about the motivation of the actors they study. This minimalist approach asserts only that human agents will choose rationally among the choices they face. This statement can be framed as a deduction from the human condition or asserted as the single fact most easily proven by empirical observation. In either case, it hardly fits the common definition of an "assumption."

Rather than claim to know or to judge an agent's values, economists speak of revealed preferences, that is, those values revealed by the act of choosing one item or course of action over another. Rational choice theory is silent on whether or not the agent's ends are rational or desirable in any way except that they are voluntarily chosen by the agent over other ends. According to Favell (1996):

> [The rational choice principle] is not psychological reductionism, nor does it imply reductionism in any way. Quite the contrary, methodological individualism can fairly be called psychologically minimalist in that it starts with an absurdly rudimentary model of the acting self and then borrows from psychology only the barest minimum required for fitting this model to observed social reality. (p. 156)

The same kind of reasoning shows why perfect competition, perfect information, and other implications of economic systems are not properly called assumptions, though this is the shorthand expression commonly used even by economists. Properly speaking, these are parameters set forth when framing the economic institution to be studied. They have been identified because they result from propositions that have been validated by empirical tests or deduced from the underlying rigorous theory of human action. Once again, it would require us to assume more, not less, if we opened the model to consider every fact or theory that might play a role in a given economic transaction.

Milton Friedman (1953/1982) pointed out that conformity of a hypothesis' assumptions with reality is not a test of the validity of the hypothesis. Indeed, he wrote, just the opposite is more often the case:

> Truly important and significant hypotheses will be found to have assumptions that are wildly inaccurate descriptive representations of reality, and, in general, the more significant the theory, the more unrealistic the assumptions (in this sense). The reason is simple. A hypothesis is important if it explains much by little, that is, if it abstracts the common and crucial elements from the mass of complex and detailed circumstances surrounding the phenomena to be explained and permits valid predictions on the basis of them alone. To be important, therefore, a hypothesis must be descriptively false in its assumptions; it takes account of, and accounts for, none of the many other attendant circumstances, since its very success shows them to be irrelevant for the phenomena to be explained. (pp. 14–15)

The great virtue of economic methodology, then, is that it uses a model of human action that is free from assumptions about values, cultures, or norms and a model of economic transactions that is free from easily manipulated assumptions about ignorance (e.g., Rawls' differentially permeable *veil of ignorance*), unexamined transaction costs, or ill-defined limitations on choices (Coleman, 1990; Popper, 1962/1971). As Favell (1996) put it:

> [The result is a] sober and materialist frame [that] offers a great improvement on normative social science saturated with reifications about culture and value: all the shrill talk of inviolable ethnic and cultural identities, collective norms so often obtuse to any kind of elementary analysis or breakdown to the individual level. (p. 294)

Public Choice Theory and Market Failure

Public choice theory is the application of economic methods to the study of social and political institutions. Modern public choice theory began in 1928 when mathematician John Von Neumann and economist Oskar Morgenstern applied the mathematical theory of strategy games to the problem of human action in the context of social rules. The following passage, written in 1944, shows that Von Neuman and Morgenstern (1944/1964) clearly understood the significance of their accomplishment for bringing economic reasoning to bear on matters that previously were thought to be outside of the domain of economists:

> We think that the procedure of the mathematical theory of games of strategy gains definitely in plausibility by the correspondence which exists between its concepts and those of social organizations. On the other hand, almost every statement which we—or for that matter anyone else—ever made concerning social organizations, runs afoul of some existing opinion. And, by the very nature of things, most opinions thus far could hardly have been proved or disproved within the field of social theory. It is therefore a great help that all our assertions can be borne out by specific examples from the theory of games of strategy. (p. 43)

Starting with simple two-person games, Von Neumann and Morgenstern showed how the economic model of rational choice and methodological individualism could be used to predict the conduct of people facing certain incentives, rules of conduct, and other environmental considerations. The result was a rich vein of research into the behavior of voters, members of interest groups, bureaucrats, and elected officials (Buchanan & Tullock, 1974; Gwartney & Wagner, 1988; Mueller, 1977/1987; Ross, 1987).

Positive public choice theory explains why some decisions are made collectively and others privately, and how rules and other institutional constraints influence the outcome of decision-making processes. *Normative* public choice theory asks whether the results of such decisions are optimal in a social sense or whether a different set of rules would generate more beneficial results.

Probably the best known and most important insight of game theory is the Prisoners' Dilemma. The hypothetical situation involves two prisoners being interrogated separately for a crime they committed together. Each prisoner is offered a sentence of just 1 year if he con-

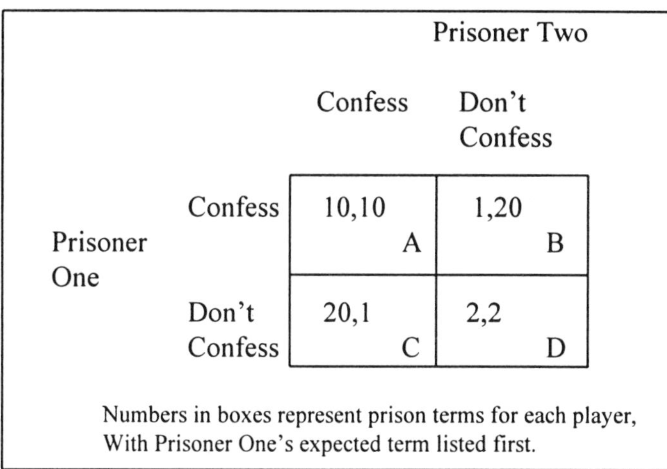

FIG. 1.1. Prisoners' Dilemma

fesses and his fellow prisoner does not; 2 years if both refuse to confess; 10 years if both prisoners confess; and 20 years if the other prisoner confesses and he does not. Each prisoner's choices are shown in Fig. 1.1.

Both prisoners would be better off if neither confesses (Box D) than if both confess (Box A). Nevertheless, it is in each prisoner's best interest to confess, with the result that both prisoners will receive 10-year sentences instead of 2-year sentences (Box A).[7]

Instead of two prisoners, the game could involve two persons deciding whether to contribute to the support of a local school. Both players might recognize that the community would be better off if everyone contributed to the school. Each player would benefit most if he or she could free ride on the contributions of the other player (in Fig. 1.1, this would be Box C for Player 1 and Box B for Player 2). Each player may also be motivated by the fear of being a sucker by paying more than his or her fair share while the other player avoids payment by misrepresenting his or her ability or willingness to contribute to the school (Box B for Player 1 and Box C for Player 2). The result is strategic behavior that results in less money being spent on the school than the players genuinely desired.

Game theory helps economists better understand instances where markets fail to arrive at optimal results. These cases frequently involve "spill-over effects" called *negative* externalities when an activity (e.g., confessing to a crime) imposes costs on third parties to the action or exchange and *positive* externalities when the activity (e.g., supporting a school) creates benefits for third parties. In such cases, buyers and sellers might not consider these externalities when making their decisions, resulting in over- or underinvestment in the activity.

Game theory shows that market failure may also occur when one person's consumption does not diminish the ability of others to also consume the product, a condition called *nonrivalous consumption* or *jointness of consumption.* Market failure can also occur when people who have not paid cannot be prevented from consuming the good, a condition called *nonexcludability. Public goods* by definition exhibit both jointness of consumption and nonexcludability.[8]

Whereas game theory helps economists understand how markets can fail, it also shows how markets often solve problems involving externalities and public goods. When a game is repeated many times, conventions and expectations develop that increase each actor's confidence that others will act reliably. Contracts can make these conventions well known and enforceable. For example, Beito (1988) described the use of restrictive real estate covenants obligating homeowners and any future homeowners to pay assessments levied by an owner's association.

Researchers have found that the vast majority of exchanges produce positive or negative externalities, meaning the presence of externalities is not sufficient grounds for government intervention (Kahn, 1970/1988). Most externalities are too small to attract the attention of policymakers or are solved by voluntary contracting among the affected parties (Coase, 1960). Seemingly indivisible goods can be broken up and sold (or resold) with value-added features to discourage free riding (Poole, 1980, 1982, 1985). Like externalities, *competition* has been found to be ubiquitous even in fields once thought to be natural monopolies (Kahn, 1970/1988).

Public Choice Theory and Government Failure

Applying economic theory to politics *does not* mean challenging the widespread notion that people who work for government have different values than those who choose to work in the private sector, or that voters do not take into account altruism and compassion when deciding how to vote (Hotelling, 1929). Public choice theory merely states that individual actors use reason to choose among ends that, to the economist, are given. The ends could include benevolence, patriotism, and so on. From this perspective, the public sector differs from the private sector only in the rules and institutions that prevail, not because the actors in each sector differ from one another in any way (Musgrave, 1959).

Public choice theory produces testable propositions predicting the behavior of elected officials and other government employees using a model that does not assume that benevolence, compassion, or altruism play a bigger role inside government than outside it. The behavior of voters, too, can be so modeled:

> Since there is no evidence that entrance into a voting booth or participation in the political process causes a personality transformation, there is sound reason to believe that the motivation of participants in the market and political processes is similar. (Gwartney & Wagner, 1988, p. 3)

Many testable propositions derived from public choice theory have been validated by empirical research. The following are most relevant to our purposes:

1. *Bureaucrats will tend to favor higher spending by their bureau.* Rather than passively implement policies adopted by elected officials, bureaucrats will act in ways that increase their income, authority, and prestige. In government, this frequently means expanding the size, jurisdiction, and budgets of their departments (Borcherding, 1977; Niskanen, 1971).

2. *Regulators will tend to represent the interests of those they are supposed to regulate.* Regulators will often be captured by the industries they are supposed to be regulating because of the latter's ability to influence political decisions affecting the regulator's budget, restrict access to information needed to implement regulations, and promise employment after regulators leave government service (Stigler, 1971).

3. *The most effective special interest groups will tend to favor higher spending.* Small groups of actors who receive *concentrated benefits* from government spending or regulation will tend to out-organize and have greater influence than the general public that pays the *widely*

disbursed cost of the benefits. Members of the latter group will tend to be rationally ignorant and vote on the basis of nonpolicy factors (name recognition, party label, etc.) or not vote at all (Olson, 1965/1971; Payne, 1991).

4. *The votes of Congress and other legislative bodies will not always reflect the wishes of the majority of their members.* Votes by deliberative bodies can be and often are manipulated by changing the order of a series of either–or choices (cycling) and by creating a secondary market for votes (logrolling). Both practices produce outcomes different from what would be produced by simple majority voting and that are undesirable in terms of the objectives identified by the elected officials (Buchanan & Tullock, 1974).

5. *Elected officials will not share most of the views of most of their constituents.* Voters typically have a choice between two candidates for public office, each representing a position on many issues of interest to a voter. The odds that the candidates' views on even a handful of major issues will match those of any one constituent are small, and the odds of the winner in the election sharing that constituent's views are even smaller (Hotelling, 1929; Mueller, 1979/1987).

6. *Elected officials will use the powers of their offices to entrench themselves in office, making them less accountable to voters.* The rate at which incumbents are reelected is more than 90% at both the national and state levels. Incumbents use free postage, generous office budgets, restrictive ballot access laws, district gerrymandering, and limits on campaign contributions to preserve their status (Payne & Jerbich, 1992; Polsby & Popper, 1991).

7. *Elected officials will tend to favor higher spending.* Recognizing the political influence of organized beneficiaries of government largesse, elected officials will build political constituencies by promising new entitlements and subsidies financed by higher spending. Focused primarily on reelection, the long-term consequences of creating new programs will be discounted (Neustadt & May, 1986; Payne, 1991).

8. *The longer an elected official is in office, the more he or she will favor higher spending.* An elected official's ability to dispense favors by increasing spending rises with tenure and experience. Because dispensing favors is a way to build dependent constituencies and reward campaign supporters, the typical elected official will increasingly favor higher spending (Payne, 1991).

9. *Government officials elected or appointed at the local level are more likely to be held accountable to taxpayers than are state or nationally elected and appointed officials.* The relatively small size and open borders of local political jurisdictions allows taxpayers to "vote with their feet" by moving to jurisdictions that better meet their needs. The result is competition among political units for residents, resulting in greater efficiency and accountability (Hirschman, 1970; Mueller, 1979/1987, Tiebout, 1956). Federal systems of government therefore "function more like markets than like single firms or hierarchical bureaucracies" (Bish, 1988, p. 366).

Many of these propositions predict that government spending and regulating will increase over time to levels that exceed those that would have been voluntarily chosen by voters or newly elected officials. This robust finding has convinced some public choice theorists to enter the modern-day political debate on the side of fiscal conservatives and libertarians, but it should not be confused with the philosophies of those groups (Friedman, 1980, 1984). That government tends to grow beyond what its participants themselves believe to be its appropriate size and role is a factual, not an ideological, claim.

Public Choice Theory and Education

Public choice theory has produced many testable propositions concerning education. Next, we introduce eight propositions and summarize some of the empirical research that has supported them. The research cited is only meant to be suggestive and not a complete survey of the literature.

Proposition 1: In school systems where there are no consequences for either success or failure, higher spending will not produce better results.

Empirical Data: Repeated studies by independent researchers have found minimal or no positive correlations between higher spending on government schools and student achievement (Berthoud, 1996; Hanushek, 1994, 1996; Walberg, 1993, 1998; Walberg & Fowler, 1987).

Huge spending increases on troubled school districts, such as Kansas City, have failed to produce any improvement in test scores or reduction in Black–White test score gaps ("The Cash Street Kids," 1993; Ciotti, 1998; Presser, 1991).

Research published by the W. E. Upjohn Institute found that "higher teacher salaries have had little if any discernible impact on the quality of newly recruited teachers" (Ballou & Podgursky, 1997, p. 163).

Proposition 2: As the source of a school's funding shifts further away from those who benefit from the school, the school's cost-effectiveness will fall.

Empirical Data: Student achievement is closely and positively related to the percentage of funding derived from local sources (Hoxby, 1997, 1998; Walberg, 1997).

As responsibility for school funding has shifted from local governments to state governments and, to a lesser extent, the federal government, government school productivity has fallen approximately 2.5% to 3% a year (Hanushek, 1996; Vedder, 1996).

Waste and lack of measurable results is greatest for Title I and Head Start programs, programs that rely on federal rather than local funding (Shokraii & Fagan, 1998; Walberg, 1997).

Proposition 3: Competing special interest groups will capture the surplus "rent" generated by the government schools' monopoly on tax funding.

Empirical Data: Teachers, not concerned parents or idealistic elected officials, led the movement for government schooling in the United States during the mid-19th century and were later instrumental in the government take-over of private schools in England (Spring, 1982; West, 1965, 1967).

Average government teacher salaries and benefits are significantly higher than those of comparable professions (Bast et al., 1996; Vedder, 1996).

Bureaucracies in government school systems are far larger and more costly than those in private school systems (Chubb & Moe, 1990; Walberg et al., 1988). Public elementary and secondary schools in 1995 employed 2.3 million people who do not teach, compared to approximately 2.5 million teachers (Organization for Economic Cooperation and Development [OECD], 1996).

Whereas less than 11% of the private-sector workforce was unionized in 1995, government schools are nearly 100% unionized (Lieberman, 1997; Peltzman, 1996).

Proposition 4: Because they can be held accountable to their customers, private schools (all other things held constant) should produce larger gains in student achievement per dollar spent as well as report superior results by other measures than their government school counterparts.

Empirical Data: Catholic schools in the United States spend significantly less per student than government schools (Boaz & Barrett, 1996; Genetski & Tully, 1992).

Though early attempts to find a private school effect met with mixed success (Clune & Witte, 1990; Haertel, James, & Levin, 1988; James & Levin, 1988), later research has found a significant positive impact on student test scores (Coleman & Hoffer, 1987; Patrinos & Ariasingam, 1997; Sander, 1995; Vedder, 1996).

Catholic schools dramatically increase educational achievement among minorities in urban areas compared to minorities attending government schools, even after the schools' allegedly tighter admission criteria have been taken into account (Neal, 1997a, 1997b; Shokraii, Olson, & Youssef, 1997).

Catholic schools have more of the characteristics of effective schools than their government counterparts (Chubb & Moe, 1990; U.S. Department of Education, 1987). Private schools tend to be more racially integrated and successful in teaching racial tolerance and public spiritedness than government schools (Greene, 1998).

Proposition 5: Opposition to cost cutting and reforms that would provide greater accountability to customers will come primarily from the interest groups benefiting from the government school monopoly.

Empirical Data: Teacher unions spent $30 million to defeat Proposition 226 (the Paycheck Protection Act) in California in 1998 and were expected to spend $4 million attempting to defeat Measure 59, a similar measure on the ballot in Oregon in late 1998 (NEA, 1998). Litigation against tax credits, charter schools, and voucher bills has been initiated and is usually funded by teacher unions (Lieberman, 1997).[9]

Teacher unions uniformly and adamantly oppose contracting out—even when it could save a school considerable amounts of money—because it threatens their own job security (Foer, 1997).

The strength of public-sector unions has a statistically significant negative effect on the likelihood of U.S. county governments contracting for goods and services (Lopez-de-Salinas, Shleifer, & Bodjmu, 1995).

Proposition 6: School board members are likely to be "captured" by administrators and teacher unions.

Empirical Data: Local school boards around the country are thoroughly cowed by teacher unions (Finn, 1995). Historically, school boards did not resist teacher unionization or collective bargaining (Lieberman, 1993, 1997).

In deference to their unions, school boards "show no preference for applicants [for teaching positions] who have strong academic records.... Public schools are no more likely to hire these candidates than those with far weaker academic records" (Ballou & Podgursky, 1997, p. 164).

The National Association of School Boards adopts positions that are largely indistinguishable from those of unions, including calling for more funding and opposing school choice (Clowes, 1998).

Proposition 7: Because they are more likely to be held accountable to parents, private schools are more likely to adopt policies popular with parents than are government schools.

Empirical Data: Polling reveals that parents and the general public are more likely to agree with private school administrators and teachers than with government school administrators and teachers on issues such as discipline, core curriculum, and the goals of education (Harwood Group, 1995).

Polling data reveal that parents of students attending charter schools are more likely to approve the policies of their chosen school than are parents of students attending government schools (Greene, 1998; Vanourek, Manno, Finn, & Bierlein, 1997a).

Polls show that a large majority of parents (and about 80% of Black families) would choose private schools over government schools if tuition was not a consideration (Harwood Group, 1995; Styring, 1998).

Case studies in Chicago show that Catholic schools were more likely than government schools to change curriculum and other school policies in response to enrollment loss (Cibulka, 1993).

Proposition 8: Programs that require schools to compete for tuition dollars should show improvements in student achievement and in measures of effective organization.

Empirical Data: Student achievement is statistically and negatively related to the degree of market concentration in the local school market, meaning that policies that allow competition result in higher student achievement (Borland & Howsen, 1992, 1993).

Early evaluations suggest that charter schools are very successful (Cheung, Murphy, & Nathan, 1998; Gifford & Keller, 1996; Nathan, 1996; Vanourek, Manno, Finn, & Bierlein, 1997a, 1997b).

In initial evaluations of the Milwaukee program, John Witte, choice skeptic, found high levels of parental satisfaction and participation, high student retention levels, and "more than adequate educational institutions," but little effect on student test scores (Witte, 1991, p. 17). Witte (1992) called for further experimentation with private school choice.

The latest studies of student achievement in schools participating in the pilot voucher programs in Milwaukee and Cleveland show positive results (Greene, Peterson, Du, Borger, & Frazier, 1996; Greene, Peterson, & Howell, 1997; Peterson, Greene, & Howell, 1998; Rouse, 1996, 1998).

Studies of students in private voucher programs show significant positive results (Beales & Wahl, 1995).

Student achievement and parental satisfaction is high in Vermont, a state in which public payment of private school tuition is widespread and of long standing (Doyle, 1981; McClaughry, 1984, 1995; Walberg & Bast, 1993).

These propositions make a strong case for continued movement toward market-based school reform. In the next section, different *strategies* for implementing these reforms are examined.

PRIVATIZATION AND SCHOOL REFORM

Proposals for market-based school reforms are part of a larger movement taking place in the United States and internationally to shift responsibility for producing goods and services from the public sector to the private sector. The strategies and vocabulary of the privatization movement, therefore, provide useful background for understanding market-based school reform proposals.

Privatization Defined

The word *privatize* (actually *reprivatize*) first appeared in print in 1969 in a book by management guru Peter F. Drucker. A 1971 essay in *Harper's Magazine* written by E. S. Savas marked the first presentation of outsourcing and service shedding as a strategy for reducing government costs and improving the quality of services. The word *privatization* did not appear in a dictionary until 1983.

Writing in 1992, Savas gave two definitions of the word *privatization*:

> In the broadest definition, one which emphasizes a philosophical basis, privatization means relying more on the private institutions of society and less on government (the state) to satisfy peoples' needs. These private institutions include: the marketplace and businesses operating therein; voluntary organizations (religious, neighborhood, civic, cooperative, and charitable); and the individual, family, clan, or tribe. According to a second and more operational definition, privatization is the act of reducing the role of government or increasing the role of the private sector in an activity or in the ownership of assets. (p. 821)

Privatization, as defined, is a global phenomenon. Research conducted by the World Bank in the 1980s found that 87 countries had completed 626 privatization transactions and planned to undertake 717 more (Savas, 1992). In 1994, an estimated $60 billion worth of state-owned enterprises were sold to the private sector ("How to Privatize," 1995).

Savas organized privatization options into three methods: divestment, delegation, and displacement. Each of these methods has several specific approaches, as identified in Table 1.1.

Though most attention has focused on proposals to use vouchers or contracts (charters) to introduce elements of free-market competition and accountability into education, virtually all of the options in Table 1.1 have been used by school reform advocates (Coons & Sugarman, 1971, 1978; Kirkpatrick, 1990; Lieberman, 1989; McGarry & Ward,

TABLE 1.1
Forms of Privatization

I. By Divestment	A. Sale	1. To private buyer 2. To the public 3. To employees 4. To users or customers
	B. Free transfer	1. To employees 2. To users or customers 3. To the public 4. To prior owner (restitution)
	C. Liquidation	
II. By Delegation	A. Contract	
	B. Franchise	1. Public domain (concession) 2. Public assets (lease)
	C. Grant	
	D. Voucher	
	E. Mandate	
III. By Displacement	A. Default	
	B. Withdraw	
	C. Deregulation	

Note. Source: Savas, E. S. (1992). Privatization. In M. Hawkesworth & M. Kogan (Eds.), *Encyclopedia of government and politics* (Vol. 2, pp. 821-835). New York: Routledge.

1966; Walberg et al., 1988). Considerable experience with privatizing education internationally also provides a wealth of models, case studies, and experience to reference when planning school reform (Glenn, 1989, 1995).

Britain in particular has considerable experience privatizing social services and transferring assets from the public sector to the private sector. Madsen Pirie, who played a major role in many of those successful privatization initiatives, assembled a list of 21 strategies that tailor privatization to fit many situations. His list of getting out techniques and strategies appears in Table 1.2.

Several books provide detailed guidance for policymakers on how to implement privatization strategies (Eggers, 1997; Hatry, 1983; Hill, Pierce, & Guthrie, 1997; Marlin, 1984; Valente & Manchester, 1984). The U.S. General Accounting Office (GAO) has published several useful studies and overviews of privatization (U.S. GAO, 1997a, 1997b, 1997c). The Reason Foundation, based in Los Angeles, published a series of how-to manuals and produced a newsletter covering every aspect of designing and implementing privatization plans (Eggers, 1998).

The Heartland Institute's *PolicyFax '98* catalog offers the complete text of 10 market-based school reform bills and proposals dated between 1995 and 1997 (Heartland Institute, 1998). An older collection of legislation, also published by the Heartland Institute, compares and contrasts 13 comprehensive educational choice bills and one public school deregulation bill (Wittmann & Hetland, 1991). Also in 1991, Heartland published a 52-page design manual for tax credits and voucher programs (Bast & Wittmann, 1991). Heartland's work generally builds on and updates the plans crafted by John E. Coons and Stephen D. Sugarman during the 1970s (Coons & Sugarman, 1971, 1978).

Evidence of Effectiveness

The results of research on the effectiveness of experiments with market-based reform in education to date are reported in the previous section. Extensive reporting exists on the results of privatization of other services (Eggers & O'Leary, 1995; U.S. GAO, 1997a; Linowes, 1988; Moore, 1997; Poole, 1980; Roth, 1987; Savas, 1982, 1987, 1992; Stevens, 1984; Valente & Manchester, 1984; Wolf, 1988). With the exception of a few reports sponsored by public-sector unions, the litera-

TABLE 1.2
Getting Out Techniques and Strategies

1. Selling the whole by public share issue
2. Selling a proportion of the whole operation
3. Selling parts to private buyers
4. Selling to the work force or management
5. Giving to the work force
6. Contracting out the service to public business
7. Diluting the public sector
8. Buying out the existing interest groups
9. Charging for the service
10. Setting up counter groups
11. Deregulation via voluntary associations
12. Encouraging alternative institutions
13. Making small-scale trials
14. Repealing public monopolies to let competition grow
15. Encouraging exit from state provision
16. Using vouchers
17. Admitting demand pressures
18. Curbing state powers
19. Applying closure procedures
20. Withdrawal from the activity
21. Right to private substitution

Note. Source: Pirie, M. (1988). *Privatization: Theory, practice and choice*. Aldershot, England: Wildwood House.

ture invariably finds significant cost savings, service quality equivalent or superior to public-sector delivery, and greater accountability and responsiveness to consumers and elected officials. The results of one especially rigorous study are shown in Table 1.3.

The evidence of savings from privatization is so compelling that experts speak of "the bureaucratic rule of two": It typically costs two times as much for a government agency to produce a product or deliver a service as it does a private firm (Bennett & Johnson, 1981; Borcherding, 1977; Savas, 1987).

TABLE 1.3
Cost Savings for Eight Public Services Due to Outsourcing

Service	**Scale**	**Percent Savings** Municipal–Contracted
Street Cleaning	Curb miles cleaned	43%
Janitorial	Square feet cleaned	73%
Refuse Collection (residential)	Cubic yards of refuse collected	28%–42%
Payroll	Checks issued	None
Traffic Signal Maintenance	Intersections maintained	56%
Road Repair	Tons of asphalt laid	96%
Turf Maintenance	Acres mowed	40%
Tree Trimming	Tree trimming visits	37%

Note. Source: Stevens, B. J. (1984). *Delivering municipal services efficiently: A comparison of municipal and private service delivery* (p. 13). New York: Ecodata.

Why Privatization Works

The broad success of privatization shouldn't be a surprise. Many of the propositions of public choice theory predict that entities in the private sector will be more efficient and more accountable than government agencies. Most public services do not fit the definition of a public good, so there is little chance that market failure will prevent private companies from providing them efficiently.[10]

It is also forgotten that many services delivered by government were once delivered privately by firms, civic organizations, or individuals (self-help) (Beito, 1988; Davies, 1987; Johnson & Pikarsky, 1984; Poole, 1985; Warner, 1962). The list includes basic services such as sewers and drinking water, roads, parks, zoning, traffic lights, mass transit, and education.

School vouchers have been in use for more than 100 years in Vermont and Maine (McClaughry, 1984, 1995).[11] Government aid to private schools was common in the United States until the 1830s, when it fell victim to rising anti-Catholic sentiments (Blume, 1958; Brickman, 1966; High & Ellig, 1988; Hummel, 1996; Johnson, 1997; Spring, 1982, 1986).

Savas addressed the question of why privatization works in his original 1971 *Harper's Magazine* article:

> Therein lies a key problem of American cities: monopolies, whether public or private, are inefficient. Since most city agencies are monopolies, their staffs are automatically tempted to exercise that monopoly power for their own parochial advantage—and efficiency is rarely seen as an advantage. When a municipal monopoly no longer serves any interest but its own, the citizenry is left quivering with frustration and rage. (p. 55)

Savas reported that:

> Between 1940 and 1965, the number of policemen in New York City increased by 50% (from 16,000 to 24,000), but the total number of hours worked by the entire force in 1965 was actually *less* than in 1940. The increase in manpower was completely eaten up by a shorter work week, a longer lunch break, more vacation days, more holidays, and more sick leave. By comparison, during the same period, the length of the average work week throughout the U.S. declined by only 8%. (p. 57)

Savas, Stevens, and other experts identified less bureaucracy and higher worker productivity attributable to better supervision, less paid time off, and superior equipment as the reasons for cost savings by private-sector contractors (Savas, 1992; Stevens, 1984). All of these policies would be expected to appear in a private-sector setting where competition, rather than monopoly, is the rule.

SUMMARY AND CONCLUSION

> Because education involves teaching children about right and wrong, about what is important in life, it must be controlled by individual families, not by politicians or bureaucrats. No monopoly system can adequately reflect the values of all parents in a diverse society.
>
> Boaz (1997, p. 242)

The movement toward market-based school reform is gaining strength across the country. Charter schools, private scholarship programs, tuition tax credits, and pilot voucher programs for low-income students are all operating in various states. It is perhaps just a matter of time before a state allows all parents the choice of a government or private school for their children.

We hope we have corrected the following common misperceptions about economic methodology:

- Economists do not assume that people are blank slates or perfectly rational. Rather, they assert (on deductive or evidentiary basis) that representing people as rational choosers among competing values or ends is more reliable than relying on assumptions about human psychology and motivation.

- Economists do not assume perfect competition, perfect information, and so forth. The accuracy or realism of these assumptions is not the test of the validity of a hypothesis. They represent the *least amount of information* necessary to create a model that reveals how economic exchange works.

- Economics is not biased toward markets and against government. Economics is only a language for describing the results of human action in situations where the goals and the institutions are taken as givens. The precision and discipline of the economic method give it a power to unveil the structure and operation of systems and institutions that other social scientists have been unable to penetrate.

When economics is applied to social and political institutions, it produces propositions and predictions that have been validated by empirical research. Part of this body of thought—public choice theory—identifies situations where institutions prevent us from achieving those goals we reveal by our actions. The eight empirically confirmed propositions the authors arrived at in the third section can be summarized as follows:

1. As long as there are no consequences for either success or failure, higher spending on government schools will not produce better results.

2. Shifting the source of school funding from local taxpayers to state governments has made schools less efficient and less accountable to parents.

3. Teachers and administrators, not children, are the principal beneficiaries of the current system of government-funded education.

4. Private schools outperform government schools because they must compete every day for the loyalty of the parents of every child.

5. The biggest obstacles to better schools are not ill-prepared students, lazy parents, or stingy taxpayers; they are teacher unions and their allies in government school administrations.

6. School boards have been captured by administrators and teacher unions and will be of no assistance to a true reform movement.

7. Parents prefer private schools because they deliver what parents want: a focus on core curricula, safe and orderly classrooms, and high academic expectations.

8. Programs that allow parents to choose the schools their children attend—private or government—will improve the quality of the participating schools.

Our survey of privatization techniques and their successful use in other areas gives the reader an idea of the large body of laws, contracts, experience, and literature available to those who wish to pursue market-based reforms. Because education was once predominantly provided by private institutions, the task is actually to *reprivatize* education. The fact that it was done before should make the task easier.

By way of a final observation, the authors find it discouraging that critics of market-based school reform seem uninformed of the issue. Maribeth Vander Weele, for example, is a former newspaper reporter whose articles exposing waste and fraud in the Chicago Public Schools won her a position on Mayor Richard Daley's reform team. Her otherwise excellent 1994 book, *Reclaiming Our Schools: The Struggle for Chicago School Reform*, neglects to include a single market-based reform in a list of 26 "measures of holding schools accountable." Her call for "raising the income tax to address inadequacies and disparities in the funding of education" is a policy that has been tried and failed in Illinois and many other states (Vander Weele, 1994, p. 280).

School choice critics Bruce Fuller and Richard Elmore appear to be similarly myopic, falsely placing the origins of the school choice movement in anti-integration sentiments in the South in the 1950s, then repeatedly misrepresenting the economic approach to understanding social action (Fuller & Elmore, 1996). Paul T. Hill and Mary Beth Celio's (1998) book, *Fixing Urban Schools*, purports to find common ground with advocates of market-based reforms, yet is filled with antimarket rhetoric and incorrect notions of how markets work. At one point, the authors said disagreements between those who favor market-based reforms and those who oppose them are "ultimately ideological and cultural" (p. 36). But to understand the economic approach to school reform means understanding that it is the rejection, not the embrace, of ideological and cultural assumptions.

ENDNOTES

1. Herbert J. Walberg is a research professor of psychology and education at the University of Illinois at Chicago and Chairman of The Heartland Institute, a nonprofit research organization based in Chicago. Joseph L. Bast is President and CEO of The Heartland Institute. The views expressed in this chapter do not reflect the views or positions of The Heartland Institute.
2. Since January 1997, The Heartland Institute has chronicled the market-based school reform movement in *School Reform News,* a monthly newspaper.
3. Many private schools, particularly those in inner cities, have open enrollment policies, while many public schools restrict enrollment by exams, racial quotas, and residency requirements. For this reason, the authors use the terms government and private to distinguish the two main ways to organize public education.
4. Lawsuits in Maine and Vermont were initiated by voucher proponents who want to include religious schools in programs that use tax dollars to pay tuition for students attending private schools in rural communities. These programs included religious schools until the 1960s.
5. The two schools of thought being portrayed here are commonly called the Chicago School and the Austrian School. Rather than choose sides, the authors demonstrate how both methodologies arrive at testable propositions about school reform.
6. Education occurs without schooling, and schooling apparently takes place without education occurring. The authors use the two terms interchangeably.
7. Prisoner one's logic is: If I don't confess, I'll get 20 years if the other prisoner confesses or 2 years if the other prisoner doesn't confess. If I confess, I only get 10 years if the other prisoner confesses and 1 year if he doesn't. Either way, I'm better off confessing.
8. The other three possible combinations are *private goods* (rival and excludable),

common resources (rival), and *natural monopoly* (excludable); see Mankiw (1998).

9. Evidence that this opposition to public aid for private schools is based on self-interest rather than ideology can be found in the fact that in 1947 the NEA/AFT and the AFL supported federal aid for private schooling (see Lieberman, 1997).
10. The fact that many public services are private goods raises the question of how they came to be delivered by the public sector. Historian Robert Higgs (1987) proposed what he called the *Crisis Hypothesis*: "Under certain conditions national emergencies call forth extensions of governmental control over or outright replacement of the market economy" (p. 17). After the crisis passes, interest groups created by the new regulations or spending programs prevent the withdrawal of government control or funding, resulting in a gradual ratcheting upwards in the size and cost of government.
11. Approximately 25% of Vermont high school students receive taxpayer-financed scholarships to attend private schools. This long-standing program and the history of public support for private schools prior to the mid-19th century cannot be reconciled with Fuller and Elmore's (1996) statement that school choice was "originally advocated in the South as a way to avoid the desegregation of public schools" (p. 6). They repeated that falsehood two pages later in the same book.

REFERENCES

Abell, P. (1992). Is rational choice theory a rational choice of theory? In J. S. Coleman & T. J. Fararo (Eds.), *Rational choice theory: Advocacy and critique* (Vol. 7, pp. 183–206). Newbury Park, CA: Sage.

Allen, J. (1997, August 14). *Summer delivers success for charter school movement.* (News release). Washington, DC: The Center for Education Reform.

Ballou, D., & Podgursky, M. (1997). *Teacher pay and teacher quality.* Kalamazoo, MI: W. E. Upjohn Institute for Employment Research.

Bast, J. L., Harmer, D., & Dewey, D. (1997). Vouchers and educational freedom: A debate. In *Policy Analysis* (No. 269). Washington, DC: Cato Institute.

Bast, J. L., & Walberg, H. J. (1994). Free market choice: Can education be privatized? In C. E. Finn Jr. & H. J. Walberg (Eds.), *Radical education reforms* (pp. 149–171). Berkeley, CA: McCutchan Publishing Corporation.

Bast, J. L., Walberg, H. J., & Genetski, R. J. (1996). *The Heartland report on school finance reform for Illinois.* (A Heartland Policy Study, Parts 1–2, Nos. 72–73). Chicago: Heartland Institute.

Bast, J. L., & Wittmann, R. (1991). *Educational choice design guidelines.* (A Heartland Policy Study, No. 39). Chicago: Heartland Institute.

Beales, J. R. (1994). Teacher, Inc.: *A private-practice option for educators* (Analysis). Portland, OR: Cascade Policy Institute.

Beales, J. R., & Wahl, M. (1995). *Given the choice: A study of the pave program and school choice in Milwaukee.* (Policy Study, No. 183). Los Angeles: Reason Foundation.

Beito, D. T. (1988). Voluntary association and the life of the city. *Humane Studies Review, 6*(1), 1, 2, 17–22.

Bennett, J. T., & Johnson, M. H. (1981). *Better government at half the price.* New York: Caroline House.

Berthoud, J. E. (1996). *A fiscal analysis of NEA and AFL-CIO contributions to 1996 Congressional races*. Arlington, VA: Alexis de Tocqueville Institution.

Bish, R. L. (1988). Federalism: A market economics perspective. In J. D. Gwartney & R. E. Wagner (Eds.), *Public choice and constitutional economics* (pp. 351–368). Greenwich, CT: JAI.

Blume, V. C. (1958). *Freedom of choice in education*. New York: Macmillan.

Boaz, D. (1997). *Libertarianism: A primer*. New York: The Free Press.

Boaz, D., & Barrett, R. M. (1996). *What would a school voucher buy? The real cost of private schools* (Briefing paper). Washington, DC: Cato Institute.

Borcherding, T. E. (Ed.). (1977). *Budgets and bureaucrats: The sources of government growth*. Durham, NC: Duke University Press.

Borland, M. V., & Howsen, R. M. (1992). Student academic achievement and the degree of market concentration in education. *Economics of Education Review, 11*(1), 31–39.

Borland, M. V., & Howsen R. M. (1993). On the determination of the critical level of market concentration in education. *Economics of Education Review, 12*(2), 165–169.

Brickman, W. W. (1966). Historical background for freedom in American education. In D. D. McGarry & L. Ward (Eds.), *Educational freedom* (pp. 1–22). Milwaukee, WI: Bruce.

Buchanan, J. M. (1979). *What should economists do?* Indianapolis, IN: Liberty Press.

Buchanan, J. M., & Tullock, G. (1974). *The calculus of consent*. Ann Arbor, MI: University of Michigan Press.

The cash street kids. (1993, August 28). *The Economist*, p. 23.

CEO America. (1998, September). Cities with private voucher programs. *Voucher Voice*. pp. 4–5.

Chancellor, J. (1990). *Peril and promise* (p. 5). New York: Harper & Row.

Cheung, S., Murphy, M. E., & Nathan, J. (1998). *Making a difference? Charter schools, evaluation and student performance*. Minneapolis: University of Minnesota, Humphrey Institute of Public Affairs.

Chubb, J. E., & Moe, T. M. (1990). *Politics, markets and America's schools*. Washington, DC: Brookings Institute.

Cibulka, J. G. (1993). School improvement processes: A comparative study of Chicago high schools. In R. P. Niemiec & H. J. Walberg (Eds.), *Evaluating Chicago school reform* (pp. 69–80). San Francisco: Jossey-Bass.

Ciotti, P. (1998). *Money and school performance: Lessons from the Kansas City desegregation experiment* (Policy Analysis). Washington, DC: Cato Institute.

Clowes, G. (1998). The empire strikes back. *School Reform News, 2*(9), 1, 4.

Clune, W. H., & Witte, J. F. (Eds.). (1990). *Choice and control in American education* (Vols. 1–2). New York: Falmer Press.

Coase, R. (1960). The problem of social cost. *Journal of Law and Economics*, *2*, 1–44.

Coleman, J. S. (1990). *Foundations of social theory*. Cambridge, MA: Harvard University Press.

Coleman, J. S., & Hoffer, T. (1987). *Public and private high schools: The impact of communities*. New York: Basic Books.

Coons, J. E., & Sugarman, S. D. (1971). *Family choice in education: A model state system for vouchers*. Berkeley, CA: Institute of Governmental Studies.

Coons, J. E., & Sugarman, S. D. (1978). *Education by choice: The case for family control.* Berkeley: University of California Press.

Davies, S. (1987). The suppression of private provision. *Economic Affairs, 7*, 27–29.

Doyle, D. P. (1981). Public funding and private schooling: The state of description and analytical research. In E. M. Gaffney, Jr. (Ed.), *Private schools and the public good* (pp. 71–78). Notre Dame, IN: University of Notre Dame Press.

Drucker, P. F. (1969). *The age of discontinuity.* New York: Harper & Row.

Eggers, W. D. (1997). *Cutting local government costs through competition and privatization.* Los Angeles: Reason Foundation.

Eggers, W. D. (1998). *Complete neutrality: Ensuring a level playing field in managed competitions.* Los Angeles: Reason Foundation.

Eggers, W. D., & O'Leary, J. (1995). *Revolution at the roots: Making our government smaller, better, and closer to home.* New York: The Free Press.

Favell, A. (1996). Rational choice as grand theory: James Coleman's normative contribution to social theory. In J. Clark (Ed.), *James S. Coleman* (pp. 285–298). New York: Falmer Press.

Finn, C. E., Jr. (1995, September 25). Blindspots on the right. *National Review. 47*(18), 68–69.

Foer, A. (1997). Contract-free education. *Technos Quarterly, 6*(2), 27–28.

Friedman, M. (1976). *Price theory.* Chicago: Aldine.

Friedman, M. (1980). *Free to choose.* New York: Harcourt Brace.

Friedman, M. (1982). *Essays in positive economics.* Chicago: University of Chicago Press. (Original work published 1953)

Friedman, M. (1984). *Tyranny of the status quo.* New York: Harcourt Brace.

Fuller, B., & Elmore, R. F. (1996). *Who chooses? Who loses?* New York: Teachers College Press.

Genetski, R. J., & Tully, T. (1992). *A fiscal analysis of public and private education.* Chicago: Robert Genetski & Associates.

Gifford, M., & Keller, T. (1996). *Arizona's charter schools: A survey of parents.* Phoenix, AZ: Goldwater Institute.

Glenn, C. L. (1989). *Choice of schools in six nations.* Washington, DC: U.S. Department of Education.

Glenn, C. L. (1995). *Educational freedom in Eastern Europe.* Washington, DC: Cato Institute.

Greene, J. P. (1998). Civic values in public and private schools. In P. E. Peterson & B. Hassel (Eds.), *Learning from school choice* (pp. 83–106). Washington, DC: Brookings Institute.

Greene, J. P., Peterson P. E., Du, J., Borger, L., & Frazier, C. L. (1996). *The effectiveness of school choice in Milwaukee* (Program in Education Policy and Governance). Cambridge, MA: Harvard University, Kennedy School of Government.

Greene, J. P., Peterson, P. E., & Howell, W. (1997). *Test scores from the Cleveland voucher experiment* (Program in Education Policy and Governance). Cambridge, MA: Harvard University, Kennedy School of Government.

Gwartney, J. D., & Wagner, R. E. (Eds.). (1988). *Public choice and constitutional economics.* Greenwich, CT: JAI.

Haertel, E. H., James, T., & Levin, H. M. (1988). *Comparing public and private schools* (Vol. 2). New York: Falmer Press.

Hanushek, E. A. (with Benson, C. S., Freeman, R. B., Jamison, D. T., Levin, H. M., Maynard, R. A., Murnane, R. J., Rivkin, S. G., Sabot, R. H., Solmon, L. C., Summers, A. A., Welch, F., & Wolfe, B. L.). (1994). *Making schools work: Improving performance and controlling costs.* Washington, DC: Brookings Institute.

Hanushek, E. A. (1996). *The productivity collapse in schools* (Working Paper No. 8). Rochester, NY: University of Rochester, W. Allen Wallis Institute of Political Economy.

Harwood Group. (1995). *Halfway out the door: Citizens talk about their mandate for public schools.* Dayton, OH: Kettering Foundation.

Hatry, H. P. (1983). *A review of private approaches for delivery of public services.* Washington, DC: Urban Institute Press.

Hayek, F. A. (1968). *Individualism and economic order.* Chicago: Henry Regnery.

The Heartland Institute. (1998). *PolicyFax '98.* Chicago: Author.

Hendrie, C. (1996, August 7). In Chicago, it's full speed ahead as Vallas & Co. begin second year. *Education Week, 1,* 22–23.

Higgs, R. (1987). *Crisis and leviathan: Critical episodes in the growth of American government.* New York: Oxford University Press.

High, J., & Ellig, J. (1988). The private supply of education: Some historical evidence. In T. Cowen (Ed.), *The theory of market failure: A critical examination* (pp. 361-382). Fairfax, VA: George Mason University Press.

Hill, P. T., & Celio, M. B. (1998). *Fixing urban schools.* Washington, DC: Brookings Institute.

Hill, P. T., Pierce, L. C., & Guthrie, J. W. (1997). *Reinventing public education: How contracting can transform America's schools.* Chicago: University of Chicago Press.

Hirschman, A. (1970). *Exit, voice, and loyalty.* Cambridge, MA: Harvard University Press.

Hotelling, H. (1929). Stability in competition. *Economic Journal, 39,* 41–57.

How to privatize. (1995, March 11). *The Economist,* pp. 16–17.

Hoxby, C. M. (1997). *Local property tax-based funding of public schools.* (Heartland Policy Study, No. 82). Chicago: Heartland Institute.

Hoxby, C. M. (1998). What do America's "traditional" forms of school choice teach us about school choice reform. *Economic Policy Review, 4*(1), 47–59.

Hummel, J. R. (1996). Emancipating slaves, enslaving free men. Chicago, IL: Open Court.

Institute for Justice. (1997). *The case for school choice: Raymond, Maine* (Litigation backgrounder). Washington, DC: Author.

James, T., & Levin, H. M. (1988). *Comparing public and private schools* (Vol. 1). New York: Falmer Press.

Johnson, C. M., & Pikarsky, M. (1984). Toward fragmentation: The evolution of pubic transportation in Chicago. In C. A. Lave (Ed.), *Urban transit: The private challenge to public transportation* (pp. 49–77). San Francisco: Pacific Institute for Public Policy Research.

Johnson, P. (1997). *A history of the American people.* New York: HarperCollins.

Judy, R. W., & D'Amico, C. (1997). *Workforce 2020: Work and workers in the 21st century.* Indianapolis, IN: Hudson Institute.

Kahn, A. E. (1988). *The economics of regulation: Principles and institutions.* Cambridge, MA: MIT Press. (Original work published 1970)

Kirkpatrick, D. (1990). *Choice in schooling: A case for tuition vouchers.* Chicago: Loyola University Press.

Kirkpatrick, D. (1997). *School choice: The idea that will not die.* Mesa, AZ: Blue Bird.

Kittower, D. (1998). Counting on competition. *Governing, 11*(8), 63–74.

Landmark Legal Foundation. (1998). Wisconsin Supreme Court upholds expanded Milwaukee school choice program. *Landmark, 2*(2), 1, 6.

Lieberman, M. (1989). *Privatization and educational choice.* New York: St. Martin's Press.

Lieberman, M. (1993). *Public education: An autopsy.* Cambridge, MA: Harvard University Press.

Lieberman, M. (1997). *The teacher unions.* New York: The Free Press.

Linowes, D. F. (1988). *Privatization: Toward more effective government* (Report of the President's Commission on Privatization). Washington, DC: Government Printing Office.

Lopez-de-Salinas, F., Shleifer, A., & Bodjmu, R. W. (1995). Privation in the United States (Working Paper No. 5113). Cambridge, MA: National Bureau of Economic Research.

Mankiw, N. G. (1998). *Principles of economics.* New York: Dryden Press.

Manno, B. V. (1998). The coming transformation of America's schools. *American Outlook, 1*(1), 40–43.

Marlin, J. T. (1984). *Contracting municipal services: A guide for purchase from the private sector.* New York: Wiley.

McClaughry, J. (1984). Who says vouchers wouldn't work? *Reason, 15*(9), 24–32.

McClaughry, J. (1995). Educational choice: It really works in Vermont. In *Heartland Perspective, 11*(4), 1–3. Chicago: Heartland Institute.

McGarry, D. D., & Ward, L., C.S.C. (Eds.). (1966). *Educational freedom.* Milwaukee, WI: Bruce.

Moore, A. T. (1997). *Privatization '97: Eleventh annual report on privatization.* Los Angeles: Reason Foundation.

Mueller, D. C. (1987). *Public choice.* New York: Cambridge University Press. (Original work published 1979)

Musgrave, R. A. (1959). *The theory of public finance.* New York: McGraw-Hill.

Nathan, J. (1996). *Charter schools: Creating hope and opportunity for American education.* San Francisco: Jossey-Bass.

National Education Association. (1998). *The real story behind "paycheck protection."* Washington, DC: Author.

National Scholarship Center. (1994). *Just doing it.* Washington, DC: Author.

Neal, D. (1997a). The effects of Catholic secondary schooling on educational achievement. *Journal of Labor Economics, 15*(1), 98–123.

Neal, D. (1997b, Spring). Measuring Catholic school performance. *The Public Interest (127)*, 81–87.

Neustadt, R. E., & May, E. R. (1986). *Thinking in time: The uses of history for decision-makers.* New York: The Free Press.

Niskanen, W. A., Jr. (1971). *Bureaucracy and representative government.* Chicago: Aldine-Atherton.

Olson, M. (1971). *The logic of collective action: Public goods and the theory of groups.* Cambridge, MA: Harvard University Press. (Original work published 1965)

Organization for Economic Cooperation and Development. (1996). *Education at a glance: OECD indicators.* Paris: Author.

Patrinos, H. A., & Ariasingam, D. L. (1997). *Decentralization of education: Demand-side financing.* Washington, DC: World Bank.

Payne, J. L. (1991). *The culture of spending.* San Francisco: ICS Press.

Payne, J. L., & Jerbich, M. (1992). *Curbing the governmental class.* (A Heartland Policy Study, No. 51). Chicago: Heartland Institute.

Peltzman, S. (1996). Political economy of public education: Non-college-bound students. *Journal of Law and Economics, 39,* 73–120.

Peterson, P. E., Greene, J. P., & Howell, W. (1998). *New findings from the Cleveland scholarship program: A reanalysis of data from the Indiana University School of Education evaluation (Program in Education Policy and Governance).* Cambridge, MA: Harvard University Press.

Peterson, P. E., & Hassel, B. C. (Eds.). (1998). *Learning from school choice.* Washington, DC: Brookings Institute.

Phi Delta Kappa/Gallup. (1998). *Thirtieth annual PDK/Gallup poll.* Bloomington, IN: Phi Delta Kappa.

Pirie, M. (1988). *Privatization: Theory, practice and choice.* Aldershot, England: Wildwood House.

Polsby, D. D., & Popper, R. D. (1991). *Partisan gerrymandering: Harms and a new solution.* (A Heartland Policy Study, No. 34). Chicago: Heartland Institute.

Poole, R. W. (1980). *Cutting back city hall.* New York: Universe Books.

Poole, R. W. (Ed.). (1982). *Instead of regulation: Alternatives to federal regulatory agencies.* Lexington, MA: Lexington.

Poole, R. W. (1985). *Unnatural monopolies: The case for deregulating public utilities* Lexington, MA: Lexington.

Popper, K. R. (1971). *The open society and its enemies* (Vol. 2: Hegel and Marx). Princeton, NJ: Princeton University Press. (Original work published 1962)

Presser, A. L. (1991). Broken dreams. *ABA Journal, 91*(20), 60.

Ross, M. N. (1987, June). Public choice: The new political economy. *The AEI Economist,* pp. 1–8.

Roth, G. (1987). *The private provision of public services in developing countries.* New York: Oxford University Press.

Rouse, C. E. (1996). *Private school vouchers and student achievement: An evaluation of the Milwaukee Parental Choice Program* (Executive Summary). Cambridge, MA: National Bureau of Economic Research.

Rouse, C. E. (1998). *Schools and student achievement: More evidence from the Milwaukee Parental Choice Program.* (Working Paper No. 396). Princeton, NJ: Princeton University, Industrial Relations Section.

Sander, W. (1995). *The Catholic family: Marriage, children, and human capital.* San Francisco: Westview Press.

Savas, E. S. (1971, December). Municipal monopoly. *Harper's Magazine*, pp. 55–60.

Savas, E. S. (1982). *Privatizing the public sector: How to shrink government.* Chatham, NJ: Chatham House.

Savas, E. S. (1987). *Privatization: The key to better government.* Chatham, NJ: Chatham House.

Savas, E. S. (1992). Privatization. In M. Hawkesworth & M. Kogan (Eds.), *Encyclopedia of government and politics* (Vol. 2, pp. 821–835). New York: Routledge.

Savas, E. S. (2000). Privatization and public-private partnerships, p. 127 (Table 5.2). New York: Chatham House.

Shokraii, N. H., & Barry, J. S. (1998). Education: Empowering parents, teachers and principals. In *Issues '98: The candidate's briefing book* (pp. 253–293). Washington, DC: Heritage Foundation.

Shokraii, N. H., & Fagan, P. F. (1998). *After 33 years and $30 billion, time to find out if Head Start produces results* (Backgrounder, No. 1202). Washington, DC: Heritage Foundation.

Shokraii, N. H., & Hanks, D. (1997, April 21). School choice programs: What's happening in the States. In *FYI* (No. 138). Washington, DC: Heritage Foundation.

Shokraii, N. H., Olson, C. L., & Youssef, S. (1997, September). A comparison of public and private education in the District of Columbia. In *FYI* (No. 148). Washington, DC: Heritage Foundation.

Spring, J. (1982). The evolving political structure of American schooling. In R. B. Everhard (Ed.), *The public school monopoly: A critical analysis of education and the state in American society* (pp. 77–108). San Francisco: Pacific Institute for Public Policy Research.

Spring, J. (1986). *The American school: 1642–1985*. White Plains, NY: Longman.

Staley, S. (1996). *Competitive contracting in public schools* (Policy Report). Columbus, OH: Buckeye Institute for Public Policy Solutions.

Stevens, B. J. (1984). *Delivering municipal services efficiently: A comparison of municipal and private service delivery*. New York: Ecodata.

Stigler, G. (1971). The theory of economic regulation. *Bell Journal of Economics and Management Science, 2,* 3–21.

Styring, W. (1998). Teachers and school choice. *American Outlook, 1*(1), 49–51.

Tiebout, C. M. (1956). A pure theory of local expenditures. *Journal of Political Economy, 64,* 416–424.

U.S. Department of Education. (1987). *The condition of education: A statistical report.* Washington, DC: U.S. Government Printing Office.

U.S. General Accounting Office. (1997a). *Privatization: Lessons learned by state and local governments*. Washington, DC: Author.

U.S. General Accounting Office. (1997b). *Social service privatization: Expansion poses challenges for ensuring accountability for program results*. Washington, DC: Author.

U.S. General Accounting Office. (1997c). *Terms related to privatization activities and processes*. Washington, DC: Author.

Valente, C. F., & Manchester, L. D. (1984). *Rethinking local services: Examining alternative delivery approaches* (Management information service special report No. 12). Washington, DC: International City Management Association.

Vander Weele, M. (1994). *Reclaiming our schools: The struggle for Chicago school reform*. Chicago: Loyola University Press.

Vanourek, G., Manno, B. V., Finn, C. E. Jr., & Bierlein, L. A. (1997a). Charter schools as seen by those who know them best: Students, teachers, and parents. In *Charter schools in action* (Final report, Part I). Washington, DC: Hudson Institute.

Vanourek, G., Manno, B. V., Finn, C. E., Jr., & Bierlein, L. A.. (1997b). The educational impact of charter schools. In *Charter schools in action* (Final report, part V). Washington, DC: Hudson Institute.

Vedder, R. K. (1996*). The three Ps of American education: Performance, productivity, and privatization* (Policy Study No. 134). St. Louis, MO: Center for the Study of American Business.

Von Mises, L. (1966). *Human action: A treatise on economics* (3rd Rev. ed.). Chicago: Henry Regnery. (Original work published 1949)

Von Mises, L. (1978). *The ultimate foundation of economic science*. Kansas City, MO: Sheed Andrews & McMeel. (Original work published 1962)

Von Neumann, J., & Morgenstern, O. (1964). *Theory of games and economic behavior.* New York: Wiley. (Original work published 1944)

Walberg, H. J. (1993). *Losing local control of education: Cost and quality implications* (A Heartland Policy Study, No. 59). Chicago: Heartland Institute.

Walberg, H. J. (1997). *Time to change federal government's role in education* (Testimony before the Committee on Education and the Workforce, U.S. House of Representatives). Chicago: Heartland Institute.

Walberg, H. J. (1998). Spending more while learning less. *Fordham Report, 12*(6), 1–32.

Walberg, H. J., Bakalis, M. J., Bast, J. L., & Baer, S. (1988). *We can rescue our children: The cure for Chicago's public school crisis.* Chicago: Heartland Institute.

Walberg, H. J., & Bast, J. L. (1993, Spring/Summer). School choice: The essential reform. *The Cato Journal, 13* (1), 101–121.

Walberg, H. J., & Fowler, W. J., Jr. (1987). Expenditure and size efficiencies of public school districts. *Educational Researcher, 14,* 5–13.

Warner, S. B., Jr. (1962). *Streetcar suburbs: The process of growth in Boston, 1870–1900.* Cambridge, MA: Harvard University Press.

West, E. G. (1965). *Education and the state*. London: Institute of Economic Affairs.

West, E. G. (1967). The political economy of public school legislation. *Journal of Law and Economics, 10,* 101–128.

Witte, J. F. (1991). *First year report: Milwaukee parental choice program*. Madison, WI: Department of Public Instruction.

Witte, J. F. (1992). Public subsidies for private schools: What we know and how to proceed. *Educational Policy, 6*(2), 206–227.

Wittmann, R., & Hetland, T., F.S.C. (1991). *Sample educational choice legislation.* (Heartland Policy Study, No. 42). Chicago: Heartland Institute.

Wolf, C., Jr. (1988). *Markets or governments: Choosing between imperfect alternatives.* Cambridge, MA: MIT Press.

BIBLIOGRAPHY

School Choice

Bast, J. L., & Wittmann, R. (1991). *An educational choice bibliography.* (A Heartland Policy Study, No. 43). Chicago: Heartland Institute.

Frumkin, P. (1992). Analytic review of educational choice literature and annotated bibliography (Working paper, No. 73). Chicago: University of Chicago, Center for the Study of the Economy and the State.

Kirkpatrick, D. W. (1990). *Choice in schooling: A case for tuition vouchers* (pp. 175–210). Chicago: Loyola University Press.

Model Legislation and Bills

Anderson, P. L., McLellan, R., Overton, J. P., & Wolfram, G. (1997, November). *The Universal Tuition Tax Credit: A proposal to advance parental choice in education* (A Mackinac Center report). Midland, MI: Mackinac Center for Public Policy.

Bast, J. L., Walberg, H. J., & Genetski, R. J. (1996). *The Heartland report on school finance reform for Illinois* (A Heartland Policy Study, Part 2, No. 73). Chicago: Heartland Institute.

Bast, J. L., & Wittmann, R. (1991). *Educational choice design guidelines* (A Heartland Policy Study, No. 39). Chicago: Heartland Institute.

Coons, J. E., & Sugarman, S. D. (1971). *Family choice in education: A model state system for vouchers*. Berkeley, CA: Institute of Governmental Studies.

Harmer, D. (1994). *School choice: Why you need it—How you get it.* Washington, DC: Cato Institute.

Heartland Institute. (1998). *PolicyFax '98*. Chicago: Author.

Quade, Q. L. (Ed.). (1995). *Paths to parental freedom and school choice*. Milwaukee, WI: Blume Center for Parental Freedom in Education.

Wittmann, R., & Hetland, T. F.S.C. (1991). *Sample educational choice legislation.* (A Heartland Policy Study, No. 42). Chicago: Heartland Institute.

2

Chartered Governance of Urban Public Schools

Bruno V. Manno
The Annie E. Casey Foundation

The motto *Climbing New Heights Together* was chosen by the struggling Fenton Avenue School when it decided to go charter in 1994. Located in the northeast San Fernando Valley in the city of Lake View Terrace, Fenton Avenue was a troubled Los Angeles Unified District elementary school in the late 1980s when Joe Lucente was assigned as its principal. It had the usual ills of urban schools: meager pupil and teacher attendance, weak student achievement, scant parent involvement, gang activity, and dilapidated facilities.

Lucente was warned that a major challenge faced him. "I heard stories of how bad it was at the school," he recalled. "It went through four principals in 5 years. But I never realized it was as bad as it was until that day I met with the superintendent and he told me for just over an hour in graphic terms about the school."

The new principal struggled like Sisyphus within the confines of the district system to turn his school around. And though some things did improve, overall the system cramped Lucente and his team in too many ways. He saw key staff people leaving in frustration. He, too, began to think about leaving:

> We had reached the point where we couldn't go any further unless we got the state and the district with all their rules and regulations

> and bureaucracy off our back. The charter approach offered us a way to do that. And now under the charter, I'm doing more and enjoying it more—the main reason being that I now answer to a community composed of the staff who work here and the families that send their kids to the school. You can't beat that.

Lucente and his colleagues began to talk about becoming a charter school shortly after California enacted the enabling legislation in 1992. The Fenton Avenue team believed that it could operate the school more effectively and efficiently than the district if it—as a community—had site control over all elements of the school's life. As they moved through the process of writing a charter, they engaged parents and other members of the school community.

The staff agreed that charter status would confer complete freedom for the school in every facet of school life, including governance, fiscal planning, spending, student instruction, professional staff development, parent involvement, continuing education, employment, support staff training, food services, and pupil transportation. At a meeting, 95% of Fenton Avenue's professional staff voted by secret ballot to seek charter status with full autonomy from the Los Angeles district. In effect, they signed a declaration of independence that would establish a self-governing school. (To this day, only a handful of California charter schools have full autonomy from their districts.) The school filed its charter application to the board of education on April 30, 1993, received its charter on July 26, and began functioning as a charter school in January 1994.

Fenton Avenue now controls 97% of its operating budget, $8.2 million in 1998–1999 (3% goes to the district for administrative support). It contracts with the county board of education for many fiscal services, and offers its staff a choice of health plans and dental benefits.

The school operates year-round. It serves nearly 1,300 youngsters, making it one of the largest U.S. charter schools. Those youngsters include 78% Hispanics and 17% African Americans. Over three fifths have limited English proficiency and participate in a bilingual program. Eighty-five percent qualify for federal Title I services and nearly all participate in the free-lunch program. After-school enrichment classes and study halls are offered Monday through Thursday.

Parents are key, and forging a strong bond with them is central to the school's success. At the start of each year, they receive information (in English and Spanish) on school policies and standards. This includes a home–school contract (with a return sheet saying that all the material that was sent home has actually been read), homework policy, student responsibility code, general school rules, dress code (uniforms are required), rules of student behavior, discipline procedures, and a textbook contract.

Monthly Saturday workshops for parents, led by Fenton teachers, focus on techniques for working with students at home. These sessions cover topics such as how to deal with homework problems and discipline issues. The school also has a family center staffed by two community representatives that offers citizenship and English classes. It operates a food pantry for families and offers computer classes for adults. A member of the professional staff said of the school's approach to parents:

> We're clear with them about what we expect. It's nearly unanimous that they are appreciative and supportive of our clarity. And no matter how limited they are in their own knowledge, they want the best school right here for their kids and they know that this is exactly what we're trying to create.

School leadership is shared by Lucente, now the executive director, and Irene Sumida, director of instruction. Lucente is responsible for finance, operations, and external relations. Sumida is responsible for the school's education program. They complement one another but can interchange responsibilities at a moment's notice. Lucente said of their approach to running the school, "Not everyone could run a school like we do here at Fenton. I'm not bragging. That's just a fact. People aren't prepared to run schools with all the autonomy and teamwork we have."

Fenton Avenue has 65 teachers, all certified. Approximately 30% hold advanced degrees or multiple credentials. They are joined by about 20 full-time classified staff members and another 50 part-timers, mostly teacher aides. The school negotiated a sidebar agreement with the United Teachers of Los Angeles and another union that enrolls teacher assistants, instructional aides, and classified employees. The unions agreed "to subrogate current Los Angeles Unified School District contractual rights to those procedures established by the Fenton Avenue Charter school governing body."

The school's governance structure—simplified over the years—consists of four large working councils: budget, facilities, and safety; curriculum and assessment; human resources and personnel; and school–

community relations. Each council is comprised of teachers, parents, staff, and community members. Overseeing them is the Council of Councils, or governing board, with 20 voting members—16 staff, 3 parents, and 1 business or community member.

The working councils schedule their meetings at 7:00 AM. Sumida described how this works:

> The council structure makes it possible for teachers to run this school.... [T]he teachers...trust each other to run the school. At first, there was a great deal of fear about what might transpire at the council meetings. But no more. We no longer have to belabor every issue or point.

Lucente added his own reflection on governance:

> It's been fascinating to see what happens when you give staff more freedom than they're accustomed to having.... [Y]ou never know who will push the envelope and move into uncharted paths.... I don't do much exit counseling. One way or the other, the teachers communicate to those who aren't making it that this school is not for them. Their peers do a better job moving them out than I could do.

A teacher commented, "It's been a lot of hard work. But we've been able to do it."

FENTON AVENUE'S SUCCESS

Fenton Avenue's success illustrates how the charter idea is inspiring educators and parents to create independent public schools of choice, freed from most bureaucratic hassles and focused on superior educational results. Charter schools are helping the nation reinvent America's public education system.

As of January 2000, nearly 1,700 of these schools were in operation in 31 states and the District of Columbia, enrolling around 350,000 youngsters. Thirty-six states and the District of Columbia have authorized a charter school law (though not all charter school laws are created equal). The charter notion enjoys wide bipartisan support, with President Bill Clinton calling for 3,000 charter schools by 2002. Charter schools may well be the most vibrant force in American education today, foreshadowing a revitalized K–12 public education system—even in urban areas.

A report prepared for The Annie E. Casey Foundation observed:

> For several decades, desegregation and resource equalization were seen as the primary mechanisms for improving educational opportunities for poor and minority students. Recently, many urban leaders have concluded that, while these were important undertakings, they have not accomplished enough. (Bryk, Hill, & Shipps, 1998, p. 3)

The working assumption of urban school reform should be that the school system is in large part the problem. In an extensive study of urban education, the editors of *Education Week* concluded:

> It's hard to exaggerate the education crisis in America's cities.... [I]t is here that most states face the greatest gap between their expectations for students and the current reality. Urban students perform far worse, on average, than children who live outside central cities on virtually every measure of academic performance. The longer they stay in school, the wider that gap grows. Somehow, simply being in an urban school seems to drag performance down. Students in urban schools where the majority of children are poor and far more likely to do poorly on tests than their peers who attend high-poverty schools outside cities. (1998, pp. 6, 9–10)

The charter school's approach to educational governance can be helpful to those in urban areas laboring to broaden and improve the educational opportunities available to families and the educational outcomes achieved by urban school children. The conventional approach to the governance of public education views schools as uniform instrumentalities of government. In other words, they are owned and operated by school boards, staffed by government employees, and held accountable to government regulations, central office prescriptions, and union contract provisions.

The education historian Diane Ravitch (1998) succinctly described urban school reform and public education governance in the following comments:

> Many school reformers believe that the current governance system is incapable of improving the achievement of inner-city students or creating the kind of schools that can successfully educate poor children. Urban schools continue to work on the assumption that there is one best way to manage every issue and that those who work in the central offices know best. Regardless of who is superintendent, administrators

> in the central office control the budget, hire and assign staff, and issue directives to the school. (p. 3; see also U.S. Department of Education, 1996)

The charter strategy challenges this current understanding of public education governance. It views a public school as any school that accepts all comers, is paid for by the public, and is accountable to a public authority for the results of student learning. Families should be free to choose among different, autonomous, and self-governing schools.

This chapter examines four assumptions underlying the conventional approach to the governance of public education and contrasts them with four assumptions that undergird the charter idea. The chapter begins with a brief overview of school and student data on urban charter schools and concludes with a brief discussion of how the regular system of public education is responding to the existence of charter schools.[1]

URBAN CHARTER SCHOOLS

Charter schools tend to be an urban phenomenon. Table 2.1 illustrates that in 1996–1997, 51% of the then-existing 457 charter schools were located in large cities or on the urban fringe of a large city (27% and 24% respectively).[2] Another 25% were located in a midsize city or on their fringe. In states with charter laws, charter schools are almost twice as likely as other public schools to be in large cities: 27% compared to 15%. States without charter laws have 7% of their public schools in large cities. In states with charter laws, there are fewer charter schools in rural areas compared to other public schools: 8% versus 19%. States without charter laws have 31% of their schools in rural communities.

Table 2.2 provides information on charter school students by type of locale. Nearly a third (32%) of the nation's charter school students attend schools in large cities. Compared to other public school students, charter school students are much more likely to attend schools in large cities (32% vs. 19%) and more likely to attend schools on the urban fringe of these cities (35% vs. 29%). Only 5% of charter school students attend schools in rural areas, compared to 11% of other public school students in those states (and 20% of students in states without a charter law).

TABLE 2.1
Number of Schools, 1996-97, by type of locale

Type of community	Charter schools		Other public schools in "charter school states"		Schools in non-charter school states		All public schools	
	Number	Percent	Number	Percent	Number	Percent	Number	Percent
Total	457	100%	38,412	100%	47,147	100%	86,016	100%
Large city	123	27%	5,727	15%	3,494	7%	9,344	11%
Mid-size city	91	20%	6,524	17%	6,591	14%	13,206	15%
Urban fring of large city	111	24%	9,446	25%	7,880	17%	17,437	20%
Urban fring of mid-size city	25	5%	3,003	8%	4,661	10%	7,689	9%
Large town	19	4%	608	2%	1,025	2%	1,652	2%
Small town	51	11%	5,753	15%	8,667	18%	14,471	17%
Rural	37	8%	7,351	19%	14,829	31%	22,217	26%

Note. Locale codes classify the location of a school relative to populous areas. The classifications are:

1. **Large city** – A central city of a metropolitan statistical area (MSA) or a consolidated MSA (CMSA), with the city having a population greater than or equal to 250,000.
2. **Mid-size city** – A central city of a CMSA or MSA, with the city having a population less than 250,000.
3. **Urban fringe of a large city** – Any incorporated place, CDP, or non-place territory within a CMSA or MSA of a Large City and defined as urban by the Census Bureau.
4. **Urban fringe of a mid-size city** – Any incorporated place, CDP, or non-place territory within a CMSA or MSA of a Mid-size City and defined as urban by the Census Bureau.
5. **Large town** – Any incorporated place or CDP with a population greater than or equal to 25,000 and located outside a CMSA or MSA.
6. **Small town** – Any incorporated place or CDP with a population less than 25,000 and greater than or equal to 2,500 and located outside a CMSA or MSA.
7. **Rural** – Any incorporated place, CDP, or non-place territory designated as rural by the Census Bureau.

Table 2.2 provides information on charter school students by type of locale. Nearly a third (32%) of the nation's charter school students attend schools in large cities. Compared to other public school students, charter school students are much more likely to attend schools in large cities (32% vs. 19%) and more likely to attend schools on the urban fringe of these cities (35% vs. 29%). Only 5% of charter school students attend schools in rural areas, compared to 11% of other public school students in those states (and 20% of students in states without a charter law).

Table 2.3 provides information on charter students by racial and ethnic groups. Approximately 7 out of 10 (68%) charter school students in large cities are from minority groups, compared to almost 8 out of 10

TABLE 2.2
Number of Students, 1996-97, by type of locale

Type of community	Charter schools		Other public schools in "charter school states"		Schools in non-charter school states		All public schools	
	Number	Percent	Number	Percent	Number	Percent	Number	Percent
Total	108,262	100%	22,273,962	100%	22,964,517	100%	45,346,741	100%
Large city	34,736	32%	4,237,279	19%	2,448,976	11%	6,720,991	15%
Mid-size city	16,221	15%	4,100,052	18%	3,849,021	17%	7,965,294	18%
Urban fring of large city	37,952	35%	6,501,918	29%	4,689,097	20%	11,228,967	25%
Urban fring of mid-size city	4,551	4%	1,860,691	8%	2,775,099	12%	4,640,341	10%
Large town	2,854	3%	340,031	2%	514,980	2%	857,865	2%
Small town	7,026	6%	2,776,021	12%	4,038,226	18%	6,821,273	15%
Rural	4,922	5%	2,457,970	11%	4,649,118	20%	7,112,010	16%

(78%) other public school students in those communities. A charter school, therefore, is about as likely as a conventional urban public school to have a large minority enrollment. Charter schools in large cities are likely to have fewer Hispanics (31% vs. 36%) and Native Americans (2% vs. 7%) than regular urban public schools, though in urban fringe areas of a large city, charter schools are likely to have a smaller percentage of Hispanics (17% vs. 22%) and Asians (3% vs. 7%). Minority enrollment in mid-size cities is comparable: 48% in charter schools versus 49% in regular public schools (Research, Policy, & Practice [RPP] International & U.S. Department of Education, 1998).

Table 2.4 provides an interesting contrast. The median school size of a large-city urban charter school (137 students) is much smaller than other public schools (625 students) in large cities. The median school size in a large-city urban fringe charter school (242 students) is significantly larger than that of a large-city urban charter school (137 students), though it is still smaller than other public schools found in the urban fringe area of a large city (582 students). But the median student–teacher ratio for large-city charter schools (21.1) is greater than that of other public schools in charter school states (19.3 students).

TABLE 2.3
Number of Students, 1996-97, by racial/ethnic group and type of locale

Charter Schools

Type of community	White		Black		Hispanic		Asian		Amer. Ind.		Total	
	Number	Percent	Number	Percent	Number	Percent	Number	Percent	Number	Percent	Number	Percent
Total	56,980	53%	17,078	16%	23,353	22%	5,122	5%	5,388	5%	107,921	100%
Large city	11,201	33%	9,166	27%	10,684	31%	2,638	8%	609	2%	34,298	100%
Mid-size city	8,361	52%	3,022	19%	3,401	21%	863	5%	527	3%	16,174	100%
Urban fring of large city	25,294	67%	4,309	11%	6,455	17%	1,199	3%	672	2%	37,929	100%
Urban fring of mid-size city	3,466	76%	327	7%	432	9%	175	4%	162	4%	4,562	100%
Large town	2,170	76%	66	2%	419	15%	74	3%	123	4%	2,852	100%
Small town	4,480	62%	152	2%	1,153	16%	94	1%	1,305	18%	7,184	100%
Rural	2,008	41%	36	1%	809	16%	79	2%	1,990	40%	4,922	100%

Other schools in charter states

Type of community	White		Black		Hispanic		Asian		Amer. Ind.		Total	
	Number	Percent	Number	Percen	Number	Percent	Number	Percen	Number	Percent	Number	Percen
Total	1,265,91	52%	3,596,074	17%	5,028,536	23%	1,114,720	5%	526,724	2%	21,531,967	100%
Large city	974,222	22%	1,287,354	28%	1,641,445	36%	308,288	7%	311,113	7%	4,522,422	100%
Mid-size city	2,087,228	51%	829,575	20%	947,033	23%	198,984	5%	29,449	1%	4,092,269	100%
Urban fring of large city	3,857,810	59%	709,306	11%	1,458,862	22%	437,203	7%	39,845	1%	6,503,026	100%
Urban fring of mid-size city	1,229,822	67%	248,436	13%	265,877	14%	89,592	5%	10,714	1%	1,844,441	100%
Large town	222,060	65%	44,789	13%	59,688	18%	6,633	2%	6,861	2%	340,031	100%
Small town	1,963,030	71%	286,866	10%	427,238	15%	35,270	1%	63,010	2%	2,775,414	100%
Rural	931,741	64%	189,748	13%	228,393	16%	38,750	3%	65,732	5%	1,454,364	100%

THE RISE OF THE ONE BEST SYSTEM

Today's system of public schooling is a 19th-century creation. In the 1840s and 1850s, states began to establish public schools as an explicit government function. Until Horace Mann and his associates crossed this bridge, there had been no real distinction between public and private schools. They were simply community institutions, run under lay or

TABLE 2.4
Median School Size, 1996-97, by type of locale

Type of community	Charter schools	Other public schools in "charter school states"	Schools in non-charter school states	All public schools
	Median	Median	Median	Median
Total	130	495	421	450
Large city	137	625	572	602
Mid-size city	104	537	496	512
Urban fring of large city	242	582	516	550
Urban fring of mid-size city	128	528	526	526
Large town	105	492	424	448
Small town	108	443	420	429
Rural	55	267	257	260

religious control, funded by a mix of town and private funds, and managed in whatever manner each community thought best. As historians David Tyack and Elisabeth Hansot (1982) explained the pre-1850 view of education, "Many forms of schooling deserved the favor of government [and] citizens tended to have an attitude toward education that Americans today have toward religion: attend the school of your choice" (pp. 28–29).

This view of education began to change when crusaders like Mann inaugurated an arrangement called the *common school*, the precursor of today's public school. The shift of initiative and responsibility from community toward government took a giant leap around the end of the century, as progressive reformers transferred to education the principles of scientific management and the factory model of the nascent industrial age. This move to make schools efficient and orderly was thought necessary for two primary reasons: to combat widespread municipal corruption and to assimilate the influx of new immigrants. The result was what Tyack in his history of American urban education called "the one best system" that would insulate schools from politics and place them under the control of experts. As Tyack (1974) summarized this approach to education reform:

> An interlocking directorate of urban elites—largely business and professional men, university presidents and professors, and some "progressive" superintendents—joined forces to centralize the control of schools. They campaigned to select small boards composed of "successful" people, to employ the corporate board of directors as the model for school committees, and delegate to "experts" (the superintendent and his staff) the power to make most decisions concerning the schools.... [T]his movement glorified expertise, efficiency, and the disinterested public service of the elites. (p. 7)

As this approach to schooling spread across the continent, each of the 50 states assumed responsibility for providing its citizens with education, including compulsory school attendance to a specified age and the universal availability of public schools. Families could comply with the attendance law without patronizing the government-run schools, but today nearly 9 out of 10 children attend the taxpayer-subsidized public schools rather than paying tuition to private schools. That means 46 million youngsters enrolled in 85,000 public schools.

The state also began to specify qualifications for teachers and administrators, and set graduation requirements for students. It entrusted, however, the actual governance and operation of the schools to local education agencies. Today, about 93% of public school funding comes from state and local tax funds (most of the rest comes from Washington in the form of assistance for low-income and disabled youngsters).

Though the United States had over 127,000 local school systems in 1931–1932, today it has about 15,000, each with its own board and superintendent. The total public school payroll numbers nearly 5 million persons, and the schools spend about $255 billion, which averages to almost $5,700 per student. It is one of the largest bureaucracies in the world.

THE AGING FACTORY

For much of this century, the one best system served the nation well. It helped millions of immigrants assimilate into American society, fueled economic growth, and advanced the national culture and principles of democratic government. Access to education has been expanded and services extended to nearly everyone. For example, at the turn of the century, just 6% of American adults finished high school. By the mid-1960s, half of the adult population over the age of 25 had high school diplomas. Today almost 95% of young adults have completed high school or the equivalent. A K–12 education is now available to anyone who wants one.

It has been an extraordinary achievement. Yet today that is a bit like praising an immense horse-and-buggy factory for succeeding in providing everyone with a two-wheeled carriage drawn by one horse. The system is universal but it is also antiquated. One form of obsolescence can be glimpsed in Jacques Steinberg's (1995) poignant *New York Times* article that profiled Brunel Toussaint, the coal stoker at Junior High School 99 on East 100th Street. There he daily shovels anthracite into the school's twin boilers, installed in 1924. It turns out that coal furnaces are still the primary source of heat in more than a quarter of New York City's thousand-plus school buildings. The reporter noted, "It could have been a scene out of early industrial England" (p. B1).

Forget the coal furnaces: The very system itself is outdated. Its decision-making process has evolved from the deliberations of selfless elites into the brokering of competing interests including instructional aides, textbook and test publishers, social workers, administrators, bus drivers, maintenance staff, and teachers. The system frustrates parents who seek the best for their children and thwarts educators like Joe Lucente and Irene Sumida who yearn for autonomy and professionalism. Essentially every group must agree to a change before any change can be made. Since many of those interests have been codified into law—teacher certification and tenure, for example—even when agreement is reached, its implementation occurs at glacial speed.

Exceptions to this bleak description are often the outcome of idiosyncratic, even heroic efforts, which make more vivid the norm: the near immunity of public education to fundamental change. The expansive and expensive public education system is reminiscent of the command-and-control economy of the former Soviet Union. It is a big, lethargic, hyper-regulated, all-powerful, one-size-fits-all government bureaucracy that does not have to change because it enjoys a virtual monopoly. Even the late Albert Shanker (1989), president of the American Federation of Teachers, said, "It's no surprise that our school system doesn't improve. It more resembles the communist economy than our own market economy" (p. A22).

Four key yet outdated assumptions form the foundation on which today's public education edifice rests:

1. Public schools are instrumentalities of government, managed in a classic bureaucratic mode by lay boards that employ experts to carry out their directives.
2. Since public school systems are monopolies that deliver education through essentially identical schools, reforms must be systemic. And only the well-to-do have easy access to alternatives for their children.

3. Education quality is gauged by inputs, resources, and compliance with rules. Results-based accountability is largely absent and resisted.

4. Power rests with producers. The consumer is marginalized.

Outdated Assumption 1. Public schools are instrumentalities of government, managed in a classic bureaucratic mode by lay boards that employ experts to carry out their directives.

States have organized the public schools in geographically defined systems or districts. Governing each district is a school committee or board of education, usually elected, sometimes appointed. The board creates the policies and establishes the rules for all the public schools in its jurisdiction, also subject to a plethora of additional regulations from the state and federal governments. The board also employs state-licensed professionals to operate its schools, using classic civil-service-style personnel procedures.

Most of the money that flows into the district's coffers from local, state, and federal tax receipts has strings attached. Money for textbooks can be spent only to purchase books on a state-approved list. The elementary school principal can be hired only from among individuals certified by the state education agency. If a school receives federal money for bilingual education, it must follow the regulations of the federal bilingual program about who qualifies for the program, what instructional methods a teacher must use, and so forth.

The local board customarily hires a superintendent to oversee a central office staff that acts as the board's administrative arm. Decision making is centralized, much as in a turn-of-the-century industrial firm with its command-and-control hierarchy and assembly line production system.

Labor relations are industrial style, too. In most districts, collective bargaining agreements control teacher assignments, working hours, class size, teacher evaluation, and so forth. Uniform salary schedules treat everyone alike, whether they are good, bad, or mediocre at their jobs. Salary increases are given for time spent in the system. Life-long employment (i.e., tenure) is usually granted after 2 or 3 years.

The concept of schools run by government, staffed by government employees, and run by lay boards was created as a reaction against circa-1890 patronage and municipal corruption. The idea was to place nonpartisan boards in charge of certified professionals and thus extricate the public schools from the grasp of corrupt politicians. But the structure has grown creaky and self-serving, partly because it is insulated from conventional politics and has developed a peculiar self-serving politics of its own. Because board members are responsible to the constituencies that elect them (or the individual who appoints them), they are inevitably embroiled in political disputes and interest-group pressures, thus making it extremely difficult to keep their eye on the ball of producing proficient graduates.

Outdated Assumption 2. Because public school systems are monopolies that deliver education through essentially identical schools, reforms must be systemic. And only the well-to-do have easy access to alternatives for the children.

School boards enjoy exclusive franchises in their districts. In the words of Ted Kolderie (1990), "Public education is organized as a pattern of territorial exclusive franchises" (p. 69). Only school boards have the authority to finance, build, own, and operate public schools within a predetermined geographical location.

This monopoly does not allow families the option of fleeing a bad public school to attend a better one. Whereas the well-to-do can break free by taking up residence in another neighborhood or school district or by paying for their children to attend private schools, other families are stuck with what they are given in the place where they live.

District boards also exert monopoly control over the education process within the schools. Today's near-ubiquitous model follows an outmoded design. According to David Osborne and Ted Gaebler (1993):

> Public education's customers—children, families, and employers—have changed dramatically over the past 50 years. Yet most schools look just like they did 50 years ago. We still require most children to attend the school closest to their home, as we did in the days of the horse and buggy. We still organize school calendars as if children were needed on the farm all summer. We still schedule the day as if Mom will be home at 3 p.m. We still put each student through the same 12-year program, grade by grade. We still measure students' progress in course credits, using a system designed in 1910. And we still put teachers in front of rows of children, primarily to talk. (pp. 314–315)

Exceptions to this archaic model require circumvention of cumbersome bureaucratic processes, but such end runs are often stymied by the provisions of the union master contract and innumerable other special interests, all jealously protecting their turf. That is one of the primary reasons why most schools, and the systemic efforts to reform them, are essentially alike.

Changing a bureaucratic monopoly means laboriously and ponderously changing the whole thing at once. The underlying assumption behind systemic reform is that education can be thoroughly rationalized and upgraded by a command-and-control system as long as all schools receive the same marching orders. If everyone is following the same script written by the same experts, then the schools should, in theory, achieve the same outstanding results. The mandates and policies are developed by a central planning authority drawn primarily from the ranks of established administrative leadership, approved interest groups, and other such stakeholders. Despite lip service to decentralization and school-site management, the systemic model holds that reform is best accomplished through top-down mandates and uniform policies (see also Hill, Pierce, & Guthrie, 1997).

Outdated Assumption 3. Education quality is gauged by inputs, resources, and compliance with rules. Results-based accountability is largely absent and resisted.

Standards of performance for school personnel are almost nonexistent, and for students, they are vague and unclear. Attempts to specify outcomes have focused on attitudes and behavior rather than knowledge and skills, resulting in a backlash against standard setting itself.

Neither do external audits furnish clear, comparable, and timely information about educational results. There are good national and international data on student achievement, and there is ample information about school resources and programs. Yet anyone seeking solid data on educational performance at the student, classroom, school, and district levels will look long and hard and, in most jurisdictions, will not find much.

The U.S. education system is endlessly forgiving. Poor performances and shoddy achievements have little consequence. Nobody loses jobs when test scores fall and students are hardly sanctioned for coasting. The inverse is also true. Great educators rarely get bonuses and students find few rewards for studying hard and excelling in school.

The public school system is a vast no-fault enterprise for its adults as well as children. One avoids trouble by obeying all the rules, not by ensuring that students learn. Typical accountability procedures concentrate on measuring services provided and regulations met.

Outdated Assumption 4. Power rests with the producers. The consumer is marginalized.

One might assume that public education serves the public interest and is accountable to the public for its performance. Yet most operational power rests with the producers of education, not with consumers, taxpayers, or the citizenry. Most decisions are made by an education establishment that would put to shame the cartels and interlocking directorates of the robber barons. This producer-dominated establishment group includes: the two big teacher unions; other employee groups representing principals, superintendents, and supervisors; state departments of education; textbook publishers; colleges of education; custodians and coal stokers; bus drivers and cafeteria workers; school psychologists and software vendors; even the boards of education themselves. They are frequently joined by sheepish business groups, even by a docile PTA, particularly when it comes to lobbying for more resources and power.

Yet it is a familiar tale: the story of sealed policy arenas, monopoly, and creeping self-interests. It is no surprise that a century without competition and meaningful accountability would result in these self-serving ideas and interests.

Power in the hands of producers means power not in the hands of consumers. Schools profess to want more parent involvement and they often solicit help for fundraisers and field trips. They may even require attendance at parent–teacher conferences. But parents seldom have real power over what the school is or does. They seldom enjoy the viable alternative of another school. And traditionally it has been folly to think that they could start their own.

Parents are essentially marginalized even before their children enter school. A computer in the superintendent's office assigns a youngster to a school, usually without regard to special needs, family preferences, or exceptional circumstances (and sometimes acting on the basis of court-prescribed racial-balancing requirements). If parents want their child to attend a different school, they must fight the system. The assumption is that family choices are secondary to bureaucratic assignments and that parents do not know what is best for their children.

THE CHARTER REVOLUTION

Charter schools point us toward a new conception of public education, one that discards the factory model, rejects the one best system, breaks the monopoly, views stakeholders in a completely different light, and replaces the outdated assumptions with a strikingly new paradigm. The charter movement rests on four new assumptions:

1. A public school is any school that is open to the public, paid for by the public, and accountable to the public. Government need not run it.

2. Public schools should be different in myriad ways, and all families should be able to choose among them.

3. What matters most is not the resources a school commands or the rules it obeys, but the results it produces.

4. Each school is a small, self-governing community in which parents, teachers, and the community have valued roles.

New Assumption 1. A public school is any school that is open to the public, paid for by the public, and accountable to the public. Government need not run it.

The charter idea begins with the conviction that sound school choices can be provided to families under the umbrella of public education without micromanagement by government bureaucracies. Indeed, a charter school can be organized and run by almost anyone, including a committee of parents, a team of teachers, private corporations, or community organizations like the Urban League or the YWCA. Some schools achieve charter status by opting out from their local school system; others are new institutions started from scratch.

The charter concept affirms that schools need not be regulated into conformity by platoons of assistant superintendents, staffed only by government employees, or bent to the thousand clauses of union contracts. Charter schools require less bureaucracy and fewer regulations because the charter idea rejects the proposition that schools must be centrally managed and regulated according to a single formula. Instead, the charter—a license to operate for a certain period (usually 5 years)—lays out how the school will organize and govern itself and what results it intends to produce. The charter-issuing body is typically a state or local board of education, though sometimes a university, state administrative office, or special chartering board is invited to shoulder this responsibility.

The charter principle of deregulation also applies to teaching. Charter schools in states with laws that provide schools with a strong dose of operational autonomy do not confine their pool of potential instructors and principals to graduates of teacher- or administrator-training programs. Individuals with sound character who know their subjects well and want to teach children can work in a charter school. This opens the classroom door to scientists and engineers who know their biology, chemistry, physics, and math, are interested in teaching, and are willing to work with a master teacher to acquire the necessary pedagogical tools. It also allows individuals trained in the leadership, management, and financing of organizations to apply their knowledge and skills to public education. These new public teachers and administrators are creating a new education profession where individuals are paid (and retained) on the basis of their performance and are encouraged to be enterprising.

In short, the charter idea keeps education public in every important sense of the word: Schools receive public funds and charge no tuition; have no admission standards and accept all comers; remain accountable to public authorities for high standards of student learning (and other results); and are subject to basic health, safety, and nondiscrimination requirements. It does not matter who owns and operates the schools or what formal credentials are held by the individuals working in them hold.

New Assumption 2. Public schools should be different in myriad ways and all families should be able to choose among them.

The charter idea recognizes that people differ from each other along countless dimensions, from the loftiest (values, beliefs, and goals) to the most mundane (daily schedules, work lives, and entertainment preferences). If U.S. families can choose their own cars, houses, spouses, tennis partners, grocery stores, doctors, communities, appliances, and clothes, why should they not also be free to choose the school that suits them best?

Whatever else the charter movement has accomplished since 1991, it has certainly loosened the imaginations of individuals and organizations that have made these schools genuine centers of policy imagination and educational innovation. The charter idea takes for granted that schools should be different from each other so that the needs of a pluralistic society can be met. It allows for traditional schools, progressive schools, virtual schools, Montessori schools, Waldorf schools, Comer schools, Core Knowledge schools, Edison schools, schools for children at risk of failure, alternative schools, and all manner of public–private hybrids.

There is no single charter design. These schools are free to differ in their curriculum, instruction, and assessment; school organization; leadership and governance; staffing; parent and community involvement; scheduling; technology; and financing. Some charters also incorporate comprehensive efforts to take most or all of the "moving parts" of a school (whole-school designs) and re-create the school in an integrated fashion. With a charter school, you can start from scratch and build an entire house or just renovate the kitchen.

New Assumption 3. What matters most is not the resources a school commands or the rules it obeys, but the results it produces.

The genius of the charter concept is that it is demanding with respect to results but relaxed about the means whereby those results are produced—the opposite of most conventional schools with their rigid adherence to bureaucratic requirements and obliviousness to pupil achievement. In other words, charter schools are engaged in what former education secretary Lamar Alexander called “old-fashioned horse-trading” (National Governors’ Association, 1986): swapping rules and regulations for results. This is what makes charter schools so vibrant a force and promising an education reform strategy—that is, they are accountable for results rather than following rules. In short, a charter school is what James S. Coleman (1994) called an “achievement-oriented school” (p. 1).

Under the charter approach, public authorities set academic, fiscal, and other performance standards and hold the providers of education accountable for meeting them. This approach distinguishes between policy management and service delivery. Osborne and Gaebler (1993) described the organizations that operate in this fashion as “steering organizations...[that] set policy, deliver funds to operational bodies (public and private), and evaluate performance—but they seldom play an operational role themselves” (p. 30).

Some call this approach to overseeing public institutions a “tight, loose” strategy. This means that a public entity is tightly controlled with respect to the goals it sets, the standards it honors, and the results it achieves, but it is loose as to the means used to produce those results. Education bureaucracies typically take the opposite approach: rigid control regarding how it does things but relaxed about achieving the desired results. Yet success in attaining results can be known only if there are clear standards for student learning and school effectiveness—and, of course, if there are good tests and other assessments of student performance that tell us whether the standards are being mastered. Moreover, accountability mechanisms are needed that include real consequences for all involved.

Charter accountability is actually twofold: to the market—the families of those who choose to attend a given school—and to the public authority that charters the school. The charter approach is not an unbridled, *laissez faire*, free-market mode. Though market forces are necessary, they are not sufficient to provide suitable quality control. Neither is the charter strategy an example of privatization, which means selling or transferring public assets to private owners who are accountable to their shareholders but not to any public authority. With the charter idea, the public will always retain an interest in the successful delivery of educational services paid for by public funds (see also Brandl, 1998, pp. 84–85).

Such public sponsors have the responsibility for setting academic, fiscal, and other performance standards for all schools receiving public funds and then holding the providers accountable for meeting those standards. They should also be able to warn, intervene in, and, if necessary, withdraw public funds from any school that fails to meet those standards. While public officials retain the power to close a school, they do not directly manage the schools, or tell them how to allocate their resources, whom to employ, or how or what to teach. This kind of standards-driven accountability by public authorities has little to do with inputs, processes, or uniformity. The charter idea views public authorities as purchasers of services, not owners or operators of those services. They steer but do not row. This approach preserves an important public role in education, in addition to—not instead of—marketplace forces.

New Assumption 4. Each school is a small, self-governing community in which parents, teachers, and the community have valued roles.

The charter idea focuses on individual schools, not school systems. The school, which includes parents, teachers and other education professionals, is the "production unit" of the restructured education enterprise. It makes its own decisions, as long as its results are satisfactory. Planned results and shared values are prized over all. Because schools are autonomous, educators are free from the micromanagement and constraints that come with central bureaucracies. Educators retain a wide latitude of decision making and responsibilities. As long as students attain the promised results and the customers remain satisfied, the school's staff can operate as it thinks best.

Charter schools are also voluntary communities. No one is sent to a charter school or forced to enroll or teach in one. Individuals are there—families, students, and educators—because they choose to be there. They are excellent illustrations of Alexis de Tocqueville's (1984) observation about the penchant of Americans to form voluntary associations that accomplish community purposes. Charter schools are good examples of people rolling up their sleeves and working voluntarily side-by-side to improve their lives—and thus rebuild America's social capital.

The scale of a charter school is far smaller than most conventional public schools. Though the charter world is beginning to develop some multisite operations and chains of schools, most charter schools are self-contained and nearly all are small. Sometimes they are truly tiny—20 or 30 pupils—but even a very large charter school is apt to enroll less than a thousand youngsters. The fourth-year federal charter school study estimates that their median enrollment is 137 students, whereas for other public schools it is about 475 students. Newly created charter schools are smaller still, with a median enrollment of 128 students (RPP International & U.S. Department of Education, 2000). With their small scale comes intimacy and familiarity, often missing from the larger and more anonymous institutions that typify American public education.

Finally, charter schools are not gated communities. They interact with the larger communities within which they exist. For example, they present opportunities to begin schools to nonprofit institutions and community organizations that would not ordinarily be much involved with public education. Charter schools are, to borrow from Peter Drucker (1993), "not the collectivism of organized governmental action from above...[but] the collectivism of voluntary group action from below" (p. 9).

THE DISTRICT RESPONSE

The charter phenomenon reaches beyond the boundaries of individual schools like Fenton Avenue Charter School and the people directly affected by them. It is beginning to affect education systems. A significant by-product of the charter movement is the fact that the regular school system is responding to competition from charter schools.

Eric Rofes (1998) of the University of California studied the effects of charter schools on districts and documented the response in 25 communities, located in eight states and the District of Columbia. His empirical work generally supports the anecdotal evidence from the Hudson Institute project on Charter Schools in Action (2000). The traditional system response typically goes through four phases.

First, there is the political effort to keep the charter from happening: Quash the charter bill in the legislative committee or in the state legislature, or file suit against the charter program if the bill has been signed into law, or make sure the teachers' union kills the contract with a for-profit education management organization.

Second, if change cannot be prevented altogether, keep it within bounds. Keep the charter schools few and weak. Seize every opportunity to reregulate them. Do not outsource whole schools, maybe just the Title I program or the special education program.

Third, fight back in the marketplace. Get those kids back. This is perhaps the most interesting phase. The superintendent wakes up to discover that students are fleeing the district's schools. What does he do to retrieve them? He changes the district's accustomed mode of operations. For example, he may survey the market to determine what parents want and then advertise new services in district public schools based on his findings. In other words, the public school system begins responding to the signals coming from its own marketplace. So, we find a new after-school program, a Montessori school, a back-to-basics school, perhaps even an Edison school contracted by the system in order to draw people back from the charter schools.

The fourth response is to take advantage of opportunities provided by charter laws to do things differently within the school system. The superintendent may start his or her own charter school to take advantage of the personnel flexibility or to serve as a research and development center or demonstration site for the district. For example, Houston contracted with Thaddeus Lott, director of the path-breaking Wesley Elementary School, to operate Wesley and several nearby schools as a charter cluster, partly to liberate him from the district's own bureaucratic burdens. Lott now reports directly to Houston's superintendent, Rod Page. Or perhaps the entire district should go charter (as has been the case in at least two small districts, one in California and one in Georgia).

These constructive responses, although not yet the norm, are gaining ground, proving that if the public school monopoly is cracked, competition allowed, and alternative methods of schooling encouraged, educational goals and practices once unimaginable become imaginable.

CLIMBING NEW HEIGHTS

When Joe Lucente, Irene Sumida, and the Fenton Avenue community decided to secede from the Los Angeles Unified School District to start a charter school, they probably did not realize that their ideas would begin to penetrate the entire system of public education.

The charter strategy is unquestionably starting to change the education world. But how much of that change is long lasting? Now that we are beginning to discern a visible impact from the charter movement, attention must be turned to the important question of how these schools are actually doing. Are they successful enterprises? Are they boosting student achievement? How innovative are they? Most of the charter iceberg is still out of sight under the water, making it difficult to discern how the charter movement will ultimately affect American public education.

At Fenton Avenue, the autonomy conferred by the charter strategy has led to achievements that would have been impossible under the direction of district and union. Examples include:

- Boosting pupil test scores more than 20% in 2 years.
- Reducing class size from 30 to 20 in Grades K–3 and to 25 in Grades 4–6.
- Adding nine additional portable units to allow class size to be reduced.
- Repaving the entire three-acre playground area using private contractors at one fourth the cost quoted by the school district.
- Providing accident insurance for students and long-term disability for employees.
- Adding after-school and Saturday programs.
- Managing the school's own food service.
- Reducing administrative personnel by 25% and redirecting those dollars to provide for a music teacher and a technology consultant.
- Restoring a 10% staff pay cut that was imposed across the school district.
- Developing the school's own primary phonics instruction program in both Spanish and English.
- Creating an on-site broadcasting studio (the first in any California elementary school).
- Decreasing teacher absenteeism by 80%.

- Adding four mentor teacher positions.

Perhaps Fenton's most visible achievement has been in the area of technology, which began with a *Writing to Read* lab underwritten by the Mattel and Riordan Foundations. These grants allowed Fenton to form a partnership with General Telephone and Electronics (GTE) and Educational Management Group (EMG is a division of Simon & Schuster). The school then redirected $1.3 million from its 1996–1997 budget to spend on technology. As a result, though classes continue to meet in portable units, all classrooms are now networked and each has four multimedia computers, a television with VCR and CD player, satellite connection, and cable access. Additionally, the school's on-site studio allows students and staff to broadcast live and taped presentations on a closed-circuit TV channel—Fenton Charter Broadcasting. Two sixth-grade classrooms model Fenton's ultimate technology goal: a computer on every desk.

In 1997, Fenton Avenue was named a California Distinguished Elementary School. In the words of an outside evaluator hired by the school in preparing to renew their charter, "Fenton has come a long way from its reputation as a 'hellhole.'" In a visit to the school, State Superintendent Eastin called it "one of the nation's finest schools." Without a doubt, it has come a long way. As Lucente said, "Charter schools are not the cure-all for education's ills. They are, however, a vital force in education reform that can transform many good schools into exceptional schools."

A recent analysis of urban school reform comments that urban reformers "must start with the commitment to create a system of public governance and oversight that fosters strong, distinctive schools" (Hill & Celio, 1998, p. 71). The charter idea presents this opportunity. It has the potential to transform urban public education and its archaic and debilitating governance structure. If urban public education is to better meet the needs of families and youngsters in those comminutes, it surely will need to walk along the path that Fenton Avenue has traveled and that the charter idea portends.

ENDNOTES

1. Much of the discussion in this chapter is based on a 2-year national study of charter schools begun in July 1995, sponsored by the Hudson Institute's Educational Excellence Network through its Charter Schools in Action research team, which included Chester E. Finn, Jr., Gregg Vanourek, Louann A. Bierlein, and Bruno V. Manno. Financial support was provided by The Pew Charitable Trusts. The second-year project report *Charter Schools in Action* can be found at www.edexcellence.net. Parts of this chapter are adapted from *Charter Schools in Action: Renewing Public Education,* by Chester E. Finn, Jr., Bruno V. Manno, and Gregg Vanourek.
2. Data are from the 1996–1997 early release Common Core of Data, U.S. Department of Education, National Center for Education Statistics. The Department has not edited these files. Analysts added missing locale codes by assigning codes based on school addresses. Seventeen states had charter school laws then.

REFERENCES

Brandl, J. (1998). *Money and good intentions are not enough: Or why a liberal Democrat thinks states and communities need both competition and community.* Washington, DC: Brookings Institution.

Bryk, A. S., Hill, P., & Shipps, D. (Jan. 1998). *Decentralization in practice: Toward a system of schools.* Baltimore: The Annie E. Casey Foundation.

Coleman, J. S. (1994, March). *Achievement oriented school design.* Paper presented at the Social Organization of Schools conference, Notre Dame, Indiana.

Drucker, P. (1993). *The ecological vision: Reflections on the American condition.* New Brunswick, NJ: Transaction Publishers.

Education Week Editors, in collaboration with the Pew Charitable Trusts. (1998, January 8). "Quality counts '98: The urban challenge." *Education Week*, Vol. *XVII*(17).

Finn, C. E., Jr., Manno, B. V., & Vanourek, G. (2000). *Charter schools in action: Renewing public education.* Princeton, NJ: Princeton University Press.

Hill, P. T., & Celio, M. B. (1998). *Fixing urban schools.* Washington, DC: Brookings Institution.

Hill, P. T., Pierce, L. C., & Guthrie, J. W. (1997). *Reinventing public education.* Chicago: University of Chicago Press.

Kolderie, T. (1990, July 28). *The states will have to withdraw the exclusive.* Saint Paul, MN: Center for Policy Studies Public Services Redesign Project.

National Governors' Association. (1986). *Time for results: The 1985 governors' report on education.* Washington, DC: Authors.

Osborne, D., & Gaebler, T. (1993). *Reinventing government.* New York: Plume.

Ravitch, D. (1998). *Meeting the challenges of urban education.* Washington, DC: Brookings Institution.

Research, Policy, and Practice International & U.S. Department of Education. (2000). *The state of charter schools: National study of charter schools.* Washington, DC: Authors.

Rofes, E. (1998). How *are school districts responding to charter laws and charter schools?* Berkeley: Policy Analysis for California Education.

Shanker, A. (1989, October 2). Cited in *The Wall Street Journal*, p. A22.

Steinberg, J. (1995, November 15). "Time stands still in some school boiler rooms." *The New York Times*, pp. B1, B7.

Tocqueville, A. de (1986). *Democracy in America.* (R. D. Hefner, Ed. and Abridger). New York: Mentor.

Tyack, D. (1974). *The one best system: A history of American urban education.* (p. 7). Cambridge, MA: Harvard University Press.

Tyack, D., & Hansot, E. (1982). *Managers of virtue*. New York: Basic Books.

U.S. Department of Education. (1996). *Urban schools: The challenge of location and poverty*. Washington, DC: Author.

3

Private Vouchers: Politics and Evidence

Terry M. Moe
Stanford University

The voucher movement is the most controversial force for change in American education today. What it proposes—that government provide grants to parents who wish to send their children to private schools—may seem simple enough, a matter of expanding opportunities for American families and imposing a healthy competition on public schools. But vouchers have ignited explosive political battles, as powerful defenders of the public system have put up fierce resistance at every turn. Vouchers have also provoked heated intellectual debate, as supporters and opponents have offered conflicting claims about how these reforms would work out in practice.

While all this has been going on, a little-noticed development has been taking place outside the public sector. Individual, corporate, and philanthropic contributors in major American cities have begun setting up their own programs to offer "private vouchers" to the parents of disadvantaged children. As of the 1998–1999 school year, 41 of these programs were up and running, involving over 13,000 children[1]—with a massive expansion due to take place 1 year later, due to the newly formed Children's Scholarship Fund, which held a lottery in April 1999 extending vouchers to another 40,000 children around the nation (Hartocollis, 1999). What began only a few years ago as a charitable experiment in educational choice has grown into a full-fledged movement.

The private voucher movement has a direct bearing on both the political and the intellectual dimensions of the voucher controversy. Politically, it adds new force to the larger movement for school choice nationwide—recruiting new activists, mobilizing new constituencies, bringing new pressures to bear. More generally still, the private voucher movement is an aggressive carrier of what I call the "new politics of education": an ongoing political realignment in which the urban poor, joined by conservatives, do battle against their traditional liberal allies, who are bound to defend the existing system.

The private voucher movement is also significant, however, for its scientific and intellectual value. In a nation where political opponents have defeated (with two small exceptions) every effort to establish public-sector voucher programs—and with them, crucial opportunities for gathering direct evidence on how vouchers might work in practice—the spread of private voucher programs represents an empirical gold mine for researchers, and for the policymakers and citizens who depend on them for information. By creating a host of new settings for learning about vouchers through observation, experience, and study, these programs stand to make dramatic contributions to the nation's storehouse of knowledge—and to the politics and public policies that shape its education system.

This movement is a recent phenomenon, and little has been written about it. Particular programs and events have been publicized on occasion, but the movement itself has largely gone unstudied and remains poorly understood. In a book that came out a few years ago (Moe, 1995a), I tried to help remedy this situation by offering an overview of the two, interconnected "sides" of the movement's political story—one having to do with its origins and development as a political movement, the other having to do with the empirical evidence it has generated on the efficacy of vouchers. Much has happened since that book came out. The movement has continued to flourish. New evidence is being generated all the time. This article is an attempt to bring us up to date and, like the book, to provide a perspective on these developments that will be helpful for thinking more generally about the "new politics of education"—and where it seems to be taking us.

THE POLITICAL SETTING OF PRIVATE VOUCHERS

In some sense, the private voucher movement is purely private. Its foundations are privately organized, its grants are raised from private sources, and its children use these grants to go to private schools. Nonetheless, the best way to gain perspective on this movement is to begin with a closely related development in politics, a development that is perhaps the most symbolic event in the recent history of American education: the adoption of the Milwaukee public voucher program.[2]

Milwaukee is similar to many other American cities. The school-age population is disproportionately poor and minority, and the public school system is clearly not educating them. Most of Milwaukee's children drop out of school before graduating; and of the African-American kids who do graduate, the average grade point is a D (Milwaukee Public Schools, 1993). There is an escape hatch of sorts. A small proportion of low-income kids are bused to suburban schools, pursuant to a desegregation agreement. But the vast majority remain in the inner city, and many parents don't want their kids bused miles away to school anyway. Like parents elsewhere, they want good schools close to home.

In the late 1980s, a group of Milwaukee parents revolted against their school system. Their leader was Polly Williams, a Democratic state legislator, former welfare recipient, and former state campaign director for Jesse Jackson. Williams blasted the Milwaukee Public School System for consistently failing to educate low-income kids. She also rejected busing as a solution. Milwaukee's children deserve good schools close to home, she argued, and if they can't get them in the public sector, the government ought to give them vouchers to help them find better alternatives in the private sector.

Polly Williams' call for vouchers met with an enthusiastic response from Milwaukee's parents. But the usual allies of low-income and minority constituents—Democratic politicians, the educational establishment, and groups like the NAACP (National Association for the Advancement of Colored People)—were vehemently opposed to vouchers, which they saw as an attack on the public school system. So Williams had to look elsewhere for support, and she found it on the other side of the political fence, where Republicans, conservatives, and business groups—led by Wisconsin governor Tommy Thompson—agreed to back her cause.

After a brutal, closely fought battle, the Williams–Thompson coalition eventually created the nation's first voucher program. Its victory, however, was hedged about by debilitating compromises with the other side. It was only a pilot program, limited to a maximum of 1,000 low-income students (in a district of 100,000) and to a set of participating private schools that was guaranteed, by virtue of the program's rules and disincentives, to be exceedingly small. Although the vast majority of private schools in Milwaukee (and elsewhere) are religiously affiliated, such schools were not allowed to accept voucher students. Only a small number of schools, then, were even eligible. These schools, among other things, were required to admit new applicants randomly, without reference to their usual academic or behavioral criteria; they were required to have more than half of their student bodies made up of tuition-paying students, which ruled out new schools emerging to meet the voucher-induced demand; and they were given a voucher of just half of the public school expenditure per child, which again limited the numbers and types of schools willing to participate. (The other half of the funding, by the way, went to the school district—which was thus paid for each child it no longer had to educate.) A mere seven schools participated in the first year of the program, and they did not have anywhere near the 1,000 slots supposedly envisioned for voucher students (Witte, 1991).

The Milwaukee design, heavily shaped by the program's enemies, guaranteed that the years ahead would be difficult. But they were also difficult because opponents—including the State Department of Public Instruction, which is officially in charge of the program—continued to erect obstacles to its success. Among other things, they challenged its legality all the way to the Wisconsin Supreme Court (where they lost, after imposing almost 2 years of uncertainty on the program and its participants); they promulgated unfavorable rulings (e.g., turning away schools that wanted to participate); and they failed to publicize the program adequately to parents (Bolick, 1992; McGroarty, 1994, 1996; Mitchell, 1992; Peterson, 1993).

For both sides, the battle continued. The voucher coalition gained legislative approval for a big extension of the program, which dramatically increased the ceiling on the number of children allowed to participate (to 15,000) and for the first time included religious schools. The education establishment, which fought furiously to defeat the extension, immediately challenged its constitutionality in court, arguing (among other things) that it violated the separation of church and state. This effort met with success in the lower state courts, but in June of 1998 the Wisconsin Supreme Court issued a landmark ruling that the Milwaukee voucher program did *not* violate the separation of church and state—largely because the pivotal decisions about which schools get public support are made by parents, not the government, and because the program takes a neutral stance between religious and nonreligious schools, as well as between schools of different religions. The establishment and their allies then appealed to the U.S. Supreme Court, which, in November of 1998, refused to hear the case—mysteriously declining an opportunity to settle the issue—and let the Wisconsin court decision stand (Walsh, 1998a, 1998c).

The Milwaukee case speaks volumes about the politics of vouchers and school choice. For anyone interested in understanding the private voucher movement, there is much here to be learned.

CHOICE AND ITS SUPPORTERS

Vouchers were first proposed in the late 1950s by Milton Friedman (1955, 1962), a libertarian economist; and in the last decade, choice of various kinds has been actively supported by conservatives, Republicans, the religious right, and the Reagan administration. So a common stereotype today, not surprisingly, is that these groups provide the bedrock of political support for school choice (Cookson, 1994).

There is some truth to this, of course, but the stereotype is misleading. The fact is poor and minority people are among the strongest supporters of vouchers and choice. More generally, support for choice is *negatively* related to income and education, and its relationship to race is precisely the *opposite* of what conventional wisdom maintains (see, e.g., Cobb, 1992; Coleman, Schiller, & Schneider, 1993; Lee, Croninger, & Smith, 1994). In the 1992 Gallup Poll, for instance, the concept of vouchers was supported by 71% of Americans overall, but by 88% of Blacks and 84% of Hispanics.[3] Similar patterns, on a variety of choice-related issues, have been borne out in a large number of national, state, and local polls over the past decade or so. The flip side is that choice receives its weakest support (often outright opposition) from older, well-to-do Whites in the suburbs (U.S. Department of Education, 1992).

This makes sense. White suburbanites already have choice, which they exercise by buying houses in the best school districts they can find. They are not a natural constituency for vouchers, and indeed are often fearful of change. Poor and minority populations in the inner cities, on the other hand, tend to be trapped in the nation's worst schools—trapped because, for financial reasons, they have no choice. They want the kind of choice suburbanites already have, and they see vouchers and other choice-based reforms as instrumental to that end.

It is no accident, in view of this, that the first voucher program was for poor kids in Milwaukee, not for upper-middle-class kids in Palo Alto. Similarly, it is no accident that the most highly touted system of public school choice is to be found in East Harlem, where virtually all children are low-income and minority. As a general matter, the choice movement's most dramatic achievements around the nation have occurred in urban areas with high concentrations of poor and minority people—not in suburbia, and not in domains controlled by Republicans and conservatives, as the stereotype would suggest (e.g., Fliegel & Macguire, 1994; Nathan, 1989; Young & Clinchy, 1992).

The New Politics of Education

On school choice, a deep chasm separates poor people from the politicians and groups that normally represent them in politics. This is not due to ill intentions or bad faith on anyone's part. It is simply inherent in the structure of things, in fundamental interests, beliefs, and incentives that are deeply rooted and difficult to change.

The educational establishment is solidly behind the poor when it comes to mainstream educational programs—compensatory, bilingual, and special education, for instance. But the establishment has reasons of its own for opposing vouchers, even when poor kids are the only ones to receive them. Vouchers allow children and resources to leave the public system. A fully developed voucher system, moreover, would largely dismantle the establishment's own system of bureaucracy and political control in favor of new arrangements that decentralize power to parents and schools. From the establishment's standpoint, then, vouchers are the ultimate survival issue, and they have to be defeated wherever they are proposed.

Democratic politicians tend to be strong allies of the poor on social issues. But school choice is a glaring exception, and the educational establishment plays an important role in this. Led by the teachers' unions, they contribute enormous amounts of money and manpower to political campaigns, almost all of it to Democrats. Democrats, in turn, work closely with members of the establishment on educational policy issues—which entails, among other things, opposing vouchers. Some Democrats have broken ranks, and more may follow someday. But for now it is virtually a united front (Lieberman, 1993).

Liberal interest groups also weigh into the equation against vouchers. In general, they distrust markets and have agendas that call for extensive government regulation, so vouchers tend to conflict with their basic beliefs and issue positions. The most active in school choice battles is the NAACP. Its leaders came of age during the civil rights struggles of the 1960s, and their views on school choice are a product of those times. To them, choice is a thinly disguised strategy by which Whites seek to avoid integration. This was often accurate decades ago, especially in the South. But times have changed. Now, school choice is regularly relied on to promote integration, whereas busing and other coercive tools of yesteryear are increasingly out of favor. Indeed, some of the most comprehensive systems of public school choice—in Cambridge, Montclaire, and Kansas City, for example—have evolved in response to desegregation concerns (Nathan, 1989; Young & Clinchy, 1992).

Be this as it may, the bottom line is that, whereas poor people are highly supportive of school choice, their traditional allies are staunchly opposed. And the divide that separates them will not be bridged in the near future. For those among the poor who want choice, the only recourse in the near term is to find new allies, as Polly Williams did. This means entering into coalitions with groups they have traditionally viewed as opponents: Republicans, conservatives, and business.

Such a coalition is unorthodox, and it doesn't form automatically. The poor are reluctant to trust the motives of conservative groups that have often opposed them in the past. And Republicans and other conservative leaders are not necessarily eager to join a voucher crusade anyway, because their suburban constituents are typically not pressuring them to move in this direction. For both sides, however, there are obvious attractions to this new, if uncomfortable, political alignment. For the poor it is the only avenue to victory on the voucher issue, and a way of escaping their dependence on liberal politicians. For conservatives it offers a golden opportunity on various counts. It allows them to make inroads—perhaps enduring, enormously consequential inroads—into their opponents' core constituency. It allows them to take the moral high ground as champions of people in need. And it enhances their power, and their prospects for transforming the American education system.

This is the basis for the new politics of education: a reconfiguration of political forces in which the liberal coalition, traditionally the vanguard of change on behalf of the poor, finds itself in the distinctly undesirable position of defending an obviously deficient status quo against demands for reform by the poor and their conservative allies—an opposing coalition that is not only embarrassing to the establishment, but also threatening, for it is potentially powerful enough, if the situation is right, to force radical reforms of the system.

The upshot is that the most revolutionary movement for educational change in modern times has been the movement for low-income vouchers: vouchers targeted not at all children (as most voucher proponents would like, ideally), but solely at the inner-city poor. Intellectually, this is the easiest voucher argument to make in political debate, for the inner-city poor are clearly in the greatest educational need, and it seems obvious that, if something radical is to be done, it should start with them. More important, though, low-income vouchers offer just the right kind of reform for mobilizing a political coalition capable of taking on the established interests and their allies, which on virtually any other issue of major education reform would be unbeatable. Low-income vouchers are the perfect vehicle for the new politics of education.

The unorthodox alliance of conservatives and the poor has been growing stronger, more coherent, and more self-aware since its emergence in Milwaukee at the turn of the decade, and since then has been putting pressure on legislatures around the country to provide vouchers to disadvantaged children. As we ought to expect, most of these early attempts have failed in the face of massive establishment opposition. A number of them, however, have come just a few votes shy of approval—in Arizona and Texas, for instance. And in 1998, the U.S. Congress passed legislation authorizing a voucher plan for low-income children in Washington, DC, only to have it vetoed by President Bill Clinton. Even the most ardent foe of vouchers would have to agree, based on a hard-headed look at the constellation of political forces, that the political trajectory is clearly positive.

Along with the near misses and obvious improvements in their prospects, the voucher movement also scored two major breakthroughs. Under the leadership of Cleveland councilwoman Fanny Lewis—a Black Democrat who is that city's Polly Williams—and key Republicans, notably Governor George Voinovich, the voucher coalition succeeded in getting the Ohio legislature to approve a low-income voucher program in Cleveland. During the 1996–1997 school year, this program went into operation as the nation's second public voucher system, providing some 2,000 students with vouchers and empowering them to choose religious and well as nonreligious schools in the private sector (Center for Education Reform, 1996a, 1996b; Heritage Foundation, 1998a). The education establishment, of course, fought this proposal furiously from the outset and, once it had lost on the legislative front, immediately went to court to block implementation. The court struggle in the years since has been complicated, and has produced victories and defeats for both sides. Suffice it to say that, after the Ohio Supreme Court decided the program does *not* violate the separation of church and state, opponents shifted over to the federal district court, which decided it *does*—and, at this writing, that is where matters stand (see Walsh, 1999). The case is being appealed, and most court-watchers think it will ultimately reach the Supreme Court and serve as the basis for a landmark decision on vouchers, one way or the other.

The second major breakthrough came in Florida. Led by newly elected Governor Jeb Bush, proponents won the nation's first statewide voucher program in 1999, this one making vouchers available to all children who attend "failing" schools. (The vast majority of these kids, in practice, will turn out to be low in income.) Initially, only two schools in the entire state met the criteria of "failing" performance, so few children qualified for vouchers. But as performance standards rise, as is expected, the vouchers population could easily become quite large (see Sandham, 1999). The education establishment lost no time in trying to block its implementation in the courts, and fairly quickly met with success—although not, interestingly enough, on separation of church and state grounds (even though the program involves religious schools). Their success came via a decision by a lower level state judge, who declared that the program violated the state's constitutional duty to provide a public education system for its citizens (see Sandham, 2000). At this writing, the case is being appealed.

Whoever wins these political and legal battles in the short term, it is a sure thing that the battles will continue. And at least for the foreseeable future, the coalitions on each side will stay the same. This is the new politics of education, and it is changing the political landscape of American education reform.

ESTABLISHED INTERESTS AND THE STATUS QUO

In Milwaukee, Cleveland, and Florida, the choice issue has gotten away from the education establishment. But at least for now, this is not the norm. In American education (as in most areas of American public policy, for that matter), the established interests have far more political power than anyone else on issues within their domain. They are extremely well organized, loaded with political resources, and fully focused on education, whose details they follow with tireless determination in every nook and cranny of the political process. The norm is that the establishment dominates the politics of education.

From this flow two basic facts of political life. The first is that, if the establishment is dead set against something, it has little chance of being adopted. In this sense, Milwaukee and Cleveland are aberrations: two districts out of some 15,000 in the nation where the establishment's hammerlock was partially broken. Much the same is true of Florida: it is one state out of 50. As a rule, anyone proposing vouchers is quite likely to lose in today's politics. More generally, choice proposals that represent coherent, far-reaching plans for transforming the system are likely to be threatening to the establishment, powerfully opposed by them, and defeated.

The second is that, when choice-based reforms actually get adopted, they tend to be quite limited. Though often touted as revolutionary, they are in fact incremental changes that, of political necessity, are simply grafted onto the existing system without altering its fundamentals. Bureaucratic and political control structures remain firmly in place, as does the operational power of the establishment (Lieberman, 1993). The programs themselves, moreover, are usually not designed according to the best ideas available. They are political concoctions, built up through a patchwork of compromises as a result of which the establishment has a heavy hand in designing and later operating the very programs they oppose. The Milwaukee voucher program is a case in point. It is a symbol of revolution that is in fact a very vulnerable program: limited in scope, hobbled by purposely contrived design restrictions, and subordinated to an official power structure that wants it to fail.[4]

Expectations have to be anchored in the realities of politics. Whatever reforms poor and minority people might favor, the reforms they actually get will tend to be heavily shaped by establishment interests, submerged in the established system, and so burdened with constraints and official opposition that it is difficult for them to function very well. They may signal the beginning of a great transformation. But for now, they are incremental changes, fighting a battle against great odds.

THE EMERGENCE OF PRIVATE VOUCHER PROGRAMS

The private voucher movement is in part a straightforward exercise in philanthropy. And not a new one at that. For there is nothing new about the idea of giving low-income children private vouchers. This is just a fancier, more politically charged way of saying that they should be given financial assistance, or scholarships, so that they can attend the private schools of their choice.

The fact is, it has long been the norm for private schools of all types to have scholarship funds for low-income kids. In most private schools, some percentage of students are attending with the help of what amount to private vouchers. In addition, various foundations around the country, many in urban areas and affiliated with the Catholic Church, provide thousands of needy kids with education grants every year. The Inner-City Scholarship Fund, for instance, provided scholarships to some 2,500 low-income children for the 1992–1993 school year, enabling them to attend Catholic schools in the Boston area. Similarly, the Archdiocese of Los Angeles Education Foundation gave out grants in 1992–1993 to 3,500 low-income kids who sought to attend Catholic schools in that city (National Scholarship Center, 1994).

The private voucher movement, however, goes well beyond these sorts of purely philanthropic efforts.[5] It is, in important respects, a political as well as a philanthropic movement, and any attempt to understand why it emerged when it did, why it is gaining support and influence, and what consequences it may hold for the future must begin by recognizing its integral connection to the politics of American education.

The leading figures of the private voucher movement—people like J. Patrick Rooney, James Leininger, Michael Joyce, and John Walton—share a common vision that is very much a reflection of the political picture I sketched out in the previous section. They believe the public school system is failing to provide poor children with anything like an adequate education, and that bold, innovative steps need to be taken—now—to bring about change for the better. They also believe that school choice, in one form or another, is the key to doing this, and they see themselves as part of the larger choice movement for fundamental reform of the entire system.[6]

They are well aware, however, of the political facts of life. They know that, given the intense opposition to choice among the poor's traditional allies, getting coherent choice plans through the political process is extraordinarily difficult, and that any "victories" are likely to take the form of weak, poorly designed compromises that fail to address the urgent needs of low-income students.

The bottom line is that, if they really want to help disadvantaged children, and if they want to avoid, as far as possible, the dangers and defeats of the political battlefield, their options are limited. Their resort to privately funded vouchers is essentially an adaptation to political reality.

With private vouchers, they are in a position to bring about immediate change, and on their own terms. Assuming enough money can be raised, they can simply design coherent programs according to the best ideas available, and put them into effect quickly and with a maximum of flexibility. Low-income children get the benefits right away, and private schools are able to participate without debilitating regulatory burdens. Meantime, opponents cannot block, subvert, delay, oversee, or impose restrictions.

There is, however, one obvious drawback. The educational problems facing the entire population of low-income children are simply too overwhelming to be solved through private contributions. There is literally no way that privately funded voucher programs could extend to millions of kids. In the end, if vouchers are to bring improvements on a large scale, they must be publicly funded: The government must use tax money to finance a new system of school choice. And this runs into the same political buzz saw that has plagued vouchers from the outset.

Taking this as given, however, leaders see a second advantage in the private voucher approach: It is an innovate way of pressing for more permanent, broadly based changes in the educational system without actually becoming immersed in politics. The idea is that private voucher programs will serve as models for reform. Objectively, these programs would be providing policymakers with a storehouse of direct evidence. Such evidence is sorely lacking in the debate over vouchers, and unlikely to be generated soon within the public sphere (outside Milwaukee and Cleveland) due to the education establishment's devout opposition to the creation of new programs that would be the source of the evidence. The expectation is that, with the proliferation of private voucher programs, it will be possible to demonstrate through actual practice that vouchers do indeed work to enhance opportunities for low-income kids—thereby influencing the public debate and turning public and elite opinion in favor of vouchers. Along the way, low-income constituencies in urban areas would get mobilized, bring pressure to bear on their representatives, and create a more favorable political setting.

As all this suggests, the private voucher movement is part philanthropy, part political reform. As philanthropy, it is not so different from other charitable programs, run by individual private schools and foundations, that give educational scholarships to low-income children. The political dimension is what makes it different, and lends it much broader national significance.

The Golden Rule Model

Most activists within the private voucher movement would point to one man as its founder and guiding spirit: J. Patrick Rooney, CEO of the Golden Rule Insurance Company. In August 1991, following the defeat of a voucher proposal in the Indiana state legislature, Rooney announced the creation of the Educational Choice Charitable Trust, a private foundation whose purpose was to provide financial assistance—private vouchers—to low-income children within the Indianapolis Public School System.[7]

In principle, there are many ways to design a private voucher scheme. Rooney chose to build his Golden Rule program around the following basic elements:

1. Vouchers would be equal to half the receiving private school's tuition, subject to some ceiling amount, with parents responsible for paying or raising the remainder.

2. Only low-income children would be eligible. This included low-income children already attending private schools.

3. Families would be allowed to use vouchers at whatever private schools they wanted, whether independent or religious.

4. Low-income children would be granted vouchers on a first-come, first-served basis. There would be no requirements, academic or otherwise, aside from the admissions standards of the specific schools they chose to attend.

The idea behind the first element of the Golden Rule model was that parents should be committed enough to contribute half the tuition out of their own resources. This is useful as a practical matter, because it essentially doubles the number of parents and children the program can reach, compared to a system in which vouchers cover all tuition costs. But it is also rooted in a fundamental principle that guided Rooney's thinking. He believed that, when parents become financial stakeholders in their children's education, they are likely to be more involved and take it more seriously, and their kids are likely to gain more from the experience. The financial burden this entails, moreover, is not great, because the tuition at most Indianapolis private schools is quite low to begin with, often (when the program began) close to $1,000.

The second element of the Golden Rule model assured that vouchers would go not just to low-income kids who want to avoid or leave the public schools, but also to those already attending private schools—and whose parents, therefore, have already found a way to pay for these schools. The idea here was that poor parents who are struggling to pay full tuition for their kids should not be penalized for their motivation, commitment, and sacrifice; the program was designed to support their efforts to keep their kids in the private schools of their choice. The downside, though, was that less program money would be available to support kids who are trapped in inadequate public schools, which is presumably the more salient problem. Rooney's solution has been to compromise. In practice, the Golden Rule program has allotted about half of its new vouchers over the years to kids who were already in private schools, the other half to kids who were not.

The model's third element gave families complete freedom to choose whatever schools they want, including religious schools. This maximized the chances that parents would find schools with the desirable properties they were looking for, and that matched up well with their children's needs. The inclusion of religious schools was a crucial part of this. Many parents value the discipline, moral climate, and academic rigor of religious schools. Moreover, the vast majority of private schools, in Indianapolis and throughout the country, are religiously affiliated. Any system of educational choice or vouchers that excluded religious schools, then, would not only prevent many parents from choosing the schools they really want, it would also drastically reduce the supply of participating schools and fail to take advantage of the diversity, dynamism, and resources the private sector has to offer.

The fourth element was intended to ensure that all low-income kids were eligible for vouchers on an equal basis. Rooney's mechanism for assuring equal treatment was first-come, first-served: children received priority based on when their applications were received, and not on the basis of their aptitude, grades, behavior, or personal connections. There were, of course, implicit criteria at work here, namely those of the receiving schools. But their standards are presumably accepted by the parents who choose them, and, outside of a small number of elite schools, can readily be met by a broad cross-section of children. This is particularly true of religious schools, which are not only quite numerous, but actively concerned with aiding needy kids (Bryk, Lee, & Holland, 1993; Coleman & Hoffer, 1987; National Catholic Educational Association, 1985).

Rooney's announcement of the Golden Rule voucher program, which was publicized in the media as well as through various church, school, and community networks, produced an overwhelming response from poor parents. Initially, his plan was to create a 3-year program capable of funding 500 students per year. But within just 3 days of his announcement, more than 600 applications had come in, followed thereafter by some 900 more (Beales, 1994). Right away, then, his program was hugely oversubscribed, suggesting that Rooney was onto something: There did indeed appear to be a pent-up demand among the poor for educational choice, and many were eager to take advantage of vouchers even when asked to shoulder some of the financial burden themselves.

With the help of Eli Lilly and scores of other new contributors, Rooney responded by raising additional funds and expanding the scope of the program. During the first year, vouchers were given out to 744 kids instead of the planned 500. The numbers increased to around 900 in 1992–1993 and 1,100 in 1993–1994. The 3-year time horizon was extended to 5, with the understanding that, if more contributions could be raised, the program would likely be continued beyond that—which, in fact, proved to be the case. What began as a novel, short-term experiment rather quickly showed signs of developing into something of an institution (National Scholarship Center, 1994).

In the meantime, the innovative example and early success of the Golden Rule program—publicized through the national media, as well as through countless speeches given by Rooney and Golden Rule's administrator, Tim Ehrgott, as part of a consciously orchestrated outreach effort—attracted attention from potential organizers, contributors, and supporters in cities all around the country. The result, in very short order, was a proliferation of new private voucher programs, and the emergence of a new movement truly national in scope.

Replicating the Golden Rule Model

Two other private voucher programs, in addition to Golden Rule, stand out as pioneers within the movement and continuing influences on its growth and development. One is located in San Antonio, the other in Milwaukee. Both began operation with the 1992–1993 school year, just 1 year after Rooney's initial announcement, and both were explicitly designed in accordance with the Golden Rule model.

The San Antonio program emerged out of the leadership of Dr. James Leininger, CEO of Kenetic Concepts Inc., a medical supply company, and chairman of the Texas Public Policy Foundation, a conservative policy organization.[8] Leininger first got excited about the idea of private vouchers when he read a *Wall Street Journal* article on Rooney and Golden Rule, and he soon resolved to create such a program for San Antonio, an overwhelmingly Hispanic city in which the vast majority of families are low-income.

Leininger enlisted the support of Jack Antonini, president of the USAA Federal Savings Bank, and Larry Walker, publisher of the *San Antonio Express-News*, among others. Under the auspices of the Texas Public Policy Foundation, they set up the Children's Educational Opportunity (CEO) Foundation and endowed it with a $1.5-million fund for private vouchers. As the *Express-News* pitched in to publicize the new program, San Antonio's low-income families responded with an enthusiasm that paralleled the Golden Rule experience. The CEO program was first announced in April 1992, and by September it was flooded with some 2,200 applications, far more than could be funded (Martinez, Godwin, & Kemerer, 1995).

For the 1997–1998 school year, 850 children were granted education vouchers of at most $750 per child—amounts that, again, were generally half the receiving school's tuition in a city where the average private school was quite inexpensive (estimated at $1,100 per year in 1994—see Beales, 1994). Meantime, demand among San Antonio's poor has continued to far outstrip the program's capacity, and the waiting list—currently at almost 3,000—remains much larger than the number of children that can be funded (Center for Education Reform, 1998).

The Milwaukee private voucher program is currently much larger than the ones in San Antonio and Indianapolis.[9] Indeed, it is by far the largest in the country. Initially, it was aided by the fact that it was not built from scratch, as they were, through newly mobilized resources and newly formed organizations. Rather, the Milwaukee program arose from an institutional base, the Milwaukee Archdiocesan Education Foundation, that had been set up earlier to provide assistance to children and Catholic schools in the inner city.

The Foundation sought to address the growing crisis that afflicts not only Milwaukee Catholic schools, but urban Catholic schools throughout the nation: As Whites and the more affluent have fled to the suburbs, inner-city Catholic schools have been left with fewer resources and with a population of low-income, minority students whose families cannot afford the schools' services. The Church sees its social mission as one of helping these children, most of whom are non-Catholic; but pursuing this mission requires resources that neither the Church nor its client families can muster. As a result, Catholic schools have been closing in record numbers around the country (National Catholic Educational Association, 1985).

A prime goal of the Milwaukee Archdiocesan Education Foundation was to see that this did not happen in Milwaukee. Initially, it did this by successfully putting together a coalition of supporters, many of them from the business community, to provide financial aid to the city's Catholic schools and the inner-city children who attend them. In 1990, the Foundation formed a more broadly based coalition, representing the full range of private schools in the city, religious and nonreligious, Catholic and non-Catholic, for the purpose of raising funds to support private education and low-income students in Milwaukee.

In the midst of this campaign, Patrick Rooney announced the Golden Rule program, which quickly emerged as a focal point for the Milwaukee coalition. The Foundation then contributed its $800,000 trust toward the creation of a new private voucher program—known as Partners Advancing Values in Education (PAVE)—modeled along the lines of Golden Rule. The Bradley Foundation, under the leadership of Michael Joyce, assumed a central role in the new PAVE program and pledged another $500,000 per year for 3 years. Other foundations and businesses, many of them already part of the Archdiocese's network of supporters, joined in with major contributions.

The PAVE experience has been much the same as those of Golden Rule and CEO, but on a grander scale. From the beginning, it was overwhelmed with applications from low-income families, as the other programs were, but its extensive funding base allowed it to provide many more of them with vouchers. During its first year of operation, 1992–1993, it funded 2,089 children, and over the next few years it added about 500 more—making it larger than Golden Rule and CEO combined. Although the initial plan was for 3 years, PAVE's leaders responded to the early enthusiasm by mobilizing new resources and extending the program's time horizon, as their colleagues did in Indianapolis and San Antonio.

PAVE program temporarily moved into an echelon all its own in 1995, when its size, already bigger than that of any other program, virtually doubled overnight. The precipitating event was a court ruling in September 1995, that Milwaukee's new public voucher program, which now included religious schools, was unconstitutional. This meant that some 2,000 low-income children who had taken advantage of that program to attend private religious schools were no longer allowed to do so, and faced going back to public schools. At this point, PAVE stepped in and, with the help of new financial support from contributors, pro-vided private vouchers to enable these children to continue attending their chosen schools. It continued to do so for 3 years, until the need evaporated in June 1998, when the Wisconsin Supreme Court ruled the public voucher program constitutional. With this ruling, the newly added children streamed back into the public program, as did a number who had previously been using private vouchers, and PAVE enrollments sank to below their original levels. It will be interesting to see what happens to it in the years ahead, given that all low-income children in Milwaukee now qualify for publicly funded vouchers. In some sense, it is one of those rare programs that has actually seen its goals achieved (Heritage Foundation, 1998b).

Growth and Institutionalization

With Golden Rule as a model, the private voucher movement took off. In 1991, the Indianapolis program stood alone, enrolling 746 children. By the next year, there were five programs in operation, providing vouchers to 4,167 children. Within another year, there were 12 programs enrolling 5,003 children. And so it went, as organizers and contributors around the country sought to replicate in their own communities what Rooney had accomplished in his.

Table 3.1 summarizes the programs in operation as of the 1998–1999 school year. As of the 1998–1999 school year, 13,155 children were receiving vouchers from 41 different programs located in cities throughout the country. Enrollments are scheduled to jump by another 40,000 for 1999–2000, however, when recipients from the Children's Scholarship Fund begin to take part (see later discussion).

Virtually all of these programs have considerable waiting lists. For the 1997–1998 school year, for instance, the Los Angeles program gave out 483 vouchers and had a waiting list of 4,000. The Washington, DC, program gave out 450 vouchers and had a waiting list of 7,573. The Orlando program gave out 235 vouchers and had a waiting list of 1,800. And so on. Almost every time private vouchers are offered (but not always—again, see later discussion), they are enormously popular with low-income families, and oversubscribed (Center for Education Reform, 1998).

As the figures in Table 3.1 indicate, there is considerable variation in the size of these programs across cities. The pioneering programs discussed earlier—Indianapolis, Milwaukee, San Antonio—are unusually large, as are the newer programs in Washington, DC, New York City, and the Edgewood school district. The other programs are much smaller. All but a few provide vouchers to less than 500 students, most have enrollments below 250, and many are under 100. There is a rationale to this, of course. The proliferation of small programs gives the Golden Rule model a concrete presence in cities throughout the nation. They serve as pilot programs to demonstrate the value of vouchers. They provide a propitious and necessary basis for future growth. And they help people who need help. But the fact remains, the sheer number of cities involved is currently a rather misleading indicator of the population of children able to participate. Of the 13,155 children receiving

TABLE 3.1
Number of Schools, 1996-97, by type of locale

City (Year founded)	1991-1992	1992-1993	1993-1994	1994-1995	1995-1996	1996-1997	1997-1998	1998-1999
Indianapolis (1991)	746	895	1,075	984	1,013	1,014	1,094	1,703
Atlanta (1992)	--	200	160	160	128	128	128	40
Battle Creek (1992)	--	53	116	180	118	178	178	149
Milwaukee (1992)	--	2,089	2,450	2,699	4,465	4,127	4,268	1,000
San Antonio (1992)	--	930	950	902	940	955	850	928
Albany (1993)	--	--	25	25	105	20	20	20
Austin (1993)	--	--	46	69	78	83	48	27
Denver (1993)	--	--	42	74	78	49	49	57
Detroit (1993)	--	--	8	3	159	462	400	500
Little Rock (1993)	--	--	17	17	391	464	461	453
Phoenix (1993)	--	--	57	60	41	110	100	100
Washington, DC (1993)	--	--	57	175	180	455	460	1,300
Dallas (1994)	--	--	--	100	235	335	441	550
Houston (1994)	--	--	--	91	196	305	305	410
Los Angeles (1994)	--	--	--	775	775	776	483	300
Midland (1994)	--	--	--	8	5	4	4	4
Oakland (1994)	--	--	--	169	250	250	250	250
Bridgeport (1995)	--	--	--	--	125	122	120	107
Buffalo (1995)	--	--	--	--	150	500	400	620
Ft. Worth (1995)	--	--	--	--	59	41	49	49
Jackson (1995)	--	--	--	--	155	217	207	289
Knoxville (1995)	--	--	--	--	13	18	5	6
Orlando (1995)	--	--	--	--	196	156	235	104

Note. Source: CEO America. (1994). Mission statement, support services, history, and background. Bentonville, AR: Author.

TABLE 3.1 (cont'd.)
Number of Schools, 1996-97, by type of locale

City (Year founded)	1991-1992	1992-1993	1993-1994	1994-1995	1995-1996	1996-1997	1997-1998	1998-1999
Jersey City (1996	--	--	--	--	42	50	52	50
Philadelphia (1996)	--	--	--	--	--	100	100	130
Albany II (1996)	--	--	--	--	--	155	155	126
Pittsburgh (1996)	--	--	--	--	--	25	38	38
Seattle (1996)	--	--	--	--	--	6	0	0
New York City (1997)	--	--	--	--	--	--	1,200	1,000
Chicago (1997)	--	--	--	--	--	--	30	30
St. Louis (1997)	--	--	--	--	--	--	--	25
Birmingham (1998)	--	--	--	--	--	--	--	44
Chattanooga (1998)	--	--	--	--	--	--	--	200
Dayton (1998)	--	--	--	--	--	--	--	542
Hartford (1998)	--	--	--	--	--	--	--	200
Louisville (1998)	--	--	--	--	--	--	--	326
Memphis (1998)	--	--	--	--	--	--	--	162
Miami (1998)	--	--	--	--	--	--	--	100
Minneapolis (1998)	--	--	--	--	--	--	--	80
San Antonio (Horizon) (1998)	--	--	--	--	--	--	--	786
San Francisco/ Basic Fund (1998)	--	--	--	--	--	--	--	325
San Francisco/ Guardsman (1998)	--	--	--	--	--	--	--	25
Total Number of Students	746	4,167	5,003	6,491	9,897	11,105	12, 130	13,155

private vouchers under the Golden Rule model in 1998–1999, more than half lived in Indianapolis, San Antonio, Milwaukee, Washington, DC, or New York City. (This will change, presumably, once the massive infusion from the Children's Scholarship Fund [CSF] takes effect in 1999–2000.)

There are actually more private voucher programs, and more children being served by them, than are summarized here (see, e.g., Center for Education Reform, 1998). This list includes only those programs that are modeled after Golden Rule, because these are the ones that best reflect the rationale, growth, and development of the movement. But there are many other programs around the country that offer children scholarships to attend private schools, and some of these could readily have been included here. It is a matter of where to draw the line, and there is no obvious way to do it.

The Student-Sponsor Partnership program (SSP) in New York City, for example, has been operating since 1986—well before Golden Rule—to provide disadvantaged children with vouchers, and its founder, Peter Flanigan, has played a leading role in the national movement. SSP is fairly large, serving almost as many children as Golden Rule does, but its model is quite different. It is based on mentoring, in which adult sponsors make contributions toward the voucher expenses of particular children, and meet with them personally throughout their school years. The program chooses its kids through outreach and referrals (centering on those who are particularly needy), rather than allowing families to simply apply. And it actively places students in the private schools that SSP deems most appropriate for them, rather than relying on the families to choose. This is clearly a private voucher program, then, but in concept and operation it stands apart from Golden-Rule-type programs that have fueled the movement. The same could be said for many other scholarship programs for needy children.[10]

Although these "different" programs are excluded here, it is also important to recognize that the more typical programs listed in Table 3.1 are not identical and do not rigidly adhere to the Golden Rule model. They are clearly patterned after it and take their inspiration from it, but they often make adjustments to the original design. It is not always the case, for instance, that parents are required to pay half the tuition on their own; sometimes smaller fractions are required, and a few programs try to offer vouchers that cover full tuition (as the Horizon program in San Antonio does—see later discussion). Similarly, programs often take rather different tacks in deciding how many private school children they are willing to fund, with some clearly trying to focus their resources as much as possible on getting kids out of the public schools. And, most important, programs have increasingly gotten away from Golden Rule's first-come, first-served approach to the selection of students in favor of other approaches—often involving an extended application period, followed by a lottery—that reduce the inherent advantages of better informed, more motivated parents, and help promote equal access.

Who has been setting up these programs? As with most movements, the spread of private voucher programs has largely been driven by spontaneous action on the part of activists seeking to pioneer change in their own cities. From the beginning, however, certain individuals have taken on larger leadership roles—promoting the cause, stimulating the emergence of programs across cities, assisting with funding, coordinating far-flung people and activities—with considerable influence on the rapid growth and increasing coherence of the movement as a whole. Patrick Rooney did exactly these sorts of things in his strategic attempts to launch the movement on a nationwide basis and get it established. And once the ball got rolling, others played leading roles on a national scale as well. Michael Joyce and the Bradley Foundation clearly stand out in this regard; they not only helped fund and organize the huge Milwaukee program, but also played an active part in publicizing and promoting the movement nationally. Dan McKinley, executive director of PAVE, has been another highly influential proponent—speaking widely on the subject, sharing information about the experiences of PAVE and other organizations, and promoting the emergence of a nationwide network of supporters.

It is the San Antonio group, however, acting through the Texas Public Policy Foundation, that has probably done the most to build an organizational foundation for central leadership—and to institutionalize the movement. Aided by a grant from the Famsea Corporation in late 1992, they fashioned an organized campaign to stimulate interest in private vouchers and assist local activists in setting up their own programs, providing, among other things, a 200-page "how-to" manual offering step-by-step guidance. They also launched a comprehensive outreach effort—involving networking and travel by San Antonio activists, videotapes, brochures, and a national conference—to publicize the CEO experience and spark national interest (CEO America, 1994).

In the spring of 1994, with the help of a $2-million grant from the Walton Family Foundation, the San Antonio group followed up with what may turn out to be the most important single development since Rooney's creation of Golden Rule: They set up a new centralizing entity, CEO America, to provide institutional leadership for the movement. CEO America's mission is to serve as a clearinghouse and umbrella organization for all existing private voucher programs, and to assist in the creation of new ones. And its assistance involves more than information and advice. CEO America provides "challenge grants" (on a matching basis) of up to $50,000 to initiate programs in new cities, as well as to stimulate the expansion of smaller, existing programs. Translated into practice, these are significant amounts: A challenge grant of $50,000, matched by local donors, is enough to provide vouchers for between 100 and 200 children (CEO America, 1994).

With the emergence of CEO America, the private voucher movement came of age as an organized social and political force. Whether it will continue to grow and prosper remains to be seen. But it is no longer an uncoordinated assemblage of activists. It is increasingly a coherent, well-integrated endeavor with a firm institutional base.

Challenging the Status Quo

During the early years, the idea of private vouchers was itself a bold innovation, and the energies of the movement were invested in proliferating new programs in as many communities as possible around the country. Once these early successes were established, however, and once the movement itself achieved an institutional capacity for coordinating people and resources, raising funds, and utilizing information and knowledge, its leaders were no longer content with more of the same. They became bolder and more aggressive.

Four recent initiatives stand out. All have captured news headlines, and the attention of education and policy elites around the country—for these new programs are issuing clear, dramatic challenges to the status quo. They are throwing down the gauntlet:

1. In February 1997, Mayor Rudolph Giuliani and the School Choice Scholarship Foundation announced that a private voucher program was being set up in the nation's largest, most-watched city, to serve low-income children from the city's 14 lowest performing school

districts. The children were to be selected by lottery, and the proposal immediately met with an enthusiastic response from poor, inner-city parents, attracting more than 20,000 applications before the deadline of April 25. About 1,200 children were randomly selected and ultimately went on to use a voucher for the 1997–1998 school year, most of them attending Catholic schools. What makes this program different from all the others is not just that it is a high-profile case, guaranteeing a maximum of exposure. It is that the program is consciously designed to allow for a careful, scientific evaluation of its effectiveness. A good deal of money (more than $1 million) has been invested to ensure that the research is carried out properly and with adequate staffing and resources. The first reports have only recently appeared, and they will almost certainly have major impacts on the national voucher debate—and on the social science of school choice (Archer, 1997; Peterson, Myers, & Howell, 1998—the research is discussed later).

2. One of the most provocative new programs by voucher advocates has followed the novel strategy of focusing its attention on a single public school—a strategy that, again, has attracted nationwide publicity. Albany's private voucher program, A Better Choice (ABC), underwritten by a $1-million commitment from New York investor Virginia Gilder, offered to provide vouchers beginning with the 1997–1998 school year to every child in Albany's Giffen Memorial Elementary School—one of the worst-performing schools in the state, whose constituent families are almost entirely poor. It is unclear exactly how many of Giffen's 458 students have taken advantage of the vouchers since the program began. ABC put the figure at 105 for the first year of the program, whereas the district says the real figure is 77. But whatever the number, Giffen has suddenly become the target of serious reform efforts by the district, obviously in response to the new competition (and publicity) induced by private vouchers. Among other things, Giffen has a new principal, 2 new top-level administrators, 12 new replacement teachers, new staff workshops on teaching methods, a new mentoring program for teachers, a new telephone hotline to help students with homework, a new program to recruit parents volunteers, and a renewed emphasis on student discipline. The district has also voted to give the school an extra $125,000 beyond the funding it would normally have received. Whether these efforts will work is another matter. But the ABC program already seems to have demonstrated, at least in this one

high-profile case, that competition can indeed motivate the public schools to improve (Archer, 1998b).

3. In April 1998, another approach that is equally novel, but on a grander and more expensive scale, was announced by CEO America and its supporters in San Antonio. Called the Horizon program, its plan is to invest some $50 million over 10 years in providing full-tuition vouchers to every low-income child in the 14,000-student Edgewood Independent School District, a low-performing district that is predominantly poor and Hispanic. As in New York City, moreover, money was allocated to fund an independent evaluation to determine whether the voucher students ultimately learn more than their peers in public schools. The potential impact of the Horizon program on its home district is enormous. Most private voucher programs are very small in comparison with the total enrollment of the school districts in which they are located, but in San Antonio the situation is different, because Horizon could ultimately siphon off a large enough percentage of public school students to make a real dent in the district's enrollments and funding, and the district is well aware of this. Whether Horizon will have such an impact remains to be seen. In the first year of the program, despite concerted efforts to inform Edgewood parents of their new options, interest in the program was lower than advocates might have expected. Vouchers were given out to 740 children from the public schools (and another 46 who had already been in private schools), representing just 5% of kids in the district. Some of this is due to a shortage of slots (for now) in the private sector, as some parents who wanted vouchers could not get into their preferred school because of space limitations. Nonetheless, the fact is that there has *not* been a groundswell of demand so far for the new vouchers, as there has been in other areas of the country. At present, it is simply unclear why this is so, and whether it will change over time as Edgewood parents become more familiar with the program. Whatever the answers, they should contribute to the nation's storehouse of knowledge on vouchers—as should information on how the district responds to competition, and whether the voucher students ultimately learn more (Walsh, 1998b).

4. And now for the main event. During the summer of 1998, Theodore Forstmann and John Walton announced the most ambitious and richly funded expansion of private vouchers to date, the CSF (see

Archer, 1998a). This giant leap forward was bankrolled by their own contribution of a staggering $100 million, supplemented (within months) by some $70 million in matching contributions from local communities, and supported by a national advisory board that includes a diverse range of highly respected leaders throughout society, including a number of prominent Democrats—a signal to the liberal opponents of vouchers that their united front may be in the process of crumbling. In April 1999, after much advance work and national coordination (which included getting out the word to low-income families), and with the media watching intently, CSF carried out a lottery in which 40,000 low-income children in cities all around the country were awarded scholarships. In one fell swoop, this lottery quadrupled the number of kids nationwide served by private voucher programs, from 13,000 to 53,000. In the process, it offered dramatic new evidence of what the smaller programs (Edgewood being the major exception) had indicated before: that there appears to be a pent-up demand for vouchers among low-income families, who want better schools but don't have the means to pursue them. The evidence in this case: More than a *million* low-income children applied for the 40,000 available slots—an astounding figure that will almost surely play a role in the larger debate over school choice, and in the way policymakers see the issue in the years ahead (Hartocollis, 1999). The CSF program is just getting under way, but its emergence already marks a stunning development whose importance—for the children whose lives are affected, for the politics of vouchers and education reform, and for the accumulation of scientific evidence—is difficult to overstate.

EVIDENCE AND POLITICS

The leaders of the private voucher movement are dedicated to fundamental reform of the American school system through vouchers. They believe that their own programs, by generating hard evidence that vouchers do indeed work, can inform and shape the public debate, put substantially greater force behind the arguments for vouchers, and lead the way toward political success in state legislatures around the country.

In the short run, this is an optimistic scenario. Even if their programs turn out to be screaming successes, the fact is that politics is often unmoved by convincing evidence. Tobacco clearly kills people, but the government still subsidizes its production, because tobacco farmers and their legislative representatives are powerful. In politics, it is power that counts. Evidence is essentially a tool, and as power brokers manipulate it to their own advantage, truth gives way to interpretation, nuance, selective omission, and outright lies. And most listeners don't know the difference. So even if the evidence seems clear, convincing, and on your side, it may or may not mean much. And it certainly will not change the views of the opposition—the educational establishment will oppose vouchers no matter what, because it is in their best interest to do so.

Still, evidence does matter in politics. It matters most of all to the people, groups, and policymakers who are uncommitted. And although the educational establishment is usually powerful enough to carry the day on issues that concern it, there are special issues, times, and places when the uncommitteds turn out to be crucial, when evidence really does count, and when radical changes can be brought about because of it. So the private voucher strategy of generating evidence makes good sense, and may well pay off. But its successes will occur unpredictably, when the political stars happen to line up just right, and not simply because the empirical case has been made persuasively (Kingdon, 1984).

To the extent that evidence does matter in the voucher debate, the private voucher movement is of pivotal importance. For at this point, there is little direct evidence of how educational voucher programs actually work in practice. The reason for the lack of evidence is, again, fundamentally political: There can be no evidence without voucher programs to generate it, but the establishment has used its power to prevent the initiation of such programs, even on a limited and experimental basis—arguing, among other things, that it would be wrong to adopt vouchers in the absence of evidence that they work! If there are no programs, obviously, there can be no evidence; but if there is no evidence, they say, then there should be no programs. This is a Catch-22 that the establishment has long played upon. And because of the new evidence being generated by the private voucher movement—which does not need establishment consent to carry out its programs—the Catch-22 may soon come to an end.

OBSERVATIONS ON THE RESEARCH LITERATURE

Before I summarize what has so far been learned from these new programs, I want to provide a little background by offering some brief observations on the current research literature.

Perhaps the most important point to underline is that, because almost all efforts to enact public voucher programs have been defeated by the education establishment, and because only the Milwaukee program has been in operation long enough to generate much data, that single program has become the focus of extraordinary national attention, as though its performance is the critical test of whether vouchers work. This is unfortunate and misleading.

Voucher programs can be designed in all sorts of different ways, and Milwaukee's design is just one possibility—and a problematic one at that. As I suggested earlier, a number of onerous restrictions have been heaped on the program by its political opponents, making it difficult for market forces to work at all. Among other things, these restrictions have drastically limited (until recently, when the 1995 reforms were allowed to go into effect) the supply of schools in the program—which have limited choice, limited competition, and limited what we can possibly learn about vouchers. Indeed, as just *three* schools (until the recent changes) have enrolled the majority of the children in the program, any assessments of performance, attrition, parent satisfaction, and the like turn almost entirely on how those three schools are doing. This is hardly a solid basis for evaluating the effects of vouchers. In fact, it verges on the ridiculous.

Be this as it may, the reports coming out of Milwaukee have received enormous attention. For years, they were produced under the direction of one man, John Witte, a professor of political science at the University of Wisconsin who was anointed the program's official evaluator by Wisconsin's Superintendent of Public Instruction, Herbert Grover, himself a devout opponent of the program. Witte was given access to confidential test data on the Milwaukee public schools, authorized to carry out parent and school surveys that participating schools in both sectors were obliged to go along with, and, as a practical matter, given a monopoly over the collection and analysis of data. Rather than initiate a social scientific process in which various researchers could have analyzed the data on their own, produced their own evaluations, challenged and augmented one another's findings, and the like—which is typically how knowledge and confidence are generated in social science—opponents ensured that Wisconsin, and indeed the country as a whole, would depend entirely on John Witte to determine whether the nation's first voucher program was working.

Beginning in 1991, Witte came out with a series of annual reports evaluating the Milwaukee voucher program (Witte, 1991, 1997; Witte, Bailey, & Thorn, 1992, 1993; Witte, Sterr, & Thorn, 1995; Witte, Thorn, Pritchard, & Claibourn, 1994). Each received tremendous national and local publicity, and came to be treated in establishment, media, and policymaking circles as the definitive word on the impact of vouchers. Witte's basic themes remained the same throughout these annual reports, and their implications for vouchers were mixed—some positive, some negative. Regarding performance, his data suggested that voucher parents are more satisfied with their new private schools than public parents are, but that, on the crucial issue of student achievement, there is no indication that voucher children are learning more academically. Regarding issues of social equity, his data suggested that voucher schools are not skimming the best low-income students from the public schools, as critics had feared, and indeed are attracting children who were doing worse in public schools than other low-income kids. The data also showed, however, that voucher parents have more education than low-income public school parents, higher expectations for their children, and participate more—which suggests that the more advantaged of the low-income families are the ones getting the vouchers.

Witte quickly became the darling of the education establishment, which trumpeted his official finding that the program was failing to live up to the high ideals of its proponents—and emphasized, above all else, that vouchers had not led to greater academic achievement. It was academic achievement that parents, educators, opinion leaders, and policymakers throughout the nation seemed to care most about in evaluating education reforms. And Witte's documentation, in the nation's first voucher program, that vouchers had failed to promote achievement was portrayed as signaling the emptiness of vouchers as a productive path to school reform (Cookson, 1994). This was just the kind of research the opposition had hoped for.

Witte's monopoly over data and analysis made it impossible for outsiders, particularly those in the choice movement who questioned his findings, to carry out their own evaluations. In the realm of public opinion, as a result, Witte held all the cards and his official findings were essentially accepted without challenge. At least for a while. But in 1994, Paul Peterson, a political scientist at Harvard, took up the challenge of gaining access to Witte's data, and, after a series of legal and informal moves, eventually was successful in getting Witte to make the data public. While all this was going on, Peterson began publishing papers challenging Witte's methods and findings, and Witte responded by defending his work (Peterson, 1995; Peterson, Greene, & Noyes, 1996; Witte, 1995). Along with serious analytical argument, there was much vitriol and personal animosity on both sides. But this exchange was nonetheless quite useful, for it provided the first social scientific debate over Witte's official findings.

The debate shifted to another level when Peterson unveiled his research team's first reanalysis of the Milwaukee data (Greene, Peterson, & Du, 1998—initially released in 1996). Armed with the same data Witte had used, Peterson attempted to show more concretely that Witte's methods were indeed seriously flawed. He pointed out, for instance, that some of Witte's analyses omitted more than 80% of the students as missing cases. The most fundamental critique, however, had to do with the issue of statistical controls. Any research on the impact of vouchers must somehow deal with the fact that differences in student achievement may be due to vouchers, or they may be due to a number of other factors, particularly those having to do with family background and motivation. The challenge is to find a means of controlling for these other factors, and thus of determining what part of any achievement differences can rightfully be attributed to vouchers alone. Peterson and his colleagues argued that Witte's statistical controls did not do an adequate job of this, and led to spurious conclusions about the impact of vouchers.

More important, they went on to suggest an alternative. They argued that a better way to explore the impact of vouchers would be to take advantage of a "natural experiment" contained within the voucher program itself. Because there have not been enough private school slots to accommodate all the public school kids in Milwaukee who wanted vouchers, children were chosen by lottery—and those losing the lottery went back into the public schools. These children offer researchers a natural control group, for they ought to be virtually the same as the voucher children on all counts—background, motivation, and the like—except that, through the luck of the draw, they wound up going to public schools. According to the Peterson team, then, the best way to explore the impact of vouchers was to ask whether the voucher kids learned more in their private schools than this control group learned in the public schools.

This is an excellent idea with strong foundations in social science methodology. And when the Peterson team pursued it, they found that the voucher students in Milwaukee *did* in fact learn more, in both reading and math, than the control group of public school students (Greene, Peterson, & Du, 1998). These findings were largely verified, moreover, in a separate analysis of the same data by Cecilia Rouse (1997), who used a similar methodology.

The new research had thus turned Witte's official findings upside down: Vouchers did appear to promote academic achievement after all. Witte, of course, disputed these results (Witte, 1996, 1997). Among other things, he argued that Peterson's "natural experiment" was inappropriate, that his number of cases was too small, and that, because of attrition within the voucher program, the remaining children represented a biased sample (the better performing students, he suspected, are more likely to stay in the program) that could not properly be compared to a public school control group. The first two of Witte's arguments are unpersuasive. The third, which raises the attrition issue, is a legitimate concern that could well bias the results if true. Greene and Peterson (1996) responded to this criticism quite effectively, however, producing new evidence that suggests—although it cannot prove—that attrition has not actually produced the kind of bias Witte claimed.

It is impossible to know definitively who is right in this debate, because there is simply not enough data at this point to resolve all the issues that arise in the course of analysis. Though, overall, I find the Peterson team's arguments, methods, and findings more persuasive, it is best for now to say that the jury is still out on the question of academic achievement in Milwaukee. Even so, there is no doubt that Peterson's entry into the arena has qualitatively changed the debate over vouchers, and for the better. In years past, one person handed down the official word on how our nation's only voucher program was faring. Now there is a genuine process of social scientific analysis and debate that promises, over the long haul, to move us toward the truth of the matter.

Already, this process has produced new research—and new conflicts. Fresh from his experience studying the nation's first public voucher program in Milwaukee, Peterson moved on to study the nation's second such program in Cleveland. As in Milwaukee, he was not anointed the official evaluator. The state awarded that job to a research team from Indiana University, under the direction of Kim Metcalf from the school of education. This team, like Witte's in Milwaukee, carried out a study of student achievement showing that, during the first year of the program's operation, voucher students did not learn more than a control group of public school students (Metcalf et al., 1998). The Peterson team carried out its own study, which showed that voucher students did in fact learn more (Greene, Howell, & Peterson, 1998). And a new debate was on, with each side disputing the other's methods and findings—and the media and policymakers paying close attention.

Here again, a dispassionate observer would have to reserve judgment about whether the voucher students are or are not really learning more. There is simply not enough evidence at this point, and the available studies are too preliminary in nature, to make a confident determination. The Peterson study is based on data from just two schools, contains no control group, and does not control for family background or other relevant factors. The Metcalf study focuses just on children in third grade, uses a questionable control group, and relies on statistical methods that are problematic. For the most part, the deficiencies on both sides arise from difficulties inherent in the data, and from the early stage of the research. Future work will tell us much more. Even so, the debate itself has been productive, with each team offering critiques of the other's work, and each pushing to generate new data and analysis that will prove more convincing. If all the sound and fury can be ignored: This is what social science is supposed to be about.

One final point. We need to remember that, in all studies based on comparisons of student achievement, however sophisticated they become and however well they are ultimately carried out, care must still be exercised in drawing conclusions about the effects of vouchers. The fact is, much of what is observed in any choice system is due to the specific rules, restrictions, and control mechanisms that shape how choice and markets happen to operate in that particular setting. As any economist would be quick to point out, choice and markets do not simply have generic, uniform effects. Their effects vary, sometimes enormously, depending on the institutional setting. In Milwaukee, for instance, it is almost surely of great significance that, until very recently (too recently to have affected existing studies) three fourths of the voucher kids have attended just three private schools. There has been very little of the competition that voucher advocates premise their ideas and expectations upon, and much dependence on the idiosyncrasies of those three schools. Moreover, the system's rules—random admissions, the exclusion of religious schools (until recently), vouchers equal to just half the per-pupil expenditure of public schools, the prohibition of parent add-ons—have surely affected the way the system performs. The Witte–Peterson debate, then, is properly about how vouchers have worked *in this particular system*, and it is dangerous to conclude—however the debate may come out—that their findings have straightforward implications for the effectiveness of vouchers more generally.

The empirical literature on school choice has grown substantially over the last 10 years or so, but it has rarely paid serious attention to these institutional and design issues. Most researchers tend to portray choice and markets as generic reforms with generic effects, without recognizing that the peculiar packages of rules, restrictions, and controls that get imposed on each system have major influences on how those systems work. Properly interpreted, much of this research is probably telling us as much about institutional settings (and thus, often, about the constraints imposed through politics) as it does about choice and markets. The challenge for researchers is to be more sensitive to these institutional concerns, and to recognize that vouchers and other choice-based reforms can only sensibly be evaluated in context.

The current state of the research literature only underlines the importance of studying private voucher programs. Their value is not just that they provide additional, much-needed evidence on student performance and other issues. It is that they allow us to explore how choice and markets tend to work in the absence of most of the rules and restrictions that shape—and often suffocate—the various school choice programs in the public sector. Private voucher programs have their own rules, and these rules (as I suggest later) affect the outcomes that get generated. But by comparison to the public programs, private voucher programs give us a much simpler, more direct indication of how choice and markets actually operate when the most burdensome trappings of bureaucracy and political control are removed.

THE EARLY EVIDENCE ON PRIVATE VOUCHERS

One of the key aims of the private voucher movement is to generate evidence that will ultimately have an influence on public policy. So it is hardly surprising that, from the beginning, leaders have taken steps to see that their programs are studied by independent researchers whose evaluations would carry weight with a national audience. Each of the large-scale programs that pioneered the movement—in Indianapolis, San

Antonio, and Milwaukee—contracted early on with outside research teams to collect data, carry out analysis, and publish reports on various aspects of its performance.

In practice, the resulting research efforts were only partially successful. There was a certain amount of coordination among the various groups—all, for instance, chose to survey participating parents by using a common set of items taken from John Witte's study of Milwaukee. But for the most part, they remained separate outfits that designed and carried out their own research in their own ways, so there was not nearly as much comparability as one might like—or might have expected, given its obvious advantages to the movement.

The reality, moreover, is that they were forced to operate on tight budgets, which meant that, as a practical matter, they could not afford to pursue the kinds of comprehensive, high-tech survey operations they would surely have preferred and that many researchers at universities and think tanks have come to expect. The movement's leaders wanted data and evaluation, and they were willing to invest a certain amount of money to get it; but they also were painfully aware that every dollar spent on research was a dollar that could not go toward a voucher, and this trade-off proved a major constraint. The research, as a result, was underfunded and not as productive as it might have been.

Leaders have since realized their mistake, and are now investing more heavily and systematically in empirical research. To carry out the work, they have turned to Harvard's Paul Peterson, who, having proved his tenacity and research skills in carrying out a very complex project in Milwaukee, has now been retained—by different leaders and organizations—to carry out studies of separate voucher programs in New York City, in San Antonio's Edgewood school district (the Horizon Program), in Washington, DC, and in Dayton. In each case, Peterson has urged leaders to design programs in such a way that they can be effectively studied. This has meant, among other things, the adoption of lottery-based selection processes that make it possible for Peterson to evaluate the effects of vouchers through "natural experiments." This is a development of great importance, one that seems to have set the stage for the most sophisticated and convincing research yet on the impact of vouchers.

The research on private vouchers is just getting under way. In the sections that follows, I briefly summarize what it has had to tell us so far.

First, it is worth making a quick point that addresses a standard concern of voucher critics about what we might call top-down inequities. The concern is that private schools are essentially elitist operations that carefully select among student applicants, preferring those who are academic achievers, well behaved, and from upper-middle-income families—and discriminating against the rest, particularly those who are disadvantaged or difficult to educate. The expectation, then, is that giving low-income kids vouchers will not necessarily give them access to private schools, because the schools will not want to have them (Cookson, 1994; Wells, 1993b).

There is no evidence whatever that this is actually borne out in practice. Thousands of low-income children have now been granted vouchers for use in the private sector, and all indications are that the overwhelming majority of private schools are happy to admit them. In Milwaukee's PAVE program, for instance, low-income students attend more than 100 schools in the metropolitan area (Beales & Wahl, 1995). In Indianapolis, the number of participating private schools is about 60 (Weinschrott & Kilgore, 1998). Similar stories can be told in virtually every other city with a private voucher program.

Moreover, though parents have not been surveyed on the discrimination issue, the way they characterize their choice of private schools does not suggest that there is an underlying problem. In Peterson's study of New York City, for example, 72% of parents receiving a voucher said that their child gained entrance to one of their preferred private schools. Very few pointed to obstacles—no space available, admissions tests—that could even be construed as a cover for discrimination. The main reason parents gave for not getting into a preferred school was simply that they did not have enough money to pay the extra tuition (Peterson, Myers, & Howell, 1998).

Demographics: Vouchers and the Creaming Problem

Another standard criticism of vouchers has to do with what we might call bottom-up inequities. When families are free to choose, critics argue, the parents most likely to take advantage of it are those who are most highly motivated, well informed, and well-to-do. The result is a creaming effect, in which choice programs "skim the cream," and less fortunate or capable families are left with less desirable opportunities (Cookson, 1992; Kozol, 1991; Wells, 1993b)

In the most general terms, there is clearly some merit to this argument (Moe, 1995b). Creaming is rooted in the calculus of choice itself: in the utility functions of parents, the information they bring to bear, and their income constraints. Some parents put a higher value on education than others do, and so are willing to give up more in order to secure quality schooling for their children. Some parents have more information than others do, and thus know more about what schools are available and how good they are. And some parents have higher incomes than others, and so are better able to acquire good information and afford good schools. Unrestricted choice, then, may well lead to "selection effects" with a class bias.

In practice, I should emphasize, these creaming effects may be mitigated or even reversed by a reality of American social life: The people who are disadvantaged on these decisional grounds also tend to be stuck in the worst schools. They have *more to gain* than their advantaged counterparts do, therefore, in seeking out new opportunities that choice makes available. Nonetheless, taken by themselves, the choice-based factors I just outlined do tend to produce creaming effects, and their potential for doing so is a troublesome (and predictable) problem that needs to be clearly recognized.

It is a mistake, however, to think that creaming is somehow limited to free markets. America's education system today, for instance, is based on political control, bureaucratic management, and student assignment by geographic area—yet it still suffers from extremely serious creaming problems. The main culprit is residential mobility. People are free to live where they want, and those who value education highly and have the money to pay for it tend to move to suburban districts with good schools. In urban areas with troubled schools, the only families left are the ones with too little money to get out. The result is a public education system highly segregated by class and race. This is a creaming effect.

Two points are especially central to a balanced perspective on vouchers and the creaming problem (Moe, 1995b). First, the assessment has to be comparative, rather than riveted on vouchers per se. The issue is not whether vouchers totally eliminate all vestiges and types of creaming. The issue is whether they improve upon the current system's creaming problem or make it worse. Second, the extent of the creaming problem is highly dependent on the institutional setting of rules, constraints, and controls in which choice takes place, and this can be socially engineered through appropriate design. Any choice program, in principle, can be consciously designed to reduce creaming and promote equal opportunity.

With this background, let's consider the demographics of who participates in private voucher programs. The place to start is by underlining the most fundamental feature of these programs: they are restricted by design to the most disadvantaged members of society. Not surprisingly, then, compared to the parent population as a whole, the parents who participate are significantly lower in income, less educated, more likely to be minorities, less likely to be married, and so on. In this crucial respect, private vouchers clearly strike a blow for social equity. They engage in "reverse creaming," setting up a design in which only the disadvantaged are allowed to reap the benefits of choice.

A rather different picture emerges if we compare program participants not to the population at large, but to other low-income families. Here we should expect that, in the absence of conscious design efforts to avoid it, the sorts of class-based selection effects I discussed earlier could assert themselves, and that the "most advantaged of the disadvantaged" may be the ones who disproportionately take advantage of private vouchers. And this is pretty much what the data indicate.

A study of the PAVE program in Milwaukee, for instance, showed that participating parents were better educated than other low-income parents in that city, and more likely to be White and married (Beales & Wahl, 1995). A more detailed study of San Antonio showed much the same pattern, adding that the voucher parents were also (among other things) higher in income, less likely to be on federal assistance, more inclined to help with homework, and possessed of higher expectations about how far their children would go in school (Godwin, Kemerer, & Martinez, 1998).

Probably the most consequential feature within this pattern is that voucher parents tend to be much better educated than other low-income parents, and to have higher expectations for their kids. To see what kinds of differences are involved here, consider some figures from San Antonio. In that program, 55% of CEO (chief executive officer) female parents had at least some college, whereas just 19% of female public school parents had that much education. The same yawning gap, not surprisingly, applies to educational expectations: 52% of CEO parents expect their children to continue education beyond the college level, compared to 17% of public school parents (Martinez et al., 1995).

This is a creaming effect. It is far less important, to be sure, than the programs' larger and positive impact on social equity. But it is still an outcome that many observers would consider undesirable. The better educated low-income parents, we can presume, are likely to place greater emphasis on their children's education, to be more strongly motivated to seek out better schools for them, to be better informed about private voucher programs and what they offer, and to know how to get involved. These qualities give them pivotal advantages over other low-income parents—and the children of the latter, as a result, have less opportunity to benefit from the programs.

It is reasonable to suggest that three elements of the Golden Rule design may be allowing this creaming effect to emerge. One is that participants are asked to pay half (or some portion of) the tuition. A second is that a fair percentage of the vouchers are given out to children already in private schools. And a third is that children are admitted on a first-come, first-served basis. All three may encourage a selection bias favoring the "most advantaged of the disadvantaged."

Let's begin with the second of these, because it suggests that the creaming effect is actually more nuanced than we have been letting on thus far. This is because the evidence of bias discussed earlier—which seemed straightforward—failed to distinguish between (a) voucher parents who came to the program from the public schools and (b) those who were already in private schools to begin with. It is reasonable to think that the latter, though still low in income, are likely to be a rather advantaged group compared to other low-income parents, particularly with regard to education and expectations. It is precisely *because* they put so much emphasis on education, presumably, that they sought out private schools in the first place and found a way to pay for them without a voucher. Thus, when voucher recipients as a whole are compared to the broader population of low-income parents, the inclusion of these previously private parents could account for some of the creaming effects we see across groups. Were we to look just at *public* parents who get vouchers, on the other hand, and ask how representative they are of low-income parents generally, we may get quite a different view of the creaming problem—if there is one. And for many observers, this may be the more relevant comparison: When private parents are factored out, how well do these programs do in extending new educational opportunities to low-income parents in the public sector? Do they tend to attract and serve the more advantaged low-income public parents, or do they successfully appeal to a broader cross-section?

These issues could be addressed and possibly even settled on the basis of the existing data sets, but the figures that are actually available in research reports do not provide a clear picture. The early studies on Milwaukee and Indianapolis both argue that there are *no* significant differences (aside from race, in Indianapolis) between the public and private voucher recipients (Beales & Wahl, 1995; Heise, Colburn, & Lamberti, 1995). A later study of Indianapolis presents data to show that the public voucher recipients are actually somewhat lower in income than the privates and less likely to be White (which the earlier study found)—but also implies (without presenting any data) that the public recipients are somewhat more educated than the private recipients, which would be surprising if true (Weinschrott & Kilgore, 1998). The most comprehensive data on the subject, however, come from preliminary studies of Dayton and Washington, DC, by Peterson. These programs are built around lotteries, which surely influenced the kinds of parents who applied (see later discussion). But what they show is that—at least in these particular programs—there *are* rather striking differences between the public and private recipients. Those coming from the public sector are less educated than the private recipients, and more likely to be Black, unmarried, and on government assistance. It may still be the case that the public recipients are advantaged relative to the broader population of low-income parents (there are no data on this). But they are clearly far less advantaged than the private recipients—and more representative of low-income parents as a whole (Peterson, Greene, Howell, & McCready, 1998).

It may well be that these conflicting results are actually telling a single story. The earlier programs, which were not based on lotteries with extended application periods, probably made it rather likely that the more motivated public parents would have certain advantages in seeking out vouchers. These more motivated parents, then, would look much like the low-income parents already in private schools—who are there precisely because they are more motivated than most. The differences between the two groups would then be minimal, as the early studies seemed to show. Many of the more recent programs, however, are moving toward lotteries. And a lottery changes things. When programs publicize the availability of vouchers, have an extended application period, and then choose students at random, the whole process is more accessible and open to average parents—and it is likely, as a result, that a more representative cross-section of low-income parents will apply for vouchers. This should reduce inequities. At the same time, it should create a bigger gap between the public and private participants in the program: the parents already in private schools should still look advantaged by the usual measures, whereas the public parents should look more like the broader population of low-income parents. This is exactly what the Peterson studies reveal.

Now let's return to the three factors that, a few paragraphs ago, I suggested might account for the creaming effects associated with private vouchers. One was that these programs offer vouchers to private as well as public parents. As we have seen, including the private parents in any comparison almost guarantees that the programs will appear to be serving the "advantaged of the disadvantaged." When private parents are omitted, however, and the focus is just on whether the programs attract a representative group of public parents, there may *still* be a creaming problem of much the same magnitude. Why? Because unless the application process makes it easy for ordinary parents to learn about the program, apply, and get accepted, the more motivated parents will still have advantages. Only if procedures are adopted that reduce those advantages will the creaming problem be mitigated.

The other two factors I listed earlier as helping account for the creaming problem are of the utmost relevance in this regard. For both are rules that, rather than facilitating participation by ordinary parents, actually make their participation more difficult. One is the requirement that parents pay half the tuition. The other is the first-come, first-served method of admissions. Because of the income requirement, parents who are especially disadvantaged may find it impossible to participate in a private voucher program. And because of the first-come, first-served method of selection, which was used (in various forms) by virtually all the early programs, parents who are the best informed, most resourceful, and best connected—meaning, again, those who are the best educated and most motivated—have the clear edge in gaining access to the vouchers. As noted previously, a number of programs have moved away from first-come, first-served in recent years, and are relying instead on well-publicized lotteries as their means of selection. There is good reason to believe, then, that these programs will do a better job of attracting a representative group of parents than the earlier programs did.

The available data have something to tell us about these matters, although not as much as we might like. Regarding the income restriction, perhaps the best evidence is provided by Witte's study of Milwaukee. Although Milwaukee is not a private voucher program, it is relevant here because, unlike the private plans, it does not require its low-income parents to pay anything at all to participate in the program—which means that income should have less to do (if anything) with who participates, and enrollments should be more equitable. The facts, as Witte showed, square nicely with this intuition: The parents who participate in the Milwaukee voucher program are not higher in income than other eligible parents with children in the public schools. In fact, they have somewhat lower incomes—although they *are* better educated (Witte, 1991; Witte et al., 1992, 1993, 1994, 1995). All of the private voucher programs for which there are data, on the other hand, require participating families to pay part of the tuition—and with one important exception (a lottery system—see later discussion), studies show that the parents who do participate tend to have higher incomes than those that don't, as expected (see, e.g., Martinez et al., 1995). For first-come, first-served programs, at any rate, it appears that the income restriction does matter.

Now let's consider the first-come, first-served system itself. Under such a system, which was initially adopted precisely to ensure fairness and equal treatment, the dynamics of information and access almost surely work to favor those parents who are relatively advantaged. The research reports tend to suggest as much. For the pioneering Golden Rule type programs, getting the word out—about what the programs offer, who is eligible, when and where applications must be filed, what the procedures are for applying, and so on—proved to be an operational task that was more complicated and consequential than leaders had counted on. All relied heavily on newspapers, supplemented by churches and private schools, both of which had incentives to inform their clienteles that vouchers would be available. In addition, leaders could expect some and perhaps many people to find out through word of mouth, once the information was released through the more formal, organizational channels (Beales & Wahl, 1995; Heise et al., 1995; Martinez et al., 1995).

If admissions were based on lottery or some other random means, then the flow of information would not be so crucial. Virtually all eligible families would eventually find out, and timing would not matter. But in a world of limited vouchers, with availability determined by who gets in line first, it makes a big difference who has early access to information. And these are clearly people who read newspapers every day, who are somehow already connected to private schools and to churches, and who are motivated enough to pay attention and pick up the information they need on their own. Though all sorts of people may fall into these categories, the deck is unintentionally stacked in favor of eligible parents who are advantaged in various respects.

Some of the evidence bearing on the apparent impact of first-come, first-served has already been discussed. Programs using this hallmark of the Golden Rule model seem to attract public parents who are just as advantaged as the private parents who get vouchers, and the move to a lottery-based system seems to lessen the bias by attracting public parents who are less advantaged. We could not say, however, how close they come to being representative of the broader population of parents, because the studies being discussed (of Dayton and Washington, DC) didn't have such a control group. In the remaining literature, the study that speaks to this matter most directly is Peterson's report on New York City, which operates on the basis of a lottery. Here, Peterson's team compares the public parents who applied for vouchers to the "eligible population" of New York's low-income parents, where the characteristics of the latter are extrapolated from census data. The analysis shows that, although the low-income parents who apply are much better educated than other low-income parents, they do not have higher incomes, are somewhat more likely to be on government assistance, and are more likely to be African-American (Peterson, Myers, & Howell, 1998).

The New York results are provocative. First, they suggest that the "education advantage" continues to be profoundly influential, even in programs based on lotteries, and that any attempt to mitigate it—and thus to give all low-income families an equal shot at the vouchers, regardless of their educational backgrounds—will have to put more serious restrictions on the selection process. Second, they suggest that a lottery, combined with an extended application period, does seem to even out inequities in other respects, particularly with regard to race and income. This in turn implies that the income restriction built into these programs—that participants pay some portion of the tuition—may not be much of an obstacle to participation after all. It may be, to speculate a bit, that the greatest relevance of low income is not that it means parents can't arrange to pay their half of the tuition—which they might still be able to do via their own funds, scholarships, or help from friends and relatives—but that it is a proxy for the more general fact that they lack the "resources" to compete in a first-come, first-served kind of selection system. The main problem, on this theory, is not the price of tuition, but the price of getting to the head of the line. And when a lottery system eliminates the latter as a problem, it may well be that income will no longer keep parents out of the programs.

Ultimately, we need more data before firm conclusions can be embraced. But at this point, the bottom line is simply this. Private voucher programs are major forces for social equity, in the sense that they extend benefits and choice to the most disadvantaged members of American society. Among the disadvantaged, however, there are certain inequities in who gets to participate and who doesn't—and the pattern and extent of these inequities turns on exactly how the programs are designed. Most of these, even those based on income, might be reduced or even eliminated by the use of lottery-based selection methods, on which the more recent programs are increasingly based. But one source of inequity remains hugely important in all these programs, whether or not they use lotteries: Parents who choose to participate tend to be much better educated and more highly motivated than parents who don't.

Reasons for Participating

A common criticism from the opponents of school choice is that parents cannot be counted on to make choices on the basis of sound educational criteria or values. Parents—especially low-income parents—supposedly care about practical concerns, like how close the school is or whether it has a good sports team, and put little emphasis on academic quality and other properties of effective schooling. As a result, they not only fail to make good decisions for their children, but they also fail to give schools strong incentives, in competing for parent support, to provide high-quality education (e.g., Carnegie Foundation for the Advancement of Teaching, 1992).

These claims are based on a selective view of the earliest evidence on the subject, almost all of which comes from studies of public school choice arrangements that give parents little of substance to choose from. Why would parents choose on the basis of academic quality if the schools they are allowed to choose among are pretty much the same? Clearly, the best way to observe what motivates parental choice is to look at contexts in which they really have choices to make.

Until recently, the most suggestive data on the basis of parental choice came from the Milwaukee public voucher program. Although the number of private sector choices is limited there, parents are still allowed to choose between public and private, which is a significant choice. Witte's data on Milwaukee reveal that low-income parents in the voucher program single out academic quality as the most important reason for using the voucher, followed by discipline and the general atmosphere of the school—clear indications that their choices are driven by educational concerns. Voucher parents are also motivated by frustration with the public schools, and are much more dissatisfied with them than parents who remain in the public sector. Yet this motivation—which appears to derive from the same concerns for academics, discipline, and atmosphere—receives somewhat less emphasis (Witte, 1991, 1997; Witte et al., 1992, 1993, 1994, 1995).

Private voucher programs, as well as the Cleveland public voucher program, ought to provide even better evidence than Milwaukee has been able to generate thus far, because these programs give parents the entire private sector to choose from, and thus greater opportunities to act on their own values. As the following chapters indicate, the evidence they yield is strikingly consistent with Witte's findings for the public voucher system. Indeed, the results for the two Milwaukee voucher programs, one public and one private (PAVE), are virtually identical. More generally, across all the Golden Rule type programs for which such evidence is available—Indianapolis, San Antonio, Milwaukee, Washington, DC, Dayton, and New York City—as well as for the Cleveland public voucher program, parents uniformly indicate that academic quality is their most salient reason for participating. Discipline is typically very highly ranked, as is the school's general atmosphere. And frustration with the public schools, though not the top motivator, is a consistent complaint. In each program that asks about it—Indianapolis, San Antonio, and Milwaukee—more than 80% of the parents say that it is either an important or very important reason for wanting vouchers (Beales & Wahl, 1995; Heise et al., 1995; Martinez et al., 1995; Peterson, Greene, et al., 1998; Peterson, Myers, & Howell, 1998).

One caveat needs to be kept in mind. These programs remain rather small, and they do not reflect a cross-section of their target population. The parents who participate are a better educated, more motivated group than low-income parents who do not participate, and the fact that they rank school-effectiveness issues so highly does not mean that other parents would do the same. They may not. Additional research is needed to determine what the gap actually is, and how the full range of parents approaches the task of school choice. The "what motivates parents?" issue could look a lot different if we had data on *all* low-income parents, rather than just the motivated subset that applies for vouchers.

Still, the evidence presented here helps fill the missing contours of our knowledge. And to the extent it does, it challenges the jaundiced, often patronizing view of parents that prevails in parts of the literature—especially of low-income parents, who, critics are quick to say, cannot be trusted to make their own decisions (e.g., Wells, 1993a). It is of no small weight that the programs being studied here do not target suburbanites, or even average middle-class families, but precisely that stratum of society that critics regard as the least capable or responsible. The evidence suggests that, even within this stratum, parents who use vouchers put very substantial emphasis on educational concerns in making their choices about schools.

Parent Satisfaction

What are the impacts of vouchers on children? For most observers, the acid test is whether vouchers lead to higher student achievement—and thus, in practical terms, whether voucher children do better on standardized tests than children in public school do, once other factors are properly controlled. But although learning is certainly a crucial outcome of schooling, it is not the only aspect that contributes to the well-being of children. Standardized tests, moreover, measure only some aspects of learning, and may not always do that especially well. To get a more broadly based view of how well children are doing, we need to look at a wider range of indicators, and we need to recognize that many of the important aspects of schooling—including those that have to do with how much students learn—are intangible. They are qualities that people recognize or sense when they experience them, but that tend to defy formal measurement.

In a choice system, the people whose judgments matter most are parents. They may not be experts, but they know what they want for their children, they know what they are looking for in a school, and they can give you their summary judgments of how well schools—and their kids—are doing on a range of dimensions. Parent satisfaction, then, is important evidence. It is subjective, to be sure, but it is anchored in direct experience, reflects the kinds of judgments on intangibles that are needed to assess important components of schooling, and addresses a fundamental issue that needs answering about any school system: whether it pleases the people it is supposed to be serving. This is a performance issue, no less than student learning is.

Data on parent satisfaction offer some of the best evidence available on the impacts of vouchers. Witte's reports on the Milwaukee public voucher system have already shown that voucher parents are substantially more satisfied with their new private schools than public school parents are with their public schools. And although the size of the satisfaction gap depends on what aspect of schooling is being evaluated—from learning to discipline to textbooks to opportunities for participation—voucher parents are consistently more satisfied than their public school counterparts, whatever the issue (Witte, 1991; Witte et al., 1992, 1993, 1994, 1995). The Peterson team's study of the Cleveland public voucher program shows the same thing (Greene, Howell, & Peterson, 1998).

The data coming in from the private voucher programs strongly and consistently reinforce these results. The study of Milwaukee's PAVE program purposely surveyed its parents on the same satisfaction items that Witte used, and found that PAVE parents are not only considerably more satisfied than public school parents across all issue areas, but they are even more satisfied than the parents in the public voucher program (Beales & Wahl, 1995). This makes sense, because they have more to choose from than the public voucher parents do, and they have more opportunities to find schools they are happy with. In Indianapolis, San Antonio, and New York City, the evidence again indicates that parental satisfaction increases substantially, and across a variety of dimensions, as children shift from public to private schools as a result of vouchers (Heise et al., 1995; Martinez et al., 1995; Peterson, Myers, & Howell, 1998).

This is crucial information. But there is also a perplexing side to the satisfaction issue, one that researchers need to pay more attention to. Whereas the vast majority of voucher parents say they were "frustrated" with the public schools, far fewer say they were actually "dissatisfied" when asked about *specific aspects* of the public schools. In Indianapolis, for instance, the percentage claiming to be dissatisfied is typically between 20% and 35%, depending on the issue, with large majorities saying they were satisfied on each (Heise et al., 1995). The same is true in San Antonio, although dissatisfaction seems to run a bit higher there, varying between 25% and 50% or so; but even in that city, a majority of voucher parents typically indicate that they were satisfied (Martinez et al., 1995).

A similar phenomenon is apparent if we look at public school parents. In Milwaukee, the proportion of public school parents who actually say they are dissatisfied with their schools varies between 7% (for textbooks) and 25% (for discipline), depending on the issue, and fully 65% say they would give their schools an A or a B as a summary grade (Beales & Wahl, 1995). In San Antonio, a poor Hispanic community not known for the stellar quality of its public schools, 80% of the surveyed public school parents gave their schools an A or a B (Martinez et al., 1995).

These figures are intriguing, and may have various explanations.[11] But one deserves special mention. Attempts to measure citizen satisfaction with government services—police, fire, garbage collection, schools—have long suffered from a subtle problem that has largely gone unrecognized, both by education researchers and by students of urban government.[12] One symptom of this problem is that low-income people, who by objective standards are often provided with lower-quality services, may claim to be quite satisfied, whereas higher-income suburbanites, whose services are objectively of much higher quality, may complain and express their dissatisfaction. A plausible reason for the disparity (when it occurs) is that these groups have different *expectations*, based on their very different life experiences. Low-income people have lower expectations than high-income people do and may be more disposed to say they are satisfied. This is especially likely to be true, I suspect, among populations of recent immigrants, who are not used to the kinds of services American governments provide, and among subcultures (such as the Hispanic) that emphasize paternalism and deference to authority.

It is important to keep in mind, then, that low-income parents in general are not necessarily dissatisfied with the public schools, and that they may continue to be rather satisfied even if the performance of these schools is poor. This does not mean that they wouldn't be interested in seeking out better alternatives in the private sector. Nor does it mean, were they to transfer to private schools, that they wouldn't be even more satisfied as a result. Nonetheless, to the extent that many low-income people are inclined to be satisfied with their current public schools, it obviously does mean that their *incentives* to go private, or to seek out vouchers, are less than they would otherwise be—and this could have profound implications for the ability of the voucher movement to attract large numbers of these parents as supporters. Most of them, it appears, are not good candidates for a revolution.

Again, more data are needed to figure out exactly what is going on here. The issues are important, and surely worth exploring. What we do know, however, is that the people who do choose to participate in voucher programs—a subset of low-income parents—are considerably more satisfied with their new private schools than they were with their original public schools, and that they are much more satisfied than other parents who have been in the public schools all along. These are among the strongest findings in the entire literature. In the eyes of parents who have actually used vouchers, the verdict is that vouchers work.

Student Achievement

For almost everyone involved in the national debate over vouchers, the most salient issue is student achievement. Advocates gain credibility for their cause by showing that parents subjectively believe vouchers are working well for them. But what uncommitted people want to see—and what opponents demand—are objective assessments of whether vouchers "really are" working to promote higher levels of student achievement. Achievement is the focal point of the debate, the key political issue.

It is also an issue that, in practice, is difficult to investigate. Part of the problem is that most voucher programs are quite young, and it is a risky business to try to evaluate the impact of vouchers by studying systems that are still in their shaky, early stages. The changes that parental choice sets in motion may take time to be realized. Children have to settle into their new schools and be shaped by their new settings, and schools have to come to terms with their new incentives and have a chance to adjust. It is probably a mistake to think that, even in a well-functioning choice system, students will suddenly show huge gains in achievement (although some may). Ideally, a confident evaluation calls for studies of systems that are reasonably well established.

Even if these problems could be dealt with, studying the effects of vouchers on student achievement would still be very difficult. Among other things, for instance, researchers would need to get the same or comparable test scores for both public and private school students—which is harder than it seems, and often just impossible. Private schools may not test their students at all, or use a variety of different tests that may not match those given by the public schools. Public school test scores, meanwhile, are often subject to all sorts of legal restrictions, and may be unavailable to researchers. Simply getting test scores, then, is a forbidding task.

Once test scores are obtained, moreover, researchers have to deal with the problem of controlling for other variables—family background and the like—that could also play a role in explaining how much students learn, and that may account (via "selection effects") for why some children show up in voucher programs to begin with. A good research design must either be built around a "natural experiment," in which these factors can be implicitly controlled through the random assignment of students to treatment (voucher) and control (nonvoucher) groups. Or in the absence of an experimental design, it must control for all these variables statistically—which means that an array of background data must somehow be collected on each student. Needless to say, most schools do not have this kind of information on hand, and most school officials are not eager to authorize researchers to collect it. So it is hard to carry out research that controls for all the variables we know might be relevant, or even for the important ones.

Good research is difficult to do—and it is expensive. The leaders of the private voucher movement did not seem to appreciate this during the early going, and as a result the early research projects were neither designed nor funded in such a way that they could provide confident answers to the achievement issue. Studies of Milwaukee (Beales & Wahl, 1995), Indianapolis (Heise et al., 1995; Weinschrott & Kilgore, 1998), and San Antonio (Godwin et al., 1998) all present data on test scores, and their evidence suggests that voucher students do achieve at higher levels than comparable children in the public schools. But as the authors themselves point out, their data and controls are limited in important respects, and their analyses are best regarded as quite preliminary.

Until recently, the best data and analysis on student achievement arose out of the Milwaukee public voucher program. Here, John Witte was able to use his official status to amass a huge, multiyear data set—on test scores, background variables, parent attitudes—that he and his team analyzed on their own for several years, followed by the Peterson team and Cecilia Rouse. As we discussed earlier, these research efforts led to conflicting results, with Witte arguing that voucher students didn't learn more than comparable public students, and the Peterson team and Rouse arguing that they did. Though unresolved, this debate was a giant leap forward for the study of vouchers and student achievement, and paved the way for a new generation of research projects—projects designed to provide for even better data, and to allow for a more confident appraisal of vouchers.

At this writing, all of these projects are under the direction of Paul Peterson. And the voucher programs themselves—in New York City, Washington, DC, and Dayton—have been designed around lottery methods of selection that allow for "natural experiments." This takes care of the control problem (although it is supplemented by parent surveys that provide background and motivational information). As for the test-score problem: The Peterson team dealt with it by arranging for all student applicants—both those who get vouchers (the treatment group) and those who don't (the control group)—to take appropriate standardized tests of achievement, and by having these same students retested over time. Thus, there is no reliance on the public school system for test-score data.

This is the future of empirical research on vouchers. So far, the Peterson team (working with Mathematica, an independent research organization) has produced one new study of student achievement, a path-breaking analysis of the New York City program (Peterson, Myers, & Howell, 1998). Its key finding is that, after just 1 year in the program, voucher students *did* learn more than the control group of students who applied for vouchers but remained in the public schools. Overall, the differences were statistically significant but not especially large—2 percentile points in math and 2.2 percentile points in reading. But this is perhaps what one ought to expect, after just 1 year. It is interesting, moreover, that the differences were greater for students in Grades 4 and 5 than for students in the earlier years—a result that may make good sense (and be important on policy grounds), given that urban public school students often tend to decline relative to national norms as they get older, and thus may well get a bigger boost by attending private schools than younger students do.

This does not settle the achievement issue, of course. Indeed, it is really only the beginning. But it is a truly exciting one—based on data and methodologies that are the best yet, and that inspire a great deal of confidence in the results. Already, the New York findings have been highly publicized in major newspapers, and they will doubtless play a major role in the continuing national debate. In the near future, the Peterson team is scheduled to complete new studies of achievement that, whatever their findings, will have similar impacts. This is precisely what the founders of the private voucher movement intended from the beginning—to create programs that would generate evidence on the impact of vouchers, and to use this evidence to influence the policy-making process. After an uncertain start, it appears their goals are finally being realized. Now they just have to hope that the findings continue to go their way.

One last point. Voucher leaders are delighted by these developments (for now), but social science is also a beneficiary. The essential scientific question here is: What is the truth of the matter? Do vouchers promote student achievement or not? In years past, it was difficult or impossible to carry out well-designed studies, and one researcher, John Witte, controlled the only good data set. Now all that has changed. There is genuine debate, there are alternative data sets, and clear progress is being made. In the short term, it is something of a problem that virtually all the new-generation studies (using “natural experiments”) are being carried out by the same research team. But over time other teams will likely get in on the act—and the Peterson team is planning to make its data sets public, so that others can reanalyze their data and have the opportunity to challenge their conclusions. Finally, social science is working the way it is supposed to, and the ultimate outcome will be a clearer understanding of the truth, whether it reflects favorably on vouchers or not.

CONCLUSION

The private voucher movement is in its early stages, and research on its programs has only just gotten under way. Even at this point, however, these new programs represent a uniquely valuable source of information and insight that have begun to fill a serious gap in the existing empirical literature.

The current knowledge gap is a byproduct of politics. In the public sector, the education establishment’s staunch opposition to vouchers has so far defeated all voucher proposals but three—inner-city programs in Milwaukee and Cleveland, and a statewide program in Florida—creating a situation in which there has been little on vouchers to study and no way for researchers to gather the kind of evidence they need. By default, the pioneering program in Milwaukee has come to be regarded as the critical test of whether vouchers work, even though its program is so restricted that it makes a very poor laboratory for exploring what vouchers can or cannot do.

Thanks to the private voucher movement, there are suddenly a great many voucher systems in operation. These systems, moreover, are based on simple program designs, free of the bureaucratic and political constraints that, in the public sector, have inhibited the operation of choice and made the study of its effects an exceedingly difficult and confusing business. With the advent of private vouchers, researchers have an array of exciting opportunities for exploring how vouchers actually work, and for investigating a range of choice-related issues that in more complex settings would tend to be obscured.

On the whole, what they have to tell us about vouchers is positive and encouraging. The evidence suggests that there is indeed a genuine demand for vouchers among low-income families, who respond enthusiastically and in large numbers when given the opportunity to participate in these programs, even when they are asked to pay half the costs. Free to choose, they distribute themselves across a wide variety of private schools; and these schools, contrary to the prevailing myth about private-sector elitism, appear only too happy to take them in. When poor children have vouchers, they have access, and there is good reason to believe that their educational opportunities are expanded considerably.

Experience from private voucher programs also casts doubt on the myth of parental incompetence. The evidence suggests that participating parents make good choices for their children, or at least make a serious effort to do so; for they appear to be guided by precisely the sorts of educational criteria that concerned parents ought to be guided by—academic quality, discipline, and other indicators of effective schooling. To the extent this is so, moreover, they are probably transmitting the right kinds of incentives to participating schools, which are put on notice that they need to do their jobs well if they are to attract parent support.

The evidence also tends to suggest—at least so far—that vouchers work. Data on parent satisfaction indicate that, on a variety of different dimensions, voucher parents are highly satisfied with the schools they have chosen, think the shift from public to private has been a beneficial one, and evaluate their schools more highly than public school parents do. These are important measures of how well students and schools are doing and, even were good data available on achievement, would still deserve heavy emphasis. In the eyes of the people who use them, vouchers seem to be working well.

The data on achievement are more complicated, and there is not enough evidence as yet to say with confidence that the students who take advantage of vouchers clearly learn more than the students who don't. Yet there has been real progress in the study of student achievement. And, at this stage, the weight of the research—including the most recent work, based on the best data and methods—leads to the tentative conclusion that voucher students do indeed learn more. Additional research on the topic is forthcoming, and whether these early results will hold up over time remains to be seen. But for now, science appears to be confirming what private voucher leaders "knew" it would confirm all along.

On the negative side of the ledger, one issue stands out: These programs have given rise to creaming effects. The creaming issue is well worth attention, but it needs to be kept in perspective. The overarching fact is that private vouchers strike a forceful blow for social equity. They are premised on the goal of expanding educational opportunities for low-income families, they appear to be succeeding, and they deserve great credit for that.

The creaming effect at work here is "internal," favoring some low-income families—those who are more highly educated and motivated—over others. It is a predictable outcome, given the underlying dynamics of choice, but it is not inevitable and could readily be lessened or even eliminated with the right program design. Creaming occurs because the original Golden Rule model is not designed to prevent it. The most likely suspect is its first-come, first-served rule, which allows the best informed, most highly motivated families to snatch up a limited supply of vouchers. Were leaders to change their rules for application and acceptance, institute lotteries, and put more effort into communication and outreach, the result would likely be a dramatic reduction in internal creaming. The newer programs, of course, have been moving in precisely this direction.

The creaming issue highlights a fundamental point that is little appreciated in the debate over vouchers: *Design is the key.* How vouchers and choice work out in practice is critically dependent on the framework of rules in which they are embedded. Vouchers will not work to greatest advantage in the absence of appropriate design features. As private voucher programs expand and multiply, researchers will have increasing opportunities to observe how different designs work out in practice, and, more generally, to explore the range of issues—from student performance to parental participation to information to equity and access—that need to be jointly assessed and fitted together in any coherent treatment of vouchers. This is an exciting prospect, and for the first time promises to generate an extensive body of empirical research to inform the public debate. As it does, it may well change that debate dramatically, along with the path of American education reform.

This prospect, of course, has been at the heart of the movement's game plan from the very beginning: to generate evidence that can be used as a powerful weapon in the political struggle for choice-based reform. Whether things will actually work out as its leaders envision is another matter. Most of the evidence has yet to come in. When it does, it may or may not be as convincing as supporters hope (although I suspect it will be quite positive). And even if the empirical case is overwhelming, it may or may not have much of an impact on the rough-and-tumble world of power politics, which is often unresponsive to even the best of evidence. Time will tell.

In the meantime, we cannot lose sight of the fact that the private voucher movement is a far more important social phenomenon than a focus on evidence and research alone can suggest. It is a movement that opens new educational opportunities to thousands of disadvantaged children. It is a movement that promotes innovation and change by loosening the iron grip of established interests. It is a movement that adds fire and momentum to the larger movement for school choice. But above all else, in my view, it is a movement that embodies and advances a new politics of education—a politics that stands traditional alliances on their heads, and promises to transform the constellation of pressures that shape our nation's educational policies and practices.

The new politics of education has only just begun to emerge, but its roots are deep in the basic structure of modern American society. Low-income families are trapped in our nation's worst schools. They want the same kinds of educational opportunities that more advantaged families have, yet their interests have gone unrepresented by their usual political allies—Democrats, the educational establishment, liberal interest groups—who are tightly bound to the existing system and are committed to defending it. Accordingly, the poor are driven to look elsewhere for their champions, and they are finding them on the conservative side of the political fence, where there is a genuine willingness to take on the educational powers-that-be and, social stereotypes notwithstanding, a genuine concern for using markets and choice to promote social equity.

In the new politics of education, the conservatives have become the progressives, pushing for major change, promoting the causes of the disadvantaged, and allying themselves with the poor. And the progressives have become the conservatives, resisting change, defending "their" status quo against threats from without, and opposing the poor constituents they claim to represent. In its consequences for the American system of education, this is perhaps the most important political transformation of modern times—and the private voucher movement, as both a creature of the new politics and a major force for its expansion, is right at the heart of it.

ENDNOTES

1. These data were obtained from CEO America, from their central office in Bentonville, Arkansas.
2. The following brief overview of the Milwaukee case is drawn from McGroarty (1994), Peterson (1993), Lieberman (1993), Bolick (1992), Beales (1994), and Beales and Wahl (1995), as well as numerous newspaper articles in *Education Week* and elsewhere.
3. The general findings from this Gallup poll are presented in National Catholic Educational Association (NCEA) (1992). Although it does not indicate how public opinion on the voucher issue varies by race, I obtained the figures for African Americans and Hispanics from raw data supplied to me by the NCEA.
4. The Milwaukee case is hardly unique in its dysfunctional organizational design. For a broader perspective on why American politics inherently gives rise to ineffective, excessively bureaucratic arrangements, see Moe (1989, 1990).
5. Some of what I have to say about the movement and its leaders is based on my own involvement in the choice movement generally and the information I have picked up along the way, much of it from countless conversations with participants and their associates. I have also relied on National Scholarship Center (1994), Beales (1994), and various publications by CEO America, including *The Voucher Voice*, their newsletter.
6. Not all activists in the private voucher movement are interested in pressing the larger cause of school choice in the political arena; some, including the leaders of a few local programs, are simply concerned with helping needy children, and have no broader political agenda. The key leaders at the head of the movement, however, are clearly strong choice supporters with an agenda.
7. This summary account of the Golden Rule program is based on National Scholarship Center (1994), Beales (1994), and Heise et al. (1995).

8. My summary account of the San Antonio program is based on Martinez et al. (1995), Beales (1994), and National Scholarship Center (1994).
9. This summary account of Milwaukee's PAVE program is based on Beales and Wahl (1995), Beales (1994), and National Scholarship Center (1994).
10. Information on the Student-Sponsor Partnership program was supplied directly by the program's founder, Peter Flanigan.
11. For example, the response rates for these surveys are fairly low (they are mail surveys), and there may be a bias in the types of parents responding. The San Antonio researchers have discovered that public school parents who do not respond to the survey are less satisfied with their schools than those who do respond. It is possible, then, that the true satisfaction levels are lower than the survey data suggest, perhaps by a good bit.
12. For background on the literature on citizen satisfaction with government services, see, for example, Lyons, Lowery, and DeHoog (1992).

REFERENCES

Archer, J. (1997). 16,000 N.Y.C. parents apply for 1,300 vouchers to private schools. *Education Week, XVI*(30), 8.

Archer, J. (1998a). Millionaires to back national voucher project. *Education Week, XVII*(39), pg. 3.

Archer, J. (1998b). Voucher proponents claim victory in Albany. *Education Week, XVII*(22), 5.

Beales, J. R. (1994). *School voucher programs in the United States: Implications and applications for California*. Los Angeles: Reason Foundation.

Beales, J. R., & Wahl, M. (1995). Private vouchers in Milwaukee: The PAVE program. In T. M. Moe (Ed.), *Private vouchers* (pp. 41–73). Stanford, CA: Hoover Press.

Bolick, C. (1992). *The Wisconsin Supreme Court's decision on education choice: A first-of-its-kind victory for children and families* [Heritage Lecture]. Washington, DC: Heritage Foundation.

Bryk, A. S., Lee, V., & Holland, P. B. (1993). *Catholic schools and the common good.* Cambridge, MA: Harvard University Press.

Carnegie Foundation for the Advancement of Teaching. (1992). *School choice: A special report.* Princeton, NJ: Author.

Center for Education Reform. (1996a). *Education reform: Scrambling for the high ground.* Washington, DC: Author.

Center for Education Reform. (1996b). School reform in the United States: State by state summary. Washington, DC: Author.

Center for Education Reform. (1998). *Private scholarship programs: Statistical profiles, 1997–98.* Washington, DC: Author. Available: www.edreform.com/research/pspchart.html.

CEO America. (1994). Mission statement, support services, history, and background. Bentonville, AR: Author.

Cobb, C. W. (1992). *Responsive schools, renewed communities.* San Francisco: Institute for Contemporary Studies.

Coleman, J. S., Hoffer, T., & Kilgore, S. (1982). *High school achievement.* New York: Basic Books.

Coleman, J. S., Schiller, K. S., & Schneider, B. (1993). Parent choice and inequality. In B. Schneider & J. S. Coleman (Eds.), *Parents, their children, and schools* (pp. 147–182). Boulder: Westview Press.

Cookson, P. W. (1994). *School choice.* New Haven, CT: Yale University Press.

Fliegel, S., & Macguire, J. (1994). *Miracle in East Harlem.* New York: The Manhattan Institute.

Friedman, M. (1955). The role of government in public education. In R. A. Solo (Ed.), *Economics and the public interest* (pp. 123–153). New Brunswick, NJ: Rutgers University Press.

Friedman, M. (1962). *Capitalism and freedom.* Chicago: University of Chicago Press.

Godwin, R. K., Kemerer, F. R, & Martinez, V. J. (1998). Comparing public choice and private voucher programs in San Antonio. In P. E. Peterson & B. C. Hassel (Eds.), *Learning from school choice* (pp. 275–306). Washington, DC: Brookings Institution.

Greene, J. P., Howell, W. G., & Peterson, P. E. (1998). Lessons from the Cleveland Scholarship Program. In P. E. Peterson & B. C. Hassel (Eds.), *Learning from school choice* (pp. 357–392). Washington, DC: Brookings Institution.

Greene, J. P., & Peterson, P. E. (1996). *Methodological issues in evaluation research: The Milwaukee school choice plan.* Unpublished manuscript, Harvard University, Cambridge, MA.

Greene, J. P., Peterson, P. E., & Du, J. (1998). School choice in Milwaukee: A randomized experiment. In P. E. Peterson & B. C. Hassel (Eds.), *Learning from school choice* (pp. 335–356). Washington, DC: Brookings Institution.

Hartocollis, A. (1999, April 21). Private school choice plan draws a million aid-seekers. *The New York Times,* pp. A1, A25.

Heise, M., Colburn, K. D., & Lamberti, J. F. (1995). Private vouchers in Indianapolis: The Golden Rule Program. In T. M. Moe (Ed.), *Private vouchers* (pp. 100–119). Stanford, CA: Hoover Press.

Heritage Foundation. (1998a). *School choice programs 1998: Ohio* [Online]. Available: www.heritage.org./heritage/schools/wisconsin.html.

Heritage Foundation. (1998b). *School choice programs 1998: Wisconsin* [Online]. Available: www.heritage.org./heritage/schools/wisconsin.html

Kingdon, J. W. (1984). *Agendas, alternatives, and public policies.* Boston: Little, Brown.

Kozol, J. (1991). *Savage inequalities.* New York: HarperCollins.

Lee, V. E., Croninger, R. G., & Smith, J. B. (1994). Parental choice of schools and social stratification in education: The paradox of Detroit. *Educational Evaluation and Policy Analysis, 16,* 434–457.

Lieberman, M. (1993). *Public education: An autopsy.* Cambridge, Mass.: Harvard University Press.

Lyons, W. E., Lowery, D., & DeHoog, R. H. (1992). *The politics of dissatisfaction: Citizens, services, and urban institutions.* Armonk, NY: M.E. Sharp.

Martinez, V., Godwin, K., & Kemerer, F. R. (1995). Private vouchers in San Antonio: The CEO Program. In T. M. Moe (Ed.), *Private vouchers* (pp. 74–99). Stanford, CA: Hoover Press.

McGroarty, D. (1994, Fall). School choice slandered. *The Public Interest,* p. 117.

McGroarty, D. (1996). *Break these chains: The battle for school choice.* Rocklin, CA: Forum.

Metcalf, K. K., Boone, W. J., Stage, F. K., Chilton, T. L., Muller, P., & Tait, P. (1998, March). "A comparative evaluation of the Cleveland Scholarship and Tutoring Grant Program: Year one, 1996–97." Unpublished paper. Bloomington, IN: Indiana University, Smith Research Center, School of Education.

Milwaukee Public Schools. (1993). *1992–93 report card: District report.* Milwaukee, WI: Author.

Mitchell, G. A. (1992). *The Milwaukee Parental Choice Program.* Milwaukee: Wisconsin Policy Research Institute.

Moe, T. M. (1989). The politics of bureaucratic structure. In J. E. Chubb & P. E. Peterson (Eds.), *Can the government govern?* (pp. 267–329). Washington, DC: The Brookings Institution.

Moe, T. M. (1990). The politics of structural choice: Toward a theory of public bureaucracy. In O. E. Williamson (Ed.), *Organization theory: From Chester Barnard to the present and beyond* (pp. 116–153). Oxford, England: Oxford University Press.

Moe, T. M. (1995a). *Private vouchers.* Stanford, CA: Hoover Press.

Moe, T. M. (1995b). School choice and the creaming problem. In T. A. Downes & W. A. Testa (Eds.), *Midwest approaches to school reform* (pp. 156–161). Chicago: Federal Reserve Bank of Chicago.

Nathan, J. (Ed.). (1989). *Public schools by choice.* St. Paul, MN: The Institute for Learning and Teaching.

National Catholic Educational Association. (1985). *The Catholic high school: A national portrait.* Washington, DC: Author.

National Catholic Educational Association. (1992). *The people's poll on schools and school choice: A new Gallup survey.* Washington, DC: Author.

National Scholarship Center. (1994). *Just doing it: First annual survey of the private voucher movement in America.* Washington, DC: Author.

Peterson, P. (1993). Are big-city schools holding their own? In J. Rury, *Seeds of crisis* (pp. 269-301). Madison, WI: University of Wisconsin Press.

Peterson, P. (1995). *A critique of the Witte evaluation of Milwaukee's School Choice Program.* Unpublished manuscript, Harvard University, Cambridge, MA.

Peterson, P., Greene, J. P., Howell, W. G., & McCready, W. (1998). *Initial findings from an evaluation of school choice programs in Washington, DC, and Dayton, Ohio.* Unpublished manuscript, Harvard University, Cambridge, MA.

Peterson, P., Greene, J., & Noyes, C. (1996, Fall). School choice in Milwaukee. *Public Interest, 125*: 38–56.

Peterson, P., Myers, D., & Howell, W. G. (1998). *An evaluation of the New York City School Choice Scholarships Program: The first year.* Unpublished manuscript, Harvard University, Cambridge, MA.

Rouse, C. (1997). *Private school vouchers and student achievement: An evaluation of the Milwaukee Parental Choice Program.* Unpublished manuscript, Princeton University, Princeton, NJ.

Sandham, J. (1999, May 5). Florida OKs first statewide voucher plan. *Education Week, XVIII*(34), 1, 21.

Sandham, J. (2000, March 22). Voucher plan struck down in Florida court. *Education Week, XIX*(28), 1, 33.

U.S. Department of Education. (1992). *Public opinion on choice in education.* Washington, DC: Center for Choice in Education.

Walsh, M. (1998a, November 18). "Green light" for school vouchers? *Education Week, XVIII*(12), 1, 19.

Walsh, M. (1998b, April 29). Group offers $50 million for vouchers. *Education Week, XVII*(33), 1, 22.

Walsh, M. (1998c, June 17). Court allows vouchers in Milwaukee. *Education Week, XVII*(40), 1, 16.

Walsh, M. (1999, September 8). Rulings on voucher program cause turmoil in Cleveland. *Education Week, XIX*(1), 5.

Weinschrott, D. J., & Kilgore, S. B. (1998). Evidence from the Indianapolis Voucher Program. In P. E. Peterson & B. C. Hassel (Eds.), *Learning from school choice* (307–334). Washington, DC: Brookings Institution.

Wells, A. S. (1993a). The sociology of school choice. In E. Rasell & R. Rothstein (Eds.), *School choice: Examining the evidence* (pp. 29–48). Washington, DC: Economic Policy Institute.

Wells, A. S. (1993b). *A time to choose.* New York: Hill & Wang.

Witte, J. F. (1991). *First year report: Milwaukee Parental Choice Program.* Madison, WI: University of Wisconsin, Department of Political Science & La Follette Institute of Public Affairs.

Witte, J. F. (1995). *A reply to Paul Peterson's "A critique of the Witte evaluation of Milwaukee's School Choice Program."* Madison, WI: University of Wisconsin, Department of Political Science.

Witte, J. F. (1996). Reply to Greene, Peterson, and Du. Unpublished Manuscript. Madison, WI: University of Wisconsin.

Witte, J. F. (1997, January). Achievement effects of the Milwaukee Public Voucher Program. Paper presented at the 1997 annual meeting of the American Economics Association, New Orleans, LA.

Witte, J. F., Bailey, A. B., & Thorn, C. A. (1992). *Second year report: Milwaukee Parental Choice Program.* Madison, WI: University of Wisconsin, Department of Political Science & La Follette Institute of Public Affairs.

Witte, J. F., Bailey, A. B., & Thorn, C. A. (1993). *Third year report: Milwaukee Parental Choice Program.* Madison, WI: University of Wisconsin, Department of Political Science & La Follette Institute of Public Affairs.

Witte, J. F., Sterr, T. D., & Thorn, C. A. (1995.) *Fifth year report: Milwaukee Parental Choice Program.* Madison, WI: University of Wisconsin, Department of Political Science & La Follette Institute of Public Affairs.

Witte, J. F., Thorn, C., Pritchard, K. M., & Claibourn, M. (1994). *Fourth year report: Milwaukee Parental Choice Program.* Madison, WI: University of Wisconsin, Department of Political Science & La Follette Institute of Public Affairs.

Young, T. W., & Clinchy, E. (1992). *Choice in public education.* New York: Teachers College Press.

4

School Choice Experiments in Urban Education

Paul E. Peterson
Harvard University

Whether viewed in comparison with other countries or not, the state of American education appears grim. For example, the well-regarded international math study, which compares U.S. students with peers abroad, finds that although American fourth-graders keep pace, by eighth grade they have fallen to the middle of the pack (and below other major, industrial nations). By age 17, U.S. students trail virtually everyone. The longer U.S. students remain in school, the further behind they fall (Lawton, 1996, 1997; U.S. National Research Center, 1998).[1]

Equally dark results are emerging from the National Assessment of Educational Progress (NAEP), long known to provide the best overall estimate of the cognitive skills being acquired by the nation's young. A report issued by Paul Barton and Richard Coley (1998), researchers at Educational Testing Service (ETS), the respected firm that administers NAEP, focuses on what students are learning in school, as distinct from the educational impacts of a student's family life. ETS researchers noted that the test scores of 9-year-old students have been increasing the last two decades, but they pointed out that these scores are shaped by everything that happens to children between the day a child is conceived and the day of the fourth-grade test. The clear gains among fourth-graders, especially more prosperous and well-educated African Americans, can be attributed not only to what has happened in the first few years of schooling, but also to gains in prenatal care, birth weight, pediatrics, nutrition, and early childhood experiences.[2]

To detect what is happening strictly within schools, Barton and Coley (1998) focused on test-score growth between fourth and eighth grade. By fourth grade, much of the family background impact has already shown up in the test scores. What happens between fourth and eighth grade depends much more on what is happening *in* school.

Looked at in this way, NAEP results are of no less concern than the international math and science results. Students are learning less during the middle-school years than they once were. When test-score growth in the 1990s is compared to growth a generation earlier, students are slipping in math, science, and writing (not in reading). Blacks are slipping just as much as Whites—even more so in reading. Families without a high school education are deteriorating the most.

The problem is nationwide. One finds little difference among states, although Minnesota, North Dakota, Nebraska, and Michigan are doing the most to buck the trend. The District of Columbia anchors the bottom of the scale, trailing every state and the island of Guam. The District of Columbia's growth performance is particularly discouraging because elsewhere Black students are making as many gains as White students. Because the District of Columbia is the only "state" that is at the same time an "inner city," these results suggest that problems in American education are particularly severe within our central cities.

Many people think that school vouchers or some other mechanisms for increasing parental choice may provide a way of reversing these educational trends. However, these same people wonder whether this solution to our educational ailments, as good as it may sound in theory, may in practice be worse than the disease. As a result, the public splits its support about evenly between those who support and those who oppose government-funded vouchers.

In this chapter, the latest evidence with respect to the use of vouchers in an urban context is summarized. First, some of the major school choice experiments are described; second, information is provided on the kinds of individuals who take advantage of choice when the opportunity is available; third, the factors parents consider when choosing a school are reported; fourth, the level of satisfaction parents express with the choices they have made is presented; fifth, data are presented on the access low-income families have to choice schools; sixth, the effects of school choice on social capital, student learning, and ethnic relations are reported; and finally, the effects on students remaining in public schools are considered.

Major Choice Experiments in Central Cities

School choice experiments have been undertaken in several central cities. In Milwaukee and Cleveland, state-funded choice programs are giving eligible families a chance to pick their school. In more than 30 other cities, privately funded scholarships provide more than 30,000 students with the private school of their choice. The largest programs are in Dayton, Indianapolis, Milwaukee, New York City, San Antonio, and Washington, DC.

The most dramatic program is in the Edgewood school district in San Antonio, where CEO America, a private foundation, announced in spring 1998 that it would provide every low-income child in the district a 10-year scholarship worth as much as $4,000 a year. The Edgewood program is an expanded version of a program inaugurated in Albany by Virginia Gilder (Viteritti, 1999), a philanthropist, who provided a similar opportunity to all children attending the city's lowest-performing elementary school. In fall 1997, parents of about a quarter of the students made use of this scholarship.

The basic characteristics of the nine largest programs are in Table 4.1. The first state-funded program was established in Milwaukee in 1990. Although it has received a good deal of publicity, originally it offered the least amount of choice. Although the scholarships are generously funded at a maximum of $4,700, the program had the following important restrictions: Only secular schools could participate; half the student body had to be nonchoice students; and the family could not supplement the scholarship. Because of these restrictions, only 20 schools and 1,600 students participated in 1996, most of them in elementary schools.

However, the state legislature allowed the inclusion of religious schools in a major expansion of the program that was declared constitutional by the Wisconsin Supreme Court in the summer of 1998. Although this decision has been appealed to the U.S. Supreme Court, the expanded program opened in fall 1998, replacing a privately funded program in Milwaukee known as Partners Advancing Values in Education (PAVE). No longer in operation, PAVE was established in 1992 and in its final

TABLE 4.1
Characteristics of Big-City School Choice Programs for Low-Income Families

City[a]	First School Year	Sponsor	Religious Schools Included	Grades	Initial Enrollment	1996–1997 Enrollment	Number of Schools 1996–1997	Maximum Payment 1997–1998 (dollars)	Selection Method
Milwaukee	1990–1991	State of Wisconsin	No	pre-k–12	341	1,606	20	4,700	Lottery
Indianapolis	1991–1992	ECCT	Yes	1–8	746	1,014	70	800	First-come, first-served
Milwaukee	1992–1993	PAVE	Yes	K–12	2,089	4,465	97	1,000/ele. 1,500/high	First-come, first-served
San Antonio	1992–1993	CEO	Yes	1–8	930	995	49	One-half tuition	First-come, first-served
Cleveland	1996–1997	State of Ohio	Yes	K–3	1,196	4,000[b]	55	2,500	Lottery
New York City	1997–1998	SCSF	Yes	1–5	1,200	1,700[b]	250	1,400	Lottery
Washington, DC	1998–1999	WSF	Yes	K–12	1,000	1,000[b]	n.a.	1,700	Lottery
Dayton	1998–1999	PACE	Yes	K–12	650	650[b]	n.a.	1,200	Lottery
San Antonio	1998–1999	CEO/Horizo	Yes	K–12	700	700[b]	n.a.	3,600/ele. 4,000/high	Unlimited

Note. ECCT—Educational Choice Charitable Trust; PAVE—Partners Advancing Values in Education; CEO—Children's Educational Opportunities; SCSF—School Choice Scholarships Foundation; WSF—Washington Scholarship Fund; PACE—Parents Advancing Choice in Education; n.a.—Not available. Information obtained from program operators by author.

[a]Programs having more than 900 students.

[b]1998 –1999.

year was providing 4,465 children from low-income families as much as $1,500 to attend any 1 of 97 religious and secular schools.

The Cleveland Scholarship Program, serving students in Grades K–3, was established by the state of Ohio in 1996, becoming the first state-funded choice program allowing students a choice that included religious schools. The state scholarship amounted to as much as $2,500 and could be supplemented by families or other sources. In 1998, more than 4,000 students received scholarships enabling them to attend more than 50 schools.

The oldest, but least generous, of the privately funded programs, Educational Choice Charitable Trust (ECCT), began in Indianapolis in 1991. Six years later, ECCT provided $800 in scholarships to 1,014 students attending 70 schools, religious and secular.

In February 1997, the School Choice Scholarships Foundation (SCSF) in New York City announced it would provide 1,300 scholarships for students in Grades 1–5. More than 20,000 applications for the $1,400 scholarships were received; scholarships were awarded to students by lot; and scholarship recipients attended 1 of approximately 250 religious and secular schools. One year later, similar programs began in Dayton and Washington, DC.

In 1992, the Children's Educational Opportunity (CEO) program was established in San Antonio. In 1996, it provided nearly 1,000 half-tuition scholarships to elementary and middle school students attending approximately 40 schools. As previously mentioned, this program was expanded in the spring of 1998 to include offers to all students in the Edgewood school district within San Antonio. Finally, in June 1998, the Children's Scholarship Fund announced a nationwide program that would make available as much as $100 million in matching funds for locally funded scholarship programs for low-income families in cities across the country. New or expanded programs have been launched in Chicago, Los Angeles, New York City, Washington, DC, and elsewhere.

Characteristics of Those Who Exercise Choice

Critics of school choice have argued that choice programs do not give low-income families a viable choice of schools. In the words of educational sociologist Amy Wells (1996), "White and higher-SES [socioeconomic status] families will no doubt be in a position to take greater advantage of the educational market" (p. 47). Defenders of private schools reply that private schools have an ethnically and economically diverse population.

Information available on those who exercise choice comes from the New York City scholarship program (Peterson, Myers, Haimson, & Howell, 1997). As previously mentioned, the New York SCSF received applications from more than 20,000 students for its scholarship. To be eligible to apply for a scholarship, a family had to qualify for the federal free-lunch program, have a child currently in a public school, and live in New York City. To have one's name entered into the lottery, applicants had to participate in eligibility verification sessions. During these sessions, the children were tested and their parents filled out questionnaires. It is possible that the application process attracted a population substantially different from a cross-section of all those eligible. Those who received scholarships were educationally disadvantaged in several respects. The average pretest scores of eligible applicants were very low. The median National Percentile Ranking (NPR) score for all students throughout the United States who take the Iowa Test of Basic Skills (ITBS) is 50. For scholarship recipients, the average NPR score in reading was 27 and in mathematics it was 22.

Demographic information on the population is available for those who would have been eligible if scholarships had been offered in 1990, the last year in which a U.S. census was taken, to estimate the extent to which the social background characteristics of the applicant population differed from the potentially eligible population. The estimate of the eligible population is thus based on data collected at a time when New York's economic and social conditions differed from those prevailing at the time parents were surveyed. 1990 was a recession year and 1997, the year of application, was in the midst of an economic boom. Also, education levels of the adult population have risen. Nonetheless, these data provide a useful estimate of the differences between the applicant population and the eligible population.

Once income is adjusted for inflation between 1990 and 1997, no significant differences between the income of applicants and the eligible population are found. The employment rates and the residential mobility of the applicant population are similar to the eligible population. Applicant mothers are no more likely to be foreign-born than the eligible population. However, applicants were more likely to be dependent on government assistance for income and African American and less likely to be non-Hispanic White. If these findings suggest that the applicant population was particularly disadvantaged, other findings point in the opposite direction. Mothers and fathers are considerably more likely to have some college education, English is more likely to be the language spoken in the household, and mothers are more likely to be employed either full- or part-time. Overall, applicants for the New York program were more disadvantaged than the eligible population in some respects, less so in others.

Choosing a School

School choice advocates say they wish to empower parents by giving them a choice among schools. Critics say that parents, especially poor parents, do not have enough information to make intelligent choices, and when given a choice, academic considerations are not paramount. The Carnegie Foundation for the Advancement of Teaching (1992) claimed that "when parents do select another school, academic concerns often are not central to the decision" (p. 13). However, Hoxby (1998) found that when public schools face greater competition (because of the larger number of school districts within a single metropolitan area), parent involvement in schools increases, student achievement increases, more students attend college, and graduates earn more money.

These findings might be limited to middle-class families living in suburban areas and quite different for low-income families. A Twentieth Century Fund report claimed that low-income parents are not "natural 'consumers' of education.... [Indeed,] few parents of any social class appear willing to acquire the information necessary to make active and informed educational choices" (Ascher, Fruchter, & Berne, 1996, pp. 40–41). Similarly, the American Federation of Teachers' (AFT) report on Cleveland suggests that parents sought scholarships, not because of "'failing' public schools" but "for religious reasons or because they already had a sibling attending the same school" (Murphy, Nelson, & Rosenberg, 1997, p. 10). Public intellectual Nicholas Lemann made the point most provocatively: When a major impediment to the achievement of poor children is "their parents' impoverishment, poor education, lax discipline, and scant interest in education," isn't it absurd to think that these same parents will become "tough, savvy, demanding education consumers" once they have the right to choose (Thernstrom, 1991, p. 40)?

Not much support for such rhetoric can be found in the responses given by the parents of scholarship recipients in Cleveland. When asked why they applied for a scholarship, 85% of parents new to choice schools said they wanted to improve the academic quality of their child's education. Seventy-nine percent of the recipients ranked safety at a choice school second in importance. Location was ranked third. Contrary to AFT's suggestion, religion was ranked fourth by just 37% of the recipients. Finally, friends were ranked as very important by less than 20% of the scholarship recipients (Greene, Howell, & Peterson, 1997).

Families in Washington were also asked to state the importance of various reasons for applying for a school choice scholarship. Once again, higher standards and a better curriculum were the reasons most frequently said to be important by public school parents applying for a scholarship. More than three fourths of the applicants gave these academic reasons as an important motive for the application. More than half of the parents said they were seeking better teachers and smaller schools with smaller class sizes. Nearly half of the parents said that safety was an important reason. One of the least important reasons was the location of the school, mentioned by only 16% of the public school applicants (Peterson, Greene, Howell, & McCready, 1998).

PARENTAL SATISFACTION WITH CHOICE AND PUBLIC SCHOOLS

Many economists think that customer satisfaction is the best measure of school quality. According to this criterion, there is little doubt that school choice is a success. Both anecdotes and more systematic studies confirm that most participating families love their choice schools. When the winners of the New York lottery for choice scholarships were announced last May, winners were ecstatic: "I was crying and crying and crying. It was the best Mother's Day present I could have asked for," said Maria Miranda, a permanently disabled single mother living in Brooklyn (Steinberg, 1997). A year into the Cleveland choice program, parent Pamela Ballard said of a new choice school in Cleveland:

> HOPE Academy was my last hope. I took my third-grade child, who had been in several Cleveland schools and was labeled a "problem child." I now have a successful child. Where there were D's and C's, there are now A's and B's. ("Improving Educational Opportunities," 1997, p. 10)

In their enthusiasm, Maria Miranda and Pamela Ballard represent the norm, not the exception. According to studies of parental satisfaction in Milwaukee, Indianapolis, and San Antonio, choice schools are more popular than public schools (Peterson, 1998).

In a recent survey of choice applicants from public and private schools in Washington, DC, nearly 60% of private school parents gave their school an A, as compared to less than one fifth of public school parents (Peterson et al., 1998). Significantly, the opinions of public school applicants in Washington, DC, do not differ from the views of a national sample of public school parents who were asked about the school their oldest child attended (Rose & Gallup, 1999). A comparison of a national sample of public school applicants and private school applicants is presented in Table 4.2.

TABLE 4.2
Comparison of a National Sample of Public and Private School Applicants

	Public Schools	**DC Low-Income**	**DC Low-Income**
Grade Given to School	Parents From the National Survey (%)	Applicants From Public Schools (%)	Applicants From Private Schools (%)
A	15	18	59
B	41	42	30
C	31	31	10
D	8	7	1
F	4	2	0
Don't Know	1	0	0
Total	100	100	100

In other words, applicants from the DC public schools do not seem to be a particularly discontented group of public school parents. Their overall assessments of their children's schools were essentially similar to those of public school parents nationally. However, the parents in the national sample and the DC applicants were much less likely to give their children's school an A than the applicants from DC private schools.

The larger level of satisfaction with private schools becomes especially evident when dealing with specific aspects of school life. For example, private school applicants are the most satisfied group of parents with school safety. Two thirds of the private school parents were very satisfied with school safety, compared to one fourth of the public school parents. Nearly two thirds of the private school parents and less than one fifth of the public school parents were very satisfied with their school's academic program.

The differences between the satisfaction levels of the two groups of DC parents were not so large concerning transportation and location. For example, two thirds of the private school parents and one half of the public school parents were very satisfied with the school's location. Differences in satisfaction levels were large in teachers' skills, parental involvement, class size, school facility, respect for teachers, and teacher and parent relations (Peterson et al., 1998).

In Cleveland, one can compare the assessments of parents attending choice schools with the assessments of parents who remained in public schools after indicating an interest in the choice program. Two thirds of parents new to choice schools reported being very satisfied with the academic quality of their school, as compared to less than 30% of public school parents. Nearly 60% were very satisfied with school safety, as compared to just over one fourth of nonrecipients in public school. With respect to discipline, 55% of recipients from public schools and only 23% of nonrecipients in public school were very satisfied. The differences in satisfaction rates were equally large when parents were asked about the school's private attention to the child, parent involvement, class size, and school facility. The most extreme differences in satisfaction pertained to teaching moral values. Seventy-one percent of the recipients from public schools were very satisfied, as compared to only 25% of the nonrecipients in public schools.

It may be hypothesized that these differences in parental satisfaction might be a function of the fact that the comparison group of public school students consists of those who had applied for a scholarship but had not received it. To see whether this was the case, the author and his colleagues isolated the satisfaction levels of parents who *voluntarily* decided to leave their children in public schools. They found that students with children in established private schools scored considerably higher on a satisfaction scale than these parents (Greene, Howell, & Peterson, 1998).

It is also interesting to inquire whether scholarship families coming from public schools were as satisfied as those already enrolled in private schools. The AFT, in its report on the Cleveland program, suggested that scholarship recipients from private schools received important advantages. As stated in the report:

> Voucher students who had previously been enrolled in private schools held a "monopoly" on placements in the established private schools. In contrast, almost half of the voucher students who moved from public to private schools were enrolled in four schools with little or no educational and financial track record. (Murphy et al., 1997, p. ii)

There is some evidence from the survey that supports the AFT suggestion that scholarship recipients from public schools had a less satisfying educational experience than those from private schools. However, the differences between the two groups are, in most cases, minor. For example, 67% of recipients from private schools say they were very satisfied with the academic quality of the school, whereas 63% of those from public schools gave the same response. For school discipline, the percentages were 62% and 55%, respectively. The biggest difference was with school safety, 69% as compared to 59% (Greene, Howell, & Peterson, 1998).

Social Capital

In a well-known study of public and private schools, James Coleman and his colleagues (Coleman & Hoffer, 1987; Coleman, Hoffer, & Kilgore, 1982) developed the concept of social capital. According to Coleman and colleagues, social capital refers to the resources that are generated by accidental interactions among adults in a well-functioning community. Coleman thought that Catholic schools were effective at least in part because Catholic parents met one another at religious services, bingo parties, Knights of Columbus ceremonies, scouting events, and other community gatherings. Although these communal occasions had no ostensible educational content, the social capital generated by adult interaction had important, indirect, educational consequences. At these public gatherings, adults met the parents of their children's friends and acquaintances and could monitor their children's relationships with peers. Aware that their parents may learn what was happening, young people governed themselves accordingly. Anthony Bryk and his colleagues (Bryk, Lee, & Holland, 1993) have shown that the process, deeply rooted in Catholic traditions, is subtle, implicit, and effective.

Robert D. Putnam (1993, 1997) has documented a serious decline in the nation's social capital. People participate less in community activities, group sports, and neighborhood picnics. Television watching, going to the movies, searching Web sites, and exercising have substituted bowling, attending Elks meetings, and going to ice cream socials. According to Putnam, the consequence is a growing distrust of one another and a decline in the effectiveness of governmental services, which depend on the mutual cooperation of citizens.[3] Putnam's findings raise particularly serious implications for the state of American education, especially if schools and families must work closely together if children are to learn most efficaciously.

Not much is known about the potential of public and private schooling for the formation of social capital—even Coleman's own study of public and private schools failed to provide direct information on the amount of social capital in the two educational sectors. It is not clear whether social capital is generated more by private or public institutions. It is possible that neighborhood public schools stimulate conversations among parents at local school events, community meetings, shopping malls, and neighborhood walks. Private schools that serve different groups within a community may fragment and isolate citizens from one another. This seems to be the position taken by Amy Gutmann (1987), Princeton theorist, who argued that "public, not private, schooling is...the primary means by which citizens can morally educate future citizens" (p. 70).

All of these considerations suggest that community engagement occurs more regularly among those who send their children to the same public school as their neighbors. It is possible that this was once the case in small towns where public schools were both educational organizations and institutions of community integration. However, any such claims for public schools located in large, central cities have a quaint, romantic tinge. Many factors in today's big cities undermine the public schools' capacity to generate social capital. In order to maintain privacy and to guard against crime, public school officials are not allowed to share lists of family names and addresses. Public school families in the inner city may attend fewer school activities because teacher union contracts often sharply limit the amount of time public schools are open to the public. Adult access to school buildings is limited by metal detectors, locked doors, and stern warnings against engaging in suspicious behavior. Concerns about crime and violence make streets unsafe for unguarded neighborhood encounters. Also, many public school children are bused to schools outside of their neighborhood in response to school-desegregation orders. In summary, potential violence, regulatory constraints, and contractual obligations may restrict community discourse and the formation of social capital in publicly controlled settings.

Meanwhile, the private sector would seem to have some specific advantages. The fact that parents are choosing their child's school provides an incentive to learn more from other parents about what is happening in alternative educational settings (Schneider, Teske, Marschall, Mintrom, & Roch, 1977). Once a choice has been made, a sense of shared experience exists among those who have made a similar choice.

Private schools give parents plenty of opportunities to contact one another. It is easier for private schools to distribute lists of phone numbers and addresses, making it easier for parents to contact one another. Parents use the phone lists to enlist each other's participation in candy sales, newspaper drives, or school auctions. Also, adults may find it easier to proceed in and out of private than public school buildings.

Private schools cannot afford the elaborate bus services that transport public school children. As a result, private school families may need to talk to one another to arrange car pools and shared public transportation routes. Private school families may meet each other at religious services, bingo parties, and evening school events, which are easily scheduled in private schools and less burdened by union contracts. All of these situations provide parents with opportunities to talk to each other and school employees.

To determine whether private schools actually generate more social capital, applicants for scholarships from Washington, DC, public and private schools were asked a number of questions about their relationships with other parents and their community. The responses to these questions indicate that Coleman's hypothesis may be correct. Parents with children already in private schools were more likely to attend school activities. The parents of private school applicants were more likely to discuss school affairs with one another. Nearly one third of the parents of DC's public school applicants seldom or never discuss school affairs with other parents, whereas only about 15% of private school parents reported an equivalent paucity of such conversations. Finally, families of applicants from private schools were more likely to report that they felt that they were part of their community, saying it is more than a place to live. Approximately three fourths of the parents of private school applicants reported this feeling, as compared to two thirds of public school applicants. Private school parents were also more likely to know the parents of their children's friends. In summary, parental responses to questions about civic engagement indicate that more social capital may be formed within the private than the public educational sector (Peterson et al., 1998).

School Mobility Rates

Student retention is a major problem in low-income, central-city communities. According to the U.S. census, residential mobility rates are very high for low-income minorities. For central-city, female-headed households with children between the ages of 6 and 17, the annual residential mobility rate is 30% for African Americans and 35% for Latinos. Not every change in residence dictates a change in school attendance. In Milwaukee's public elementary schools, nearly 20% of the students leave before the end of the school year (Witte, Bailey, & Thorn, 1992). The following fall, 35% of the students are no longer attending the same public elementary school they attended the previous year.

School Choice and Retention Rates

School mobility is less when parents are given a choice of schools. All, with the exception of 23%, of the Milwaukee choice students returned to the same elementary school the following fall (as compared to 35% in Milwaukee's low-income public schools). Within the school year, the percentage of students leaving choice elementary schools was as low as 4% in 1993 and 6% in 1994—much lower than the 20% changing from one low-income public elementary school to another (Peterson, 1995a, 1995b). In Milwaukee's privately funded program, turnover rates were similar—6% within the school year and 14% from one year to the next.

The Cleveland choice schools also did quite well in retaining their students in the first year of the program (Greene, Howell, & Peterson, 1998). Only 7% of all scholarship families reported not attending the same school for the entire year. Among recipients from public schools the percentage was 10%. This mobility rate is approximately the same as the within-the-school-year mobility rate in the Milwaukee elementary school choice program and about half the mobility rate in Milwaukee public elementary schools.

The most important reason recipients new to choice schools gave for changing schools midyear, given by 3.3%, was admission to their preferred private school. Some of these changes may be because the full establishment of the voucher program was delayed by a court challenge to its constitutionality. As a result, some recipients did not receive their scholarships until after the school year had begun. If so, this cause of school mobility should attenuate over time. One percent of the students changed schools because they had been admitted to a preferred public school, whereas 0.8% of the families moved during the course of the year (0.8% moved for transportation reasons).

All of these reasons for changing schools are understandable and some can be expected to attenuate as the program becomes more established. Two percent of the parents changed schools because of the quality of the school, administrative problems, and school closure or change; and 0.5% of the families said expulsion, disability, or behavior problems had led to a school change. These reasons signalize that some private schools were not working well for some families.

Parents were also asked whether they planned on sending their child to the same school next year. A positive response was given by 81% of scholarship recipients from public schools. If actual choices are consistent with these plans, the mobility rate in Cleveland from one year to the next is approximately the same as it is in the Milwaukee choice program.

Choice critics have suggested that private schools routinely expel or not readmit students for a second year, if they are not keeping pace with their peers. Defenders of private schools say they use their authority to deny readmission sparingly. To ascertain whether low-income parents were encountering difficulties in obtaining readmission for a second year, those changing schools were asked the reason for the change. Less than one half of 1% of recipients from public schools said their child could not be readmitted to the private school in which he or she had been enrolled. In other words, though refusal to be readmitted is not unknown, neither has it been practiced to any significant degree.

Parents instead gave a wide range of other reasons for planning to move their child to another school in the fall of 1997. Six percent gave quite practical reasons, such as the family's moving from the area or the child's change in grade level (necessitating a school change). One-and-a-half percent found another private school they preferred and 0.5% found a preferable public school. Transportation difficulties or financial costs posed an obstacle for another 2.4% of the parents. Six-and-a-half percent of all recipients from public schools were leaving because they were not satisfied with the quality of the school or were disappointed in how the Cleveland scholarship program was operated. For a small but still important fraction of scholarship recipients, the program, at least in its first year, was not a success. Choice critics may see this as a sign of program failure because not all of the families' expectations were fulfilled. However, school choice supporters may interpret this as evidence that choice allows a parent to make a move when things do not seem to be working out.

Scholarship Usage

If retention does not seem to be any more of a problem for private than for public schools, can low-income voucher recipients find admission to a private school in the first place? Some answers to this question are available from the New York City scholarship program (Peterson, Myers, et al., 1997). Students received scholarships in May 1997, which could be used the following September. Despite the fact that the scholarships were made available after many private schools had already admitted students for the following year, 75% of those offered scholarships used them.

Overall, users and nonusers did not differ in their average math and reading pretest scores. The levels of current educational satisfaction and involvement were similar for those who took the scholarship and those who did not. For example, both users and nonusers gave public schools a grade of C+. Both groups reported similar levels of satisfaction with the location of the school, school safety, teaching, class size, school facility, and communications regarding student progress. They also reported similar levels of involvement with their child's education and interaction with public school officials about their child's education.

Users and nonusers have differences in some social and educational characteristics. Those who took the scholarship were likely to be African American and less likely to be White. However, some of the students who took the scholarship had higher incomes and were less likely to be dependent on federal subsidy programs, such as food stamps, welfare, and Medicaid. Mothers of those who accepted and used the scholarship were slightly better educated than nonusers, but the fathers were similarly educated. Applicants who took the scholarship were likely to come from residentially stable homes and less likely to come from homes where someone speaks English. Those who took the scholarship were less likely to have been in a special education program.

The findings from the New York scholarship program confirm evidence from other studies of participation in central-city school voucher programs. When the programs are restricted to those of low income, the programs succeed in recruiting a decidedly disadvantaged population. However, there is a modest tendency to recruit the more socially integrated segment of that population (Peterson, 1998).

LEARNING IN CHOICE SCHOOLS

These positive results would mean little, perhaps, if students did not learn more in choice schools. Because controversy over this question has raged for more than a quarter of a century, it is best to place recent findings in historical context.

Early Studies

The first large-scale study to show that students learn more in private high schools was conducted by a research team headed by James Coleman, a sociologist from the University of Chicago (Coleman et al., 1982; Coleman & Hoffer, 1987). A decade later, another national study showing similarly positive effects was carried out by Chubb and Moe (1990) at the Brookings Institution.

Choice critics attacked both studies for not adequately correcting for "selection effects," an issue that has become central to the current debate. Former Wisconsin state school superintendent and arch-choice critic Herbert Grover (1993) argued, "Do private school children outperform children in public schools? It's hard to imagine that they wouldn't, given the initial advantages they enjoy from their parents" (p. 250). Both the Coleman et al. (1982) and the Chubb–Moe (1990) studies anticipated this argument and took into account family characteristics, such as education and income. Critics say that no amount of statistical tinkering can ever fully correct the selection effect: Families who pay to send their child to private school are almost certainly more involved in and concerned about their child's education, even after adjusting for demographic characteristics (Goldberger & Cain, 1982; Wilms, 1984, 1985). Even the Coleman research team admitted that the "difference between parents, by its very nature, is not something on which students in public and private schools can be equated" in a statistical analysis (Goldberger & Cain, 1982, P. 110).

New Research Strategies

School choice experiments are providing researchers with new opportunities to circumvent this selection problem. Researchers are limited to inner-city children from low-income families. More important, to ensure fairness, scholarship winners are sometimes chosen by lottery, giving these programs the potential of becoming a classic, randomized experiment as found in the best medical research.

The advantage of a randomized experiment for researchers derives from its intrinsic simplicity. When a lottery is used to pick scholarship winners, the two groups of students are similar except for the fact that the names of one group were drawn from the hat. When one works with information from a classic, randomized experiment, one can in fact reasonably assume that students from public and private schools can be "equated." If children from the winning group do better than the remainder, one can reasonably conclude that it was the school, not the family, that made the difference.

Unfortunately, most school choice experiments conducted thus far have not conformed to a classic, randomized experiment. The privately funded programs in Indianapolis, San Antonio, and Milwaukee all admitted students on a first-come, first-served basis. These admission procedures have a fairness of their own and they are easy to administer. Test-score results from these experiments are mainly positive. For example, the scores of students participating in the school choice program in San Antonio increased between 1991–1992 and 1993–1994, whereas those of the public school comparison group fell.

Cleveland Results

Evidence with respect to test-score performance in Cleveland comes from two studies, one conducted by the Program on Education Policy and Governance at Harvard University, the other by an evaluation team at the School of Education at Indiana University. Although the findings from the two studies differ in some respects, both find positive test-score effects from participating in a voucher program.

The central component of the Indiana University study was a 2-

year evaluation of the performance of students who had used a voucher to enter Grade 3 in most of the private schools in the fall of 1996. After 2 years in the program, the students in the private schools were found to have “higher test scores than public school students in language (45.0 vs. 40.0 [National Curvilinear Equivalent points]) and science (40.0 vs. 36.0).” However, there were no statistically significant differences between the voucher students and the comparison group of public school students in three other subject areas (Metcalf, 1999; Metcalf et al., 1998). In short, the study found that students who entered the voucher program in the third grade did as well as their public school counterparts in three subject domains and significantly better in two after 2 years in private school.

Less clear are results from evaluations of two schools that were given individual attention by both evaluations. These schools, the Hope schools, are secular schools that originally participated in the voucher program but that, in the summer of 1999, closed and opened and as two new charter schools. The Indiana evaluation found that third-grade students attending the Hope schools did not perform as well as those remaining in public school (Metcalf, 1999; Metcalf et al., 1998). These results are at odds with the findings reported by the Harvard research team. These researchers found sizeable test-score gains in the first year of the program, gains that were maintained but that did not increase in the program’s second year (Peterson, Howell, & Greene, 1999). The findings from the two studies may be reconciled in the following way: (a) the Indiana evaluation looked at the test scores of only the third-graders, whereas the Harvard results are based on all the students with vouchers at the Hope schools; (b) the Indiana evaluation only looked at the third-year students’ test-score performance in the second year of the program, whereas the Harvard researchers obtained test results for students in all grades in both the first and second years, finding gains in Year 1 but no additional gains in Year 2.

Taken together, the findings seem to suggest that the voucher students in Cleveland did at least as well as—and in some subject domains better than—the students in the public schools.

Milwaukee Experiment

In Milwaukee, data are available from a randomized experiment (Greene, Peterson, Du, with Berger, & Frazier, 1996; Peterson, 1995a; Witte,

1991, 1997; Witte, Bailey, & Thorn, 1992, 1993; Witte, Sterr, & Thorn, 1995; Witte, Thorn, Pritchard, & Claibourn, 1994). The original evaluation of the Milwaukee choice program reported no systematic achievement effects of enrollment in a private school. This evaluation did not carefully analyze the data from the randomized experiment. Instead, the evaluation compared students from low-income families with public school students from more advantaged backgrounds, leaving open the possibility that unobserved background characteristics could account for these negative findings.

In 1996, the data became available on the World Wide Web. When Greene et al. (1996) examined these data, they found that enrollment in the program had only limited positive effects during the first 2 years a student was in the program. Choice students made larger gains in Years 3 and 4, as much as one fourth of a standard deviation in reading and one third of a standard deviation in mathematics (Greene, Peterson, & Howell, 1998). Similar math results (but not substantial reading results) are reported by Rouse (1998a).

That improved performance does not become substantial until Years 3 and 4 is quite consistent with a common-sense understanding of the educational process. Choice schools are not magic bullets that transform children overnight. It takes time to adjust to a new teaching and learning environment. The disruption of switching schools and adjusting to new routines and expectations may hinder improvement in test scores in the first year or two of being in a choice school. Educational benefits accumulate and multiply with the passage of time. As Barbara Lewis (1997), Indianapolis choice parent, explained the process:

> I must admit there was a period of transition, culture shock you might call it. He had to get used to the discipline and the homework.... But Alphonso began to learn about learning, to respect the kids around him and be respected, to learn about citizenship, discipline, and doing your lessons.... My son has blossomed into an honor roll student.

Future Research

Cecilia Rouse (1998b) suggested that the Milwaukee results are not a function of school choice per se but of the smaller classes in choice schools. The study in question has many technical limitations, but even if its findings are corroborated by future research, they raise a new set of questions: Why do Milwaukee choice schools, with more limited resources, have smaller class sizes than public schools? Are private schools better able to find efficient ways of using limited resources? Do they provide more effective education by concentrating resources on smaller class sizes rather than paying higher teacher salaries or hiring more administrators? These are questions well worth exploring in future studies.

We also need to conduct more carefully designed randomized experiments of school choice. The data from the randomized experiment in Milwaukee are the best available, but they are still not definitive. The number of participating schools was small and valuable data are missing. Higher quality information may emerge from evaluations of experiments now beginning in New York City, Dayton, and Washington, DC. The 1,200 students participating in the New York program were chosen by a lottery from a large pool of more than 20,000 applicants, from which a control group is being selected. Similar lotteries were held in the spring of 1998 in Dayton and Washington, DC. It remains to be seen whether the payoff from private schooling in these cities will be as great as some anticipate.[4]

College Attendance

School choice programs are too recent to provide information on their effects on college attendance, although the PAVE program in Milwaukee reported that 75% of those who have graduated from high school have gone on to college (McKinley, 1997). More systematic information on the effects of attendance at a Catholic high school are contained in a recent University of Chicago analysis of the National Longitudinal Survey of Youth, conducted by the Department of Education, surveying more than 12,000 young people. Students from all racial and ethnic groups are more likely to go to college if they attended a Catholic school, but the effects are the greatest for urban minorities. The probability of graduating from college increases from 11% to 27%, if such a student attends a Catholic high school (Neal, 1996). The University of Chicago study confirms results from two other analyses that show positive effects for low-income and minority students who attended Catholic schools, on high school completion and college enrollment (Evans & Schwab, 1993; Siglio & Stone, 1977). As one researcher summarized:

> [It] indicates a substantial private school advantage in terms of completing high school and enrolling in college, both very important events in predicting future income and well-being. Moreover...the effects were most pronounced for students with achievement test scores in the bottom half of the distribution. (Witte, 1996, p. 167)

Ethnic Relations and Political Tolerance

The purpose of education is to teach more than math and reading; it is also to prepare citizens for a democratic society. According to critics, school choice will provoke the formation of schools specializing in witchcraft, Black nationalism, and White supremacy. Former *New Republic* editor Michael Kelly (1996) said, "Public money is shared money, and it is to be used for the furtherance of shared values, in the interests of *e pluribus unum.* Charter schools and their like...take from the *pluribus* to destroy the *unum*" (p. 6). Only schools operated by a government agency, it is claimed, can preserve democracy. Princeton theorist Amy Gutmann (1987) put it this way: "Public, not private, schooling is...the primary means by which citizens can morally educate [sic] future citizens" (p. 70). Or, in the words of Felix Frankfurter, writing the Supreme Court opinion in *Minersville Board of Education v. Gobitis* (1940), "We are dealing here with the formative period in the development of citizenship.... Public education is one of our most cherished democratic institutions" (p. 598).[5]

Despite the scare tactics and the rhetorical flourishes, choice critics have failed to offer much evidence that school choice will balkanize America. No reasonable person can believe the American public would routinely turn over school dollars to extremist groups any more than it will allow airlines to fly unregulated or meat to be marketed without inspection. Only the most extreme libertarians think school choice should mean completely unregulated choice. As RAND scholar Paul Hill (1997) said, "In the long run, schools in a publicly funded choice system will be public because they'll be regulated" (p. 98). This should not mean that regulated schools are the same as government-operated schools. To make that argument is to claim that government inspection of the meat-processing industry constitutes an establishment of a nationwide system of collective farms.

Today, students in private schools are in fact less racially isolated than their public school peers. According to 1992 Department of Education data (Greene, 1998), 37% of private school students are in classrooms whose share of minority students is close to the national average, as compared with only 18% of public school students. Not only are private school students more likely to be in well-integrated classrooms, they are less likely to be in extremely segregated classrooms (either more than 90% White or 90% minority). Forty-one percent of private school students are in highly segregated classrooms, as compared to 55% of their public school peers.

Private school students also report more positive relationships with students from other racial and ethnic groups. According to the same Department of Education survey, private school students are significantly more likely to have cross-racial friendships than are students at public schools. Students, teachers, and administrators at private schools all report fewer racial problems.

Private school students are also more community spirited. According to the 1992 survey, students at private schools are more likely than public school students to think that it is important to help others and volunteer for community causes. They also are more likely to report that they in fact did volunteer in the past 2 years and to say their school expected them to do so.

Children Remaining in Public Schools

How about those left behind? For many critics of school choice, this is the critical question. Robert F. Chase (1998), National Education Association President, said:

> The real test of an urban voucher system is whether it can accommodate all who want to take advantage of it, while not simultaneously destroying the public schools by siphoning away their funding as well as their talented students and teachers." (p. 6)

Similarly, the AFT, in its critique of the Cleveland scholarship program, said that "instead of being distracted by promises to 'save' a handful of students, policymakers could be improving the achievement of all of our youngsters" (Murphy et al., 1997, p. iv).

In making these arguments, choice critics often assume that: (a) the more able children from more privileged families will be the first to leave public schools, (b) children learn mainly from their peers, and (c) public schools will not respond to the challenge posed by choice. None of these assumptions is well supported by available data.

Who Goes to Choice School

First, there is little reason to expect the best and the brightest to flee the public schools to take advantage of inner-city choice programs. Most big city school systems have their own programs—magnet schools, gifted classes, and honor's tracks—that siphon off the best into specialized educational programs. Parents can be expected *not* to change their child's school, unless they have doubts about his or her progress. In Milwaukee, for example, parents who signed up for choice schools were more likely to say the school had been in contact with them, probably because their child was having difficulties (Peterson, 1995a; Witte, 1991). Student test-score data also indicate that choice applicants are less than the cream of the crop. The percentage of applicants to New York City's choice program performing at grade level was only 26% in reading and 18% in mathematics, far below the 55% reported for all New York City elementary students (Peterson, Greene, Howell, & McCready, 1997). However, in the first-come, first-served programs in Indianapolis and San Antonio, school choice applicants may have been above the norm for the city as a whole (Godwin, Kemerer, & Martinez, 1998; Weinschrott & Kilgore, 1998).

Peer-Group Effects

Even so, to claim that those left behind suffer as a result depends on the strange assumption that children learn not from teachers but from other children. This idea can be traced back to a 1966 school desegregation study. Researchers found that most school factors (e.g., per pupil expenditures, class size, teacher salary, and the number of books in the school library) had few measurable effects on student achievement (Coleman et al., 1966). However, the socioeconomic background of other children in the school did have a detectable effect on achievement, a tantalizing fact that was overinterpreted to mean that children learned mainly from their peers. In a comprehensive review of the peer-group literature, sociologists Christopher Jencks and Susan Mayer (1990) found these effects to be small and inconsistent from one study to the next. They offered an intriguing explanation: Peer-group effects could be substantial but offsetting, they said. Students thrive by picking up facts, ideas, and phrases from their more capable associates. However, they get discouraged when they cannot keep up. The two factors, working in opposite directions, may have roughly equivalent educational effects (see also Mayer, 1991).

Jencks and Mayer may be right, but the matter deserves still further consideration. One of James Coleman's first studies indicated that, in private schools, group leaders were academics, whereas in public schools the popular students were sports stars and cheerleaders (Corwin & Borman, 1988). As Cornell professor John Bishop (1999) put it, "Popularity depends first and foremost on being good in sports.... Being smart is OK, but being studious is not" (p. 238). To explain the difference between public and private schools, Coleman (1961) pointed out that, in both types of schools, the most popular students were those who brought honor to the whole school. In private schools, the whole school benefits from high academic performance because academic achievement enhances the reputation of the school with potential customers. In public schools, it is often the sports program, more than the academic performance of a few, that brings credit to the school.

If Coleman and Bishop are correct, then peer-group effects may in fact help explain the greater learning that takes place in private schools. It is not that private school students are more capable; it is that the more capable students carry more influence in this setting and "nerds" are subject to less harassment. The problem faced by those "left behind" in the public schools is not the lack of capable peers but the fact that academic study has in most inner-city public schools negative cache.

The systemic impact of vouchers and scholarships that enhance parental school choice has been a matter of intense public and academic debate. Some have argued that school choice will segment and stratify the country's educational system, with the best and the brightest students attending private schools, while public schools are left with a particularly unmotivated and disadvantaged population.

Will Public Schools Meet the Challenge?

Choice supporters claim that a choice-based system will motivate the public schools to respond vigorously to new competitors, producing an across-the-board upsurge in U.S. education. Hoxby (1998) found that students learn more, if they live in metropolitan areas where public schools are subject to greater competitive pressures, both from private schools and other public school systems. She also found that in competitive contexts public schools are less costly and give greater emphasis to academic achievement. In a study of interdistrict choice in Massachusetts, Armour and Peiser (1998) found that when school districts lost students to neighboring districts, they developed partially successful strategies to attract students back, stemming future losses. In 1997 in Albany, the school board responded vigorously to a privately funded scholarship program that offered scholarships to all students at a particular school.

Yet all these bits of information are still fragmentary and incomplete. At this point, the Albany case is not more than a telling anecdote. Armour and Peiser's (1998) evidence comes from a few school districts. Hoxby's (1998) studies, though fascinating and important, depend upon complex econometric analyses that require strong theoretical assumptions.

The San Antonio Experiment

The scholarship program that began in the Edgewood Independent School District (EISD) in San Antonio provides an opportunity for assessing the impact of school choice for those remaining in public schools. The Edgewood voucher program, sponsored by the CEO America foundation, is offering scholarships to all low-income students in the school district. If students attend private schools within the Edgewood school district or newly established schools outside the district but within the San Antonio metropolitan area, elementary students will receive scholarships worth $3,600; high school students will receive scholarships worth $4,000. If students attend already established schools outside the Edgewood school district, students will receive scholarships that are equivalent to the tuition at the school during the 1997–1998 school year or the aforementioned amount, whichever is less. The program is projected to continue for 10 years or until a publicly funded program is established. Students accepting scholarships are guaranteed scholarships throughout their elementary and high school years.

Edgewood schools serve an economically disadvantaged, predominantly Latino population. In 1996–1997, 93% of the students attending schools in Edgewood were considered economically disadvantaged by the Texas Department of Education. Ninety-six percent were Hispanic, 2% were African American, 1.8% were White, with the remainder Asian, Pacific Islander, and Native American. Students with limited English proficiency constituted 24.3% of the population.

In 1996–1997, Edgewood had 14,180 students. The students are distributed quite uniformly across the first 10 years of schooling, Grades

K–9. However, the number of students in high school decreases dramatically. Apparently, the high-school dropout rate is a serious problem within the Edgewood school district.

Edgewood is highly dependent on state aid. As a result, any school choice program that attracts large numbers of students away from the public schools to choice schools will result in a sharp decline in state aid—as long as state-aid formulas remain conditional on the number of students enrolled in the public schools. The total revenue budgeted for the district amounted to $83,978,251, or $5,852 per pupil. Eight percent of the money is from local tax sources, 83% comes from the state, 7% comes from the federal government, and another 2% comes from other local sources. Because of the high dependence of Edgewood on external funding, the public schools will be under strong financial pressure to find ways of responding to the challenge posed by the scholarship program.

CONCLUSIONS

Many studies of school choice thus far are limited to small-scale experiments. The effects of vouchers and scholarships may be quite different once they are introduced on a larger scale. The answers may come soon. Now that the expansion of the Milwaukee choice program has been declared constitutional, as much as 15% of the Milwaukee public school population (approximately 15,000 students) may participate. How many will apply? How many will be accepted into private schools? What new schools will form? Which of the existing schools will expand?

We recommend that further large-scale experiments be undertaken. Specifically, we recommend that Congress enact legislation giving all the students living in the District of Columbia an opportunity to attend the school of their choice. The costs of public education in the District are extremely high and the quality of the services being rendered appears to be quite inadequate. The population receiving the services is among the most needy in the nation. According to a poll taken by *The Washington Post* (Horwitz, 1998), a majority of the citizens living in the district and 60% of the city's African Americans favor a voucher program for their schools. Support is particularly strong among low-income respondents.

The answers to the questions posed in this chapter do not indicate that school choice is a panacea that can resolve all of society's problems. They do suggest it is time to rethink the way we organize our public educational system; this seems to be taking place. Arthur Levine (1998), president of Columbia University Teachers College, throughout his career an opponent of school voucher programs, "reluctantly concluded" that "a limited school voucher program is now essential for the poorest Americans attending the worst public schools" (p. A28). Hugh Price, Urban League President, said:

> If urban schools...continue to fail in the face of all we know about how to improve them, then parents will be obliged to shop elsewhere for quality education. We Urban Leaguers believe passionately in public education. But make no mistake. We love our children even more." (Peterson & Greene, 1998, p. 34)

The final, succinct words are best left to William Raspberry (1997): "It's time for some serious experimentation" (p. 13).

ENDNOTES

1. Though the fourth-graders trailed students in Japan, South Korea, the Netherlands, and the Czech Republic, they did better than students in England, Norway, and New Zealand. The U.S. eighth-graders clearly outscored only seven countries—Lithuania, Cyprus, Portugal, Iran, Kuwait, Columbia, and South Africa—none of them usually thought to be U.S. peers.
2. These results constitute a half a standard deviation difference on the satisfaction scale and are significant at the .001 level.
3. For commentary and criticism of Putnam's thesis, see M. Schudson, "What if Civic Life Didn't Die?"; T. Skocpol, "Unraveling From Above"; R. D. Putnam, "Robert Putnam Responds"; and R. M. Valelly, "Couch-Potato Democracy?" (March–April, 1996), *American Prospect*, pp. 17–28.
4. David Myers at Mathematica and Paul E. Peterson plan to follow both test and control groups in New York over the next 4 years. The University of Dayton is undertaking a similar study in Dayton, and Northern Illinois University is undertaking a study in Washington, DC.
5. Frankfurter's reasoning justified a West Virginia regulation forcing Jehovah's Witnesses to salute the school flag, a decision that the Supreme Court reversed in *West Virginia State Board of Education v. Barnette* (1943) soon after the country had entered the war against Nazi Germany.

REFERENCES

Armour, D. J., & Peiser, B. M. (1998). Interdistrict choice in Massachusetts. In P. E. Peterson & B. Hassel (Eds.), *Learning from school choice* (pp. 157–186). Washington, DC: Brookings Institution.

Ascher, C., Fruchter, N., & Berne, R. (1996). *Hard lessons: Public schools and privatization*. New York: Twentieth Century Fund Press.

Barton, P. E., & Coley, R. J. (1998). *Growth in school: Achievement gains from the fourth to the eighth grade*. Princeton, NJ: Policy Information Center, Research Division, Educational Testing Service.

Bishop, J. (1999). Nerd harassment: Incentives, school priorities, and learning. In P. E. Peterson & S. Mayer (Eds.), *How schools make a difference* (pp. 231–280). Washington, DC: Brookings Institution.

Bryk, A. S., Lee, V. E., & Holland, P. B. (1993). *Catholic schools and the common good*. Cambridge, MA: Harvard University Press.

Carnegie Foundation for the Advancement of Teaching. (1992). *School choice: A special report*. Princeton, NJ: Author.

Chase, R. F. (1998). Save urban schools by bleeding them? *Brookings Quarterly Newsletter*, *8*(3), 6.

Chubb, J. E., & Moe, T. M. (1990). *Politics, markets, and American schools.* Washington, DC: Brookings Institution.

Coleman, J. S. (1961). *The adolescent society.* New York: The Free Press.

Coleman, J. S., Campbell, E. Q., Hobson, C. J., McPartland, J., Mood, A. M., Weinfeld, F. D., & York, R. L. (1966). *Equality of educational opportunity.* Washington, DC: U.S. Department of Health, Education and Welfare, Office of Education.

Coleman, J. S., & Hoffer, T. (1987). *Public and private high schools: The impact of communities.* New York: Basic Books.

Coleman, J. S., Hoffer, T., & Kilgore, S. (1982). *High school achievement: Public, Catholic and private schools compared.* New York: Basic Books.

Corwin, R. G., & Borman, K. M. (1988). School as workplace: Structural constraints on administration. In N. J. Boyan, (Ed.), *Handbook of research on educational administration* (pp. 209–237). New York: Longman.

Evans, W. N., & Schwab, R. M. (1993). *Who benefits from private education? Evidence from quantile regressions.* College Park, MD: University of Maryland, Department of Economics.

Godwin, R. K., Kemerer, F. R., & Martinez, V. J. (1998). Comparing public choice and private voucher programs in San Antonio. In P. E. Peterson & B. C. Hassel (Eds.), *Learning from school choice* (pp. 275–306). Washington, DC: Brookings Institution.

Goldberger, A. S., & Cain, G. G. (1982). The causal analysis of cognitive outcomes in the Coleman, Hoffer, and Kilgore report. *Sociology of Education, 55,* 103–122.

Greene, J. P. (1998). Private schools and civic education. In P. E. Peterson & B. C. Hassel (Eds.), *Learning from school choice* (pp. 83–106). Washington, DC: Brookings Institution.

Greene, J. P., Howell, W. G., & Peterson, P. E. (1997). *An evaluation of the Cleveland scholarship program* (Occasional paper). Cambridge, MA: Harvard University, Program on Education Policy and Governance.

Greene, J. P., Howell, W. G., & Peterson, P. E. (1998). Lessons from the Cleveland scholarship program. In P. E. Peterson, & B. C. Hassel (Eds.), *Learning from school choice* (pp. 357–393). Washington, DC: Brookings Institution.

Greene, J. P., Peterson, P. E., & Du, J., with Berger, L., & Frazier, C. L. (1996). *The effectiveness of school choice in Milwaukee: A secondary analysis of data from the program's evaluation* (Occasional paper). Cambridge, MA: Harvard University, Program in Education Policy and Governance.

Greene, J. P., Peterson, P. E., & Howell, W. G. (1998). School choice in Milwaukee: A randomized experiment. In P. E. Peterson & B. C. Hassel (Eds.), *Learning from school choice* (pp. 335–356). Washington, DC: Brookings Institution.

Grover, H. (1993). Comments and general discussion. In E. Rasell & R. Rothstein (Eds.), *School choice: Examining the evidence* (pp. 248–255). Washington, DC: Economic Policy Institute.

Gutmann, A. (1987). *Democratic education.* Princeton, NJ: Princeton University Press.

Hill, P. (1997). *Reinventing public education.* Chicago: University of Chicago Press.

Horwitz, S. (1998, May 23). Poll finds backing for D.C. school vouchers: Blacks support idea more than whites. *The Washington Post*, p. F1.

Hoxby, C. M. (1998). Analyzing school choice reforms using America's traditional forms of parental choice. In P. E. Peterson & B. C. Hassel (Eds.), *Learning from school choice* (pp. 133–156). Washington, DC: Brookings Institution.

Improving educational opportunities for low-income children: Hearing before the U.S. Senate Committee on Labor and Human Resources, 105th Cong., 1st Sess. (1997). Washington, DC: U.S. Government Printing Office.

Jencks, C., & Mayer, S. E. (1990). The social consequences of growing up in a poor neighborhood. In L. E. Lynn, Jr., & M. G. H. McGeary (Eds.), *Inner city poverty in the United States* (pp. 111–186). Washington, DC: National Academy Press.

Kelly, M. (1996, December 30). Dangerous minds. *The New Republic*, p. 6.

Lawton, M. (1996). U.S. students about average in global study. *Education Week 16*(13), 1, 32.

Lawton, M. (1997). 4th graders do well in math, science study. *Education Week 16*(38), 1, 22.

Levine, A. (1998, June 15). Why I'm reluctantly backing vouchers. *The Wall Street Journal*, p. A28.

Lewis, B. S. (1997, July 29). Families organized for real choice in education (Testimony during hearings on education opportunities for low-income children, presented before the U.S. Senate Labor and Human Resources Committee). Washington, DC: Federal Document Clearing House.

Mayer, S. E. (1991). How much does a high school's racial and socioeconomic mix affect graduation and teenage fertility rates? In C. Jencks & P. E. Peterson, (Eds.), *The urban underclass* (pp. 321–341). Washington, DC: Brookings Institution.

McKinley, D. (1997, August 25). *Memorandum for the board of directors of Partners Advancing Values in Education.* Milwaukee, WI: Partners Advancing Values in Education.

Metcalf, K. (1999). *Evaluation of the Cleveland scholarship and tutoring grant program, 1996–1999.* Bloomington, IN: Indiana University, Smith Research Center.

Metcalf, K. K., Muller, P., Boone, W., Taito, P., Stage, F., & Stacey, N. (1998). Evaluation of the Cleveland scholarship program: Second year report (1997–1998). Bloomington, IN: Indiana University, Smith Research Center.

Minersville Board of Education v. Gobitis, 310 U.S. 598 (1940).

Murphy, D., Nelson, F. H., & Rosenberg, B. (1997). *The Cleveland voucher program: Who chooses? Who gets chosen? Who pays?* New York: American Federation of Teachers.

Neal, D. (1996). *The effects of Catholic secondary schooling on educational achievement.* Chicago: University of Chicago, Harris School of Public Policy, and National Bureau for Economic Research.

Peterson, P. E. (1995a). *A critique of the Witte evaluation of Milwaukee's school choice program* (Occasional paper 95-2). Cambridge, MA: Harvard University, Center for American Political Studies.

Peterson, P. E. (1995b). *The Milwaukee school choice plan: Ten comments on the Witte reply* (Occasional paper 95-3). Cambridge, MA: Harvard University, Center for American Political Studies.

Peterson, P. E. (1998). School choice: A report card. In P. E. Peterson & B. C. Hassel, (Eds.), *Learning from school choice* (pp. 3–32). Washington, DC: Brookings Institution.

Peterson, P. E., & Greene, J. P. (1998). Race relations and central city schools. *Brookings Review, 16*(2), 33–37.

Peterson, P. E., Greene, J. P., Howell, W. G., & McCready, W. (1997). *Initial findings from the evaluation of the New York school choice scholarships program* (Occasional paper). Cambridge, MA: Harvard University, John F. Kennedy School of Government.

Peterson, P. E., Greene, J. P., Howell, W. G., & McCready, W. (1998). *Initial findings from an evaluation of school choice programs in Washington, DC* (Occasional paper). Cambridge, MA: Harvard University, John F. Kennedy School of Government.

Peterson, P. E., Howell, W. G., & Greene, J. P. (1999). An evaluation of the Cleveland voucher program after two years (Report No. 99-02). Cambridge, MA: Harvard University, John F. Kennedy School of Government, Program on Education Policy and Governance.

Peterson, P. E., Myers, D. E., Haimson, J., & Howell, W. B. (1997). *Initial findings from the evaluation of the New York School Choice Scholarships Program.* Cambridge, MA: Harvard University, John F. Kennedy School of Government, Program on Education Policy and Governance.

Putnam, R. D. (1993). The prosperous community: Social capital and public life. *American Prospect, 13,* 35–42.

Putnam, R. D. (1997). Bowling alone: Democracy in America at century's end. In A. Hadenius (Ed.), *Democracy's victory and crisis* (pp. 27–70). New York: Cambridge University Press.

Raspberry, W. (1997). A reluctant convert to school choice. *Selected Readings on School Reform, 1*(2), 13.

Rose, L. C., & Gallup, A. M. (1999, September). *The 31st annual Phi Delta Kappa/Gallup poll of the public's attitudes toward the public schools* (Vol. 81). Available: http://www.pdkintl.org/kappan/kpol19909.htm

Rouse, C. E. (1998a). Private school vouchers and student achievement: an evaluation of the Milwaukee Parental Choice Program. *Quarterly Journal of Economics, 113,* 553–602.

Rouse, C. E. (1998b). Student achievement: More evidence from the Milwaukee parental choice program. *Educational Policy Review, 4*(1), 61–78.

Schneider, M., Teske, P., Marschall, M., Mintrom, M., & Roch, C. (1977). Institutional arrangements and the creation of social capital: The effects of school choice. *American Political Science Review, 91,* 82–93.

Siglio, D. & Stone, J. (1977). *School choice and student performance: Are private schools really better?* Madison: University of Wisconsin Institute for Research on Poverty.

Steinberg, J. (1997, May 13). Students chosen for grants to attend private schools. *The New York Times,* p. B3.

Thernstrom, A. (1991). *School choice in Massachusetts.* Boston: Pioneer Institute for Public Policy Research.

United States National Research Center. (1998). *TIMMS high school results released* (Report 8). Lansing, MI: Michigan State University.

Viteritti, J. P. (1999). *Choosing equality: School choice, the constitution, and civil society.* Washington, DC: Brookings Press.

Weinschrott, D. J., & Kilgore, S. B. (1998). Evidence from the Indianapolis voucher program. In P. E. Peterson & B. C. Hassel (Eds.), *Learning from school choice* (pp. 307–334). Washington, DC: Brookings Institution.

Wells, A. S. (1996). African-American students' view of school choice. In B. Fuller & R. Elmer (Eds.), *Who chooses? Who loses? Culture, institutions, and the unequal effects of school choice* (pp. 25–49). New York: Teachers College Press.

Wilms, D. J. (1984). School effectiveness within the public and private sectors: An evaluation. *Evaluation Review, 8,* 113–135.

Wilms, D. J. (1985). Catholic school effects on academic achievement: New evidence from the high school and beyond follow-up study. *Sociology of Education, 58,* 98–114.

Witte, J. F. (1991). *First year report: Milwaukee parental choice program.* Madison: University of Wisconsin-Madison, Department of Political Science, and the Robert M. La Follette Institute of Public Affairs.

Witte, J. F. (1996). School choice and student performance. In H. F. Ladd (Ed.), *Holding schools accountable: Performance-based reform in education* (pp. 149–176). Washington, DC: Brookings Institution.

Witte, J. F. (1997, January). *Achievement effects of the Milwaukee voucher program.* Paper presented at the American Economics Association annual meeting, New Orleans, LA.

Witte, J. F., Bailey, A. B., & Thorn, C. A. (1992). *Second year report: Milwaukee parental choice program.* Madison: University of Wisconsin-Madison, Department of Political Science, and the Robert M. La Follette Institute of Public Affairs.

Witte, J. F., Bailey, A. B., & Thorn, C. A. (1993). *Third year report: Milwaukee parental choice program.* Madison: University of Wisconsin-Madison, Department of Political Science, and the Robert M. La Follette Institute of Public Affairs.

Witte, J. F., Sterr, T. D., & Thorn, C. A. (1995). *Fifth year report: Milwaukee parental choice program.* Madison: University of Wisconsin-Madison, Department of Political Science, and the Robert M. La Follette Institute of Public Affairs.

Witte, J. F., Thorn, C. A., Pritchard, K. M., & Claibourn, M. (1994). *Fourth year report: Milwaukee parental choice program.* Madison: University of Wisconsin-Madison, Department of Political Science, and the Robert M. La Follette Institute of Public Affairs.

Part II

Best Systems

5

Integrated Governance in Chicago and Birmingham (UK)

Kenneth K. Wong
University of Chicago

TRANSFORMING URBAN SCHOOL SYSTEMS

The Chicago Public Schools (CPS) and the Birmingham, England, Local Education Authority (LEA) lead their respective nations with their school reform strategies. Since Mayor Richard Daley took over the school system in July 1995, the CPS have made significant improvements in their financial management, administrative functions, and educational performance. Major initiatives that initially posed political risks, such as an end to social promotion and the creation of Summer Bridge programs, are now endorsed by national, state, and local leaders from the two major political parties, including President Bill Clinton, Texas Governor George Bush, and New York Mayor Rudolph Giuliani. In large part because of the CPS accomplishments in the absence of additional state funds, the mayor was selected as 1 of the 10 "public officials of the year" (Ehrenhalt, 1997, p. 22). The system is managed by a politically skillful school board president, a dynamic chief executive officer (CEO), Paul Vallas, and a competent administrative team, including the chief education officer.

Across the Atlantic Ocean, the Birmingham LEA has undergone a transformation. In September 1993, the Birmingham City Council reversed a decade of neglect in education with its appointment of a nationally known reformer, Professor Tim Brighouse, as the chief education officer. Brighouse's charismatic leadership has energized and inspired the rank-and-file in the teaching force. Since 1994, the city's budget for education has consistently exceeded the national spending standard. These investments have produced significant gains in student performance. As David Blunkett (1998), England's Secretary of State for Education and Employment, commented on the findings from a major external evaluation of the LEA, "This report describes a success story for Birmingham City Council.... The report describes a very well run LEA, with a sense of purpose and a carefully articulated rationale for the deployment of its resources" (pp. 1–2).

Both school systems are moving toward better student performance that coincides with new leadership at the district level. Although test scores are seen as an incomplete measure of student learning, student outcome indicators remain a widely accepted barometer of how well school systems perform. In this regard, student performance suggests that the sister systems are closing the gap with their national averages. In Birmingham, there have been significant gains in student test scores in the past 3 years. In 7 out of 10 national tests in key subject areas across four different grade levels, Birmingham students made gains at a much faster rate than the national average. In Chicago, elementary reading and math test scores have shown consistent gains over the past several years. Truancy rates have declined steadily in the last 3 years and graduation rates for high school seniors have improved to 65%.

Clearly, Chicago and Birmingham are in the midst of an unprecedented drive toward educational improvement. Current reforms in the sister cities will provide valuable lessons in urban educational transformation for other urban school systems. Recent accomplishments of the two systems must be considered significant as their schools were once publicized as the "worst" in their respective nations. The two systems also confront numerous structural constraints associated with urban society. The Birmingham LEA is the fifth most socioeconomically deprived district out of 366 in England. Twenty-five of its 39 wards are ranked in the most disadvantaged 10% in the country. Similarly, 83% of Chicago's students qualify for free and reduced-price school lunch. Most middle-class families who live in the city send their children to parochial and private schools.

INTEGRATED GOVERNANCE AS A SCHOOL REFORM MODEL

The successes of the two systems closely relate to the recent redesign of district-level governance and management. The sister systems share several institutional characteristics that can be broadly described as *integrated governance,* a framework that the author first identified in a 1997 report on Chicago school reform entitled, *Integrated Governance as a School Reform Strategy in the Chicago Public Schools* (Wong, Dreeben, Lynn, & Sunderman, 1997). The major institutional features include:

- Strong political will to improve the operation of the school system.
- A clear vision of educational accountability, focused on academic standards and performance outcomes.
- High-quality leadership at the central office committed to using a mix of intervention and support strategies to meet the challenges faced by urban schools.

More specifically, in Chicago, the Chicago School Reform Amendatory Act, which took effect in July 1995, reverses the trend toward decentralization of authority over school operations and redesigns the governance arrangement so that power and authority are now integrated. Integrated governance in Chicago is characterized by:

- A reduction of competing authorities (such as the School Board Nominating Commission) and a coordination of activities in support of systemwide goals and standards.
- Mayoral appointment of school board members and selection of top administrators.
- The creation of the position of CEO to oversee the top administrative team, including the chief education officer.
- Powers granted to the school board to hold local school councils (LSCs) accountable to systemwide standards.

With integrated governance in place, CPS has improved the conditions for teaching and learning in several ways:

- It has improved the financial and management functions of the entire system.
- It has allowed for a sharper focus on schools and students with the greatest academic needs.
- It has raised the standards in professional recruitment, academic performance, and school management throughout the system.
- It has enhanced public confidence in the city's educational system.

In Birmingham, integrated governance offers a useful framework for understanding educational management. As in Chicago, educational accountability in Birmingham is closely connected to the city's electoral institutions. The following institutional features characterize the LEA governance:

- The education committee of the city council (currently under the control of the Labour Party) functions as the school board, which oversees the entire operation of the district-level administration.
- The chief education officer is accountable to the city council, which is structured in terms of a ward-based electoral system.
- The education budget is an integral part of the city's total allocation.
- The chief education officer and his top staff in the education department regularly coordinate their activities with those of the other city departments.

Since the appointment of Tim Brighouse as the chief education officer, the Birmingham LEA has transformed the educational system in several ways:

- It counters the national tide of de-legitimizing the role of LEAs during the era of conservative party dominance in Westminster.
- It redesigns the central office as a critical friend to assist schools and teachers to improve on previous best practices, particularly through the Birmingham Advisory and Support Service (BASS).
- It offers schools a wide range of high-quality, affordable, technical services in both statutory and nonstatutory domains.
- It leads the nation in setting performance targets and in innovative initiatives, such as secondary school restructuring, early years

education, and the University of the First Age (UFA).

- It provides the critical support to schools within a national educational system that otherwise lacks sufficient checks and balances.

Clearly, the sister systems have much to celebrate and to learn from each other. Both systems can be characterized as integrated governance in that educational governance is closely connected to the electorally accountable political leadership in the city. There is a strong tendency to improve policy coherence and organizational coordination.

Variation in Pressure and Support

Though organized under an integrated governance model, Chicago and Birmingham have adopted a different mix of intervention strategies to reach the goal of improved student performance. Table 5.1 depicts the key components of the accountability framework used in the sister systems. The four major accountability mechanisms include setting standards, establishing formal sanctions, providing support to build up the capacity of schools and students, and pressure from "marketlike" competition. The two systems employ these strategies to varying degrees.

In Chicago, systemwide standards, formal sanctions, and support are used simultaneously to improve the performance of failing schools and students, although sanction-oriented policies have received the most attention. Chicago has developed systemwide standards for principals and teachers and has begun to implement curricular standards for students. The latter will serve as a basis for assessing both student achievement and teacher and school performance. They provide both curricular support to schools and a tool that the district can use to develop further sanctions.

This combination of support and pressure is also reflected in the Summer Bridge programs, which are a key element in the district's academic promotion policy. The Summer Bridge programs, as described later, offer remediation for poorly performing students while also serving as sanctions for low performance. Along with a focus on academics, the district is attempting to address the nutritional and personal needs of its most disadvantaged students. The Lighthouse Program is an after-school program that provides students who would otherwise be left alone with dinner and activities within the safe confines of the school.

TABLE 5.1
Key Components in Systemwide Accountability

Policy mechanisms	Chicago	Birmingham, UK
Setting standards	• District-wide standards in curriculum, assessment, and professional recruitment	• National curriculum and examination
Formal sanctions	• Seven schools reconstituted • 109 schools placed on probation • Social promotion terminated	• OFSTED inspection of LEA • OFSTED inspection of schools • School rankings by test performance in newspapers
Support to build up school capacity	• External partners for reconstituted and probation schools • Professional development for principals and teachers (e.g., Projects LIFT & LAUNCH) • Expanded teacher recruitment efforts	• Birmingham Advisory Support Services • LMS enables school autonomy • Chief Education Officer leadership in ensuring teacher support
Support to build up student capacity	• Summer Bridge programs • Lighthouse program	• Early years provision • Cross-agency collaboration (e.g., University of the First Age)
Pressure from market-like competition	• Limited: 15 charter schools approved; IB and magnet programs expanded • Families exit to private and suburban schools	• Grant-maintained schools opt out of LEA control • School closure • Parental preference and LMS budgeting

Note: IB—International Baccalaureate; OFSTED—Office of Her Majesty's Chief Inspector of Schools; LEA—Local Education Authority; LMS—Local Management of Schools

Finally, unlike the Birmingham LEA, which faces market competition, particularly in terms of high school enrollment, Chicago schools face limited competition. Within the system, newly formed charter schools and the expansion of magnet schools and the International Baccalaureate program create competition among schools. Unlike in Birmingham, where the national government initiates competition between schools through its parental choice program, in Chicago the district directs school competition.

In contrast to Chicago's pressure-and-support approach, the Birmingham LEA has developed a coherent set of strategies that is primarily supportive of teachers and head teachers at the school level. In part, the LEA can adopt this approach because of the nature of the English educational system. In England, the national level sets curricular standards and has established a national assessment. In addition, the national government conducts inspections of both the LEAs and individual schools. Sanctions are based largely on school rankings that are determined by the students' performance on national exams. The national government, therefore, applies much of the pressure on schools. Birmingham has used this situation to align itself with the schools and to counterbalance national-level sanctions. The LEA has created a number of support programs to help schools set performance targets and to prepare for evaluations by the Office of Her Majesty's Chief Inspector of Schools (OFSTED).

In addition, the LEA has undertaken several programmatic initiatives in partnership with other city agencies to provide schools with further support. A primary example is the UFA which provides early adolescents with unique learning experiences during school breaks and the summer.

Finally, the Birmingham LEA must contend with competition from private and grant-maintained schools. This is particularly relevant in the area of secondary schooling. The LEA controls only 7,381 of the 10,600 places available for secondary school admissions. The remaining one third of the places are controlled by selective single-sex and voluntary-aided schools. Grant-maintained schools, which are outside of the LEA control, have captured an additional 3,000 places. The LEA schools thus face the effects of creaming, which diminishes the number of high-performing students within the schools.

In summary, although the two sister systems operate within an integrated governance framework, they have developed significantly different approaches to improving school and student performance. In terms of a policy continuum between a pressure-oriented approach and a school professional-oriented approach, Chicago maintains a hybrid approach that uses both pressure and support whereas Birmingham directs more of its efforts and resources toward supporting teacher improvement at the school level.

These cross-Atlantic variations in systemwide improvements are embedded in the governance structure of the public educational systems in the two countries. The author feels that Chicago's district-level administration has few options to reduce its pressure on failing schools because it constitutes the only legitimate source of meaningful sanctions within the American governmental framework of local (i.e., district) control. In the absence of a national examination, a national curriculum, and a meaningful state monitoring system, Chicago has to assume the responsibility of ensuring systemwide performance in order to meet its vision of educational accountability. In contrast, the LEA in Birmingham can focus its attention on teacher and school support because pressure on failing schools comes from various external sources with different policy mechanisms, as Table 5.1 suggests. These include OFSTED, which applies national testing and curricular standards to monitor school performance on a regular basis, and a choice scheme that enables parents to register their schooling preferences for their children. The national government recently issued a new educational policy that is likely to give the LEAs a new role in pressuring failing schools. Both systems, therefore, face a crucial challenge of finding the proper balance between pressure and support.

Policy Challenges Defined

Despite variation in school improvement strategies, Chicago and Birmingham face several common challenges as the sister systems enter the millennium. These policy challenges can be identified as:

- The need to institutionalize key leadership qualities that would sustain administrative success for the system in the long run. The two systems currently operate under dynamic leaders. This raises the question of how Chicago will make the transition when Vallas leaves. Likewise, what kind of leadership is Birmingham going to cultivate in the post-Brighouse era?
- The challenge of broadening the academic gains in underperforming schools.
- The challenge of identifying the proper balance between pressure and support in raising performance in failing schools.
- The need to ensure equal access to quality schooling for the city's diverse student populations.
- The need to improve the quality of the teaching force and the school principals systemwide.

In the following analysis, the author specifies how school governance has been redesigned, how the change facilitates particular kinds of management and educational initiatives, and the consequences of these actions. The next section outlines the distinctive features of Chicago's integrated governance, its accomplishments, and its major intervention strategies to improve student performance. In the third section, the major reform initiatives under Brighouse's leadership in Birmingham are discussed, specifically the central administration's supportive role in promoting better teaching and learning. Then, the author briefly examines several factors in Birmingham and in the UK that have contributed to the unique LEA role. This chapter concludes with policy implications for lessons learned from a comparative study of the sister systems. Given the national prominence of the two systems, these lessons can have international significance for the redesign and improvement of urban school systems.

How the Research Was Conducted

To examine how governance redesign facilitates school management and improves educational performance, this study adopts a comprehensive institutional perspective (Wong, Dreeben, Lynn, Meyer, & Sunderman, 1996). This perspective considers how broader institutional arrangements (top-level political, policy, and administrative institutions) influence resource allocation, supportive services of the central office, intervention in failing schools, and professional development. Particular attention is focused on how systemwide institutions create the conditions that affect teaching and learning in schools and classrooms.

Several research strategies were used to collect information for this report. To gather data from the Birmingham LEA and schools, the author spent several weeks in England during the fall of 1997 and winter of 1998. The author "shadowed" Professor Tim Brighouse, Birmingham's CEO, for about 1 week, attending virtually all of his meetings at the school sites, district-level offices, and in the department of education and employment in Westminster. He also interviewed (sometimes more than once) district-level administrators and members of the education committee in the city council (an equivalent to the school board in CPS). He attended various meetings and forums, including hearings conducted by the Secondary Education Commission, consultative meetings between the unions and the education committee, and the city council's chief administrative officers' meeting. During his visits to several primary, secondary, and special schools, he observed classroom instruction and interviewed teachers and head teachers. The author collected numerous documents, including policy reports, budgets, internal memos, minutes of city council meetings, OFSTED inspection reports on the LEA and selected schools, news reports, and proposals on school reform from interest groups.

In Chicago, using semistructured questionnaires, a cross-disciplinary research team under the author's direction interviewed board members, the CEO, the chief education officer, the head of the accountability office, and others who are responsible for developing and implementing programs in professional development, curricular standards, and school improvement. Documentary materials were also collected from the board. These included board policies, budget information, and minutes of the Chicago School Reform board of trustees meetings. At the school level, the researchers selected several schools that were under probation and reconstitution for more focused data collection. In these selected schools, they interviewed the principals and teachers, conducted classroom observations, and collected school documents such as curriculum guidelines, budgets, school improvement plans, and staff development materials. To develop an understanding of the broader policy climate, the researchers developed a database of articles and editorials related to education that appeared in two major Chicago newspapers, the *Chicago Sun-Times* and the *Chicago Tribune,* since August 1, 1995 (1 month after the mayor took over the school system).

Considering the Cross-National Context

The two sister systems operate in very different policy and political contexts. The UK has instituted a national examination, a national curriculum, and a national inspectorate on schooling standards. Under the Local Management of School (LMS) scheme in the last 8 years, schools in the UK have enjoyed substantial control over financial and human resources. Parents in England can select from a broader pool of schools, which include state (government), religious (Catholic, Muslim, and Church of England), and grant maintained (those that opt out of direct LEA control but continue to receive government funding). In contrast, the United States does not maintain a national educational system. Instead, it has a strong tradition of district-level governance that is defined by the constitutional framework of individual states. Autonomy at the school level and parental choice remain largely limited in America.

At the same time, there are similarities between the two sister systems. Both Chicago and Birmingham are large, urban systems, each with several hundred schools. As Table 5.2 shows, Birmingham, the largest district in England, has 164,000 students. The LEA maintains 444 schools, including 25 nursery, 327 primary, 61 secondary, 29 special, and 2 hospital schools. Like Chicago, Birmingham has a highly diverse student population. Whereas 59% of Birmingham students are White, 41% of the students are Black and ethnic minorities. Pakistanis (17%), African/Caribbeans (7%), and Indians (7%) comprise the largest minority communities. In all, 32% of the students speak English as a second language. One of three (31%) students in Birmingham is classified as low income, compared to the national average of 19%. The mobility rate is 18% (Birmingham Local Education Authority, 1997b).

Chicago's student population has similar characteristics though the system is much larger. Chicago enrolls more than 420,000 students in 567 schools. These schools include 489 elementary schools and 78 high schools. Unlike Birmingham, the majority of Chicago's students are from minority communities. More than half, 54.5%, of the students in the CPS are African American, 31.3% are Latino, 10.8% are White, and 3.4% are Asian American and Native American. In all, 15.4% of students are classified as limited English proficient. This compares to just 5.9% of students in the state when Chicago is excluded. Approximately 83% of students in Chicago are classified as low income compared with only 17% in Illinois when Chicago is excluded. Finally, the mobility rate in Chicago is 29% (Chicago Public Schools, 1997).

TABLE 5.2
Birmingham and Chicago School Characteristics, 1997–1998

Characteristic	Birmingham	Chicago Public Schools
Number of schools	444	567
Minority students	41%	*89%
Low-income students	31%	83%
Mobility rate	18%	29%

Note: From Birmingham City Council (1997a), and from Chicago Public Schools (1998).

In short, both systems face similar challenges that arise from the socioeconomic conditions their students confront. In several ways, Chicago's challenge is more difficult given the size of the system and the higher percentage of disadvantaged students.

SYSTEMWIDE REFORM IN CHICAGO

Integrated Governance in Chicago

Decentralization is no longer the dominant reform strategy in the CPS. The Chicago School Reform Amendatory Act, which took effect in July 1995, reverses a 7-year trend toward decentralization of authority over school operations and redesigns the governance arrangement to integrate power and authority. Integrated governance reduces competing authorities and coordinates activities in support of systemwide policy goals. The 1995 law suspended the power of the School Finance Authority (SFA), eliminated the School Board Nominating Commission, and diminished the ability of the LSCs to operate independently of board policy. Further, integrated governance is designed to facilitate policy coherence and improve organizational collaboration among major actors. As a result of the 1995 reform, appointment decisions emanating from the mayor's office closely link the board, top administration, and the mayor's office. Finally, integrated governance relies on an administration that enjoys strong managerial authority. The 1995 law expanded the financial powers of the board and enhanced the powers of the CEO to manage the system.

Several questions arise concerning this redesigned system of governance. Can integrated governance effectively address the complex challenges facing the CPS? Specifically, how does the redesigned system of governance address issues of teaching and learning, failing schools, and finance and management? The author's study of the integrated system in the CPS found that the new governance system has improved the conditions for teaching and learning since July 1995 in many ways:

- Mayoral control facilitates policy coordination and reduces institutional fragmentation.

- Integrated governance improves the financial and manage-ment functions of the entire system.
- Integrated governance allows for a sharper focus on schools with the greatest academic needs.
- The public school system is able to broaden its political base of support.
- There are systemwide efforts to improve the quality of principals and teachers.

Reducing Institutional and Policy Fragmentation

Although the 1995 legislation left intact some features of the previous arrangements, it reduced competing institutional authority and recentralized administrative authority. The law decreased the size of the 15-member board to 5 and put the mayor in charge of appointing board members, the board president, and the CEO in charge of the schools. Because the board appoints the top administrative officers, these changes facilitate an effective link between the mayor's office and the central office. Under this arrangement, education becomes a part of the mayor's policy agenda and gives the mayor the option to decide the amount of political capital he is willing to invest in improving the schools.

The new administration acted swiftly to demonstrate a commitment to efficient management by adopting a business management model. The management and maintenance of school buildings, for example, was reorganized to stress customer service and contracting out. The board eliminated the Bureau of Facilities Planning in the central office (resulting in the elimination of 10 jobs), reduced the number of positions in the Department of Facilities Central Service Center by half (26 out of 50 positions were eliminated), and reduced the citywide administration of facilities from 441 positions to 34. Contracts for these services are now with private firms. To oversee the management and maintenance of school property, the board negotiated contracts with five firms to provide property advisory services for each region. Under this arrangement, the firms advise principals and the department of operations on property management and provide custodial, engineering, and construction-related services to the schools. In addition, the board prequalified a number of general construction contractors for schools to select from.

By strengthening the centralized authority of the school system, the 1995 legislation shifted the balance of power between the central office and the LSCs. Prior to 1995, the central office competed with the LSCs for authority over the educational agenda. The LSCs had broad authority, but there was little direct accountability or oversight. For example, state Chapter I funds went directly to the schools, but the board remained accountable if the money was misused. Selection of principals by the LSC was often influenced by the constituencies of the particular neighborhood.

The new administration has signaled that LSCs can no longer operate with complete independence and have incorporated the LSCs into the overall system by defining standards and responsibilities they must adhere to. This policy establishes 15 criteria covering the actions of the principal, staff, LSC, and LSC members. Under the new board policy, the board declared that an educational crisis existed at Prosser Preparatory Center and Nathan Hale School. At each school, the board disbanded the LSC. The LSC at Prosser was declared nonfunctional in part because of its failure to approve the school improvement plan or evaluate the principal. At Hale, the LSC was suspended after LSC members were found to have intruded in the day-to-day operations of the school, entered classrooms unannounced and uninvited, and failed to follow the law regarding their powers and responsibilities, among other violations. The board also requested that the state legislature tighten guidelines on the use of Chapter I funds currently controlled by LSCs. This request stems from a controversy in which LSC members at Roberto Clemente High School allegedly used Chapter I funds to send parents to Puerto Rico and to support the Puerto Rican independence movement. After a preliminary investigation, the board found the politicized climate at Clemente to be counterproductive to student learning and appointed a new principal without the LSC's consent. A special legislative committee and the Cook County state's attorney are currently investigating the use of Chapter I funds by Clemente's LSC.

Improving Financial Management and Upgrading the Physical Infrastructure

The 1995 governance redesign enhanced the ability of the central administration to perform financial and management functions efficiently. The 1995 law suspended the budget oversight authority of the SFA, removed the balanced budget requirement, and placed the inspector general under the authority of the board. In addition, the board was granted new authorities that expanded its financial powers. A number of funded programs (e.g., K–6 reading improvement, substance abuse prevention, Hispanic programs, and gifted education) and categorical funds were collapsed into a general education block grant and an educational services block grant, respectively. Although total revenues available to the board declined by 8% in fiscal year 1996 from the previous year, revenues going into the General Funds increased by about 2% (or $28.5 million). Additionally, the board acquired greater flexibility over the use of pension funds and Chapter I funds not allocated to the schools. Finally, there were no longer separate tax levies earmarked for specific purposes.

These changes increased board discretion over school revenues, allowing the board to prepare a 4-year balanced budget and negotiate a 4-year contract, including a raise, with the Chicago Teachers Union. The 4-year teachers' contract brought both financial and labor stability to the system. Indeed, by March 1996, Standard and Poor's raised the CPS bond rating from a BBB- to BBB, and Moody's from a Ba to Baa, allowing the board to issue bonds for the construction of new buildings under lower interest rates than before. By the summer of 1997, the CPS bond ratings were A- from Standard and Poor's and Baa1 from Moody's.

Enjoying its much-improved standing in the bond market, the CPS launched a major capital improvement campaign for the first time in decades. The need to upgrade the schools' physical infrastructure is long overdue. Whereas 36% of the school buildings were built more than 75 years ago, only 11% are less than 25 years old. The school where Mayor Daley announced Phase II of the improvement plan offers an example of the need. According to one report, the school's "roof leaked so badly that five third-floor classrooms had been rendered soggily unusable, thus creating overcrowding in other classrooms. Windows were broken and missing… Hallways were scarred by peeling paint and crumbling plaster" (Kogan, 1998, p. 10). After the $2.3-million renovation, the school principal summed up the impact of the capital project as causing "a transformation in learning" (Kogan, 1998, p. 10). System-wide, without board-directed capital improvement, most facilities will continue to lack the capability to make the transition to the information highway. The first two phases of the capital improvement plan are financed by $1.65-billion bond funds, with an additional $800 million in the third phase. Through the year 2003, these funds are allocated in four areas: renovation of school buildings, improvement in existing operating systems (e.g., heating), new construction, and educational enhancement projects (e.g., science laboratories and playgrounds). In response to public concerns about accountability in implementing such an ambitious plan, the school board released school-by-school information on physical conditions and a detailed timeline for repair and renovation, and organized public hearings citywide beginning in the spring of 1998.

Pressuring and Supporting Low-Performing Schools

The 1995 law incorporated a focus on accountability and academic achievement that compelled the administration to target the lowest performing schools within the system for intervention. Declaring that an educational crisis existed in Chicago, the 1995 legislation directed the board of trustees and the CEO to increase the quality of educational services within the system. It enhanced the powers of the CEO to identify poorly performing schools and place these schools on remediation, probation, intervention, or reconstitution. Prior to 1995, the subdistrict superintendent, not the school board, had the primary responsibility of monitoring the performance of the schools and identifying nonperforming schools. In the past, to place a school on remediation or probation required the approval of the subdistrict council, which was made up of parents or community members from each LSC within the subdistrict.

With the new legislation, the board and central office focused on the lowest performing schools within the system. In January 1996, the CEO placed 21 schools on remediation for failing to meet state standards on the Illinois Goals Assessment Program (IGAP) for 3 consecutive years. Only six schools were placed on remediation by the previous administration. At the same time, the board removed two elementary school principals because the schools failed to improve after a year on remediation. In September 1996, the CEO placed 20% of the district's schools on probation.

Probation. In 1996, the district placed 109 of the 550 CPS on academic probation because 15% or less of their students scored at grade level on nationally normed tests. These schools are being held accountable to their school improvement plans as well as to improvements in test scores. By the fall of 1997, 9 schools have been removed from the list, 15 have been added, and 7 have been reconstituted. In addition, 36 principals have been removed. Since spring 1998, probation schools are required to have at least 20% of their students scored at grade level on nationally normed tests. As of summer 1998, 108 schools were on probation and another 7 high schools were on reconstitution.

Table 5.3 shows the percentage of students in high schools on probation (including reconstitution) and in the district as a whole who score at the national norms on the Test of Achievement and Proficiency (TAP), the standardized test that the district uses to place schools on probation. The researchers focused on the high schools because, on the whole, high schools have not made the gains in test scores achieved by elementary schools. Students scoring at national norms in reading in probation schools range from 7.6% to 12.62% over an 8-year period. The average across the district's high schools ranges only from 17% to 23.35%. At the highest point, less than 30% of the students in the districts' high schools score at the national norm in reading. The same holds true for math (Wong & Anagnostopoulos, 1998). Clearly, the district faces severe challenges in improving probation high schools and high schools systemwide.

Whereas the district holds the probation schools accountable for improving student performance on standardized tests, it also provides several types of support. Each school must select from a list of board-approved external partners. The external partners are teams of support personnel from local universities and national reform groups who are charged with improving instruction in probation schools. The district

TABLE 5.3
Average High School Percentage of Students at National Norms on Test of Achievement and Proficiency

	Subject	1991	1992	1993	1994	1995	1996	1997	1998
District High School Average	Reading	23.35%	20.24%	21%	17.65%	19.49%	16.92%	20.92%	23.1%
	Math	17.43%	18%	20.84%	16.5%	21%	17.97%	25.83%	25.84%
Probation High School Average	Reading	12.6%	10.2%	10.2%	7.6%	9.6%	7.5%	10.5%	12.62%
	Math	8%	8.4%	10.2%	6.6%	10.8%	8.4%	14.3%	15.82%

Note: From Chicago Public Schools (1998).

paid for the external partners in full the first year of probation. Schools are expected to pick up one fourth of the cost each year of probation. The district also provides schools with probation managers who oversee the school improvement plan and assist the principal in all areas of school operations. Finally, the district provides the schools with business managers to oversee the school budget and financial operations. All of these supports are intended to enable the principal to become an effective instructional leader.

The researchers' preliminary analysis of the probation policy in their case study of high schools suggests that the policy has created new incentives for schools to examine how they allocate resources, in particular, time, teachers, and students. Schools have responded to probation by devoting more class time to test practice. In addition, schools have altered the ways in which they assign teachers to classrooms. The researchers detailed comparative case studies of four high schools indicates that the schools under probation tend to assign the most experienced teachers with the best reputations to students who are testing close to the national norms. As part of promotion policy, some schools have developed new basic math and reading skills sessions to assist low-performing students. According to our survey of high school principals in the spring of 1998, 34% of the principals reported hiring reading specialists but only one principal reported hiring a math specialist.

Reconstitution. Seven schools have been reconstituted based on continual low performance of students' test scores (none of the reconstituted schools had more than 7% of their students reading at or above grade level according to test scores). Five of the seven schools had their principals replaced, and 188 of 675 teachers, or 29%, were not rehired. These schools will have to improve their test scores or risk being shut down.

Table 5.4 shows various characteristics of reconstituted schools. The table indicates the difficult socioeconomic conditions with which the schools and students must contend. The seven reconstituted schools are located in the most racially and economically isolated wards of the city. The mobility rates reflect conditions of extreme poverty. Table 5.4 suggests that support and pressure are needed to assist both the schools that operate in these conditions and the young people they serve. Pressure alone will not be sufficient given the severe challenges both face.

The researchers' case studies suggest that principals and teachers

TABLE 5.4
Characteristics of Reconstituted High Schools, 1997-1998

School	Low-income	Mobility	Dropout	Chronic truancy	Black	Hispanic
DuSable	90.2%	70.7%	21.8%	12.6%	100.0%	0.0%
Englewood	67.5%	50.3%	23.3%	5.1%	100.0%	0.0%
Harper	83.5%	52.4%	34.5%	12.0%	99.4%	0.5%
King	91.9%	55.6%	18.6%	30.5%	100.0%	0.0%
Orr	79.5%	49.8%	29.1%	1.9%	96.3%	3.6%
Phillips	86.8%	57.0%	45.7%	9.7%	100.0%	0.0%
Robeson	87.7%	53.7%	27.5%	21.6%	100.0%	0.0%
Mean	83.9%	55.6%	28.6%	13.3%	99.4%	0.6%
All High Schools	76.0%	32.0%	17.0%	12.0%	63.0%	24.0%

Note: Based on information provided by the Chicago Public Schools, Office of Accountability (1998).

in reconstituted schools feel enormous amounts of pressure to increase test scores. This has led to an increasing standardization of instruction and even more attention being focused on test-taking practice and drill than in probation schools. A reconstituted school in this study has informally tracked students in order to provide those students near the national average access to a more effective learning environment. The school has also been affected by the district's academic promotion policy. Because of the failure of eighth-graders from the feeder schools to score at the district benchmark on the Iowa Test of Basic Skills (ITBS), ninth-grade enrollment dropped significantly. Because of this drop, the percentage of special education students in ninth-grade classrooms has increased. To date, teachers feel that they have been provided with inadequate support to deal with this situation. This suggests the need to examine how student promotion policies interact with school accountability policies, and to consider ways to link elementary and secondary schools together more effectively.

Reorganizing the Office of Accountability to Support Schools. The board and top administration reorganized the central office to reflect the focus on accountability and established the improvement of standardized test scores as the primary objective of the system. Though other departments within the central office were eliminated or significantly downsized, the administration created the Office of Accountability, which has grown from a staff of 50 in September 1995 to almost 80 in 1998. This office monitors the performance of the schools and identifies and intervenes in low-performing schools. One administrator said that the mission of the department is "to fix schools...so they won't fall below a safety net."

The Office of Accountability not only pressures schools to improve but also provides professional support. It is in the process of implementing various programs to level up schools where test scores are low. Currently, the Department of School Quality Review works with the Illinois State Board of Education to develop a review process to evaluate all schools once every 4 years. The Department of School Intervention works with schools on the state's Academic Watch List or on probation. These schools receive a 1-day visit from the staff in School Intervention, which recommends corrective actions and pairs them with consultants to provide technical support. The Office of Accountability provides a list of 21 external partners that the schools can choose from. According to the Guidelines for External Partners, each external partner is expected to have the "ability to raise student performance and...to customize the assistance to meet the individual needs of each school." In December 1995, the board approved $1.3 million in contracts for universities and colleges to work with 30 schools on the watch list. During 1996–1997, the first year of probation, the school board allocated more than $11 million to these schools in terms of support personnel and staff positions devoted to implementing and overseeing probation. In 1997–1998, the central budget for probation and reconstitution associated personnel was close to $8 million. During 1998–1999, the central budget for this purpose was about $10 million.

Few principals and teachers in our case study of schools on probation and reconstitution report satisfaction with the contracted external partners the board financed. Teachers feel that the external partners, which the district requires schools on probation to hire, offer little meaningful assistance. Teachers resent planning time being controlled by the external partners and resist attempts by the external partners to evaluate instruction. Teachers in one school actually locked their doors to prevent the external partners from entering. Similarly, principals feel that the external partners lack a focused plan for school improvement, particularly in the area of instruction. Though many principals report satisfaction with the probation managers, they feel that the external partners have not been cost-effective. Overall, the variation in terms of support provided to schools by external partners poses a serious challenge to the district. The district has delegated responsibility for improving teaching and learning in low-performing schools to external partners. The author's case studies suggest that the district needs to monitor the quality of the services provided by the external partners more closely and to consider whether or not these contracted services could be provided by district personnel like Birmingham's BASS model, thereby building the district's instructional support capacity for long-term improvement.

Pressuring and Supporting Low-Performing Students

The End of Social Promotion. In an expanded program from the summer of 1996, third-, sixth-, eighth-, and ninth-grade students who did not meet set levels on one of two nationally normed tests (the ITBS or the TAP) were required to participate in a system-sponsored summer school called the Summer Bridge program during 1997. The pressure is particularly high for the eighth-graders, because those who fail the spring tests cannot attend graduation ceremonies. In 1997, 21% of the eighth-graders failed to meet the cutoff point in the spring and were placed in the Summer Bridge program. Sixty-two percent of eighth- graders who participated in the program met the promotion requirements after 7 weeks. In other words, by the end of the summer in 1997, 92% of the 27,800 eighth-graders had met the school system's new promotion standards. In the summer of 1998, 54% of the 7,558 eighth-graders who were required to attend the Summer Bridge program passed the tests and were promoted to high school. The district provided teachers in the program with day-by-day lesson plans. Students were promoted to the next grade if they brought their scores to the established cutoff point. If they did not, they were required to repeat the grade. Repeating students returned to their original schools, unless they were older eighth-graders. Approximately one half of the repeating eighth-graders (in 1997 that constituted about 4%), who were 15 years old by December 1, were attending 1 of 13 transition centers that feature a basic skills curriculum.

Seeing the Summer Bridge program as providing an opportunity for social and academic development for many inner-city children, the school board decided to expand the program to the first and second grades beginning in the summer of 1998. From a broader institutional perspective, the expanded Summer Bridge program for students across six different grade levels constituted only a part of the district's overall summer initiatives that involve the Chicago Public Library, the Chicago Park District, and the Mayor's Office of Employment and Training. The system was expected to spend a total of $65 million to provide a variety of learning, social, and job skills to 175,000 children or about 40% of the CPS enrollment. As Mayor Daley envisioned the long-term impacts of these collaborative programs, "By providing safe and productive ways for our young people to spend their summer vacation, we help keep them away from the dangerous influences of gangs, guns and drugs" (Washburn, 1998, p. 3).

Political Will and a Broadened Base of Political Support

The link between the mayor's office and the board can facilitate political support for the school system. With the redesign of the governance system, Mayor Richard Daley has been more willing to invest his political capital in the Chicago schools. To restore public confidence, the new administration has projected an image of efficient, responsive, and "clean" government. The administration has also taken a number of steps to strengthen the support of the business community for the public schools. This support becomes crucial when appealing to the Illinois legislature because the business community can lobby in favor of the board's legislative agenda, thereby lending the board credibility.

In 1995 and 1996, the author and his colleagues issued two surveys to 100 members of the policy community from Chicago and Illinois and asked them to rate the performance of seven governance actors, the governor, the mayor, Democratic and Republican legislators, the Chicago Teachers' Union, the central office, and the school board. Their analysis of the 1995–1996 performance ratings for these seven governance actors shows that the board, the central office, and the mayor made significant gains over their 1993–1995 performance ratings. Only the performance of these three actors edged into the "satisfactory" category. The performance of the other actors remained in the "poor" category (Wong et al., 1997; see also Wong & Moulton, 1998).

Media support for the board and central administration remains strong. The authors tracked all stories and editorials concerning education that appeared in the two major Chicago newspapers from August 1, 1995 to March 31, 1997. Their analysis indicates that the two newspapers were generally supportive of the central administration. The newspapers opposed only 5% of the proposed administration policies. The most noticeable editorial pattern was a supportive response to central administration policies. Seventy-four percent of the editorials that

TABLE 5.5
New Appointments at Chicago Public Schools' Central Office (July 1995–February 1998)

	Intermediate past employers											
Area	City of Chicago		Public agencies		Non-profit		Private sector		CPS		Total	
	#	%	#	%	#	%	#	%	#	%	#	%
Education	1	2.2	1	2.2	3	6.8	—	—	39	88.6	44	39.6
Non-Education	25	37.3	4	5.9	4	5.9	9	13.4	25	37.3	67	60.3
% of total	23.4%		4.5%		6.3%		8.1%		57.6%		100.0%	

Note: From *Catalyst*, section on "Comings and goings," September 1995 through February 1998.

focused on administration policies were supportive (Wong & Jain, 1999).

The mayor's appointments to the board of trustees reflect a concern with consolidating business supporters of the schools. Most board members have extensive experience in the private sector. The distribution of appointments within the central office reflects the mayor's commitment to improving the fiscal conditions and management of the system. The top appointments in the central office made between July 1995 and February 1998 reflect a diversity of expertise: 27.9% come from city and other public agencies, 8.1% from the private sector, 6.3% from nonprofit organizations, and 57.6% from the ranks within the CPS (see Table 5.5). In areas that are not directly related to education (e.g., finance and purchasing), 63% of the appointees came from outside the school system.

The new administration reorganized the central office according to business principles that stress downsizing and privatization as a way to further enhance business support for the schools and the perception of efficient management. Within 1 year of implementing the new system, the number of staff positions in the central administration declined almost 21%. The majority of these cuts came from citywide administration and services. The reduction was achieved through awarding contracts to private providers for food services and facilities. Other reductions were obtained by consolidating the 11 district offices into 6 regional offices.

The administration's strategy of focusing on management and budget issues early on can be viewed as a serious effort to establish political credibility. Thus, the administration balanced the budget, developed a 5-year capital development plan, and negotiated a 4-year teacher's contract. In March 1998, the board initiated the negotiation with the Chicago Teachers' Union even though the teachers' contract did not expire until 1999. This strategy improved public confidence in the ability of the administration to manage the schools and stabilized relations with the union. Believing that raising test scores is the basis for long-term political support, the mayor, board, and CEO have now taken this as their primary strategy. Better test scores, it is hoped, will form the basis for increased state funding and the continuation of the current governance with the mayor in control of the schools. This arrangement is likely to shift additional power back to the central office, including the establishment of qualifications for the appointment of principals by the central office, and to further diminish the LSCs' role. Indeed, in August 1996, the legislature adopted legislation that allows the board of trustees to develop additional standards and requirements to become a principal. Taken together, the district's actions significantly improved public confidence in the ability of the board and the central administration to govern the schools, giving the top administration the legitimacy it needs to carry out its educational initiatives.

Strengthening the Quality of Human Resources

The district administration has taken several steps to improve standards for teachers and principals systemwide. The districts' teachers are predominantly from two local institutions. This administration has expanded the pool of teachers by targeting other teacher education institutions in Chicago through programs such as the Ambassador Corps, which sends teachers and principals to local colleges. The district also recruits candidates nationally through the Recruiting New Teachers Partnership Network. Overall, three fourths of the teachers are from Illinois institutions and one fourth are predominantly from other Midwestern states ("City aims to higher 'best and brightest,'" 1996).

In addition to recruitment efforts, the district has instituted a new teacher induction program that focuses on pairing new teachers with expert mentors. Mentors and new teachers meet monthly for district in-services and collaborative learning. New teachers receive detailed materials from the district that explain policies and procedures and provide overviews of different aspects of classroom management and instruction. The district also offers all teachers professional development opportunities through the Teachers' Academy.

Although the district has focused its efforts on teacher recruitment and professional development, it has developed new, more rigorous standards for principals. The 1988 reform gave LSCs the power to hire and terminate principals. Consequently, principal hiring became political. Although one of the intentions of the 1988 reform was to foster a more rigorous selection process, the vast majority of principals continue to come from the schools where they served as assistant principals. In 1997, the current administration adopted a new set of standards in an attempt to control the quality of principals. These standards require principals to reside in Chicago and to have a master's degree, a minimum of 6 years of classroom and administrative experience, 70 hours of course work in administration, and a 30-day internship. Once in office, principals are required to complete 32 hours of professional development training every 2 years. The board was instrumental in lobbying the state legislature to enact Senate Bill 1019, which codifies these standards.

In order to support new and experienced principals, the district has created the Leadership Academy and Urban Network for Chicago (LAUNCH) and Leadership Initiative for Transformation (LIFT) programs in cooperation with the Chicago Principals and Administrators' Association and local universities. In addition, the district has provided all principals with training on how to use district teacher evaluation forms. These evaluations are checklists the principals can use to assess classroom management, instruction, and the teacher's participation in the school. These evaluations are a way for principals to terminate poorly performing teachers. Although the evaluations provide principals with a tool to do this, they do not rely upon any model of effective instruction and represent a variety of items to look for in a classroom rather than an instrument for actually assessing the quality of a teacher's instruction. Although the district has increased efforts to improve the quality of the teaching pool and current principals, it has yet to develop more comprehensive standards for teachers.

An Ambitious Agenda for Systemwide Restructuring

As integrated governance operates at the end of its third year, the CEO and the school board have broadened the reform agenda. Designed to improve the quality of schools throughout the system, these new initiatives include the following:

- The system has designed and disseminated their own standards (Chicago Academic Standards) in the areas of English language arts, mathematics, biological and physical sciences, and social sciences. Benchmark exams for selected cutoff grades are being developed and piloted in June 1998 and in 1999–2000. These standards and assessments may mark a new phase of outcome-based accountability in the district. The results of the district exams may provide additional information concerning probation and reconstitution. Thus, although these standards and assessments may provide an educational vision to guide teaching and learning districtwide, they may also serve as a tool to develop further sanctions on low-performing students and schools.
- All high schools have established Junior Academies for 9th- and 10th-grade students and are creating Senior Academies for 11th- and 12th-grade students. The academy structure creates teams of teachers who are responsible for a group of students throughout the course of their high school educa-tion. Teachers advance through the grades with their students.
- The academy structure is intended to provide students with academic and personal support and provide teacher collaboration. Teachers are expected to participate in a professional development program that is supportive and consistent with their school's action plan.
- LSC elections were held on report card pickup days as a way to improve parental participation. Between 1988 and 1993, voter turnout for these elections decreased by 68%. This is consistent with a sharp decline in the number of people seeking LSC seats. In 1989, more than 17,000 candidates ran for the LSC. In 1991, that number decreased to 8,398, and to only 7,288 in 1996. This year 84 schools, or slightly more than 15% of the system, slated fewer than the six parents needed (Sall, 1998). Clearly, attracting

widespread parental support and involvement in the LSCs remains a challenge.

Under integrated governance, the CPS has tried to improve the operations of the system and the performance of its schools and students. The district administration has brought financial stability to the system and, in conjunction with the mayor, has regained public and political confidence in the schools. Whereas the administration has addressed a number of functions, including teacher recruitment, principal standards, and facilities improvement, its most visible efforts have been the policies that place pressure on poorly performing schools and students. Probation and reconstitution have served as wake-up calls for schools, teachers, and students. Yet without adequate technical support, such policies will not ensure improvement. The district has yet to develop an instructional and organizational model that provides schools and teachers with a vision to guide their improvement efforts. The new curricular frameworks and exams the district has begun to implement may provide the base for such a vision. The district has made tremendous strides in several key areas. The challenge of developing an educational vision that provides the support for improved performance lies ahead.

TRANSFORMATION IN BIRMINGHAM LOCAL EDUCATION AUTHORITY

Integrated Governance in Birmingham

Across the Atlantic, the Birmingham LEA maintains two essential characteristics of integrated governance, namely, a unified political structure that is committed to education, and a vision that aims at better student performance. In terms of governance, Birmingham's arrangements are quite similar to Chicago's post-1995 structure. The LEA is formally the Education Department in the City of Birmingham. In the city's political system, power rests in the city council, and the office of the Lord Mayor performs mainly ceremonial functions. The chief education officer is hired by the city's chief executive and serves the city council's education committee. Because the Labour Party constitutes the majority in the 117-member city council, its caucus in the education committee controls

TABLE 5.6
1997–1998 Birmingham City Budget

Function	Budget (£ millions)	Percent of total
Education total	493	47.7%
Delegated to schools	372	36.0%
Non-delegated to schools	121	11.7%
Other function total	541	52.3%
Total	1,034	100.0%

Note: From Birmingham City Council (1998).

the policy agenda. At the same time, the Labour group in the committee is responsible for the fiscal management and school performance of the educational system. The council's education committee regularly consults with organized interests (e.g., the teachers' and head teachers' unions). In other words, the council's education committee "integrates" both political and policy functions.

The direct involvement of the Labour Party caucus in allocating the educational budget is indicative of how "integrated governance" operates. Education is the largest item on the city budget. In 1997–1998 it accounted for 48% of the city's total expenditure, as suggested in Table 5.6. As a result of the 1988 national LMS reform, 75% of the resources are allocated to the schools, 16.5% is retained at the central administration, and the remaining 8% is for capital improvement projects (see Table 5.7). Not surprisingly, budgetary allocation involves political leadership, upper-level administrative staff in the city, and the LEA's leadership. During the process, political concerns and policy needs are properly balanced. For the fiscal year 1998 budget, planning began in the spring of 1997 when the baseline for both statutory and nonstatutory services was established by the LEA's director of finance. A series of strategic planning sessions then followed where the CEO, the director of finance, and other upper-level managers presented their proposed budgets before the leadership of the Labour Party and the upper-level administrative team of the city. Additional closed-door sessions were scheduled during the fall that allowed the Labour group to question the budget justifications and to pressure the CEO and his upper-level managers on savings. In late 1997, for example, the Labour group decided on a 5% reduction of the central administration's budget but

TABLE 5.7
1997–1998 Birmingham Education Budget

Allocative level	Budget (£)	Percent of total
Non-delegated		
Central administration	81,482,290	16.5%
Capital asset charges	39,755,650	8.1%
Subtotal	121,237,940	24.6%
Delegated to		
Local Education Authority schools	327,087,720	66.3%
Grant-maintained schools	44,831,340	9.1%
Subtotal	371,919,060	75.4%
Total	493,157,000	100.0%

Note: From Birmingham City Council (1998).

preserved the portion of the delegated school budget in 1998. By December 1997, the final budget for the next fiscal year was established.

Political Commitment

Like its counterpart in Chicago, the political leadership in Birmingham has made a strong commitment to education in recent years. The strongest indication of the city's political will toward educational improvement was its significant shift in educational funding that coincided with the appointment of Tim Brighouse, a nationally known school reformer, as the CEO in September 1993. Prior to Brighouse's appointment, economic development dominated the city's agenda. During the 1980s and the early 1990s, local and national revenues were shifted away from education and allocated to an ambitious renewal program in the central business district, including the construction of the international trade center, orchestra hall, and the infrastructure to expand tourism. Public works and construction programs appealed to the traditional constituency of the Labour Party, which captured the majority of city council in 1984. As shown in Fig. 5.1, during the 1980s and the early 1990s, the city did not spend up to the Standard Spending Assessment (SSA) level as recommended by the national government. The SSA is the amount of revenue expenditure that the national government considers appropriate for a local authority to incur to provide a standard level of service consistent with the national government's public expenditure plans.

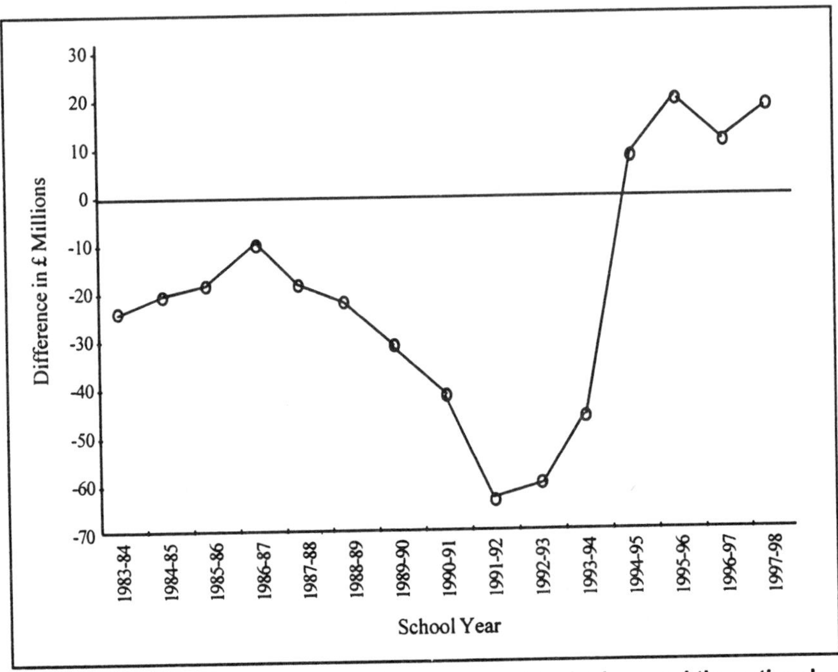

FIG. 5.1. Differences in school spending between Birmingham and the national standard. From Birmingham City Council Education Department (1998).

Between 1991–1992 and 1992–1993, the gap between actual spending and the SSA widened to more than £60 million. However, this trend was reversed following an "internal revolt" within the Labour Party in 1992. The new leadership saw the need to maintain a proper balance between public construction and human capital investment. Since 1994 Birmingham's spending on education has exceeded the SSA level. In 1997–1998, the actual education spending was £20 million above the SSA.

The shift in funding priorities represented a politically visible endorsement of the Brighouse administration. Birmingham's decision bore national significance in light of 17 years of policy dominance by the Conservative Party in Westminster. In a series of school reform legislation, the Conservative Party mandated district-level administration to delegate the majority of the funding to schools, enabled schools to opt out of the government-maintained sector, broadened parental preferences in choosing schools, and expanded the role of the OFSTED in monitoring LEA and school performance. Politically, the Conservative

Party aimed at weakening the power of the LEAs, a substantial number of which were governed by the Labour Party in the city council. Losing substantial control over both funding and the most competitive schools, LEAs across the nation faced virtual extinction. National policy allocated the majority of the funds directly to schools (LMS) and encouraged schools to opt out of direct governmental control (grant-maintained option) (Bullock & Thomas, 1997). The role of the LEA was further eroded as the national inspectorate system expanded in 1993. Given this national trend of undermining the LEAs, Birmingham's decision to renew its LEA under new leadership was unique.

As the Conservative agenda aimed at dismantling the organizational functions of the LEAs nationwide, the local scene in Birmingham was far from promising. For years, the office of the chief education officer in the city was dominated by the electoral concerns of politicians and lacked a focus on school improvement. Within the central administration, heads of services operated like warring barons. The LEA suffered from organizational fragmentation and an absence of systemwide concerns over classroom practices. Policymakers in Birmingham, thus, were at a crossroads. Should they dismantle the LEA and its functions or should they redefine the role of the LEA to fill the gap between the national policy initiatives and educational practices at the school and classroom levels?

To develop an informed basis for deciding on the future of the LEA, the city council appointed an independent education commission to review the present and the future needs of education services in Birmingham. The 13-member commission was led by Professor Ted Wragg of Exeter University, and city councilors, parents, head teachers, and teachers were represented. The commission was established in the spring of 1993. It held 34 public hearings and heard from 140 witnesses during the spring and summer of 1993. In addition, the commission received more than 100 written submissions. Its report was published in October 1993, when Brighouse began his tenure as the CEO.

Because the 1993 education commission report coincided with the arrival of the Brighouse administration, it provided useful baseline information on the quality of the educational system under the previous leadership. *Aiming High,* commonly referred to as the Wragg report, documented extensive deficiencies in the existing system. These included:

- Education was not a sufficiently important issue in the city as it integrated with the global economy.
- The LEA had difficulty transitioning to LMS by holding firm to the existing attitude that it owned schools, thereby providing an incentive for schools to choose for grant-maintained status (exiting from governmental control).
- A climate of political contention and personal favors weakened the support for education.
- It lacked a unified vision of the role of LEA.
- Achievement standards in Birmingham schools were too low.

In light of these concerns, the Wragg report concluded, "We see no point in a city with Birmingham's aspirations in aiming low. It would be a disappointment to those whose children are already in or about to enter school, as well as to those who work in the education service." The commission made 25 recommendations that covered major components of the educational institution, including educational governance, resource allocation, and standards and achievements. Many of the recommendations reflected Brighouse's vision. The major recommendations included:

- Establish a clear district organization, while allowing for local flexibility and creativity.
- Establish a process of school self-review that does not overburden schools and recognizes the work done by OFSTED.
- Place education at the top of the city's spending priorities.
- Develop individual school and citywide targets in literacy, numeracy, and staying-on rates.
- Improve the political climate for education.

In a follow-up review 2 years after its publication of the report, the education commission found that the educational system was moving in a positive direction and meeting several important targets. *Hitting the Target?,* the second Wragg report, found that education had become the city's top priority beginning in 1994–1995. Brighouse was praised for his efforts to share his vision with the broad business community, including the Technology and Education Consortium, the Chamber of Commerce, City Pride, and the Birmingham Education Business Partnership. The second report also observed an improved relationship between the LEA and the schools. Whereas 13 schools left the LEA in 1993, only 1 had opted out during 1994 and 1995. The LEA also began to establish more rigorous targets and to institute means of consultations with schools. Overall, out of the 25 original recommendations in the 1993 report, 13 showed progress made, 6 remained stable but satisfactory, and 6 remained unsatisfactory in the 2-year period. Initial accomplishments in the period between the first and the second Wragg report have turned into systemic restructuring and higher performance in subsequent years. As Table 5.8 shows, the achievement gap between Birmingham and the nation narrowed substantially in reading, writing, and math at Key Stage 1, in English at Key Stage 2, and in General Certificate of Secondary Education (GCSE) examinations. Key Stage 3 is the only level where both the national average and Birmingham declined in performance. Whereas the LEA and the national average fell at more or less the same pace in math, the LEA experienced a greater decrease in English performance. The overall picture, thus, suggests that Birmingham has made significant progress in "improving the previous best" (Birmingham City Council Education Department, 1996). By January 1998, the OFSTED (1998) report concluded that "the LEA has defined a clear aspiration to raise standards and has convinced schools and others of its determination to do so, and of the feasibility of that undertaking" (p. 1).

SCHOOL IMPROVEMENT STRATEGIES IN BIRMINGHAM

In the following sections, the author identifies strategies that the LEA has used to improve teaching and learning in Birmingham schools within a fairly short period of time. As a whole, these strategies offer a promising reform model for other LEAs to consider in their efforts to raise standards and student performance. Instead of relying on a "silver bullet," the LEA adopts a mix of informal pressure and persistent support as intervention strategies. Overall, a vision of the LEA as a critical friend to teachers and head teachers lies at the core of the Birmingham model. This vision, in turn, relies on a well-designed infrastructure at the central office focused on bringing about school improvement and academic gains.

Table 5.8
Birmingham Local Education Authority Performance Compared to National Average

Key Stage 1				
Subject	Year	LEA	National	Difference
Reading	1995	72.3	78.5	-6.3
	1997	77.3	80.1	-2.8
Writing	1995	75.2	80.4	-5.2
	1997	79.0	80.4	-1.4
Math	1995	74.2	79.2	-5.0
	1997	81.4	84.1	-2.7
Key Stage 2				
Subject	Year	LEA	National	Difference
English	1995	37.4	48.3	-10.9
	1997	56.7	62.9	-6.3
Math	1995	37.9	44.7	-6.9
	1997	53.2	61.0	-7.8
Key Stage 3				
Subject	Year	LEA	National	Difference
English	1995	59.8	61.9	-2.1
	1997	46.4	56.6	-10.2
Math	1995	50.2	63.0	-12.8
	1997	48.3	61.0	-12.8
General Certificate of Secondary Education				
% pupils 5+	1994	31.0	40.7	-9.6
A*–C	1997	36.0	43.1	-7.0
% pupils 5+	1994	78.1	87.0	-8.8
A*–G	1997	83.8	88.4	-4.6
Average points	1994	28.0	33.5	-5.5
Score per pupil	1997	33.4	36.7	-3.4

Note: From Office of Her Majesty's Chief Inspector of Schools (1998).

The Local Education Authority Leadership Matters

Just as Vallas is so closely associated with progress made in Chicago, it is virtually impossible to separate Brighouse from school improvement in Birmingham. Under the leadership of Brighouse, Birmingham went against the national tide of de-legitimizing district-level administration. Clearly, Brighouse not only resurrected but also redesigned the LEA to the effect that, to use the words of the OFSTED (1998) report, it "has helped to revive the morale of its teachers and to engender an enhanced professional commitment that has resulted in a worthwhile rise in standards" (p. 1). Teachers and head teachers have clearly regained their high level of professional respect since the first Wragg report. The district-level administration, from Brighouse's perspective, plays a unique and indispensable role that bridges the gap between national standards and school needs. In essence, the LEA needs to provide the necessary support to enhance the quality and the performance of the schools. Without the LEA's supportive functions, schools are on their own in coping with a national system of educational accountability that is primarily designed to exert top-down pressure and sanctions. Brighouse's vision of the LEA revolves around the notion of "celebrating [the] success of urban teachers and head teachers." Seeing the many challenges that teachers face on a daily basis in an urban setting, Brighouse redesigned the LEA as a critical friend to teachers. The supportive role involves several major LEA functions.

The Chief Executive Officer as Pedagogical Mobilizer

First, the CEO personifies the teacher-oriented culture of the LEA. Unlike his predecessors who were office bound, top-down managers, Brighouse decided to spend most of his time visiting schools, talking to teachers in the staff room, and observing classroom instruction. Within the first 6 months of his appointment, he established the new governing style by visiting about 200 schools. In the next 3 years, he visited all the remaining schools, developed a close working relationship with head teachers, and engaged in discussion with numerous teachers on a wide range of curricular and instructional issues. Even with his busy schedule, he regularly writes personal messages of praise to teachers identified as making important contributions in their classrooms.

Over time, the CEO has made every effort to diffuse good practices. He takes advantage of all opportunities to motivate teachers to take that extra step toward higher standards. In his writings and his lectures, Brighouse constantly reminds teachers of several broader principles that guide good practices. These include "inclusive practices," intelligence as "multi-faceted" and not inherited, education as a "life-long" activity, competition as "ipsative" and not "normative," and "celebrating success" rather than focusing on failure (Birmingham City Council, 1997c, pp. 8–9). To connect these broad principles to the school and classroom setting, Brighouse writes a regular column in the LEA bulletins that are distributed regularly to all teachers. Through both informal conversations and direct contacts with the teachers, Brighouse serves as a pedagogical mobilizer to create new energy points throughout the system. As the OFSTED (1998) inspections concluded, the CEO "has had an enormous personal impact. He has the ability to...inspire teachers to new levels of commitment..." (p. 4). Brighouse's vision is ably supported by a first-rate administrative team at the central office, including the deputy chief of education.

The Local Education Authority Offers Competitive Services

Second, the educational needs of the schools drive central office organization rather than the reverse. Because of LMS budgeting, the city delegates 75% of the operating budget to schools in Birmingham. Schools can purchase services from nongovernmental vendors or buy back services from the central administration (Table 5.9). Indicative of the LEA's success in gaining the confidence of the schools, virtually all the schools purchase from the central administration the personnel/payroll services, the general financial services, special education (statutory) services, statistical support, the advisory and support services, and information technology. According to the annual city council survey, customer (i.e., school) satisfaction with the quality of the LEA services increased from 84% in 1995 to 91% in 1997. Education was rated as the best among all municipal service areas. A survey conducted by the Audit Commission indicates that head teachers in Birmingham were much more positive about their LEA services than their peers in 10 other LEAs with similar socioeconomic characteristics (OFSTED, 1998). Of the 52 total categories of LEA activities and services, Birmingham LEA was rated first in 20, including the quality of LEA actions to achieve its priorities, openness of the LEA about the budget-making process, and help in using comparative data for target setting. The LEA was rated second in another 12 sets of activities, including its willingness to listen to schools' views, support for school self-evaluation, and curriculum support. Only four items were ranked at or below 10th place.

TABLE 5.9
1997–1998 Birmingham Central Service Budget

Central administration department	Staff (number of Full-Time Equivalent	Percent of total	Budget amount (£)	Percent of total
Special education	1,231	46.7%	31,577,880	38.8%
School services and support	303	11.5%	18,609,310	22.8%
Financial controller	150	5.7%	3,816,060	4.7%
Personnel and equalities	609	23.1%	14,368,140	17.6%
Management and coordination	125	4.7%	6,008,690	7.4%
Advisory and support service	220	8.3%	5,827,860	7.2%
Total	2,638	100.0%	81,482,290	100.0%

Note: From Birmingham City Council (1998).

An Infrastructure of Support

Third, the LEA has developed a full-scale infrastructure that provides ongoing professional and technical support to the schools, a key function of the advisory and support services. The BASS is efficiently staffed with 30 teacher advisors who provide teachers with training in classroom practices and with another 35 link advisors who assist schools in dealing with issues that affect the entire school organization. Advisors are accredited inspectors, who receive formal training and conduct school inspections in other LEAs. The basic advisory entitlement allotted to each school is two half-day training sessions each term, with additional time allocated to support new head teachers and teachers, members of the school governing body, and schools that are scheduled for the 4-year national inspection cycle. Twice a year advisors report on the organizational health of the schools and once a year they rate the schools' effectiveness in meeting the national standards. Schools that show serious weaknesses in attendance, achievements, and curricular delivery can then purchase additional, sustained intervention strategies from the advisory and support services. A key function for the advisors, then, is to prepare schools to pass the rigorous test of national inspection. Each advisor serves as a "critical friend" to an assigned cluster of schools, challenging schools to improve on their delivery standards and student performance. About 4 to 6 months prior to the scheduled visit of the national inspection team to the schools, the advisors identify and coach those teachers who are not meeting the national standards. The key challenge for the schools and their advisers is to pass the inspection by making sure that at least 80% of their performance indicators meet the satisfactory level in the national framework.

Establishing Performance Targets

The Birmingham LEA was touted as a national model when it first introduced the process of target setting at the school level. Its vision was to "improve on the previous best" (Birmingham City Council Education Department, 1996). Using their 1996 performance level as the baseline, all secondary schools have set millennium targets in terms of raising achievement at Key Stage 3 and GCSE. More than 70% of primary schools have set targets for literacy and numeracy. This process of target setting has been reinforced by the LEA's yearlong focus on a particular subject matter. For example, the LEA launched the "Year of Numeracy" and the "Year of Reading" and planned to implement the "Year of the Arts" in the next academic year. Target setting is also aided by new assessment initiatives, for example, creating families of schools that share similar socioeconomic characteristics.

The OFSTED evaluation of the LEA suggests that the targeting process, though seen as beneficial by the schools involved, needs to be elaborated more clearly. Some schools report feeling that they did not know the specific components of the process, although the LEA's support was helpful. In addition, declaring a different focus for each year may distract teachers from improving their core practices as much as it provides a goal to mobilize their support. Schools that have adopted the targeting approach have seen improvements in student achievement. The challenge for the LEA is to expand this support to more schools. As we see in Chicago, this requires enormous resources. As the LEA expands its support and advisory model to more schools, this challenge will become more significant.

To summarize, Birmingham's LEA approaches the challenge of improving school and student performance by creating a professionally oriented culture and providing schools with expertise in the areas of school management and instructional improvement. Brighouse emphasizes the key role teachers play in improving school and student performance. His charismatic leadership has mobilized teachers' support for systemwide improvement and innovation. In conjunction with this cultural shift, the central administration has developed its capacity to provide schools with technical support. Through the BASS and its advisors, the central administration assists schools in setting and attaining improvement targets. This twofold approach has enabled Birmingham to make significant gains in student performance. The LEA is helping to narrow the gap that has long existed between the nation and the city.

VARIATION IN PRESSURING AND SUPPORTING FAILING SCHOOLS

Whereas the Chicago administration is pressing low-performing schools and low-performing students with sanctions and support, the Birmingham LEA restrains from applying formal pressure on their schools. For Brighouse, publicly labeling schools as failures would distract from serious efforts at school improvement. Instead, the LEA prefers to rely on a combination of constructive persuasion and technical support. Why do Birmingham and Chicago adopt such different approaches toward systemwide educational improvement? Here are some of the institutional factors that may explain these policy differences.

Major Versus Small Crisis

First, the educational challenge differs in terms of its magnitude and urgency between the two districts. Chicago is confronted with a wide scale of failing schools. The key challenge is to bring up the enormous number of students who are performing very poorly at all elementary and secondary grade levels. For example, only 12 of the district's 80 high schools have at least 30% of their students performing at the national average on the standardized TAP tests. In the seven reconstituted high schools, only about 7% of their students have met the national norm for several years. At the end of their eighth grade, 22% of the 27,800 students failed to read and calculate at the seventh-grade level and were required to attend summer school in 1997. For the 33,300 third-grade students, more than one third of them fell significantly behind in their basic academic skills. The magnitude of these challenges required the school board to take immediate and broad-scale action. If the school board had been indecisive, more than 6,000 eighth-graders would have been promoted into high schools even though they were 2 years behind in their academic performance. Districtwide sanctions visibly create new and higher expectations for many schools and students in terms of academic outcomes.

Compared to Chicago, Birmingham faces the challenge of "improving their previous best" (Birmingham City Council Education Department, 1996). Though Birmingham has schools that are performing poorly, most of the schools are getting close to the national averages in meeting academic outcome standards. In the author's analysis of the 61 LEA-maintained secondary schools, only 16 (or 26%) fell below the district's average in both the 1996 General Certificate of Secondary Education point score and a 5-year percentage change (see Table 5.10). The magnitude of failing schools and low-performing students in Birmingham is clearly nowhere near that of its sister district. It should be noted that within its own national context, Birmingham does have some room for improvement. The gap between the LEA and the national average remains considerable in several areas of assessments. For example, 48% of the LEA's pupils achieved at a satisfactory level in Key Stage 3 math assessment as compared to 61% at the national level. In Year 11, GCSE results for 1997, 36% of students in the LEA earned five or more top grades (A to C) as compared to 43% of the national population.

Local Control Versus National Standards and Local Competition

The United States has a strong tradition of local control. Schools are not required to meet national standards in the absence of a national examination and national curriculum. Outcome-based pressure, if any, would have to come from the school board and its administration. There is no appropriate governmental agency other than the Chicago district administration to enforce systemwide standards.

The Birmingham LEA is positioned in a national system of checks and balances. Pressure on schools comes from the national inspectorate that evaluates both the schools and the LEAs. The Birmingham LEA responded to this systemic pressure by aligning itself with the schools. To assist schools in coping with this external threat, the LEA becomes a "critical friend" of the schools. Between October 1997 and January 1998, a team of national inspectors conducted an extensive review of the LEA and its schools. In preparing for the inspection, the LEA had to organize an enormous number of documents. As shown in Table 5.11,

TABLE 5.10
General Certificate of Secondary Education Points Score for Birmingham Schools

	1991–1996 Change in Performance		
1996 Performance	Above LEA Average	Below LEA Average	Total (Number of Schools)
Above LEA average[a]	8	23	31
Below LEA average	14	16	30
Total (number of schools)	22	39	61

Note: LEA = Local Education Authority. From Birmingham City Council (1998).
[a]In 1996, the average GCSE points score was 26.9.

there were 572 pieces of documents in 20 major areas submitted by the LEA to the inspection team. These included 209 policy documents on curriculum and assessment, and another 40 reports and records on admissions and student placement. Further, OFSTED inspectors conducted extensive interviews and classroom observations in 20 primary, 14 secondary, and 3 special schools. Data collection at the site level focused on the effectiveness of the LEA strategy in school improvement. According to the LEA's own estimate, the entire OFSTED inspection costs £180,000.

The 1998 White Paper published by the Blair government alters the LEA's role. The White Paper restores the LEA's evaluative function and requires LEAs to intervene more directly into low-performing schools. The White Paper provides a significant challenge for the LEA. It will have to renegotiate its relationship with schools and determine how much pressure it can and should place upon poorly performing schools within the framework of its supportive approach.

Limited Institutional Competition Versus the Market for Schooling

In Birmingham, schools have to compete with non-LEA schools in order to keep their student enrollment, and thus their budget, at their usual levels. Competition has had the most effect on the LEA at the secondary level. As noted earlier, the LEA-maintained schools enroll approximately 54% of the possible secondary students in the district whereas 46% of students attend grant-maintained, selective single-sex, and voluntary-aided schools. This has resulted in a large number of undersubscribed secondary schools. Twenty-two of the LEA-maintained secondary schools are undersubscribed. Nine of these schools have more than 40% of their classrooms vacant. Two schools are scheduled to be closed because of low enrollment. Because funds follow the pupils, schools need ongoing support from the LEA advisors to avoid any negative findings from the OFSTED inspection. In contrast, student enrollment in the Chicago public schools is not significantly threatened by a competitive sector. Exiting demands to the suburbs and nonpublic schools affect both districts.

In short, given the American tradition of local control, Chicago's district administration has to perform multiple functions, namely both pressuring and supporting schools. In Birmingham, given the checks and balances within a national system, the LEA joins the schools as a "critical friend." A proper balance between pressure and support is a challenge for the leadership in both districts.

DEFINING THE POLICY CHALLENGES

Having outlined the institutional changes in the two sister systems, in this section the author identifies several policy challenges and their implications for policymakers, practitioners, and researchers. For policymakers, the key is to develop strategies that will sustain and broaden the accomplishments of the last 3 years. For practitioners, there is a need to improve organizational coherence and programmatic alignment between the central administration and the site level to meet the challenge of educational accountability. For researchers, the challenge is to raise analytical standards in conducting research that is less grounded in advocating a particular ideological or partisan point of view. The challenges the author has defined may provide a preliminary basis for a policy and research agenda in the next several years.

The Challenge of Leadership Succession

The two sister systems are currently under exceptionally capable leadership. As we look to the future, a critical issue is whether those qualities that help the transformational process can be institutionalized beyond the Vallas and the Brighouse era.

In Birmingham, the OFSTED (1998) report recognized the immeasurable contribution of the chief education officer. It concluded, "[The chief education officer] has the ability to articulate a very particular educational vision.... His accessibility to schools is much appreciated.

TABLE 5.11
Documents Prepared for 1997 Office of Her Majesty's Chief Inspector of Schools

Section	*Number of Documents*
Strategic planning within the Local Education Authority	19
Organization of decision making and the council	5
Local Education Authority provisions supporting schools	34
School places, admissions, and appeal procedures	40
Behavior plan and supporting provisions	20
Pupils educated outside of school	18
Supporting school attendance	11
Maintenance and repair of schools	15
Financial regulation	37
School governance	35
Employment of staff	29
Special education needs	17
Health, safety, and welfare	9
Curriculum and assessment	209
School transport	1
Discretionary and mandatory awards	1
Youth service	5
Adult education	11
Performance data on pupil attainment	39
School improvement	17
Total	572

Note: From Birmingham City Council (1997b).

The LEA would not have made anywhere near as much progress without his leadership" (p. 4). Restructuring of the LEA leadership already began with the departure of the deputy chief education officer and the head of BASS in 1998. Together with the CEO, these top-level administrators played a crucial role in school improvement in the LEA. The key question is what kind of leadership culture will occur once Brighouse leaves office. This is particularly critical as several units within the LEA central administration have slowly adapted to the Brighouse vision.

Similarly, in Chicago, the successful operation of the system currently depends on the managerial and leadership qualities and skills of Paul Vallas. Vallas' strong management expertise and leadership skills complement the educational expertise of the chief education officer, Cozette Buckney. However, the risk of putting power at the top of the system is that the system is dependent on the capabilities of the leadership. The question arises: How can the system maintain effective leadership beyond a few years? Currently, leadership relies on the mayor's ability to appoint competent managers. If the mayor appoints a strong leader, good things will happen. If not, the whole system could flounder. The city needs to develop a more systematic means of leadership succession. Toward this end, the author has identified several qualifications that contribute to the effective leadership of the current administration that may serve as a starting point. They include (Wong et al., 1997):

- Ability to articulate a clear mission and realistic policy goals.
- Knowledge of the local political scene and understanding of the connections between the schools, city hall, the state legislature, the business community, LSCs, and local reform groups.
- Political skills to manage the conflicting interests of these various groups.
- Ability to manage competing demands without arousing the animosity of particular groups.
- Ability to focus on the collective enterprise rather than disaggregate school management in terms of racial and ethnic considerations.
- Administrative, managerial, and negotiation skills.

The Challenge of Broadening Academic Gains: Implications for Pressure and Support Policies

Redesigning Secondary Education. For the sister systems, a major challenge is to broaden the academic gains from the primary to the secondary level, in poorly performing schools, and systemwide. In this regard, secondary education is a central challenge for both systems. In Birmingham, according to OFSTED, the percentage of city primary schools in the special measures/failing category is lower than the national average, whereas the comparable figure for secondary schools is higher. In Chicago, standardized test scores at the elementary level for both math and reading have been improving in recent years. At the high school level, however, though math scores have improved, reading scores remain low.

Both Birmingham and Chicago are currently in the process of redesigning secondary schooling. In Birmingham, the city council's Secondary Education Commission has begun to rethink secondary admissions arrangements. An LEA position paper that led to the creation of the commission focuses on the effects of market competition and LMS on the distribution of students (Birmingham Local Education Authority, 1997a). The paper argues that the creaming of the highest performing students by selective schools has resulted in an increasing number of both underperforming schools and school closures. Furthermore, different admissions and exclusion policies and varying rates of subscription have led to a chaotic transfer of students, both from primary to secondary schools and across secondary schools. The paper suggests that admission policies be centralized to reduce this confusion and ensure a more equitable distribution of students. In addition, the LEA administration is attempting to build its capacity for supporting secondary schools. Currently, most of the LEA school support personnel associated with the BASS have primary school expertise. The Brighouse administration needs to focus on bringing more secondary education expertise to the LEA.

Chicago has initiated several organizational changes at the secondary level. In order to personalize relations between students and teachers, the district has implemented Junior and Senior Academies. The central focus of the academies is to have teachers stay with one group of students through 2 or 4 years of high school. Similarly, the district has begun to implement advisory periods intended to create supportive relations between teachers and students. The district recently published a curriculum guide for this program. Teachers have disagreed with the advisory periods. It will be vital to have teacher support for this initiative.

In an effort to improve student performance, the district has increased math and science graduation requirements and developed standards and assessments for core subject areas. The district has also expanded specialized programs, including magnet schools, the International Baccalaureate program, scholars honors programs, and career training. Several new schools are slated to open over the next 2 years, including 11 high schools redesigned as Career Academies, several charter schools for high school students, and 7 "small school" high schools. The district's reform plan, Design for High Schools, is an ambitious effort to ensure that all high school students receive a strong core academic curriculum and to offer several different avenues for achievement.

Improving Teaching and Learning in Poorly Performing Schools. Along with efforts to improve secondary education, both districts face crucial challenges in improving teaching and learning in poorly performing schools. Birmingham's "critical friend" approach to school improvement is facing many alternative strategies that are under consideration by the national government.

One option is closing failing schools. Stephen Byers, the schools standards minister until recently, considered the option of closure if a school fails the OFSTED inspections and has at least 25% of their places vacant (Carvel, 1998). In the last 4 years, the Birmingham LEA has closed five schools because of poor performance and undersubscription by parents. The second option being considered is contracting private service providers. Michael Barber, a key education adviser to the Blair administration, introduced the option of contracting failing school management to private vendors in a speech in January 1998 ("Schools. Labour's learning," 1998). As part of the proposed "Education Action Zones," private firms can take over some or all of the 20 low-performing schools within each zone. To create a flexible climate for whole-school improvement, the education action zones are likely to relax national curricular standards and national union provisions.

The third option is the pressuring strategy (without proper support) that OFSTED inspections are associated with. The head of OFSTED, Chris Woodhead, insists that failing schools ought to be publicly labeled and that poor teaching should be sanctioned. The league tables report school rankings on the national assessments and further stigmatize schools that serve disadvantaged students. The tables do not take into account either this disadvantage or the gains made by these schools and their students. In contrast, Brighouse sees that public blaming is counterproductive and that failing schools need proper support and encouragement. In recognition of these two opposing strategies—pressuring and support—Brighouse and Woodhead have been appointed by the government to serve as vice-chairmen of a national commission on school standards.

The Birmingham model has to contend with several competing approaches. Yet, precisely because of these contending models, Brighouse's approach to school improvement constitutes a necessary counterbalance to the other strands of governmental intervention, thereby providing the proper checks and balances within a national educational system.

In Chicago, whereas the media and the public have focused on probation, reconstitution, and academic promotion, the CPS have expanded their policy options in addressing educational failure. With the

CPS board's approval, seven charter schools started fall of 1997 and six new charter schools were in operation during 1998–1999. These schools are selected based on state and district provisions, including services targeted to at-risk student populations. Although receiving public funds, these schools enjoy substantial autonomy from both CPS central direction and union work rules. In return for programmatic flexibility, charter schools are held accountable for student performance through a 4-year contract agreement. Because of political opposition from the teachers' union, existing failing schools are not likely to become charter schools. Further, many schools in CPS are adopting the small-school strategy, broadening their school-to-work programs, and bringing in external expert partners to address their own needs. Although there is no lack of innovative strategies, CPS is somewhat behind in assessing the effectiveness of these initiatives in improving student achievement. Clearly, the district needs to strengthen its monitoring and evaluation functions as it proliferates innovative practices systemwide.

Providing Ongoing Support to Schools

Another major challenge in the area of broadening academic gains is the need to develop the systems' capacity to provide ongoing support to schools. The sister systems differ in the capacity of their central administrations to assist schools and teachers in their efforts to improve student performance. Whereas Birmingham has developed a strong advisory and support system that provides schools with expertise in these areas, Chicago relies heavily on consultants. Table 5.12 shows the decline in the number of central office staff in Chicago involved in curriculum, instruction, and professional development that has occurred over the past decade. Almost one half of these positions have been eliminated. Currently, the central administration does not have the technical capacity to assist schools in their improvement efforts.

This downsizing has resulted in the district relying on external consultants to assist schools in efforts to improve core instructional activities. This policy is problematic in terms of the support the district offers poorly performing schools. As previously mentioned, the quality of the external consultants provided to schools on probation is highly variable. Although these consultants have the best intentions, helping schools improve their performance and that of their students requires

TABLE 5.12
Central Office Staff in Curriculum, Instruction, and Professional Development

	Number of Staff		
School Year	*Curriculum, Instruction, and Professional Development*	*Total Central Office*	*Percent of Total*
1988–1989	404	4,881	8.3%
1989–1990	471	4,328	10.9%
1990–1991	371	3,632	10.2%
1991–1992	237	3,404	7.0%
1992–1993	201	3,126	6.4%
1993–1994	166	3,266	5.1%
1994–1995	221	3,456	5.7%
1995–1996	197	2,739	8.1%
1996–1997	143.2	2,712	5.3%
1997–1998	138	2,505	5.5%

Note: Data taken from Chicago Public Schools annual budgets 1988–1989 through 1997–1998. Calculations are author's own.

intensive, long-term efforts. Many of the external partners do not have the staff to provide such support. The reliance on external consultants also results in the lack of a unified educational vision at the district level. Whereas Brighouse and the central administration in Birmingham offer a coherent vision of school improvement, Chicago's approach offers a variety of models. This policy should be reconsidered, particularly in light of the district's drive to raise standards systemwide. Providing support to schools requires a long-term institutional commitment that may be undermined by the overreliance on competing consultants.

The Challenge of Diversity

The districts are facing two kinds of diversity challenges. First, the school systems have to ensure equal access for their disadvantaged populations. Second, the districts need to maintain a middle-class presence by allowing for institutional diversity.

For Birmingham, a longer term challenge is to improve performance among its immigrant student populations. Whereas 14% of the White boys failed in all subjects in the GCSE examinations in 1996, these numbers are higher for the Bangladeshi boys (24%) and the Pakistani boys (17%). There are significant gender differences. Whereas 37% of the girls achieved 5 or more A–C grades in the GCSE in 1996, only 28% of the boys did. Although African/Caribbean children performed well in the primary level, African/Caribbean boys as a group underperformed at the secondary level. Birmingham's recruitment of teachers and head teachers also showed a significant underrepresentation of ethnic minorities. In light of these concerns, Birmingham has initiated several strategies. Particularly innovative is the UFA, which is a cross-agency initiative designed to complement and enrich school learning for early adolescents. The UFA offers interest-led, intensive, and accelerated learning opportunities during holiday breaks and also provides distance learning and debating opportunities through the Young People's Parliament. In its first year, the UFA was piloted in Aston, a City Challenge area.

With its diverse student body, the Chicago school board is weighing the proper balance between second language instruction for Limited English Proficient (LEP) students and the need for mainstream English-based instruction. In February 1998, the board approved a 3-year limit to instructional programs for most of the district's LEP students. The limit is coupled with additional support for professional development and multicultural programs. The challenge is for the CPS to create the necessary conditions for LEP students to make a meaningful transition to the mainstream classroom.

The other dimension of the diversity issue is how to retain the middle class. Central-city educational systems have to cope with the exiting of the middle class to both suburban and nongovernmental schools. As public institutions, urban school systems need to maintain a healthy mix of students with different socioeconomic backgrounds. Thus, the sister systems, though focusing on raising the lower-performing schools, cannot afford to neglect the needs of the middle class. Innovative programs that emphasize high-quality curriculum and outcome performance are designed to address these structural challenges. In Chicago, magnet schools with distinct curricular programs have been a successful tool for maintaining a more heterogeneous student population. In spring 1998, the board revised the magnet school admission policy in part to accommodate the schooling demand of middle- class parents in regentrified neighborhoods. In March 1998, the school board approved an expansion of the International Baccalaureate program from 1 school to as many as 13 in the next few years. These programs are intended to become regional centers of academic excellence as students would be drawn from those who score above the 60th percentile within a specific regional boundary.

If successful, these initiatives may bring about more integrated schools in terms of income, ethnicity, and race.

CONCLUSION

Integrated governance has accomplished much in a relatively short period of time in both systems. This reform model fosters educational improvement through the coordination of activities in support of system-wide goals and standards. Integrated governance enables central administrators to develop a strong political base on which to improve system operations.

In Chicago, the central administration under integrated governance has successfully addressed fiscal and managerial problems. It has raised performance standards for the whole system and instituted an ambitious accountability agenda that provides both pressure and support for school improvement. Several urban school districts in the United States, including Cleveland, are following Chicago's lead.

The Birmingham LEA has had similar success under integrated governance. The LEA has significantly improved its fiscal operations and has mobilized teachers and head teachers around its innovative educational agenda. Its professionally oriented support model has led to significant school improvement and improved student achievement. As the national government in the UK reinforces the LEA's monitoring function, Birmingham offers a promising model for balancing pressure and support.

Integrated governance appears to be a promising strategy for the improvement of urban school systems. Although the sister systems have made significant gains, their approaches to school improvement reflect both differences in the educational visions that guide the leadership of each system and the organizational and political realities in which both systems are located. As the educational visions of both administrations continue to evolve and as the political and organizational realities change, continued study of how integrated governance operates within each system may provide further insights into successful strategies for improving urban schools.

REFERENCES

Birmingham City Council. (1997a). *Birmingham LEA and PICSI commentary* (Version 2). Birmingham, England: Author.

Birmingham City Council. (1997b). *Directory of documents prepared for OFSTED inspection.* Birmingham, England: Author.

Birmingham City Council. (1997c). *An education development strategy for Birmingham towards the year 2000.* Birmingham, England: Author.

Birmingham City Council. (1998). *Education Budget Book, 1997–98.* Birmingham, England: Author.

Birmingham City Council Education Department. (1996). *Improving on previous best: An overview of school improvement strategies in Birmingham.* Birmingham, England: Author.

Birmingham City Council Education Department. (1998). *Education budget book, 1997–98.* Birmingham, England: Author.

Birmingham Local Education Authority. (1997a). *Briefing note for the commission investigating the future of secondary school needs in Birmingham.* Birmingham, England: Author.

Birmingham Local Education Authority. (1997b). *PICSI and commentary* (Version 2). Birmingham, England: Author.

Blunkett, D. (1998, February 6). *News: Education "success story" for Birmingham city council.* London: Author.

Bullock, A., & Thomas, H. (1997). *School at the centre?* London: Routledge.

Carvel, J. (1998, February 27). Under-used schools get ultimatum. *The Guardian.*

Chicago Public Schools. (1997). *1997–98 final budget.* Chicago: Author.

Chicago Public Schools. (1998a). *Annual budget 1997–1998.* Chicago: Author.

Chicago Public Schools. (1998b). *Chicago Public Schools fact sheet.* Chicago: Author.

Chicago Public Schools. (1998c). *Test of achievement and proficiency reading and math, 1991–1998.* Chicago: Author.

"City aims to higher 'best and brightest.'" (1996, May). *Catalyst.*

Ehrenhalt, A. (1997, December). Master of the detail. *Governing*, pp. 19, 22.

Kogan, R. (1998, March 8). Do you know where your children are? *Chicago Tribune Magazine.*

Office of Her Majesty's Chief Inspector of Schools (OFSTED). (1998). *Inspection of Birmingham local education authority* (Final Report). London: Author.

Sall, Jon. (1998, Aoril 6). "School races attract few candidates." *Chicago Sun-Times*, p. 8.

"Schools. Labour's learning." (1998, January 10). *The Economist.*

Washburn, G. (1998, April 3). City summer school required for more kids. *Chicago Tribune.*

Wong, K. K., & Anagnostopoulos, D. (1998). Can integrated governance reconstruct teaching?: Lessons learned from two low-performing Chicago high schools. *Educational Policy, 12*(1&2), 31–47.

Wong, K. K., Dreeben, R., Lynn, L. E., Jr., Meyer, R., & Sunderman, G. (1996). Systemwide governance in the Chicago public schools: Findings and recommendations for institutional redesign. In K. K. Wong (Ed.), *Advances in educational policy: Vol. 2. Rethinking school reform in Chicago* (pp. 225–251). Greenwich, CT: JAI.

Wong, K. K., Dreeben, R., Lynn, L. E., Jr., & Sunderman, G. (1997). *Integrated governance as a reform strategy in the Chicago public schools*. Chicago: University of Chicago, Department of Education.

Wong, K. K., & Jain, P. (1999). Newspapers as policy actors in urban school systems: The Chicago story. *Urban Affairs Review, 35*(2), 210–246.

Wong, K. K., & Moulton, M. (1998). Governance report cards = accountability in the Chicago public school system. *Education and Urban Society, 30*(4), 459–478.

6

Turning Around Low-Performing Schools: The Case of the Washington, DC Schools

Margaret C. Wang
JoAnn Manning
Temple University

As we enter the next millennium, the United States is experiencing marked transformations in a variety of critical realms. What was once a land of secure jobs, effective laws, and well-knit homes is rapidly becoming defined by the homeless, the jobless, and the lawless. This is especially true in urban communities across the country, where rates of poverty, crime, and unemployment far exceed those of suburban and rural areas. In the end, the schools are hardest hit. Their students are often woefully unprepared, lacking good nutrition, medical care, safe transportation, and adequate academic preparation. Urban schools in their current condition are clearly unable to withstand the social forces that affect them. For the nation and its cities to remain vital, schools must not only anticipate changes but also lead toward solutions. Otherwise, the current generation of children in urban communities, which are plagued with modern morbidities of our time, will be consigned to lives of academic, economic, and social marginalization.

Making these general statements about the severity of urban problems (e.g., widespread academic failure) is relatively easy; the real challenge is finding feasible, practical, affordable solutions to these problems. How can we transform our urban schools to achieve student success? We contend that information already exists from research and practical application of innovative school reform approaches that work and would be useful in the ongoing efforts to revitalize this nation's urban schools. Research and practical experience indicate that the capacity for school success is not mysterious. It is a capacity that can be developed and nurtured even in some of the most challenging circumstances. What is certain is that transforming low-performing schools to work better is difficult but does not, and cannot, take years. Genuine improvements can come about in short order, provided certain conditions are created for success.

In this chapter we describe one approach that is feasible and has shown to be promising in helping restore failing urban schools. This is an illustration of how schools can defy adversity and restore and nurture the expertise and talents of their teachers and students to achieve the vision of schooling success.

BACKGROUND AND CONTEXT

During the summer of 1996, the superintendent of the District of Columbia Public Schools (DC Schools) asked the Laboratory for Student Success (LSS), the mid-Atlantic Regional Educational Laboratory at the Temple University Center for Research in Human Development and Education, to assist the District in designing a comprehensive school reform initiative to help its lowest performing schools to significantly improve their capacity to increase student achievement. An implementation plan for a collaborative demonstration project to implement a comprehensive approach to whole-school reform was developed by the DC Schools and LSS. In September 1996, the plan was unanimously approved by the DC school board and the project officially began its implementation in October.

Five elementary schools were selected by the DC Schools to participate in the demonstration project. These schools were identified as some of the lowest performing schools in the District and had shown a continuous pattern of decline in student achievement. The schools were mandated by the superintendent to implement a research-based comprehensive school reform plan, with implementation assistance from LSS. The schools were not given a choice about their participation. The school staff had the option to ask for a transfer without losing seniority. None of the staff requested a transfer.

The superintendent who initiated the project was fired by the school board at the end of October. This is the month when the project began implementation. The project was implemented under three superintendents during its first 2 years of operation.

THE PROJECT

The project began during the 1996–1997 academic year with five schools, and included a sixth school during the 1997–1998 academic year. The overall goal of the project was to demonstrate the feasibility of turning around the lowest performing schools by implementing a comprehensive school reform model, known as the Community for Learning program, to significantly improve student achievement.

The Community for Learning Program

The Community for Learning (CFL) program was developed at the Temple University Center for Research in Human Development and Education (Wang, 1992, 1998). It is an implementation delivery framework designed to assist schools in implementing a comprehensive approach to school reform that is systemic and sustainable in achieving student success. CFL was field-tested with much success in several major cities, including Houston and Philadelphia (e.g., McComb, 1999; Oates, Flores, & Weishew, 1998; Wang, Oates, & Weishew, 1995). Implementation focuses on a coordinated process of uniting the expertise and resources of the school, family, and community to ensure a high standard of achievement of each student. A high degree of program implementation of CFL is expected to strengthen the capacity of schools to mobilize and redeploy school and community resources to support a comprehensive, coordinated, inclusive approach to achieving schoolwide student success. Education programs implemented in CFL schools are connected with broad-based efforts of students' families and the community to significantly improve student achievement and the expertise of adults—a *community for learning.* A synopsis of the design of CFL is provided in the Appendix at the end of this chapter.

Roles and Responsibilities

As a part of the implementation design, specific roles and responsibilities were delineated for the participating demonstration DC Schools and LSS.

The School District of the District of Columbia agreed to:

- Designate a District official to serve as the coordinator of the project. The primary responsibility of this individual was to oversee the project's implementation in the collaborating demonstration schools and to serve as a liaison for the DC Schools' central administration, the demonstration schools, and LSS. The project coordinator also worked with the LSS program implementation staff and the school staff in designing and implementing professional development and technical assistance programs to meet the implementation needs of the staff at the demonstration schools.
- Provide a full-time facilitator for each of the five schools to assist the principals and teachers in achieving a high degree of program implementation.
- Provide LSS with School District-collected student achievement data and other relevant data to conduct evaluative analyses of program progress and impact on student achievement, and assist schools in using the database for making programming decisions and professional development plans.

The demonstration schools continued to receive the same support and resource allocation from the School District. No extra resources were given to or withdrawn from the schools.

The responsibilities of the school staff included the following:

- The demonstration schools were responsible for demonstrating a high degree of implementation of the CFL program.
- All school staff were to begin implementation of CFL by the beginning of the 1996–1997 academic year.
- The principals of the demonstration schools were to work closely with the project coordinator, their respective facilitators, and the LSS implementation staff in developing an implementation assistance plan that closely aligned the re-

sources, organization support mechanisms, and personnel deployment of each school to ensure a high degree of program implementation by the school staff.

- The school staff were to participate in professional development workshops and planning sessions to learn about CFL, and develop implementation plans and strategies to achieve a high degree of program implementation.
- School staff were to participate in collecting program implementation and outcome data to document program implementation and outcomes.

The Laboratory for Student Success agreed to provide the following implementation support services to the DC demonstration schools at no cost to the School District for at least 3 years:

- Assist the School District and the five participating demonstration schools in conducting needs assessments for developing an implementation plan that determines the support needs of each school.
- Provide preimplementation training and continuing professional development support to each school through on-site assistance to teachers and professional development support for the principals and facilitators.
- Provide ongoing professional development and technical assistance that focuses on capacity building. This capacity-building role will vary from school to school, based on their needs and implementation progress.
- Assist the schools in collecting and analyzing implementation and program outcome data to inform the School District and schools of their implementation progress and program impact on student achievement and other program outcomes.
- Work with the District and demonstration schools in developing a plan to establish the demonstration and professional development capacity at each of the schools to assist the School District in replicating CFL in other, interested schools in subsequent years.

TABLE 6.1
Demographic Characteristics of Students (1997–1998 Academic Year)

School	Free or Reduced Price Lunch	Race (African-American/other)	Attendance Rate	Mobility Rate
A	86.8%	92.0%	92.0%	19%
B	87.5%	89.9%	89.9%	28%
C	93.1%	99.8%	98.1%	16%
D	94.1%	99.6%	96.3%	12%
E	97.6%	99.6%	93.0%	18%
F	94.3%	98.4%	96.3%	20%

THE DEMONSTRATION SCHOOLS

The five schools began implementation during 1996–1997, the project's first year. One additional school was added to the CFL network of demonstration schools during Year 2. This school was also identified as one of the low-performing schools by the District that required "special intervention." However, it was the decision of the staff from this school, not the School District administration, to implement CFL as the core reform program for improving the achievement of the students.

Table 6.1 provides a synopsis of the demographic characteristics of the students in the six CFL demonstration schools. Figure 6.1 shows the geographic location of the schools.

As is typical of most, if not all, schools in large urban school districts, the six Year 2 CFL demonstration schools experienced a significantly large teacher and student turnover rate, and changes in their administrative staff, including the appointment of two new principals, one new assistant principal, and three new facilitators. Furthermore, many of the replacement administrators and teachers were not appointed until several months after the schools had opened. As a result, although five of the six schools were entering their second year of implementation, they opened the school with many disadvantages and implementation problems. While the challenges faced by schools in overcoming these implementation problems are not unique, the degree of program implementation and program impact must be viewed in light of these ongoing implementation challenges. Table 6.2 shows the statistics that illustrate some of the challenges faced by the schools as they addressed

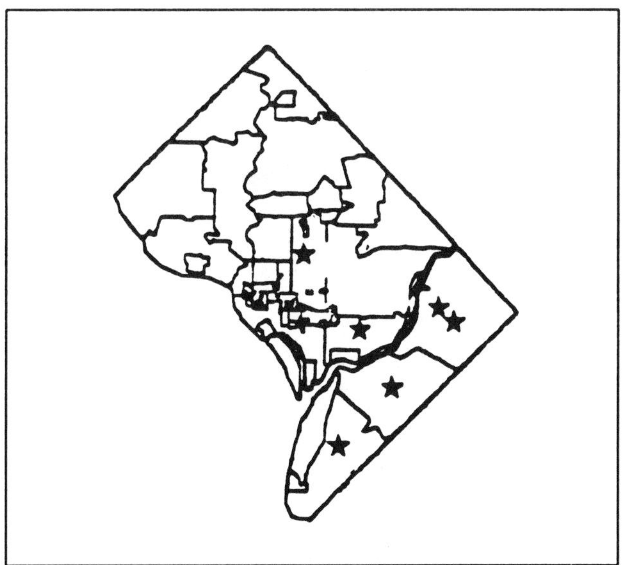

FIG. 6.1. Geographic Location of CFL Demonstration Schools Across the District of Columbia

the implementation needs resulting from the changes.

As shown in Table 6.2, during the 1997–1998 academic year, major personnel changes took place in all six demonstration schools. These changes resulted in the need for intensive implementation training and professional development support, despite the fact that five of the six demonstration schools were entering their second year of CFL implementation.

For example, for School F, the near-50% teacher turnover rate meant that the school began the academic year with an insufficient number of teachers. The school did not have a consistent number of teachers throughout the school year and did not have a full complement of teachers until June 1998. The staffing situation necessitated the continuous reassignment of students to classes, while coping with the pressure of providing on-the-job implementation training for new teachers.

School B began the school year with a new principal and a high percentage of new teachers (39%). The school was without a facilitator until December 1997, and an assistant principal was not appointed until February 1998.

School D began the academic year with several break-ins during

TABLE 6.2
Changes in the Composition of the Schools (1997–1998 Academic Year)

School	New Principal	New Assistant Principal	New Facilitator	New Teachers	New Student
A				30%	47%
B	Aug. 1997*	Feb. 1998*	Dec. 1997*	39%	51%
C	Aug. 1997*	—		16%	51%
D		—	Feb. 1998*	13%	39%
E**	Aug. 1997*	—	April 1998*	0%	43%
F		—		48.2%	30.9%

— Indicates no change.
* Indicates date of appointment.
** First year implementation school for the 1997–1998 academic year.

the first 3 weeks after the school's opening. All of the school's computers and high-tech equipment were stolen.

School C began the academic year with a new principal and a high percentage of new students (more than 50%). The principal not only had to be a quick study of the design and implementation requirements of CFL, but also had to provide implementation and professional development support to new and returning teachers faced with the larger number of new students while working on establishing and maintaining a high degree of program implementation.

School F, a new CFL school for the 1997–1998 academic year, started with a new principal who did not have a choice in using CFL as the school's reform strategy. The school staff made the choice at the end of the 1996–1997 school year. This school is one of the designated targeted assistance schools, that had to implement one of the externally developed research-based school reform models identified by the School District. CFL was the consensual choice. The school, however, did not get a facilitator until April 1998.

FINDINGS ON PROGRAM IMPLEMENTATION AND OUTCOMES

The findings on program implementation and outcomes for the first 2 years of program implementation indicated an overall positive pattern toward program outcomes, including changes in teacher and student classroom behaviors, and the degree of program implementation and student achievement.

Year 1 Findings

All of the 142 staff members in the five demonstration schools participated in the program's implementation during the 1996–1997 school year. Implementation was initiated in three cohort groups. The first cohort began implementation training in October 1996, the second cohort began training in January 1997, and the third cohort began training in March 1997.

The initial implementation of CFL in the five schools focused on addressing the following questions about CFL implementation and impact: (a) Is it feasible to establish schoolwide implementation of CFL during the first year of the program initiative? (b) To what extent does CFL implementation lead to positive changes in the patterns of classroom processes and behaviors of teachers and students? (c) Does implementation of CFL lead to changes in teachers' perceptions about their school learning environments? and (d) Can program implementation lead to improved student achievement after less than 6 months of program implementation?

The following highlight findings that specifically address the questions just listed:

- Preimplementation training was provided to all school staff in the five schools within a 6-month period. After receiving preimplementation training, school staff were able to initiate program implementation immediately. Many staff were able to achieve a moderate to high degree of program implementation within less than 6 months.
- On-site facilitators at each school were able to provide ongoing implementation support to meet the training and technical assistance needs of the individual teachers with support from the LSS.

The phase-in process of training teachers in the three teacher cohorts made it possible to achieve the project's goal of initiating program implementation schoolwide during Year 1.

- As the degree of program implementation improved, a concomitant pattern of positive changes in the classroom processes and teacher and student classroom behaviors was observed.
- Changes in classroom instruction and learning processes were observed as a result of program implementation. Teachers substantially reduced time spent in whole-class instruction and focused class time on small-group instruction and working individually with students. Teachers spent more time interacting with students for instructional rather than managerial purposes.
- Teachers expressed more positive perceptions about their ability to provide for student diversity when survey results from preimplementation and postimplementation periods were compared. Among the two most salient changes were (a) an increase in teachers' perceptions of the feasibility and effectiveness in using individualized instruction and cooperative learning strategies to effectively respond to student diversity in their respective schools, and (b) teachers reported an increase in using instructional materials that stimulated varied student interests and encouraged collaborative learning and small-group instruction.
- Achievement scores suggested that students functioning in the program for a greater period of time (first cohort) performed better than their peers who had less time in the program (second and third cohorts). This was a positive trend that matched the expectation that program implementation and positive changes in classroom process would lead to improved achievement of students.
- Positive changes in student achievement were also reflected when comparing the fall 1996 and spring 1997 Stanford Achievement Test, 9th ed. (Stanford 9) test results. Furthermore, an overall pattern of positive changes in achievement among students in the CFL schools was observed, when compared with students in the other elementary schools in the District.
- The school that had the fewest teachers in the first-cohort implementation group was the school that showed the minimal improvement in student achievement.

- There was a consensus among the principals and program facilitators that a kindred sense of accomplishment was evident among the staff. The staff in all five schools have expressed this sense of accomplishment despite being designated by the District as "targeted assistance schools" and implementing the changes required by the CFL design. They were pleased with what they had been able to achieve within a short period of time. Most important, they were most encouraged by the positive changes they observed and thought were not possible.

Year 2 Findings

A major concern of school reformers is program maintenance after the initial implementation success of innovative programs. A detailed discussion of the Year 2 findings is provided under four headings: (a) degree of program implementation, (b) patterns of changes in classroom processes, (c) relationship between degree of program implementation and classroom process, and (d) student achievement.

Degree of Program Implementation

In this section, a summary of the implementation progress across the six demonstration schools during the 1997–1998 school year is discussed. Because of school-specific variations (e.g., the percentage of new teachers and new principals, organizational structure, student turnover rate, and other site-specific factors), there were variations in implementation progress across the schools. However, overall across the six CFL demonstration schools, the degree of implementation data indicated an overall pattern of improvement in the degree of implementation across all demonstration schools. The cross-site improvement in the degree of implementation from fall 1997 to spring 1998 was statistically significant at the $p < .0001$ level.

The Degree of Program Implementation Assessment Battery was used to collect information on the extent to which the 12 critical dimensions of the instructional component of CFL (known as the Adaptive Learning Environments Model [ALEM]) were implemented in each class in all six demonstration schools. The ALEM critical dimensions were identified through a synthesis of the research base on effective classroom instructional practices and were refined through many years of field-based development and implementation in more than 200 schools with a wide spectrum of demographic and socioeconomic characteristics across different geographic regions (Wang & Zollers, 1990).

In analyzing the degree of program implementation data, the following questions were addressed: (a) To what extent did teachers in the CFL demonstration schools already demonstrate a high degree of performance in the 12 critical dimensions of ALEM prior to implementation training? (b) To what extent did teachers show implementation progress after initial training and ongoing data-based staff development support by the facilitators and the LSS implementation staff? and (c) What were the areas that required targeted assistance by LSS to ensure that a high degree of program implementation was achieved by the end of Year 2 by every teacher across all six demonstration schools?

The Degree of Program Implementation Assessment Battery is routinely used in all CFL implementation schools to assess program implementation progress. In general, formal assessments are conducted in the fall and spring of each year to collect information on the extent to which the 12 critical program dimensions are implemented in each CFL classroom. Based on the information from the fall data, a data-based staff development plan is developed and implemented to assist individual teachers in achieving a high degree of implementation of the 12 critical dimensions of the program.

Degree of program implementation data are also used by the school staff to document improvements over time and to identify specific areas of improvement. Teachers are encouraged to use the degree of implementation measures on a periodic basis to check their implementation progress and to determine their own professional development and/or implementation support needs.

Table 6.3 shows the results of the cross-site mean degree of implementation scores for fall 1997 and spring 1998 for each of the six demonstration schools.

The fall and spring changes were statistically significant for 11 of the 12 dimensions. The two areas that had the lowest percentage of indicators implemented to a high degree across the demonstration schools included managing assistance from support staff and conducting diagnosis and testing to assess student learning needs. Other areas that did not meet the high degree of implementation criterion included

TABLE 6.3
Degree of Program Implementation: Cross-School Means (1997-98 Academic Year)

	Percentage of Performance Indicators Implemented		
Program Dimensions	**Fall 1997 Mean**	**Spring 1998 Mean**	**ANOVA F**
Arranging Space and Facilities	72.13	91.31	34.36**
Creating/Maintaining Instructional Materials	51.45	79.96	25.61 **
Establishing/Communicating Rules and Procedures	52.55	77.09	32.07**
Managing Assistance from Support Staff	39.14	48.33	1.28
Record Keeping	44.45	76.30	25.79**
Diagnosis/Testing	63.04	81.52	10.48*
Prescribing	37.90	78.06	44.20**
Monitoring and Diagnosing	56.96	86.81	63.79**
Interactive Teaching	54.10	83.51	37.24**
Instructing	75.30	93.75	29.69**
Motivating	64.35	86.67	28.22**
Developing Student Self Responsibility	40.99	78.64	91.97**
Total	54.35	80.14	55.62**

* Change in scores from fall to spring is significant at p<.001.
** Change in scores from fall to spring is significant at p<.0001.

establishing/communicating rules and procedures, record keeping, and using curriculum-embedded tests to assess student learning needs. Although all of these areas showed close-to-criterion degree of implementation levels (i.e., 80% of the indicators of a given dimension were in place), they were targeted as the focus of an ongoing professional development program at each school.

Patterns of Changes in Classroom Processes

One of the expected improvements in the degree of implementation of CFL is a concomitant pattern of change in classroom processes. Classroom observations were conducted in all six demonstration schools during the fall and spring to obtain information on teacher and student classroom behaviors and to examine the pattern of classroom process changes resulting from program implementation.

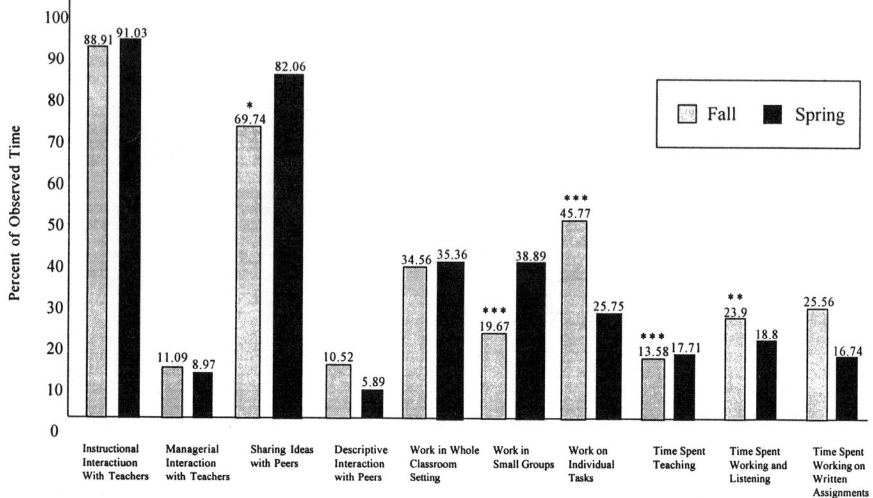

Differences between fall and spring were:

* A statistical test of the difference between fall and spring was significant at $p < .05$.

** A statistical test of the difference between fall and spring was significant at $p < .01$.

*** A statistical test of the difference between fall and spring was significant at $p < .001$.

FIG. 6.2. Patterns of Changes in Student Behaviors Cross-Site Analysis (Fall 1997–Spring 1998)

Figure 6.2 shows the patterns of changes in student behaviors between fall and spring in terms of how students spent their class time, including time spent with teachers on instructional versus managerial interactions, time spent with peers in sharing ideas versus causing disruption, and time spent interacting versus doing seat work and watching and listening. In general, findings suggested an overall pattern of active and task-oriented classroom behavior from the students. Results of the teacher observations between fall and spring were consistent with the student observation findings. Changes were observed between fall and spring in terms of teachers spending more time instructing rather than managing students, and increasing the amount of time spent conducting small-group lessons and working with individual students.

Relationship Between Degree of Program Implementation and Classroom Process

To determine the extent to which the positive changes in the patterns of classroom processes and behaviors could be attributed to changes in the degree of program implementation, a multiple correlation analysis was performed. Using the results from the classroom observation study performed for the pre- and postimplementation periods and the degree of implementation measures, the degree of implementation was found to be significantly correlated with classroom processes and student behaviors ($p < .05$).

The incremental increase in the degree of implementation and concomitant changes in classroom behaviors and the instructional/learning process were significant in two ways. First, these findings validate the CFL program design in terms of its feasibility and positive impact on the classroom process and how teaching and learning take place in CFL classrooms. Second, and perhaps more important, these findings provided reassurance to school staff that their efforts in achieving a high degree of program implementation resulted in observable, positive changes in their classrooms.

The correlation between program implementation and changes in classroom process was also verified by the informal observations reported by the school staff. In addition, the teachers, facilitators, principals, and project coordinator have consistently shared their observations of the correlation between degree of program implementation and the patterns of positive changes observed in classroom processes and student behaviors. The positive changes in classroom process were cited by the school staff as most reinforcing—according to teacher reports, implementing CFL made an observable difference in the classroom environment and the teaching and learning process.

Student Achievement

Student achievement gains between fall and spring testing districtwide were analyzed for each of the CFL schools. Findings are shown in Table 6.4. Only students with both fall and spring scores were included in this analysis. Student achievement gains were analyzed to address the following questions: (a) Did the CFL schools meet the improvement standards stipulated by the superintendent for the 1997–1998 academic year? (b) What was the pattern of progress across the four performance standard levels according to the norm established for the Stanford 9 (below basic, basic, proficient, or advanced)? and (c) Were there differences in the patterns of progress between CFL schools and other targeted assistance schools?

TABLE 6.4
Student Achievement Changes
Stanford 9 Test Results*
(Fall 1997 and Spring 1998)

	NCE						Percentage Rank					
	Reading			Math			Reading			Math		
School	Fall	Spring	Change**	Fall	Spring	Change	Fall	Spring	Change	Fall	Spring	Change
A	34.8	48.1	13.3	28.4	47.9	19.5	28	47	19	20	46	27
B	26.1	33.1	7.0	22.4	34.9	12.5	18	26	8	14	29	15
C	32.7	46.7	14.0	30.3	41.7	11.4	27	46	19	24	39	14
D	26.4	34.9	8.5	21.4	35.2	13.8	19	28	10	13	29	16
E	25.2	38.0	12.8	22.8	41.2	18.4	17	35	18	15	42	27
F	35.8	46.4	10.6	29.5	49.0	19.5	30	44	15	22	48	26
CFL Schools ***	30.2	41.2	11.0	25.6	41.3	15.7	23	38	15	18	38	20
Other Targeted Assistance Schools	33.4	44.4	11.0	27.4	44.4	17.0	26	41	15	19	42	23

* Only students with both fall and spring scores are included.
** All change in scores from fall to spring are statistically significant at <.0001.
*** Mean difference in NCE and percentile rank for math between CFL and other targeted assistance schools is not statistically significant

For the 1997–1998 academic year, the superintendent stipulated that all of the schools must show at least 10% gain between fall and spring testing as measured by Stanford 9 for both reading and math. All of the six schools implementing CFL exceeded this District-mandated improvement standard.

For example, for School A, the reading Normal Curve Equivalent (NCE) score for the fall Stanford 9 testing was 34.8. School A would have met the 10% gain standards established by the superintendent if the reading NCE score had shown a 3.5 gain. The reading NCE gain for School A was 13.3, which was significantly higher than the School District's improvement standard of a 10% gain. Similarly, the change in percentile rank for reading for School A was 19, a significantly greater change than the 3-percentile rank gain that School A had to make to meet School District standards. This example of "exceeding the standards gains" was observed for every school, even for Schools B and D, which showed the least gains among the CFL demonstration schools.

Although the CFL demonstration schools began the 1997–1998 academic year with lower scores when compared with the other targeted assistance schools (targeted assistance schools are designated by the School District as low-performing schools requiring special intervention by the School District; the CFL schools were designated as Level 1 targeted assistance schools, the lowest performing schools among the targeted assistance schools), the CFL demonstration schools made equal gains in reading, and a slightly lower (1.3 NCE score) gain in math. The 1.3 NCE difference is not statistically significant.

Figure 6.3 shows the NCE gains in math and reading made by each CFL demonstration school. Figure 6.3 also shows the cross-site means in comparison with the mean of other targeted assistance schools (see the last two columns shown in Fig. 6.4).

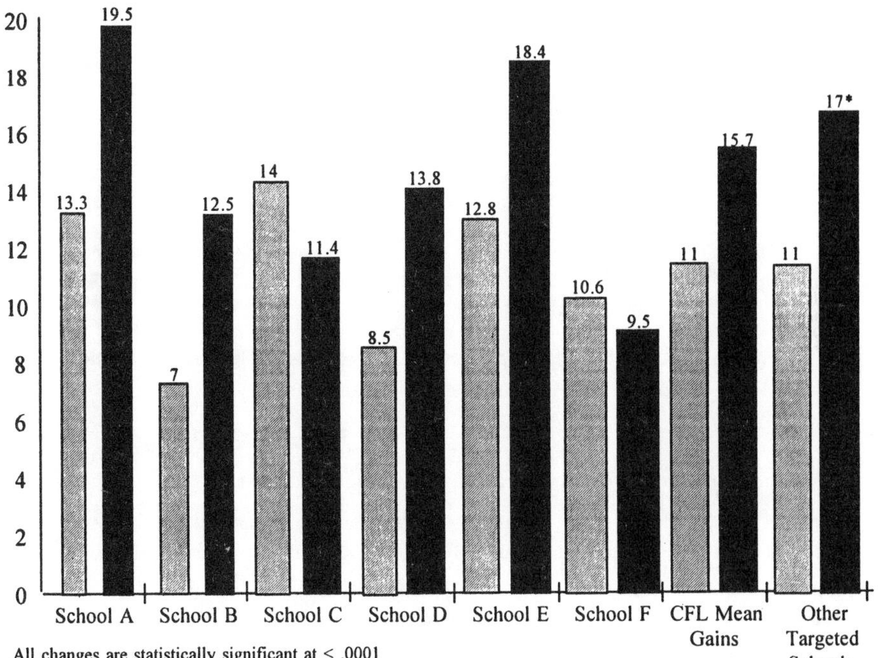

FIG. 6.3. Changes in Stanford 9 Test Results (Fall 1997–Spring 1998)

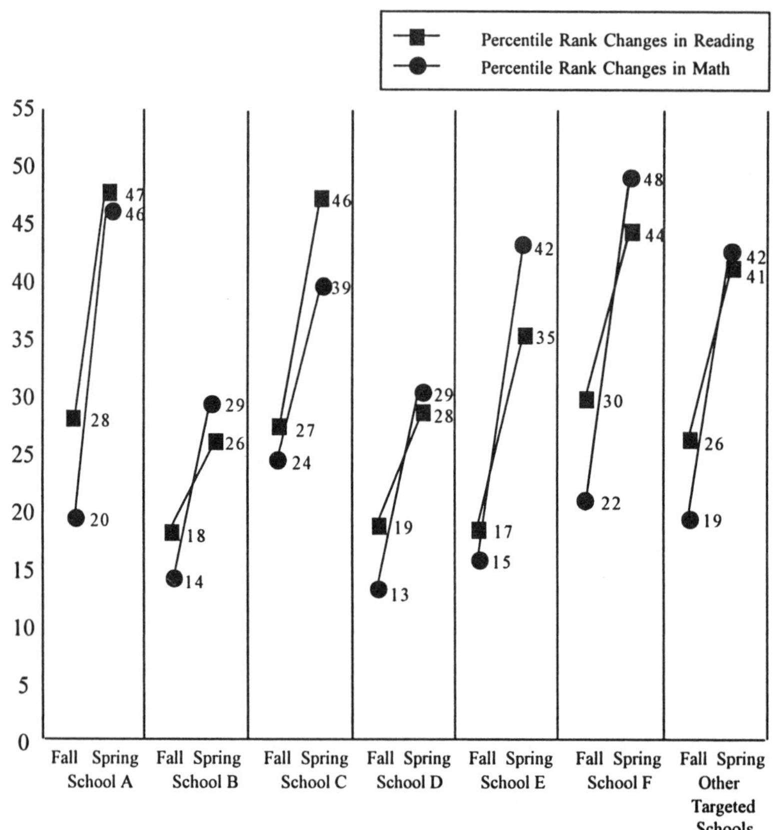

FIG. 6.4. Stanford 9 Test Results–Changes in Percentile Rank 1997–98 Academic Year)

Figure 6.4 shows the changes in percentile rank for each demonstration school in both math and reading. Although the CFL demonstration schools were still below the 50th percentile (based on Stanford 9's national norm) in both reading an math, significant progress was made in all schools. The mean scores for students from four demonstration schools moved from the bottom fourth to close to the 50th percentile. This included the two schools that began the year with percentiles in the low teens.

Degree of Implementation and Student Achievement

One central concern about the effectiveness of any innovative program is whether program implementation leads to improved student achievement. Toward this end, a correlational analysis of the degree of program implementation and student achievement across the CFL demonstration schools was performed. The correlation was found to be statistically significant at $p < .001$.

Comparative Analysis of Student Achievement Based on Performance Standards Established by Stanford 9

Two sets of comparative analyses of student achievement were conducted. The first examined the changes in the percentage of students in CFL demonstration schools whose scores fell within each of the four performance standards as measured by the Stanford 9 achievement test in reading and math. The percentage of positive progress made by students between fall and spring testings was analyzed to examine: (a) the change in the distribution patterns of the achievement scores across the four performance standards levels for each school, (b) the change in the distribution pattern for students whose scores placed them at the bottom 20% based on the fall 1997 testing, (c) the change in the distribution pattern for students whose scores fell within the middle 60% range based on the fall 1997 testing, and (d) the change in the distribution pattern for students whose scores fell in the top 20% based on the fall 1997 testing.

The second set of analyses focused on comparing student progress across the four performance standards for students attending the CFL demonstration schools and students attending other targeted assistance schools.

Student Achievement Patterns in CFL Demonstration Schools

Student progress in math and reading is summarized in Tables 6.5 and 6.6, respectively. As shown in Table 6.5, for example, although the schools varied in the amount of progress made, a pattern of positive progress was reflected in the results across all four performance standards in math achievement by all six CFL school. The math test results listed under the "All Students" section in Table 6.5 show, for example:

TABLE 6.5
Stanford 9 Math Test Results
Performance Standards Levels

Performance	School																	
	School A			School B			School C			School D			School E			School F		
	Fall	Spring	Change	Fall	Spring	Change	Fall	Spring	Change	Fall	Spring	Change	Fall	Spring	Change	Fall	Spring	Change
All Students																		
Below Basic	52.5	36.6	-15.9	69.4	63.0	-6.4	56.8	44.8	-12.0	72.8	61.1	-11.7	74.9	37.9	-37.9	60.0	38.2	-21.8
Basic	41.4	40.1	-1.3	28.6	32.2	3.6	36.7	35.8	-0.9	25.5	32.2	6.7	23.6	37.4	13.8	34.6	45.9	11.3
Proficient	6.1	18.3	12.2	1.9	4.8	2.9	5.0	19.4	14.4	1.7	5.7	4.0	1.5	18.2	16.7	4.4	13.0	8.6
Advanced	0.0	5.1	5.1				1.5	0.0	-1.5	0.0	1.0	1.0	0.0	6.6	6.6	1.0	2.9	1.9
Bottom 20%																		
Below Basic	100.0	100.0	0.0	100.0	100.0	0.0	100.0	100.0	0.0	100.0	100.0	0.0	100.0	76.9	-23.1	100.0	100.0	0.0
Basic													0.0	10.3	10.3			
Proficient													0.0	2.6	2.6			
Advanced													0.0	10.3	10.3			
Middle 60%																		
Below Basic	53.4	28.3	-25.1	81.0	71.2	-9.8	62.8	40.0	-22.8	83.3	68.3	-15.0	85.1	38.1	-47.0	64.7	29.8	-34.9
Basic	46.6	65.8	19.2	19.0	28.8	9.8	37.2	56.0	18.8	16.7	31.7	15.0	14.9	58.5	43.6	35.3	67.7	32.4
Proficient	0.0	5.8	5.8				0.0	4.0	4.0				0.0	3.4	3.4	0.0	2.4	2.4
Advanced																		
Top 20%																		
Below Basic				4.9	0.0	-4.9				12.3	0.0	-12.3	22.0	0.0	-22.0			
Basic	69.2	0.0	-69.2	85.4	74.4	-11.0	65.8	5.6	-60.2	79.0	65.5	-13.5	70.7	2.4	-68.3	72.5	26.8	-45.7
Proficient	30.8	74.4	43.6	9.8	25.6	15.8	26.3	94.4	68.1	8.8	29.3	20.5	7.3	75.6	68.3	22.5	58.5	36.0
Advanced	0.0	25.6	25.6				7.9	0.0	-7.9	0.0	5.2	5.2	0.0	22.0	22.0	5.0	14.6	9.6

TABLE 6.6
Stanford 9 Reading Test Results
Performance Standards Levels

Performance	School																	
	School A			School B			School C			School D			School E			School F		
	Fall	Spring	Change	Fall	Spring	Change	Fall	Spring	Change	Fall	Spring	Change	Fall	Spring	Change	Fall	Spring	Change
All Students																		
Below Basic	34.8	22.5	-12.3	59.9	61.2	1.3	50.5	28.6	-21.9	59.8	55.7	-4.1	62.6	35.9	-26.7	38.3	34.7	-3.6
Basic	45.1	48.9	3.8	31.7	32.4	0.7	33.2	42.4	9.0	32.0	36.9	4.9	28.6	44.1	15.5	46.8	46.8	0.0
Proficient	19.0	20.9	12.2	7.2	5.9	-1.3	14.2	21.9	7.7	7.7	7.4	-0.3	8.8	18.2	9.4	12.8	15.8	3.0
Advanced	1.1	7.7	5.1	1.2	0.6	-0.6	2.1	7.3	5.2	0.4	0.0	-0.4	0.0	1.8	1.8	2.1	2.9	0.5
Bottom 20%																		
Below Basic	100.0	100.0	0.0	100.0	100.0	0.0	100.0	100.0	0.0	100.0	100.0	0.0	100.0	88.2	-11.8	100.0	100.0	0.0
Basic													0.0	8.8	8.8			
Proficient													0.0	2.9	2.9			
Advanced																		
Middle 60%																		
Below Basic	26.6	4.6	-22.0	63.4	69.5	6.1	51.7	14.4	-37.3	100.0	88.2	-11.8	69.1	30.4	-38.7	28.8	25.2	-3.6
Basic	69.0	80.9	11.9	36.6	30.5	-6.1	48.3	68.6	20.3	0.0	8.8	8.8	30.9	67.6	36.7	71.2	73.9	2.7
Proficient	4.4	14.6	10.2				0.0	17.0	17.0	0.0	2.9		0.0	2.0	2.0	0.0	0.9	0.9
Advanced																		
Top 20%																		
Below Basic																		
Basic	13.5	0.0	-13.5	57.6	67.6	10.0	18.4	0.0	-18.4	60.4	62.0	1.6	55.9	8.8	-47.1	24.3	10.5	
Proficient	81.1	61.1	-20.0	36.4	29.4	-7.0	71.0	61.1	-9.9	37.7	38.0	0.3	44.1	82.4	38.3	64.9	76.3	11.4
Advanced	5.4	38.9	33.5	6.1	2.9	-3.2	10.5	38.9	28.4	1.9	0.0	-1.9	0.0	8.8	8.8	10.8	13.2	2.4

- A decrease in the percentage of students who scored in the below-basic performance level for the spring testing compared to fall testing (e.g., School E showed the greatest decrease in the percent of students who scored at the below-basic level—a decrease of 37%. School B, which showed the least gain among the six schools, showed a decrease of 6.4% in the below-basic level).

- An increase in the percentage of students who scored in the basic, proficient, and advanced levels (e.g., 63.5% of students in School A scored at the basic performance level or above during the spring testing, compared to 47.5% during the fall testing).

Another finding in the pattern of progress in student achievement in math and reading was the gains made by students who scored at the top 20% across all CFL demonstration schools. All students in the top 20% of each school were performing at the basic performance level or higher for both math (see Table 6.5) and reading (see Table 6.6). In fact, many of these students were performing at the proficient or advanced levels (for math, e.g., 100% of the top 20% of the students performed at the proficient or advanced level for School A; 95% for School B; 94% for School C; 34.5% for School D; 97.6% for School E; and 73.1% for School F).

The significant progress made by students in the top 20% was reflective of the design focus of the CFL program. A major lack in education reform programs that aim to improve student achievement in schools with a high concentration of children from economically and educationally disadvantaged backgrounds is a deliberate strategy for nurturing the academic talents of children at the top range of the achievement distribution. Improvement efforts to increase student achievement tend to focus on the lower levels of student achievement. A key design principle of CFL is the ability of staff to adaptively respond to the diverse learning needs of all students, including those at both the bottom and the top range of the achievement distribution. All students should be provided with the most powerful instruction and learning opportunities to ensure maximum progress in achieving educational success.

Figure 6.5 shows the pattern of achievement for mathematics across the four performance levels for fall and spring testing. As shown in Figure 6.5, whereas 65.1% of the students attending the CFL demonstration schools were performing at the below-basic performance level at

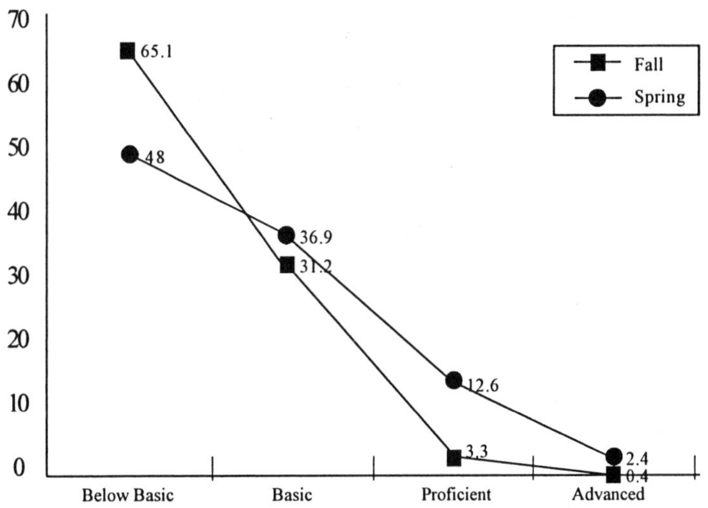

FIG. 6.5. Progress Patterns Across Stanford 9 Performance Levels for Math (CFL Schools, 1997–98 Academic Year)

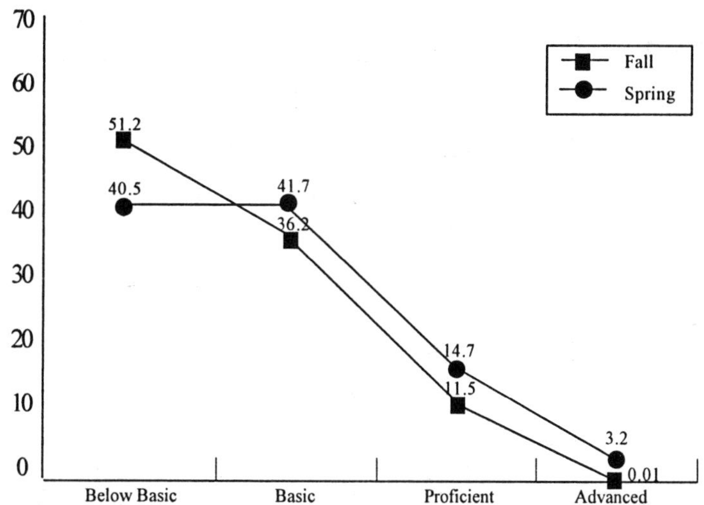

FIG. 6.6. Progress Patterns Across Stanford 9 Performance Levels for Reading (CFL Schools, 1997–98 Academic Year)

TABLE 6.7
Comparison of Student Performance Between CFL and Other Targeted Assistance Schools*
Stanford 9 Math Test Results: Performance Standards Levels (1997–1998 Academic Year)

	Percent of Students					
	CFL Schools			Other Targeted Assistance Schools		
Performance Standards	Fall	Spring	Change	Fall	Spring	Change
All Students						
Below Basic	65.1	48.0	-17.1	57.8	42.6	-15.2
Basic	31.2	36.9	5.7	35.9	38.6	2.7
Proficient	3.3	12.6	9.3	5.7	16.3	10.6
Advanced	0.4	2.4	2.0	0.5	2.5	2.0
Percent Positive Changes			34.1			30.5
Bottom 20%						
Below Basic	100.0	96.4	-3.6	99.6	994	-0.2
Basic	0.0	1.6	1.6	0.4	0.6	0.2
Proficient	0.0	0.4	0.4			
Advanced	0.0	1.6	1.6			
Middle 60%						
Below Basic	72.8	48.0	-24.8	61.9	38.1	-23.8
Basic	27.2	49.6	22.4	38.1	57.4	19.3
Proficient	0.0	2.4	2.4	0.0	4.5	4.5
Advanced						
Top20%						
Below Basic	7.0	0.0	-7.0	3.6	0.0	-3.6
Basic	74.2	31.9	-42.3	64.9	19.3	-45.6
Proficient	16.8	57.1	40.3	28.8	68.4	39.6
Advanced	2.0	11.0	9.0	2.6	12.4	9.8

* Targeted assistance schools are schools designated by the school district as low-performing schools requiring "special intervention" to significantly improve student achievement. CFL schools were identified as the lowest performing schools (Level I targeted assistance) among the targeted assistance schools.

TABLE 6.8
Comparison of Student Performance Between CFL and Other Targeted Assistance Schools*
Stanford 9 Reading Test Results: Performance Standards Levels (1997–1998 Academic Year)

	Percent of Students					
	CFL Schools			Other Targeted Assistance Schools		
Performance Standards	Fall	Spring	Change	Fall	Spring	Change
All Students						
Below Basic	51.2	40.5	-10.7	39.3	30.3	-9.0
Basic	36.2	41.7	5.5	45.0	49.3	4.3
Proficient	11.5	14.7	3.2	14.3	18.2	3.9
Advanced	1.1	3.2	2.1	1.5	2.2	0.7
Percent Positive Changes			21.5			17.9
Bottom 20%						
Below Basic	100.0	98.2	-1.8	99.2	95.4	-3.8
Basic	0.0	1.3	1.3	0.8	4.6	3.8
Proficient	0.0	0.4	0.4			
Advanced						
Middle 60%						
Below Basic	52.1	35.1	-17.0	32.4	18.5	-13.9
Basic	47.2	59.4	12.2	64.5	74.4	9.9
Proficient	0.7	5.5	4.8	3.1	7.1	4.0
Advanced						
Top20%						
Below Basic						
Basic	39.2	26.8	-12.4	30.0	17.7	-12.3
Proficient	55.2	57.0	1.8	62.6	70.9	8.3
Advanced	5.6	16.2	10.6	7.4	11.3	3.9

* Targeted assistance schools are schools designated by the school district as low-performing schools requiring "special intervention" to significantly improve student achievement. CFL schools were identified as the lowest performing schools (Level I targeted assistance) among the targeted assistance schools.

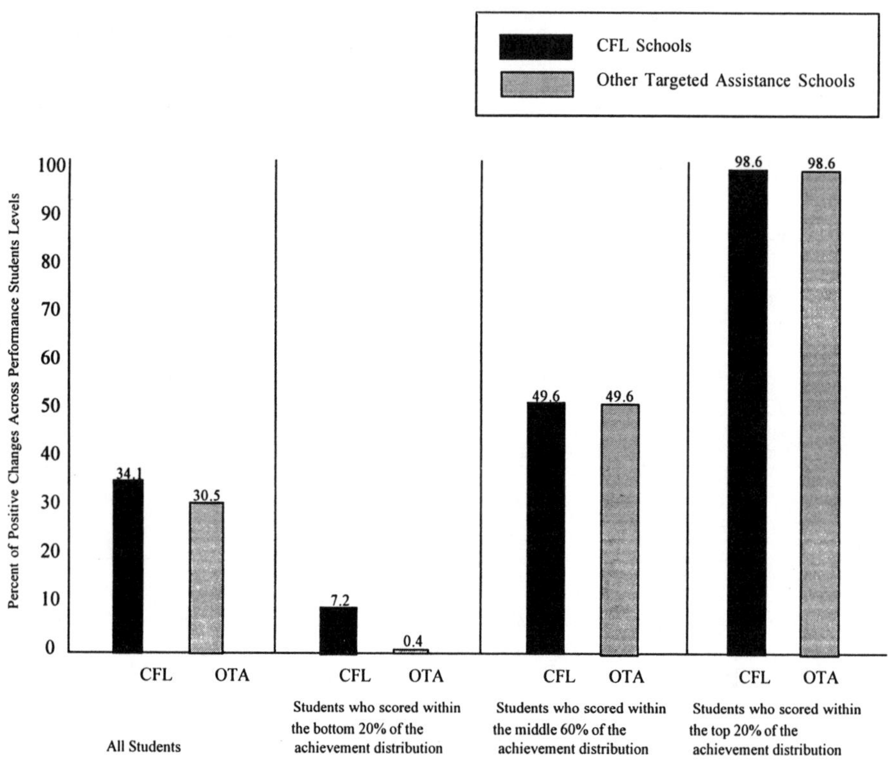

FIG. 6.7. Comparisons of Mean Percent of Positive Changes Across the Four Categories of Performance Standards Between CFL and Other Targeted Assistance Schools Stanford 9 Math Test (Fall 1997–Spring 1998)

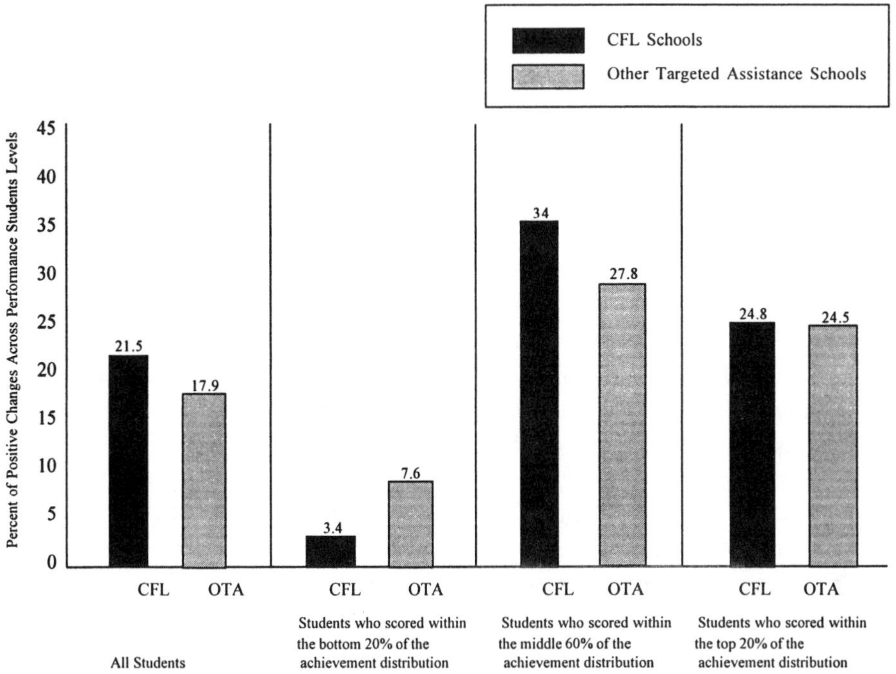

FIG. 6.8. Comparisons of Mean Percent of Positive Changes Across the Four Categories of Performance Standards Between CFL and Other Targeted Assistance Schools Stanford 9 Reading Test (Fall 1997–Spring 1998)

the beginning of the school year, 52% were achieving at the basic performance level of achievement or higher at the end of the school year. Also, whereas only 3.7% of students were performing at the proficient and advanced levels across the CFL schools, 15% of the students were performing at the proficient and advanced performance levels.

Table 6.6 shows the student achievement patterns in reading. A similar overall pattern of improvements in reading was achieved across all schools. More students moved from the below-basic performance level to more advanced levels of performance.

As shown in Figure 6.6, a similar pattern of changes was observed in reading achievement for students attending the CFL demonstration schools. Figure 6.6 shows a decrease from more than half of the students performing at the below-basic level in reading at the beginning of the school year to 60% performing at the basic level of performance and higher at the end of the year. Also at the end of the school year, approximately 18% of the students attending CFL demonstration schools were achieving at the advanced performance level compared to 11.6%.

Tables 6.7 and 6.8 show the results of a comparative analysis of the changes in student progress across the four performance standards levels assessed by Stanford 9. The mean change in the percentage of students who scored at each of the four levels in the CFL demonstration schools and the other targeted assistance schools were compared across the following categories: (a) all students, (b) students whose fall 1997 scores are in the bottom 20% of the distribution of the achievement scores in their respective schools, (c) students whose fall scores were in the middle 60% range, and (d) students whose fall scores were in the top 20% range.

As shown in Figures 6.7 and 6.8, CFL students made greater positive changes across all performance standards levels in math (Fig. 6.7) and across all levels in reading (Fig. 6.8). The mean percent of positive changes for the CFL demonstration schools for math was 34.1%, whereas the mean positive percent of positive change for the other targeted assistance schools was 30.5%. For reading, the CFL demonstration schools on average made a 21.5% positive change, compared to a mean of 17.9% for the other targeted assistance schools.

CONCLUSION

The findings from the Year 2 implementation of the project confirmed the complexity of implementing and maintaining school reform efforts in large, urban school systems with a high concentration of students from economically and educationally disadvantaged circumstances, including high levels of student mobility and turnover rates of teachers and principals.

Despite the seemingly insurmountable odds, the progress in program implementation and student outcomes that was achieved during the first year of the project's implementation was maintained and continued to progress in each participating school. All six schools met the District standard of achievement gains and showed greater achievement gains than the other District-designated targeted assistance schools.

In addition to the outcome data presented, the overall climate of the schools changed. The children's learning was displayed on every wall. Students were bursting to open their classroom doors to visitors, and the principals and teachers were visibly elated by the results of their efforts.

The ability of the CFL demonstration schools to maintain the initial gains they made during Year 1 of the program, in spite of the turbulent start and implementation challenges the schools faced, was particularly noteworthy. The resilience of the school staff to overcome the many challenges they face in bringing about changes in the learning of children in their schools was indeed encouraging. Nevertheless, though the "value added" analysis of improvement and the continuous upward trend in student achievement patterns was impressive, particularly in light of the continuing pattern of decline prior to CFL implementation, developing strategies to provide the support required to ensure high achievement standards that were comparable to the national and regional norms remained a challenge.

DISCUSSION

The DC story described in this chapter is one example of what can be expected when systematic attention is attributed to the lessons from decades of research and practical applications. The remarkable transformations of the six schools described in this chapter were no miracles. What have we learned from the DC experience? The two most salient ingredients to their implementation successes were: (a) focusing on each student's learning needs and tailoring the instructional program to address them, and (b) using a school's (and a community's) strengths instead of focusing solely on what is broken. Although these are key elements in many other comprehensive school reform programs (Wang, Haertel, & Walberg, 1998), what distinguished the DC implementation was what it did not do:

- Thrust a different curriculum on the school.
- Throw out everything old in favor of something new.
- Hire hordes of new staff.

Instead of starting from scratch, they used the schools' resources—financial, human, and instructional capital—preserving what worked and supplementing with improved practices. They built elements that reinforced each teacher's competence, which helped sustain the changes and continued to keep the momentum.

One flaw in some promising school reform programs is their dependence on the skills and charisma of a uniquely inspiring individual. Leadership is indisputably essential for reform to succeed, but programs must be able to replicate even without a colossus at their helm. If all teachers and staff members receive ongoing professional development, and feedback to build their competence, then they as individuals—and thus the whole institution—become more resilient. With this strength embedded in the school, improvements can be sustained through personnel changes, budget problems, student population shifts—all inevitable stresses faced by schools in communities with high concentration of families living in poverty.

Schools that do the best job of bolstering resilience and academic success among their students share similar critical features, as evidenced in the six DC Schools described in this chapter. They all hold high expectations for student success, employ effective classroom management practices, offer feedback to students with praise, help teachers use powerful strategies that tailor instruction to the individual learning needs of the students, provide a professional climate and supportive working conditions, and stress a learner-centered approach to foster students' problem-solving skills and their ability to be responsible for their learning and behavior. They also recognize that factors that breed confidence and competence are not only found in schools, but also within the family, among peers, and in the community, all of which can be strengthened by what goes on in schools.

What is needed to turn low-performing schools around is restoration, not new construction. We can work with the features and structures that are already in place, making needed changes to achieve the vision of stronger and more functional schools with systemic improvements. It has taken a long time and a great deal of research to build a successful reform prototype. With the knowledge on how to replicate effective prototype reform approaches, a high degree of implementation can result in significant improvements in student achievement and, significantly, they can occur during the same academic year the program is put in place—the turnaround that the six DC Schools were able to demonstrate; genuine improvement does not need to take years.

REFERENCES

McComb, B. (1999). *Evaluation of the CFL program: Based on the learner-centered principles developed by the American Psychological Association.* Denver, CO: University of Denver, Denver Research Institute.

Oates, J., Flores, R., & Weishew, N. (1998). Achieving student success in inner-city schools is possible, provided... *Research in Middle Level Education Quarterly, 21*(3), 51–62.

Wang, M. C. (1992). *Adaptive education strategies: Building on diversity.* Baltimore, MD: Paul H. Brookes Publishing Co.

Wang, M. C. (1998). *The Community for Learning program: A planning guide.* Philadelphia: Temple University Center for Research in Human Development and Education.

Wang, M. C., Haertel, G. D., & Walberg, H. J. (1998). Models of reform: A comparative guide. *Educational Leadership, 55*(7), 66–71.

Wang, M. C., Oates, J., & Weishew, N. (1995). Effective school responses to student diversity in inner-city schools: A coordinated approach. *Education and Urban Society, 27*(4), 484–503.

Wang, M. C., & Zollers, N. J. (1990). Adaptive instruction: An alternative service delivery approach. *Remedial and Special Education, 11*(1), 7–21.

Appendix A

The Community for Learning Program: A Synopsis

by
Margaret C. Wang
Laboratory for Student Success at Temple University Center for Research in Human Development and Education

Nothing can be counted as progress in a community until its children and youth are well served and show healthy development and steady, sustained advances in learning. When children and youth lack the care they need, when they see too little progress and promise in their own lives as well as in their families and neighborhoods, they lose hope and motivation for schooling success. Such is the sad story of many students in our nation's schools, where disinvestment of all kinds—economic, professional, and social—is the pattern. There is simply no justification for inaction in the face of this serious deterioration in the lives and learning opportunities of so many of our children and youth.

But this view is only part of the entire picture. Despite various difficulties, many children and youth manage to rise above their problems and mature into healthy, competent, well-educated adults who lead productive lives. Children are remarkably resilient; they respond readily to caring adults and a supportive community. If only we can find the means to magnify the "positives" in the life of every child, we can rekindle the hope for transforming education into a system that fosters the educational resilience and learning success of the diverse students in our nation's schools.

This concern for improving the prospects for educational success and life circumstances of children and families sparked the design and implementation of the Community for Learning program at the Laboratory for Student Success, the Mid-Atlantic Regional Educational Laboratory at Temple University Center for Research in Human Development and Education.

A Call to Action

Schools must remain the primary focus of all efforts to improve our capacity for education, for other efforts will surely come to naught if schools fail to offer powerful forms of instruction to ensure high standards of academic outcomes for all students. However, significant learning also occurs outside of the school; indeed, the conditions for learning both in school and outside are established both at home and in the community. Thus, the search for answers to the fundamental question, "What conditions are required to cause massive improvements in the learning of this nation's children and youth?" must embrace families and all elements of the community.

In improving our capacity for achieving student success, insights drawn from many disciplines and professions and collaboration among a wide range of public and private institutions are required to link the work of schools with all other learning environments, including homes, libraries, museums, the workplace, higher learning institutions, and other public and private sector establishments. Education programs conducted in these environments are coordinated with community revitalization efforts to create a broad-based commitment to improved learning and competence of all children and the adults who serve them—*in short, a Community for Learning.*

A Framework for Program Delivery

Figure 1 is a schematic representation of an integrated framework for the design and implementation of the Community for Learning program. The nascent Community for Learning reflects the educational goals as operationalized through site-specific program design elements being implemented in the schools and connected with a wide range of learning opportunities in varied environments, including the school, the home, and the community. Although it is anticipated that the Community for Learning will vary across sites based on site-specific needs and capacity, the various components shown here comprise the core design elements of the Community for Learning program.

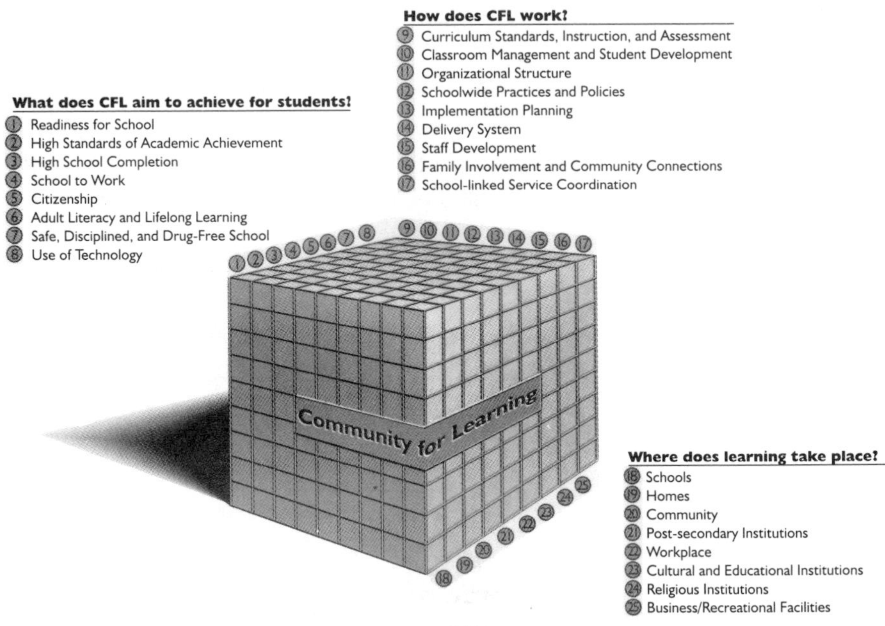

FIG. 1. The Community for Learning Program: Program Goals, Design Elements, and Learning Environments.

A centerpiece of the Community for Learning program, as shown in Figure 1, is the integrated framework for a collaborative process of uniting people and resources in initiating schoolwide restructuring efforts to ensure student success. At its most effective, the process strengthens the school's capacity to mobilize and redeploy community and school resources to support the implementation of a comprehensive, coordinated, inclusive approach to service delivery.

Key Program Components

The Community for Learning program consists of the following key program components that address the learning needs of the students, the organizational and administrative support requirements for achieving a high degree of program implementation, and the staff development needs of the school staff and related service providers:

- A site-specific implementation plan that takes into account the school's program improvement needs, the learning characteristics and needs of the students, staff expertise and staffing patterns, curricular standards and assessment, and other implementation-related concerns.

- A schoolwide organizational structure that supports a teaming process by involving regular and specialist teachers in the planning and delivery of instruction in regular classroom settings.

- A data-based staff development program that provides ongoing training and technical assistance tailored to meet the needs of the individual staff and program implementation requirements.

- An instructional-learning management system that focuses on developing student self-responsibility for behavior and learning progress.

- An integrated assessment-instruction process that provides an individualized learning plan for each student, utilizing multiple approaches like whole-class and small-group instruction, as well as one-on-one tutoring, based on an ongoing analysis of student needs, resources, and expediency.

- A family and community involvement plan that aims to enhance communication between the school and families and to forge a shared responsibility partnership and community connections to achieve schooling success of every student.

- A school-linked comprehensive, coordinated health and human services delivery program that focuses on the wellness and learning success of each student.

How the Community for Learning Program Impacts Student Learning

Implementation of the Community for Learning Program impacts three major areas of student outcomes: (a) improved academic achievement of all students, including and particularly those at the margins; (b) patterns of active learning and teaching processes that are consistent with the research base on effective practices; and (c) positive attitudes by students and staff toward their school, and, most importantly, the expectation that every student has the capacity for educational success.

Findings from implementation studies in a variety of inner-city school settings to date show a positive pattern of changes in student achievement. Community for Learning students consistently outperform comparison students in both reading and math, and show more positive attitudes about learning and their classroom and school environments when compared with students in nonprogram schools. Students in the Community for Learning Program also tend to perceive better and more constructive feedback from teachers about their work and behaviors; hold higher aspiration for academic learning; have a better academic self-concept; and more clearly understand the rules of behavior and class/school operations. Data also show that Community for Learning families and communities become increasingly active in a wide range of school activities and in the decision-making process.

Expected Outcomes

A major expected outcome of the implementation of the Community for Learning Program is the development and demonstration of a capacity-building process for establishing a restructured school organization that strengthens, mobilizes, and redeploys school, family, and community resources to implement and institutionalize a coordinated system of education and related service delivery. The focus is on breaking down artificial barriers within the school and across the multiple service-providing agencies to ensure the healthy development and educational success of every student. The premise is that a strong effort toward these ends will require collaboration and focused work performed on a scale never previously attempted.

Many students have difficulty achieving schooling success and need better help than they are now receiving. If all students are to successfully complete a basic education through equal access to a common curriculum, the way schools respond to diverse student needs must undergo major conceptual and structural changes. Improvement efforts must consider the learning context and require broad collaboration and coordination among educational professionals. The Community for Learning Program provides a delivery framework that mandates a coherent and coordinated system of service delivery emphasizing rooted connections with the family and the community in the service of the students.

No single approach or practice can achieve the magnitude of improvements required. Of critical importance is the way in which successful practices are combined in an integrated system of delivery that considers the needs of the students, site-specific strengths and constraints, the professional development needs of the school and other service-provider staff, and alignment of resources, policy, and administrative support. Poorly implemented versions of demonstrably successful practices are unlikely to achieve dramatic outcomes. Furthermore, some practices that work well in some settings and with some students may not have the same effects with others. Nonetheless, the research base and practical knowledge on implementing the Community for Learning approach as a systemic strategy for achieving student success provide a promising basis for formulating improvement that is both strategic and site-specific.

— Margaret C. Wang, Executive Director

For more information about the Community for Learning program, contact Tina Caldwell, Director of Information Services.

Laboratory for Student Success
The Mid-Atlantic Regional Educational Laboratory at Temple
University Center for Research in Human Development and Education
1301 Cecil B. Moore Avenue
Philadelphia, PA 19122-6091
Tel: 800-892-5550; Fax: 215-204-5130
E-mail: lss@vm.temple.edu; Web: http://www.temple.edu/LSS

7

Redefining Success: The San Antonio Case

Diana Lam[1]
Providence School Department

In a *Harvard Business Review* article, "From Affirmative Action to Affirming Diversity," Roosevelt Thomas (1990) noted that "mistakes at the cutting edge are different—and potentially more valuable—than mistakes elsewhere" (p. 117). He argued that people on the cutting edge "need some kind of pioneer training. But at the very least they need to be told they are pioneers, that conflicts and failures come with the territory, and that they will be judged accordingly" (p. 117).

At the height of the polio epidemic in the United States, there was a great deal of debate and dissent over which direction future research should take. At the time, there was not yet a clear understanding of how polio was transmitted. There was naturally a great concern for those stricken with polio, particularly children, and tremendous efforts were made to find new ways to ameliorate their suffering.

The prevailing treatment was the use of the iron lung, and it was here that the debate raged within the professional field and among the public. Should scarce dollars be directed toward improving—hopefully perfecting—the iron lung or should funds go into research that may or may not yield a vaccine? Development of the vaccine by Jonas Salk and his colleagues was the first breakthrough after many years of research. A successful public education campaign for the vaccine's acceptance and use was the second breakthrough, making iron lungs obsolete.

In education today, we get sidetracked by a similar debate over restructuring schools. Are we focusing our energies on building better iron lungs or are we being creative and persistent in designing and testing new solutions to old problems? In education, much of what we need to know has already been researched; in a sense, we already have the vaccine. The challenge is to apply new methods—getting a whole industry to dismantle production and promotion of iron lungs—and to gain parental and professional acceptance of new approaches in light of current research.

Dr. Salk was one of the first people to take the vaccine, leading other brave persons to participate in the first drug-efficacy trials. They sincerely believed, because they did not know otherwise, that they could be risking their lives. The naysayers wondered if it was worth the risk because medical treatment had advanced to a point where—thanks to the iron lung—people did not die of polio.

Taking a risk for a purpose beyond one's personal gain presupposes a compelling rationale for one's actions, which are not in any obvious sense in one's self-interest. Restructuring schools is not in any obvious sense in one's self-interest; it means more time, more work, and a greater chance of personal and professional failure. So why do we take the risk? In San Antonio, it is because we want to free children from even the most sparkly, shiny, and technologically advanced iron lungs that we have.

Helen Keller said that she always considered her birthday March 5 rather than the day she was born because it was on that day that she met Annie Sullivan, her teacher, and she equated that with being her soul's birthday (Lash, 1981). This is the sole purpose of restructuring: to create structures whereby those meetings and the rich relationships between teachers and students are celebrated as "birthdays of the soul." It is for this vision of education that we are working so hard in the San Antonio Independent School District (ISD).

More than any other organization, a school district must draw upon and encourage each person's capacity to learn. Our mission of education is one that requires us to think about learning, not only for our students but also for the teachers and administrators who work with them. To this end, we believe our district must offer rewarding opportunities that allow our students, our community, and members of our organization to be lifelong learners.

Beginning in 1994, the San Antonio ISD engaged in a quest for academic excellence and sustained student learning. The experience of engaging in change—whether attitudinal or behavioral—can be jarring and unbalancing. Even when an approach does not work, our impulse is to stick with it simply because we know what to expect; we cling to our mastery, even when it is dysfunctional. Though change can be exhilarating and energizing, we recognize that it can also be frightening and chilling. Change almost always initially involves extra work and certainly involves taking a risk—the risk that we may fail or appear foolish.

Change is often difficult and children and adults striving to change need support in their efforts. Thriving on change is a major characteristic of systems that work well. Every healthy organization is dynamic, changing, growing, evaluating its performance, and assessing strengths and areas of improvement. Organizations that do not change stagnate. We chose growth, and with that choice came the full responsibility of evaluating our programs, monitoring compliance with school laws, and reviewing the performance of people and programs.

For a very long time, we did not believe that all children could learn. The expectations were low for poor and minority children, voices were not raised, and there were no protests when almost half of our schools were identified as low-performing. We decided, however, to change this and to face the future with an ambitious agenda that puts children and their learning first. We committed ourselves to a fundamental shift in how we viewed our school system. Every decision flows from this premise: The school system exists to support students' learning and growth. Those closest to students, namely their teachers and their parents, are the adults the school system must primarily support. We mean to educate the children well, so that their years in the San Antonio ISD will be springboards to a lifetime of learning, achievement, and service.

This chapter relates the changes and struggles we have undergone to provide the children and adolescents of San Antonio with a quality education. It tells of our systemic school district reform focused on student learning and achievement, and of our efforts to strengthen parental and community involvement, to improve communication and collaboration, build an infrastructure for professional development for teaching and learning, and provide appropriate school facilities.

In order to achieve systemic reform in an organization, one must have a vision of the organization's future. Getting to that vision is not simple. It requires that the old system be restructured, the old ways of doing things be reformed, and the new ways of doing things be so different that individuals are forced to change their behaviors. In *Transitions,* William Bridges (1991) talked about three stages of the change process:

the ending, the neutral zone, and the beginning. In systemic reform, the challenge is to push changes in the organization and its culture as quickly as possible into the neutral zone. The neutral zone is a particularly unsettling stage because the organization can no longer go back, yet everyone is fearful of moving forward. The leader must care deeply about the changes in order to take the system through the tough, unpopular struggle of culture change. The change effort must become a crusade so that all participants are willing to let go of the past in order to move beyond the neutral zone. Only then will the system become committed to a new beginning that embraces the new vision of the system.

San Antonio is known for The Alamo, "the cradle of Texas Liberty," and for its historic missions, beautiful river walk, and annual *Fiesta.* We are doing our best in the San Antonio ISD to make the city famous for its high-achieving students as well. Our district includes 97 square miles in the heart of the city. Our student population of 61,000 students is 85% Hispanic, 10% African American, and 5% other. Approximately 92% of our students come from low-income families, 16% have limited English proficiency, and 10% receive special education services.

With these demographic characteristics, it was not surprising that in 1994, student academic achievement in the district consistently ranked below the state average in all areas of testing. All public school districts in the state use the Texas Assessment of Academic Skills (TAAS), a state-mandated test for Grades 3 through 8 and Grade 10, (Exit) in mathematics and reading and Grades 4 and 8, (Exit) in writing. The TAAS is a high-stakes achievement test—a student must pass all the three parts of the exit-level test before he or she can graduate from high school. In 1994, the percent of students across the district mastering the TAAS in writing was 60.8%, in reading 56.2%, and in mathematics 34.8%. The first time our students took the end-of-course algebra test, only 3% passed compared to the state's 17% average. In biology, 38% passed compared to the state's 84% average. Consider the following:

- In all three areas, San Antonio was 20 to 25 points below the state average on the TAAS tests.
- Student attendance was 94.2%.
- The student dropout rate was 5.5%, considered high enough for the district to have received an "unacceptable" rating from the State of Texas.

- Less than 5% of the seniors in the district met the state criteria for performance on the SAT and ACT.
- Student test scores were so low that 42 of the 94 schools in the district were rated as low-performing by the state in 1994. At that time low-performing meant that fewer than 20% of the students in the school passed the state examinations. Several schools were in the single digits.

San Antonio ISD was also a school district riddled with self-doubt and a school culture that was conservative and traditional. The organizational culture of the district had a long-established hierarchical structure, deeply entrenched practices, and very narrow and rigid job descriptions. An independent audit described the district structure as inefficient, bureaucratic, and plagued with communication gaps. Accountability was insufficient and the mechanisms for ensuring it were either lacking or unclear. The district espoused the rhetoric of wanting more parental involvement, but was only minimally receptive of parents who desired to become involved. The opportunities for employees to engage in personal and professional growth were limited.

Today, San Antonio is a school district in transition. We have accomplished much in recent years in our quest for academic excellence, but at this point we are a long way from our destination. The transitions give some idea of where we are going and where we want to be:

- We are a district moving from *the education of some students* to *a commitment to educate all children*. In the past, it was acceptable for students to fall through the cracks, to drop out and enter the work force or the military. In today's society, this is no longer a viable option. We must educate all children through graduation to ensure that they will lead a productive, meaningful life.
- *The role of principals is changing from building manager to instructional leader*. For years in San Antonio, principals were trained to be good administrators and managers. Our emphasis today is on instructional leadership. We expect the principal to know the curriculum, recognize good instructional practices and programs, and be familiar with student achievement data to provide direction and make sound instructional decisions. Administrative and managerial skills are

important, but instructional leadership is critical for student success.

- *The role of teachers is changing from working in isolation to working as members of teams.* The days when a teacher could close the door and teach in isolation are ending. Teachers work in teams examining data, discussing reform designs, and sharing teaching strategies. They also work together on implementing the content standards and aligning the curriculum from one grade to another and from class to class. Teachers are discovering that group learning is rewarding and that working together takes advantage of the collective thinking and wisdom of the group.
- *The San Antonio community is beginning to change from being dormant and compliant to engaged and active.* For many years, although everyone criticized San Antonio ISD for low test scores and high dropout rates, the community at large showed little interest in joining with the district to change the situation. In recent years, the district and its schools have encouraged parents, community members, businesses, and others to join efforts to improve student learning. The response has been positive although we still do not have a fully active, engaged community.
- *The business community has moved from ignoring the district to being very supportive of its efforts.* Business leaders, community leaders, city government, community action groups, and even parent organizations were either disinterested or devoted their time and resources to activities unrelated to student achievement. They provided annual financial support by paying their property taxes, but showed very little commitment or emotional support. Last year, business and community leaders took the initiative in our bond election and they continue to be supportive of our efforts to increase student achievement. They realize that well-educated students who graduate from high school and college are the foundation of a strong economy in San Antonio.
- Finally, *we are shifting from having little or no accountability to accountability for student learning.* In the past, it was convenient to blame others for low student achievement. No one was accountable or, even worse, everyone was ac-

> countable (with no means of ensuring accountability). The mechanisms for ensuring accountability are now in place, and this is fostering a new attitude that everyone is responsible for student learning.

Where is San Antonio ISD today? In the period 1994–1998, the district made modest increases in student achievement in reading and writing and significant gains in mathematics.

In reading, the percentage of students mastering the TAAS test increased by 15.5% to 71.7%. In writing, the gain was 14.9%; in 1998, 75.7% of our students mastered the writing TAAS test. Our greatest gains were in mathematics—since 1994, district scores increased 30.6%. As of 1998, 65.4% of our students mastering the math TAAS test. During this same period, the student dropout rate declined from 5.5% to 1.6%. (See Fig. 7.1.)

What did we do during this 4-year period to make this happen?

We faced two types of challenges in San Antonio. First, we faced cultural challenges—changing the organizational culture and belief system, raising expectations, and sharing accountability for results. We also faced challenges that involved changes in the system: alignment of improvement initiatives, adjustment of policies and practices to support redesign, reallocation of resources, shared decision making, and building capacity.

We set out to create the conditions in the district and in schools that need to be present to ensure teacher and student success. Often it is hard to describe the support structure that makes possible the kind of improvement that we have made. It is sometimes useful to think about it as scaffolding—planks of wood assembled in a way that makes it possible to reach great heights. We are climbing together in San Antonio ISD to create something new. It would be easy to take scaffolding for granted because it's not very glamorous; it is behind-the-scenes work, convening meetings, sharing ideas and resources, keeping focused, demanding accountability, asking the tough questions, and not being afraid to make difficult decisions. It is providing the kind of leadership that inspires others to achieve sustained student success.

Some of the first planks of the scaffolding were laid early on, when the district operations were reviewed and numerous meetings were held with parent and community groups, as well as conversations with individual parents and business and community leaders. The district stra-

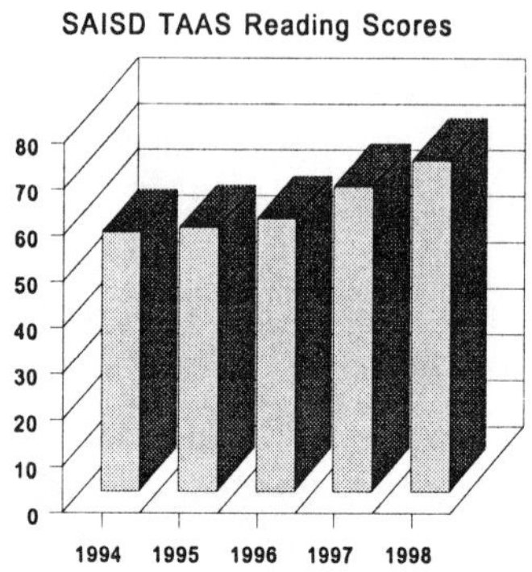

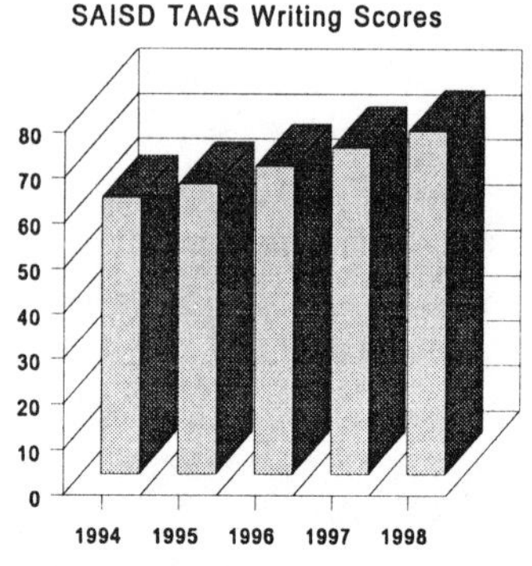

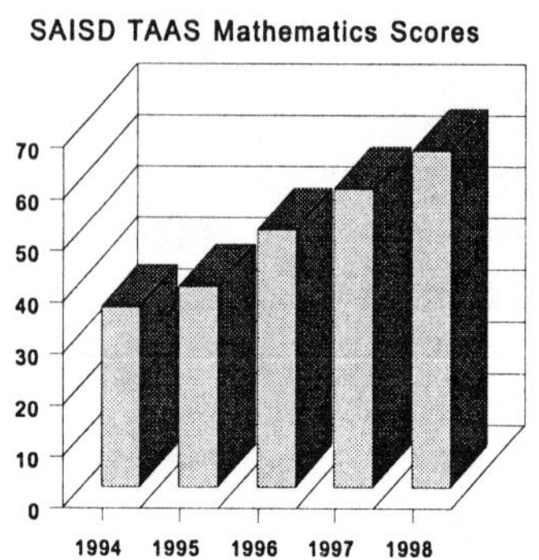

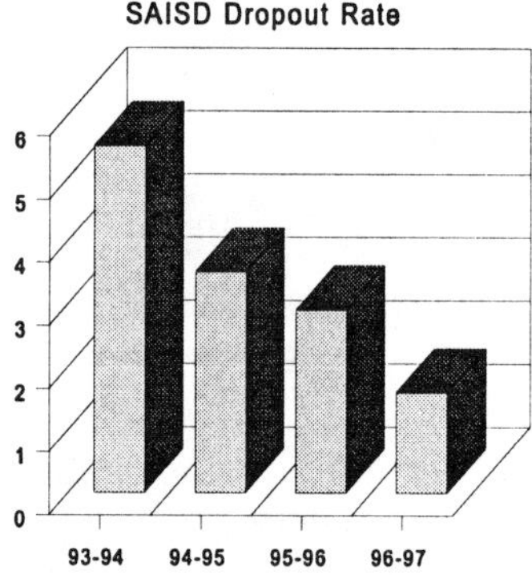

FIGURE 7.1
San Antonio Independent School District Scores on the Texas Assessment of Academic Skills, and Dropout Rate

tegic plan, the district improvement plan, and other relevant documents about the school district were examined. All this information was gathered into a report entitled *Where We Stand and Where We Are Going* (Lam, 1995). In this report, which was presented to the board of education in March 1995, we not only shared the findings and reflections about the district, we also presented a vision for change, a new organizational structure, and our goals for the district.

The five goals outlined in our report were embraced by the school board and incorporated into the district improvement plan. The goals, which have driven the district strategies, initiatives, and activities, are:

- Increasing student achievement.
- Building an infrastructure for professional development.
- Strengthening parent and community involvement.
- Fostering collaboration and communication.
- Providing appropriate school facilities to all students.

These goals provide a framework for the changes needed for improvement in the district and for our vision of all students achieving success. They are broad enough to foster consensus among the stakeholders, but also focus attention on a limited and manageable number of areas in which we can direct our resources, energies, and commitment.

In order to facilitate the implementation of our district goals, we put into place a new organizational structure focusing on instruction and the needs of students in the summer of 1995. Under the old structure, all of our schools were under the supervision of an elementary or secondary education director, two assistant superintendents, and three associate superintendents. The new structure divides the district into four learning communities, each headed by an instructional steward who is responsible for the instructional and professional development needs of 20 to 25 schools. The title of the position was selected purposefully because the position's main responsibility is instruction; a steward knows no rank or hierarchy, and puts service to others above self-interest. The main responsibilities of the instructional stewards are focused on teaching and learning, not administrative details. The instructional stewards do not conduct disciplinary hearings or hear grievances and are not responsible for the operational functions of the district.

The instructional stewards have vertical as well as horizontal responsibilities. For example, one of our instructional stewards is responsible for bilingual education in addition to her learning community. Another is responsible for the fine arts. Stewards also act as conveners for different grade levels. They constantly emphasize quality and accountability in academic programs, staff development, curriculum, and instruction. In 1997, we added a department of curriculum and instruction to facilitate the development of content standards and alignment of curriculum and instruction with assessment. The traditional operational functions of finance, personnel and records, transportation, food services, and technology operate as a network. All of the support services for students were brought together and a new parent and community partnership network was formed to increase involvement of these critical stakeholders in our school system.

As a key element of our restructuring, we also created the new position of instructional guide at each school. Instructional guides support the principal in providing meaningful instructional leadership. They link research findings to professional development and classroom practices. They train, coach, and offer technical assistance to teachers in supporting the use of quality instructional strategies and the demonstration of good practice.

The five goals of the district provide a convenient means of describing what has happened in San Antonio from 1994 to 1998.

INCREASING STUDENT ACHIEVEMENT

We struggle with the larger public to fulfill our commitment to educate every child for the 21st century. No child should be left behind or excluded from this right. Every child is our child. We do not believe the accident of birth predetermines life's script or consider it a crime to be poor in material possessions. Public education asserts that every child has a right to unlock the riches of the world's greatest literature, art, and scientific and mathematical thinking and discoveries. This planetary cultural and intellectual heritage belongs to all.

It is this philosophy that drives our planning. The five areas that are integral to our plan to increase student achievement are: developing content and performance standards; implementing district initiatives such as the restructuring of bilingual education, middle and high school practice, and intervention plans for low-performing and priority schools; emphasizing reading and mathematics; being a New American Schools

(NAS) jurisdiction; and using data for planning and accountability purposes.

Development of Standards

In 1995, when we began examining practices in middle schools, we found inconsistencies in what was taught across campuses or on the same campus. A curriculum audit revealed that many concepts and activities were taught in multiple grades at the same level of instruction. For example, a science unit on the solar system was being taught using the same basic content and instructional methodology in Grades 3 through 9. There was a need for coordinated and consistent standards that provided high expectations for all students and teachers. The quality of children's education should not be left to chance. Content and performance standards ensure that all students are held to the same benchmarks of quality, regardless of the neighborhood school they attend or the teacher to whom they are assigned. Standards help give us quality and consistency.

Our district engaged in a 3-year process to develop and implement curriculum content and performance standards for core academic subjects. The first year was the development phase, when content-area action teams formulate standards for their respective subjects. In Year 2, these content standards were field tested, refined, and changed as needed. In the third year, teachers implemented the content and performance standards in their classrooms. As of 1998, the middle schools were beginning the third year of the process, the high schools were in the second year, and the elementary schools were in Year 1.

At the beginning of the development of curriculum standards, the four subject-area teams posed the question of what they want their students to accomplish by the end of a particular grade level. Each team aligned its content area with the national standards, the Texas Essential Knowledge and Skills, and the TAAS. This alignment also identified the major strands within a discipline that need to be developed. The next phase involved both horizontal and vertical curriculum analyses. The horizontal analysis looked within grade levels to ensure that what was taught in each subject complemented lessons in other subjects. The vertical analysis, meanwhile, examined subjects across grade levels to ensure that each grade level built on the last, and that repetitious content was reduced or eliminated. From this work, we aimed to identify content gaps and determine what should be kept and what should be dropped from the curriculum.

In the future, it will be critical for this process to determine the benchmarks for each subject in each grade level. Benchmarks are important because they indicate whether a student has mastered a subject. However, before benchmarks can be developed, interim assessments need to be created and administered.

District Initiatives

Bilingual Education. In 1995, we looked critically at our bilingual program. Bilingual students were scattered over a multitude of classes, with some translation services available. We created a program with academic integrity: Our bilingual students are now clustered, and the program builds a strong foundation in Spanish and helps children learn English. We expect all of our bilingual students to read and write in their native language as well as in English. Our bilingual students took the TAAS in Spanish and their scores were included in the state accountability system for the first time in 1998. Our bilingual students also took advantage of other reform efforts in the district. For example, in schools that have chosen "Roots and Wings," a New American School design, as their framework for change, bilingual students participated in the program. They can participate in either language, depending on their individual needs. All bilingual students in Grades K–6 are learning mathematics through the Everyday Mathematics program developed by the University of Chicago.

Middle School Restructuring. Our middle school reform started with a year of study by the principals and other middle school staff. They examined national research and the state board policy statement on middle grade education. They studied current practice, identified critical needs, and prioritized actions to be taken. The approved plan incorporated three of the areas targeted to increase student achievement—use of data, content-specific emphasis on reading and mathematics, and development of content and performance standards. The data analysis began at the middle school level, as did the development of content and performance standards. Development of a consistent discipline plan and a supportive transition program became a focus as we examined the expansion of student support services and ways to increase parental involvement.

In addition, we offered specific professional development sessions for middle school teachers in the areas of teaming, cooperative discipline, and adolescent development, among others. Additional sessions on scheduling, wellness, data analysis, and urban middle school reform were offered to principals.

High School Redesign. In 1995, all eight of our high schools implemented magnet school programs. Each magnet school or program operates as a school within a school, providing students with the core curriculum needed for graduation as well as special courses with a focused theme or specialized area of study. As of 1998, we had nine magnet schools that are open to students from across the district and from surrounding school districts. The nine magnet school programs are:

- Communication technologies
- Fine arts
- Health professions
- International banking and business
- Law and research
- Science, engineering, and technology
- Media productions
- Multilingual studies
- International baccalaureate

The implementation of the magnet school programs paved the way for the comprehensive high school redesign process underway in 1998 in all of our high schools. For more than a year, the parents and community members of one of our high schools had expressed concerns about the decline of the school. Community meetings were held over the summer and special task forces of all stakeholders formed to gather ideas and strategies to bring about a renaissance at the school. In January 1998, plans were announced to reorganize the high school into four smaller, academically challenging academies, each headed by its own principal. This reorganization was designed to create a high-performing high school in which all students could be successful. All of the traditions of the high school continue through a common program of extracurricular activities such as athletics, band, and pep squad.

In March 1997, we invited the teachers and administrators of the other seven district high schools to begin to explore ways to transform their schools to meet the needs of all their students. Since then, the high school staffs as well as parents and community members have been exploring, planning, and designing schools where all students are successful and will graduate. We assured schools that there was not a single way to redesign a school, but emphasized that their plans had to address four different parameters: the formation of small, caring teaching and learning environments; academic rigor and high standards for all students; an infrastructure of support for student success; and curriculum alignment. We have supported each high school by making available the services of a facilitator, funds for study materials, and summer stipends for redesign teams. We suggested that high schools consider the recommendations made by the National Association of Secondary School Principals and the Carnegie Foundation (1996) in *Breaking Ranks: Changing an American Institution* and the elements of comprehensive reorganization identified by Gordon Cawelti (1997) in his *Effects of High School Restructuring: Ten Schools at Work.* At the request of the high-school principals and their redesign teams, we also put together a time line with a list of products and benchmarks to help them through the planning process. In early November, each high school had the opportunity to present a draft of their plan to a group of "high school experts." Each team had time to present its plan and to receive feedback. As part of the process of evaluation, the district compiled all the data for high schools and shared it with the schools. District and school staff and community and business members also worked on a profile of a San Antonio ISD graduate. The final plans were presented to the superintendent in February 1998 and then went to the school board for approval. Our goal was to open the 1998–1999 school year with all our high schools reorganized.

Targeted Assistance. The schools that we targeted for intervention assistance were those that were designated as low-performing according to established state accountability standards. We also intervened in priority schools, in which less than 50% of students pass any subject at two or more grade levels. The plan for supporting these schools has four components:

- The district-level intervention team is composed of the associate superintendent for curriculum and instruction, an instructional steward, a peer principal, a special education and a bilingual supervisor, math and reading curriculum specialists, a parent and community network member, and a specialist from advanced academic studies. They are committed to providing strong instructional support and feedback gathered through unscheduled classroom and school observations. Data gathered through these observations are shared with the school staff through reports and debriefings. The team examines the quality of curriculum and instruction, planning, and assessment.

- On-site technical assistance is provided to help the school in the identified areas of greatest need. In addition, the peer principal acts as a critical friend and resource for the school principal in a mutually agreed-upon role.
- The school-level intervention team is composed of the principal, an instructional guide, one teacher per grade level and/or subject area, one special education and one bilingual teacher, one teacher certified in gifted and talented education, and the administrative assistant or assistant principal. They are responsible for working with the district team and leading the school staff in thoughtful analysis and planning for improvement. They provide guidance, support, and encouragement throughout the year. This team also works closely with the district team to review and intensively analyze data, attends debriefing sessions, and communicates results to the entire staff.
- Data analysis is provided to each campus in several formats as part of a campus briefing session. Data are examined both annually and longitudinally to provide a clear picture of instructional patterns on the campus. In addition, data specific to individual teachers are analyzed to provide a picture of instructional strengths and weaknesses. After analysis, as part of the on-site visit debriefing sessions, the school formulates a plan of action to build on areas of strength and improve areas of weakness.

Content-Specific Emphasis

Balanced Literacy. In reading, we decided to implement a balanced literacy approach with a curriculum framework that gives reading and writing equal status. This framework combines explicit instruction in skills and content with skills taught in the context of a variety of reading experiences. These include modeled reading by the teacher, shared reading in which the teacher shares a text with the class and gradually releases responsibility for "reading" to the students, guided reading in which the teachers assist students in the use of strategies for making sense of texts, and finally independent reading in which the students select their own texts and apply what they know while reading. Writing instruction provides a variety of opportunities for students to generate ideas, shape their ideas into drafts, revise their drafts to make meaning clearer to readers, and edit their texts for publication. The most important balance is that between student-centered instruction and specific grade-level goals and expectations. This delicate balance is achieved by providing continuous professional development that allows teachers to develop their repertoire of strategies, instructional expectations, learner outcomes, benchmarks to monitor progress, and intervention strategies to help all students improve.

As part of our reading program, we have created a literacy center in one of our schools and we expect to create at least one in each of the other learning communities. The literacy center provides on-site demonstration of research-based literacy practices, offers mentorship and classroom support for reading teachers, builds model literacy-based classrooms throughout the school, and collects data to assess the effects of specific reading practices on student achievement.

This literacy center is led by a master teacher who works with two classroom teachers during their regularly scheduled reading period for a 3-week rotation:

- Week 1—Teaching of a balanced literacy program is modeled by the master teacher. The master teacher also assists the classroom teachers in assessing students, organizing reading groups, and selecting materials and strategies appropriate for beginning readers. Classroom teachers are given an opportunity to observe and plan new lessons.
- Week 2—The master teacher team teaches with the individual classroom teacher. The master teacher and classroom teacher plan and work with small groups on guided reading. This allows classroom teachers the rare opportunity of having a respected colleague help them support the varied reading needs of their students.
- Week 3—The coaching phase of the cycle allows for coaching and conferencing. The master teacher steps back and the individual classroom teacher assumes the responsibility for instruction. During this phase, other teachers on the campus are invited to observe instruction. The master teacher also facilitates discussion groups to address any issues that arise.

Everyday Mathematics. In mathematics, we started with a small cohort of volunteer schools that were willing to implement Everyday Mathematics, developed by the University of Chicago. This curriculum explores the various strands of math, including the basics of data gathering and analysis, probability, geometry, and algebra. The curriculum's strength is its use of mathematics in real-world applications. Its instructional design takes advantage of the ways in which children naturally learn. Mathematics concepts and ideas are visited informally several times before they are formally taught, allowing students time to build a conceptual foundation. Once formally introduced, each topic is revisited in a variety of contexts, deepening understanding about the patterns and relationships inherent in mathematics. Because students use what they learn over time and in a wide variety of activities, they more easily understand mathematics' complex web of connections.

The use of Everyday Mathematics started as a voluntary effort on the part of the schools. We offered it to schools three times and each time more schools opted to use the materials. As we were preparing for the 1997–1998 school year, there were only 10 schools that had not voluntarily chosen to be involved. At that time, the decision was made for all schools to use Everyday Mathematics. It was a hard decision to make, but by the end of the school year even former critics acknowledged that it had been the right decision.

New American Schools

Another key part of the scaffolding was erected in July 1996, when San Antonio ISD became a NAS jurisdiction. The district had posted achievement gains, attributed mainly to a renewed focus on academic achievement. We felt that to continue improving, we needed to engage in comprehensive reform. NAS was interested in urban partners and we wanted external help on how to continue to improve as the state standards kept moving higher. Each NAS design seeks to increase student achievement through comprehensive reform that focuses on strengthening learning in core academic areas and helping students learn more complex skills. As of 1998, 70% of our schools are committed to a design and three additional schools are working with one of our unions, the San Antonio Teachers Council, using the KEYS program, to evaluate their current programs before deciding on a framework for change. We expect 100% of our schools to participate in the future.

NAS has no equivalent counterpart on the national scene. It plays a unique leadership role in convening district, state, and national leaders and design teams to set an agenda for change, particularly in underperforming districts that commit to ambitious goals for raising student achievement. NAS has taken some of the best ideas and practices from the private sector—most notably the idea of comprehensive organizational change instead of piece-by-piece programs—and infused them into public education. NAS is not a "one-size-fits-all" approach to school transformation. Instead, NAS provides leadership to partner districts and design teams in forging continuous improvement against benchmarks, time lines, and specific goals and products. NAS is among the forerunners in addressing issues of bringing change to scale.

NAS began as a national competition for design teams in 1992 with a commitment to funding the research, development, and early implementation phases of new designs for 5 years. It created or helped create seven viable design teams that in turn are working with schools. The idea of focusing on urban partner districts emerged in 1994, and San Antonio ISD has benefited as a partner district from the continuing ideas and support of NAS and the NAS network. We cannot change our public schools alone. Our partnership with NAS gives us a vital national perspective and access to the best thinking and practices being used in school reform as we join with other districts in bringing comprehensive school reform to scale. NAS helps keep us from "reinventing old wheels" and simultaneously helps us create new ways to deliver services to the children and families we serve.

In San Antonio, we use the following NAS designs:

- The *Co-NECT* design structure allows small multigrade clusters of students to use technology as a tool for learning and communication in a project-based and interdisciplinary curriculum.
- *Expeditionary Learning Outward Bound* offers a curriculum centered around purposeful learning expeditions that develop intellectual and physical skills as well as character and service.
- The *Modern Red Schoolhouse* design combines traditional curriculum and education principles of high student achievement and community support with modern instructional methods and technologies.
- *Roots and Wings* uses intensive reading instruction to ensure that every child meets high academic standards, and an inter-

disciplinary science and social studies curriculum, early childhood education, and family support services to help all students.

Three of our schools are using the Accelerated Schools design, which is based on democratic principles and a commitment to providing powerful learning opportunities to all students.

Use of Data

Since 1992, the State of Texas has had an accountability system that disaggregates achievement data and other indicators by subgroup. The subgroups used in the accountability system are Hispanic, African American, Other, and Economically Disadvantaged. No school can be acceptable, recognized, or exemplary unless all its subgroups meet the same standard. In other words, no single group can skew the school results.

In San Antonio, we have redefined success. We will be successful only when every student is learning and achieving above the national and state standards. Our greatest decision in our school district's transformation has been the use of data to inform choices about teaching and learning at every level of our system. The data from 1994 proved to be a strong impetus for change. Schools were striving to get off the state's "low-performing" list and become "acceptable." They were ready to look closely at the data to identify areas of weakness.

In the past, data examination was limited to moving large printouts from the principal's office to the counselor's filing cabinet. Our first important task, therefore, was getting data into teachers' hands and helping them to understand how to use it. We wanted teachers and administrators to be able to:

- Identify the factors affecting performance.
- Determine which factors have the greatest influence on student achievement.
- Assess student performance at a single point in time and over periods of time.
- Predict how changes will affect instructional outcomes.
- Apply a combination of judgment and data analysis in deciding how to improve performance.
- Compare actual effects of changes to predicted effects.

- Analyze student data for specific strengths and weaknesses in skills and concepts.
- Use data to drive curriculum and instruction.
- Use data to promote ownership and accountability.

We developed several tools for teachers and principals to use as they analyzed individual and group performance and, just as important, we communicated clear expectations about their use and connection to classroom and campus improvement planning. An analysis of student performance data over time both by grade level and by content area highlights two areas of interest. Scores that are consistently low generally indicate deficits in curriculum and instructional methodologies. Patterns that show over time in data generally reveal teaching issues rather than learner problems.

These profiles reveal the strengths and weaknesses of the school as a system and show how the same group of students achieves over time within that system. Analysis of each objective over 3 years or more adequately reveals the strengths and weaknesses at specific grade levels and how they are impacting the system.

We emphasize the importance of looking at data patterns over time. Our aim is to identify areas where we are growing and to determine the factors in our curriculum and/or instructional practices that support learning. We also look for areas where we are not growing, analyze our curriculum and/or instructional practices to identify possible reasons why, and then determine what we can do to improve.

We insist that teachers prepare student profiles that track individual performance over time. These individual student profiles show the teacher which specific TAAS objectives have and have not been met. This identification helps the teacher to spot class patterns, identifying strengths and weaknesses in a visual manner. We also ask teachers to conference with their students and explain the profile to them. The completed profile ensures that teachers know the strengths and weaknesses of each student, including state test performance, report card grades, interim assessments, and informal reading inventories. This comprehensive look at our students leads us to better decisions about what we ought to teach and how we ought to teach it.

At another level, we review classroom-level (or teacher-level) data. We can use a graph to illustrate the aggregate performance of several teachers' classes over a 2-year instructional period. Then, we can graphically "place" these students in relation to their performance on different objectives (sections) of the test. For example, if eighth-grade "teacher P" had students whose average math score in one particular objective (section) in the seventh grade was 71% and after 1 year of instruction these same students scored 60%, we want to know how this teacher addressed this objective. How does this compare to "teacher D" or "teacher O" whose students scored 72% on the same objective in the seventh grade and 88% to 90% after the eighth grade? Each school is able to look at these data by objective or by test. Thus, they can begin to identify effective teaching strategies or curriculum alignment problems.

Classroom-level data can be broken down into individual student data. Using the same type of graph and displaying the performance of each student, we can quickly determine whether students, individually and as a group, have progressed. We can also tell how many have met the minimum standard and we can identify those students who still have not met the minimum standard, those who improved, and those who did not improve.

In addition, we can look more deeply into the data to examine the performance of the subgroups that make up our student body. The results are equally significant for these groups. Achievements of African Americans, Hispanics, economically disadvantaged students, and other groups can be presented in graph format. Using a bar graph, the user/reader quickly visualizes performance of these groups by building and by district. The percentage of students who passed the state test in reading, writing, and arithmetic shows a steady increase from 1994 to 1998. The same is true for those students enrolled in Algebra I and Biology.

The use of data for planning and accountability is institutionalized in every school. An instructional guide from one of our high schools stated:

> It has been pretty amazing what only ONE year of data use at our high school has produced. In the past people just tossed numbers around with no concept of what they meant or what they related to.... One of the most powerful aspects here has been bringing the students into the loop. Students now walk around saying, "Yes, my Texas Learning Index [TLI] was 68, I only missed it by two...if I had just answered one more correctly under objective 6... I really need to study that part...." Two years ago,

> students could fail six times and not know what their score was.

The TLI is a score that describes how far a student's performance is above or below the passing standard.

Building an Infrastructure for Professional Development

A key to increasing student achievement is an infrastructure for professional development. In *Where We Stand and Where We Are Going: Reflecting on the District, A Vision for Change* we observed that the district lacked "an infrastructure and framework for professional development that would be predicated upon the views of teachers as reflective practitioners and the need for district- and school-level supports to enable teachers to construct and act upon knowledge about their craft" (Lam, 1995, p. 13). During the last 3 years, we have found that many people struggle with the concept of an infrastructure for professional development.

In San Antonio, we use the term *infrastructure* to mean anything that facilitates the professional development of teachers and others. Among the components of infrastructure are:

1. *Time*. Any change requires time and it must be made available if we want to be successful. We have increased the number of professional development days from 2 in 1994 to 8 this year. Teachers have 3 additional nonteaching days, which they use as workdays. We schedule creatively during the school day in order to provide teams of teachers with common planning time, and we also conduct summer and weekend institutes.

2. *Policy*. An official acknowledgment that professional development is important and necessary to student success is required. We were able to increase the number of professional development days, which are clustered in groups. Some of our schools had waivers that allowed them to extend the school day 4 days each week and let students out early 1 day in order to have weekly professional development time. The district regularly reviews its policies and practices in order to foster professional development and growth. For example, we invested a large amount of money in buying hardware and software, but most schools did not use the technology to its potential. In 1997, the school board approved a change in school employees' contracts that called for demonstration of

technology competencies. All employees need to ensure their compliance with this clause—the district offers training at times that are convenient to staff.

3. *Reallocation of resources.* Increasing the capacity of staff requires appropriate funding. We finance the position of at least one instructional guide in every school and we spend approximately 3% of our budget on professional development. Most school districts spend less than .5% on training, compared to businesses that spend anywhere between 10% and 20%.

4. *Reculturing.* We have shifted thinking about professional development from the narrow view of "sitting and getting" workshops to a broader understanding that professional development comprises all the activities that teachers and others engage in to improve teaching and learning.

5. *Technology.* In the last 3 years, the district has built a wide-area technology network that connects all schools to each other, the central administrative offices, and the Internet. This connectivity encourages teachers (and their students) to communicate with each other and exchange ideas, information, practices, and lesson plans.

6. *Public engagement.* This was identified as a critical factor in developing an infrastructure for professional development. It is also one of the district's goals and is addressed in more detail later in the case study.

7. *Reconfiguring the organization.* In the summer of 1995, the San Antonio ISD began building an infrastructure for professional development that focused on instruction and student learning and achievement. We have already described the reorganization of the district into four learning communities under the leadership of instructional stewards. Another critical element of the restructuring was the creation of the position of instructional guide.

The instructional guide position at every school is the backbone of our efforts to build an infrastructure for professional development. The position provides a critical link between professional development and classroom practice. Although the role of the instructional guides continue to emerge and evolve, the instructional guides' main purpose is to provide teachers with staff development, training, coaching, and technical assistance to implement new instructional strategies and practices. The guides act as catalysts who facilitate the creation of an instructional focus and support that focus through planning, conversations, data analysis, acquisition of resources, and evaluation.

A recent grant from the Spencer Foundation is funding a 3-year study by Policy Studies Associates to examine the guides' work and their impact on teacher professional growth and the improvement of classroom instruction. The preliminary report states that guides are having a significant impact on individual teachers and groups of teachers. However, more time should be spent coaching teachers. The report recommends a clarification of the instructional guides' role, particularly as it is linked to district priorities.

A reorganized delivery of services for professional development has also been critical to building our new infrastructure. We are committed to making professional development more than passive training sessions, and are working to implement an effective model of staff development that includes theory, demonstration, practice/feedback, and practical application. In 1997, for the first time, we published a comprehensive *Resource Guide for School Improvement* (San Antonio Independent School District, 1997), a handbook that contained all district professional development opportunities for the 1997–1998 school year, standards for professional development, and a guide for campus improvement planning. The eight San Antonio ISD standards for high-quality professional development provide schools and departments with criteria that can be used to evaluate the quality of prospective professional development opportunities. The list of professional development opportunities is updated every year.

The Rockefeller Foundation has been a major partner in our efforts to build an infrastructure for professional development. In 1995, we were chosen as one of four school districts across the nation to participate in a Rockefeller Foundation initiative, "Building Infrastructures for Professional Development." Involvement in this initiative has prompted key district personnel to reconceptualize thinking about an infrastructure for professional development. We have used $750,000 in funding from the Rockefeller Foundation to train the instructional guides in cognitive coaching, provide them with access to computers and the Internet through the districtwide area network, develop a closer connection with parents and the community, and enhance communication among professionals by publishing a teacher journal.

In the 1998–1999 school year we built more choice into professional growth in the district through the "Teachers and Teaching Initiative" and the "Teacher Incentive Program." These two programs provide dedicated teachers, librarians, and instructional guides with opportunities to grow professionally and personally. School employees can choose to participate in several different areas that foster growth:

1. *Certification by the National Board for Professional Teaching Standards.* The district has 20 teachers and instructional guides who are candidates for certification by the National Board for Professional Teaching Standards (NBPTS). The district is committed to paying the $2,000 application fee, and teachers who achieve National Board Certification will receive an additional annual stipend. The National Board Certification Program has high standards for teachers. Because of its rigorous requirements, the district sponsored a precandidacy year in 1997–1998 to prepare interested teachers for the candidacy year. We have also created a partnership with the University of Texas in San Antonio to support the candidates by offering graduate credits, planning regular meetings of this cohort group, and providing trained facilitators to work with the candidates. During the candidacy year, each candidate will spend at least 100 hours developing a comprehensive portfolio and completing several assessment exercises.

2. *Mentoring of new teachers.* There are four specific objectives of this program: to improve teacher performance, to increase retention of promising beginning teachers, to promote the personal and professional well-being of beginning teachers, and to provide quality opportunities for the professional growth of beginning teachers and mentors. We use an application and a screening process to identify a pool of master teachers to work with our beginning teachers. These mentors are trained and matched with beginning teachers at the same school and same subject area or grade level whenever possible. Mentors receive a stipend for their work and we also provide a financial incentive for beginning teachers (San Antonio Independent School District, 1998).

3. *Professional development residency.* This involves a 5-week internship of a teacher with a resident master teacher in mathematics. During the residency, an experienced and highly qualified substitute will work at different times in both classrooms, freeing the intern and resident master teacher to visit one another's classrooms to observe and refine teaching strategies.

4. *Sabbaticals.* Teachers may opt to participate in a sabbatical program to pursue graduate work, individual study, reflection, or other interests. Participating teachers defer 20% of their salary for 4 years and get paid 80% of their salary during their sabbatical (the 5th year). The

district recognizes the sabbatical year as a year of service and continues to pay the participants their contractual benefits.

5. *Teacher networks*. Participation is voluntary but the district supports and encourages the development of teacher focus groups by providing them with necessary resources. For example, in the summer of 1998 a group of teachers participated in the Expeditionary Learning Poetry Summit. Upon their return, they formed a network and now hold poetry readings on a regular basis. They share their own poems as well as those of their students and exchange ideas on how to make the teaching and learning of poetry more exciting. These teachers had not thought of themselves as poets and had not emphasized poetry in their teaching prior to attending the Poetry Summit.

6. *Incentives*. An incentive of $500 was given to teachers who participated in activities that supported the district's goals of increasing student achievement, staff development, student and parent involvement, good attendance, collaboration, and professional growth.

The district has also implemented the required technology competencies for all teachers and professionals in the district. The competencies, which will be achieved in 3 years after regular access to a computer, are:

- To model and enforce responsible and ethical use of technology.
- To operate a computer, demonstrate proficiency in word processing, and use e-mail and online communications.
- To acquire critical competencies in the applications of databases, spreadsheets, graphing, and multimedia/graphics presentation software.

One of the district's greatest professional development priorities is content deepening and resources have been committed to develop teachers' subject-area expertise. Test results have driven the decision to place a major emphasis on mathematics, with extensive district-level staff development.

Our training for instructional guides has been in cognitive coaching, TAAS preparation, and content-area subjects. Other important professional development includes training for principals and administrators on leadership skills, the change process, and systems thinking. The district has also formed partnerships with two universities in the city; one provides school administrators with opportunities for professional and intellectual growth and both offer master's degree programs in school leadership and administration.

Strengthening Parent and Community Involvement

For years, people viewed schools as walled fortresses, keeping communities out and children in. What happened in the nearby housing development was not seen as connected to what happened in school. Every school was its own fiefdom. More recently, people see schools as anchors in a community, and as forces for its revitalization. An anchor, however, is very heavy and keeps a boat from drifting out to sea. As we enter the new century, we understand that schools are neither anchors nor fortresses, but integral lively members of complex learning communities of adults and children.

Our third goal is to strengthen parent and community involvement. In the past, parental involvement in schools was limited. In the fall of 1995, the Parent and Community Partnership Network was created to coordinate all parent activities and ensure more parent and community involvement in district activities. The network is designed around the Partnership 2000 framework developed by Dr. Joyce Epstein (1995) and her colleagues at Johns Hopkins University in order to promote more creative avenues in designing effective partnerships. The Partnership 2000 framework consists of six key components: parenting, communication, volunteers, learning at home, decision making, and business/community collaboration.

The new network has fostered increased parent and community participation through the expansion of mentoring and partnership programs, increased offerings in community and adult education, and the expansion of parent and community membership on school instructional leadership teams. The network acts as an advocate for parents and community residents and helps them to access the school system.

The Parent and Community Partnership Network actively engages parents and community members in the learning of children through a number of different strategies:

1. *Parent Academy*. This school for parents consists of four major strands and 20 sessions conducted in both English and Spanish. The four strands are How To Be an A-Plus Parent, Tools for Success, Community Connections, and Parents and Teachers: The Winning Team.

More than 1,500 parents and community members have attended at least one session of the Parent Academy in the last 18 months, and last year 123 of them attended 15 or more classes. We also have a core group of parents who have participated in leadership development sessions conducted in collaboration with the Mexican American Legal Defense Education Fund (MALDEF).

2. *Parent and community help line.* Parents and community members can call to get the answers they need about how to contact the department or school that can help them.

3. *Home-based parent education services.* Through an agreement with the Mental Health Association in Texas, AmeriCorps members are assigned to elementary school communities where each member provides 1,700 hours of community service to low-income parents with children from birth to age 5.

4. *Migrant education Even Start grant.* This federally funded family-literacy program provides for improved educational opportunities for migrant families in the district by integrating early childhood education, adult education, and parenting education in a home-based setting.

5. *Conflict resolution training and mediation services.* The Parent and Community Partnership Network staff provides conflict resolution training: More than 100 individuals have been trained in cooperative problem solving and nearly 80 others have signed up for future training sessions. The network staff also provides mediation services on request.

6. *Project Milagro.* This collaborative venture of AT&T and the Texas A&M University System ensures that *all* children in one of our high school feeder patterns will graduate from high school fully prepared for the global society. Its theme is "100% in to get 100% out, by 100% of the community." Project Milagro seeks to integrate all health care, educational, and social services available to children and adolescents into one coordinated effort.

7. *Seamless Support for Academic Success (SSAS).* This is presently a planning grant by the Ford Foundation to enable a coalition of partners to develop a strategic plan to help students experience academic success. This project addresses a common problem that families and children in San Antonio face—that many children lack the academic, physical, and emotional support necessary for negotiating the challenging transitions in their lives. Such transitions include those from home to

school, from elementary to secondary, and from high school to higher education or the workplace.

The district and its schools also continue to increase business partnerships with schools to provide mentoring and other assistance. At present, more than half of our schools have one or more business partners. Approximately 270 businesses and agencies are partnered with one or more of our schools.

Fostering Collaboration and Communications

Engaging in comprehensive school district reform requires high-quality communication. We use existing means of communication and develop new means to share information with our employees and the community. Our main avenues of communication with our employees are a twice-a-month employee newsletter, a monthly newsletter from the superintendent to all teachers and professionals, a weekly report from the superintendent to the school board, a weekly update of upcoming district events, a weekly packet of memos sent electronically to all principals and departments, a journal written by and for teachers, and the annual district improvement plan. We communicate with parents and the community through a monthly activity calendar and notes to parents, a monthly cable television program, a quarterly community newsletter, a fact sheet about the district, and an annual progress report.

We do not underestimate, however, the importance of personal communication. We hold monthly teacher coffees, community forums, and administrators' coffees. These occasions provide staff and parents with an opportunity to speak to the superintendent in an informal way. There is no set agenda and no appointment is necessary.

Our strategic communications plan for the district is designed to provide a comprehensive overview of the district's efforts to improve communications with both internal and external audiences. The fundamental purpose of these activities is to build sustained public support for student learning and achievement. The district's communication plan has four major areas:

1. *Employee communication.* The main purposes of internal communications with district schools, departments, and employees are to share information about the district and its schools and to ensure that the district's vision, goals, and initiatives are clearly understood, supported, and shared throughout the school system.

2. *Communication with parents and the community.* The main purposes of external communications with parents, community members, and other district partners are to share information, report on the progress of the district and its schools, and build public support for the district's vision and goals.

3. *Public engagement and involvement.* Public engagement and involvement are intended to gather public opinions on issues of concern to the district and its community, to recruit and involve community members as partners in education, and to provide parents and others with information and opportunities to build their capacity in supporting students in their learning.

4. *Communication of the shared vision.* Communication of the shared vision to the news media, the public, parents, and other partners of the district is meant to provide timely and accurate information about the district and its schools and to improve understanding of the district and its vision for student learning and achievement.

San Antonio has also been very active in forming collaborations with national groups and other school districts throughout the United States. For example:

- The Rockefeller Foundation grant for building infrastructures has linked San Antonio ISD with the Learning Community Network of Cleveland, OH, and the school districts of Albuquerque, NM; Flint, MI; and San Diego, CA.
- The NAS design involves collaboration with four design teams along with the Rand Corporation, the Spencer Foundation, and Policy Studies Associates.
- The National Commission for Teaching and America's Future counts San Antonio as one of its urban school district partners in improving the quality of teaching by transforming how teachers are prepared, recruited, selected, and inducted, and how schools support, assess, and reward their work.
- The National Science Foundation's Urban Systemic Initiative grant is a collaboration of San Antonio and eight other Bexar County school districts and the University of Texas at San Antonio to improve the quality of curriculum and instruction in science, mathematics, and technology education.
- The Department of Education Technology Challenge grant collaboration with Northeast Independent School District, the

Archdiocese of San Antonio, and the University of Texas at San Antonio will build an infrastructure for technology at one of our high schools and two of our middle schools.

The district has two other important local collaborations. One is a partnership with Citizens Organized for Public Service (COPS) and Metro Alliance, two community-based advocacy groups. Its purpose is to develop a strong community-based constituency of parents, teachers, and community leaders who work to dramatically improve student achievement in our schools. At present, 30 of our schools are Alliance schools.

The other collaboration is with H.E.B., a regional grocery store chain, which committed $1 million for a Teacher Reward and Recognition Program for campuses that are exemplary, recognized, or score 10% above district average on the TAAS. The "most-improved" campuses also received a monetary award based on the most improvement with the same group of students.

Providing Appropriate Facilities for All Students

On September 27, 1997, voters passed, by a two-to-one margin, the largest bond issue in the history of Texas: $483 million. The district last passed a bond issue for general school construction in 1968. Our success resulted from a year-long process during which the district and individual schools held community meetings; surveyed parents, employees, and other patrons; conducted facility tours for the public; and publicized efforts to develop a building improvement plan. Passage of the bond package meant that we were within reach of our goal of providing appropriate facilities for all students. It also sent a strong and clear message to students and their parents that, despite living in an inner city, they are entitled to modern facilities like those in the surrounding suburbs.

A Quick Recap

The key components of systemic reform efforts in the San Antonio ISD include:

- Identifying five goals that support the district's vision of all students being successful.

- Reorganizing the district to focus efforts and resources on teaching and learning.
- Developing high standards in the core academic subjects.
- Improving teaching in the areas of math, reading, middle school, and bilingual education.
- Building an infrastructure to ensure quality professional development, especially by placing an instructional guide at every school to mentor, coach, and train teachers.
- Providing support for teacher growth through mentoring of new teachers, National Board certification, teacher sabbaticals, professional development residencies, teacher networks and inquiry groups, and incentives for teacher activities that support the district goals.
- Embracing comprehensive school reform by adopting one of the NAS designs.
- Providing magnet school programs in all of our high schools and beginning the process of high school redesign.
- Establishing important links to national foundations, the federal government, and other school districts.
- Creating a parent and community partnership network to promote parent and community involvement in San Antonio schools.
- Improving both the internal and external communication of the district.
- Passing the largest bond package for school facilities in the history of the State of Texas.

The Lessons We Have Learned

Here are a few of the lessons we have learned while engaging in systemic school reform in San Antonio:

1. *Always put children first, above personal interest.* Putting children first, especially if personal interest is jeopardized, raises the reform efforts above personal motives. Putting children first forces the critics—and there will always be critics opposed to the changes—to address the real issue: student learning and achievement. More important, *always putting children first is the right thing to do.*

2. *Vision building is a continuous process.* A vision cannot be set at the onset of the reform effort and remain static. It needs to be revisited on a regular basis as new players, new influences, and even new directions emerge and develop. Refinement of the vision is necessary not only to provide clarity but also to encompass more stakeholders. The vision needs to be revisited and refined constantly in order to maintain the creative tension between it and current reality.

3. *Data are our best friend.* Data help create the sense of urgency needed for change to occur. Good use of data also provides information for planning and accountability purposes.

4. *The old basics are not enough; we also need to deal with the new basics.* Too often we hear the cry, "Back to basics!" Competence in reading, writing, and arithmetic is only part of the answer to improved student achievement. The new basics—problem solving, critical thinking, analysis and synthesis of data, collaboration, use of technology, and so on—demand that students perform at higher levels.

5. *District leadership must support and drive the implementation of reform efforts.* Without leadership from the top, reform efforts will fail. District leaders must define the reforms, communicate those reforms to others, involve everyone in the changes, and ensure that the reforms are implemented. They must also lead the celebrations of success—the times when the system reflects on "where we are, where we were, and where we want to be." The district must balance setting parameters for action with providing enough flexibility for school-based decision making.

6. *Capacity building is multifaceted and continuous.* The changes necessary for systemic reform often require a school system to rely on most of the same people that were in the system before the reform efforts began. Part of the reform effort, therefore, is to build capacity in each and every one of the employees and stakeholders of the school system. We cannot focus only on principals and selected teachers; we must include all teachers, paraprofessionals, administrators, parents, and other community members. Capacity building must also be continuous. The goal is to build a community of lifelong learners with a focus on and commitment to student learning and achievement.

7. *Change that is linear, small, and limited will not work.* Change that is piecemeal, like pilot programs, will not cause organizational or cultural change. Every school, department, and classroom must be involved in change. Change must be massive, rapid, and geometric to make a difference. Price Pritchet and Ron Pound (1998) claim you must "Start out fast and keep trying to pick up speed. *Leave skid marks"* (p. 43). A linear change rarely leaves skid marks; indeed, it is more likely not to leave a trace at all. It is important to understand the need for scaling up reform. The district is responsible for creating conditions that will encourage simultaneous changes in many of the schools. The challenge is to make it more difficult for an institution and its people to go backwards than to go forward. With 70% of our schools implementing a NAS design, it is not a matter of whether the other 30% will agree to do it, but rather of when and what design framework for change they will choose.

8. *Spending more dollars on doing the same thing does not work.* In San Antonio, this mistake cost more than a million dollars. In its visit in 1995, the state accreditation team recommended that the district provide more money and resources for low-performing schools. In the 1995–1996 school budget, an extra million dollars was allocated for these schools to assist them in improving student achievement. The schools were asked to submit simple plans outlining how they would like to spend the additional money. They responded by proposing to buy more workbooks, computers, and books for the library; to create tutorial classes after school and/or on Saturdays; and to provide student incentives for attendance. All of these ideas, of course, were good, but schools did not focus on strengthening or changing the interaction between teacher and student, the most important interaction that happens on any given day in a school.

We have also learned lessons related to the process of scaling up comprehensive school district reform. In some small way, our experiences in San Antonio have provided insight into how to break the cycle of inertia. We are not saying we have all the answers or that we have engaged in systemic school district reform in the only possible way. The process is very complex and perhaps unique to every system. Our experiences, however, can provide a point of departure for other school districts that choose to engage in systemic reform. From our perspective, we think that scaling up for comprehensive school district reform can work if the following factors are considered:

1. *Connect the reform efforts to the vision and the mission of the school district.* Usually the vision or mission of the district is very general with lofty expectations. The statement, therefore, can be used as a way to rally everyone around the reform efforts. Taking this high road elevates the conversations and discussions. Few people will want to challenge a vision of having all students be successful in school. This shifts the discussion from whether to engage in reform to how to implement reform efforts.

2. *Integrate the reform efforts into a systemic school district plan to improve performance.* In Texas, all school districts and schools are required to develop an improvement plan for student achievement. We have used the district improvement plan as a vehicle to move our reform efforts forward. The formative and summative assessments built into the planning process provide us with periodic checks on where we are and where we need to go to achieve our goals. The reorganization of the district, all of our initiatives, the adoption of NAS designs, our focus on quality professional development, and many other activities were built into the district improvement plan.

3. *Link comprehensive reform to all school improvement efforts.* School district reform will be more successful if it is directly tied to improvement efforts in the schools. In fact, systemic district reform will probably fail unless many schools engage simultaneously in reform efforts. While reform is often initiated at the district level, reform at the school level is the foundation for comprehensive school district reform. Involving San Antonio schools in the different NAS designs has caused a quantum leap in our reform efforts.

4. *Create a supportive operating environment.* One key ingredient of a supportive operating environment is a sense of urgency to change the structure and culture of the system. We cannot afford to wait and see if a pilot program will be successful because every year we are losing thousands of children in San Antonio and millions more across the nation. The supportive operating environment also requires individuals to adapt or grow into new, more general roles with new respon-

sibilities. Consequently, the need for clear policies, rules, procedures, and routines is essential. Also necessary is a general understanding of the realities of the new expectations and culture of the system. District leadership must provide all these components of a supportive operating environment if systemic reform is to succeed.

5. *Create dynamic interactions among all people in the district.* The more people are involved in the process, the more likely they are to commit to the reform efforts. Communication, partnerships, and shared accountability are critical to the success of these interactions and the reform efforts. Taking the reform efforts to parents and the community, rallying them around the vision, and valuing their opinions and support will provide an impetus for the more reluctant educators to commit. It will also encourage everyone to talk about what needs to be done in order to achieve the vision.

6. *Balance accountability and support.* Everyone must be personally accountable and have the support needed in order to ensure student success. This means that we must build capacity in both individuals and teams. The accountability measures must be objective: that is, we must move to results-oriented evaluation systems.

Though our current successes are encouraging, San Antonio as a school district still has a long way to go. In Bridges' stages of change, we are still in the neutral zone. Our vision has recently been revised. Today, our vision is ambitious. We want to be the first urban school district where all students achieve above the state and national standards, exhibit personal growth, and serve others in the community. In stressing the academic, personal, and service dimensions of learning, our vision encompasses the whole child. Though academic achievement is still the first priority, we recognize the importance of the social, emotional, and personal growth of children and adolescents, and their development into model citizens who see service to others as an integrative part of themselves.

Most of us chose to be educators because we wanted to make a difference in the lives of children. That's what education is all about: our ability and commitment to make a difference in the lives of children.

In their book *Leading with Soul: An Uncommon Journey of Spirit,* Lee Bolman and Terrence Deal (1994, p. 32) told a story about a stream.

This stream flowed around many obstacles until it arrived at a desert. The stream tried to cross the desert, but its waters disappeared into the sand.

Then the stream heard a voice saying, "The wind crosses the desert. So can the stream." The stream protested, "The wind can fly but I cannot." The voice responded, "Let yourself be absorbed by the wind." The stream rebelled, "I want to remain the same stream I am today." "That is not possible," said the voice. "But your essence can be carried away and become a stream again. You've forgotten your essence."

The stream remembered dimly that she had once been held in the wind. She let her vapor rise into the arms of the wind, which carried the vapor across the desert and then let it fall in the mountains. There it again became a stream.

Our essence as educators is helping children learn. We must remember and rekindle our zeal and commitment to do whatever it takes to educate each and every child. We must be willing to let go of old ways and embrace new ones. We must foster a culture of revision where change, growth, and risk-taking in the service of children are welcomed, appreciated, and encouraged. Like the stream, we must act with courage and be willing to change. We must continue to develop the capacity to act with flexibility and vision.

ENDNOTE

1. Superintendent of Schools in San Antonio, TX from 1994 to 1998, Diana Lam is now Superintendent in Providence, RI. This chapter profiles San Antonio's school reform efforts through the end of 1998.

REFERENCES

Bolman, L. G. & Deal, T. E. (1995). *Leading with soul: An uncommon journey of spirit.* San Francisco: Jossey-Bass.

Bridges, W. (1991). *Managing transitions: Making the most of change.* Reading, MA: Addison Wesley.

Cawelti, G. (1997). *Effects of high school restructuring: Ten schools at work.* Arlington, VA: Educational Research Service.

Epstein, J. (1995). School/family/community partnerships: Caring for the children we share. *Phi Delta Kappan, 9*(76), 701–712.

Lam, D. (1995). *Where we stand and where we are going: Reflections on the district, a vision for change.* San Antonio, TX: San Antonio Independent School District.

Lash, J. P. (1981). *Helen and teacher: The story of Helen Keller and Anne Sullivan.* New York: Delacorte Press/Seymour Lawrence.

National Association of Secondary School Principals and the Carnegie Foundation. (1996). *Breaking ranks: Changing an American institution.* Reston, VA: NASSP.

Pritchet, P., & Pound, R. (1998). *High-velocity culture change: A handbook for managers.* Dallas, TX: Pritchett & Associates, Inc.

San Antonio Independent School District. (1997). *Developing a community of learners: A resource guide for school improvement.* San Antonio, TX: Author.

San Antonio Independent School District. (1998). *Beginning teacher mentoring program: Program description.* San Antonio, TX: Author.

Thomas, R. R. (1990). From affirmative action to affirming diversity. *Harvard Business Review, 68*(2), 107–117.

8

Strategies for Reforming Houston Schools

Rod Paige
Susan Sclafani
Houston Independent School District

As the largest district in Texas and sixth largest in the nation, the Houston Independent School District (HISD) confronts many of the same challenges as other urban school systems. Covering 312 square miles with a population of more than 210,000 students in 280 schools, HISD includes students from 90 countries, of which 52% are Hispanic American, 35% African American, 11% White, and 2% Asian American. In 1996–1997, HISD identified 57,076 limited English proficient students and approximately 73 home languages. As reflected by free- and reduced-lunch statistics, the number of economically disadvantaged students, currently at 73%, increases annually. The district mobility rate is 38.2%. HISD is fiscally independent of municipal or county government, with state-level oversight and governance provided by the Texas Education Agency.

HISD has seen its commitment to improving student achievement begin to produce success. Student performance increased significantly on the Texas Assessment of Academic Skills (TAAS). Since 1993, reading scores are up 42%, mathematics up 53%, and writing up 20%. The average SAT scores have improved 95 points since 1985, with more students taking the test than ever before.

Since 1990, the annual dropout rate has fallen from 10.4% to 2.8% as a result of dropout prevention initiatives at the school and district levels. In addition, HISD's crime rate decreased 22% in 1997 and an additional 14% in 1998 because of better school security, drug-free school programs, new at-risk student programs, a citywide gang task force, and a new alternative educational program for disruptive students. Additional student data are provided in the Appendix at the end of the chapter.

A further sign of HISD's success is the increased decentralization of decision making to schools organized in 12 semiautonomous administrative districts. Each school uses its total budget as it sees fit through the district's school-based budgeting system. Shared decision-making committees of staff and parents advise principals on the allocations of funds to specific projects and for staffing. The district has also encouraged within-district charter schools that are approved by the school board to operate in compliance with basic life safety codes and their own best practices. The schools are held accountable for improved student performance, as all schools are on the district's accountability system. There were more than 20 charter schools operating in the district during the fall of 1998, some as whole-school charters and others as schools within schools.

There are a number of areas that are critical to urban school improvement: establishment of a coherent organization, a governance system aligned to core values, improved academic performance, decentralization, quality of staff, and efficiency and effectiveness of services provided to schools and students. In each area, the district established initiatives that are aligned to the core mission of the district.

ESTABLISHMENT OF A COHERENT ORGANIZATION

Though many call for school reform by focusing on the reform of individual schools, they do not appear to recognize that schools exist within organizations. Although the school is the unit of accountability within the organization, individual schools cannot achieve outstanding results on a long-term basis unless they are imbedded in a coherent organization. One cannot reform schools without reforming the district that provides the goods and services, policies and procedures, and selection, training, and compensation of the employees within those schools. HISD has recognized that the organization is more than a system of schools. In addition to the pedagogical issues that must be addressed to meet HISD's core mission of teaching and learning, HISD must recognize that there is a business side to the organization. HISD has organized the district into a bifurcated system, with educational principles governing the teaching and learning components of the organization and business principles governing the business components. In the same way, HISD seeks assistance in improving the education side of the organization from experts in content, professional development, and pedagogy, but it looks to the business community for assistance in business areas, including organizational development.

Working with Main Event Management (MEM), developed by Harold Hook, retired chairman of the board of American General Corporation in Houston, HISD analyzed its organization and identified specific improvement efforts. The first improvement effort is the culture of the organization. Main Event Management is a systems approach for building and maintaining the information, control, and communication infrastructure necessary for managing an organization as a whole.

Large urban school districts are like many large organizations in the private and public sectors. They are open, complex, and dynamic institutions that require organization. Without a plan, institutions self-organize, but they organize toward chaos. Therefore, the district must establish procedures for accomplishing routine tasks that allow employees to apply their energies to solving the nonroutine problems. Employees must understand where they have discretion to act so that they are not dependent on their superiors for accomplishing routine activities.

To achieve coherence within its district, HISD determined that it must create a culture that influences its employees to work to achieve the common mission and purpose of the school district. To become a high-performing institution, HISD must identify and communicate internally and externally the district's enduring purpose, a purpose that overrides the difficulties, energizes the employees, and gives them the will to move forward to the goal. As *Built to Last* by James C. Collins and Jerry Porras (1994) noted, this is the difference among the visionary organizations that have lasted over time and outperformed their competitors. The district's enduring purpose follows: HISD exists to strengthen the social and economic foundation of Houston by assuring its youth the highest quality elementary and secondary education available anywhere. Achieving that commitment to a common purpose requires that common beliefs, assumptions, and values are proactively developed throughout the organization through an enculturation process. With 27,000 employees and 280 schools, the district needed a method to develop a common culture based on the mission and purpose of the school district. Just as corporations require franchisees to attend their training programs and the armed forces require basic training, school districts must do the same thing. HISD has adopted an enculturation process for all current employees through a communications and leadership development program entitled Model-Netics. This course teaches HISD employees how an organization works and provides a common language they can use to communicate effectively. All new principals and higher level administrators participate in this course either before or immediately following their appointments.

Core Values

The district has identified a set of core values that its employees believe in and are committed to implementing. They are:

- Safety above all else.
- Student learning is the main thing.
- Focus on results and excellence.
- Parents are partners.
- Common decency toward all.

These core values are the frame against which all decisions are measured. They provide a coherent backdrop for the individual actions of all employees.

Governance

The results in Houston could not have been achieved without the focus of a reform-minded school board, first elected in 1990. The HISD board of education has nine members elected by single-member geographic districts and serving staggered 4-year terms. Since 1990, the elected school board has focused on four basic tenets of improvement, embodied in its Declaration of Beliefs and Vision:

- Redirect the district's focus back to its core mission: teaching and learning.
- Reestablish pedagogical validity so that all students may be provided with the best opportunity to develop authentic mastery

of skills of high intellectual quality in a core curriculum.

- Decentralize its operations to create an organizational structure that will increase the connection between those served (pupils, their families, and their communities) and those providing the service (public school educators), and that will efficiently and effectively deliver to schools the goods and services that school-based personnel need to do their jobs.
- Redirect the district's major operational tenet from compliance to performance, so that goals are articulated clearly, resources are provided quickly, accountability is established at all levels, and innovation and the entrepreneurial spirit are encouraged.

The struggle in Houston, as in many urban districts, is to maintain the focus on the children of the entire district, rather than fractionalizing into concerns about specific ethnic groups or board districts. The board has worked hard to avoid the parochial view, but the tension remains as a result of the board's single-member district structure. With new board members elected every 2 years, the board must constantly reinvent itself, developing consensus around the mission and beliefs.

IMPROVED ACADEMIC PERFORMANCE

Accountability for Results

The state moved into strict monitoring and prescription of practices and results in its 1984 legislation. However, over the last 6 years, the state has removed the requirements and mandates and replaced them with an accountability system focused on results. This has enabled the district to make major changes in the ways it organizes and provides educational services to children. In addition, state statutes since 1990 have provided greater flexibility to schools to redesign their educational programs to meet individual student needs. Requirements for specified time periods for each subject, specific instructional strategies, and documentation were exchanged for definitions of outcomes and accountability for student performance on state-mandated, criterion-referenced tests. Smaller class sizes mandated in 1984 have continued to provide better learning conditions for students in prekindergarten through fourth grade.

Texas Accountability System. The State of Texas established an accountability system in 1991 that focused on student dropout rates and student performance on state-mandated, criterion-reference tests, which are based on statewide essential elements required in each subject area. The system established levels of performance based on the percentage of students passing the tests in reading, mathematics, and writing at the 70% level. The categories were:

- Low-performing—fewer than 20% of the students passing.
- Acceptable—more than 20%, but fewer than 70% passing.
- Recognized—more than 70%, but fewer than 90% passing.
- Exemplary—more than 90% passing.

The levels have been raised each year. The state required 40% to pass for *acceptable* and 80% for *recognized* in 1998. The state also refined its testing program in 1990 to go beyond minimum skills and focus on application and analysis of knowledge and skills. In 1992–1993, the state tested Grades 3, 5, 7, and 10. In 1993–1994, testing moved to Grades 4, 8, and 10. Testing finally stabilized for Grades 3–8 and 10 for reading and mathematics, Grades 4, 8, and 10 for writing, and Grade 8 for science and social studies.

The accountability system has also changed over time in two ways. At first, the system used the number of students passing all tests taken, but it now considers the total number of students passing each test. However, the easing of standards in the first case was more than compensated for by changes in the consideration of the test scores and dropout rates by student subgroups (i.e., African American, Hispanic, and economically disadvantaged). A school's accountability rating is now based on the performance rating of the lowest performing subgroup in any subject area or dropout rate. For example, if 92% of the students at a school of 2,000 students pass TAAS, but there is a subgroup of as few as 30 students on the campus whose passing rate is 38%, the school is ranked as low-performing. This rule has had the desired impact of focusing the school's attention on the performance of all students, rather than ignoring minority-group performance. In one school, middle-class parents were spurred to action by the low performance rating of their school based on the dropout rate of one subgroup.

The district's performance on the Texas Accountability System has improved annually. The number of exemplary schools increased from zero in 1993 to 36 in 1998, even with the higher standards. On the other hand, the number of low-performing schools decreased from 55 in 1993 to 8 in 1998, all 8 of which are based on the performance of the school's subgroups in academic performance or dropout rates. The improvement in schools designated as *low-performing* in 1993 has been largely the result of the district's targeted schools program. Many of the schools that were *low-performing* are now *exemplary.* As one principal noted: "We did not change the teachers or the students, we changed our attitudes." Through the targeted schools assistance program, schools have received training and support in data analysis, program planning, identification of effective strategies, implementation of professional development designed to address the weaknesses in student performance, and acquisition of resources to improve the program.

District Accountability System

The district established a matrix accountability system in 1992, which considered a snapshot of performance, as the state system does, but adds a component of progress from the previous year. Thus a school might be *acceptable* in performance, but *exemplary* in the level of progress it has achieved since the previous year. This enables the district to recognize those schools that are making dramatic progress, even if their performance levels are less than *recognized.* The district has kept the criteria constant, except for raising the achievement levels for each category. From 1993 to 1998, the number of schools rated as *low-performing* and *acceptable* has dropped from 30 *low-performing* and 57 *acceptable* to zero *low-performing* and zero *acceptable* schools. In addition, the number of *exemplary* schools rose from 10 in 1993 to 83 in 1998. In 1998, all but 50 schools were either *recognized* or *exemplary.*

Targeted Schools Assistance

Each targeted school is paired with a team of principals, curriculum specialists, and researchers to observe current practices, discuss issues and data with the staff, and assist in the development and implementation of an improvement plan that is funded by the district. Originally, the targeted schools were the 55 *low-performing* schools. In 1998, targeted schools were those with fewer than 50% of the students passing. Targeted schools can receive additional funds for up to 3 years that can be used for teacher training, extended-day or Saturday tutorial programs, additional teachers to lower the student–teacher ratio or provide expertise in specific subject areas, manipulatives, books and materials, and/or establishment of computer-assisted instruction laboratories. Funding amounts range from $25,000 to $150,000, depending on the size of the school and the severity of the problems.

Team visits are made to targeted schools at least quarterly to monitor the effectiveness of the implementation and to consider revisions to the improvement plan. Many of the schools that were targeted in 1993–1994 are now *recognized* or *exemplary* schools. Schools that do not improve are analyzed to determine the appropriate actions. In some cases, a new administrative team is put in place or a significant portion of teachers is transferred. In one case, the school was totally restaffed. In most cases, however, the staff at the school have been able to improve and maintain their performance with the assistance of the targeted assistance team.

District-wide Initiatives Contributing to Academic Success

The district attributes the improvement in school performance to several factors. The primary factor is the alignment of the state's curriculum, assessment tools, and accountability system. This alignment eliminates the discrepancies between what is taught and what is tested, as well as what is placed before the public as the measure of a school's or district's quality. The district's progress is, in fact, accelerated by the public nature of the measurement system— annually, the district publishes the accountability matrix of schools and honors those schools that have achieved *recognized* and *exemplary* status. This provides an impetus for lower performing schools to improve their performance. It also provides role models for them to observe and emulate.

A second factor in the improvement is the instructional assistance provided to schools. This included district-wide initiatives to increase graduation requirements, define successful reading programs, and improve the quality of mathematics instruction. It also included the targeted assistance program described previously.

Graduation Requirements. Since 1994, the school board has worked closely with parents and the business community to develop and approve expanded graduation requirements to include 3 years of mathematics and science, 1 year of computer applications, and a three-unit focus on career and technology, science/mathematics/technology, or the humanities. In 1996–1997 HISD eliminated all remedial mathematics and science courses. Algebra is the first course required for all students, and Integrated Physics and Chemistry, Biology, and either Chemistry or Physics are the minimum graduation requirements in science.

Reading Initiative. The district established reading as a priority in 1996 through the creation of a Peer Examination, Evaluation, and Redesign (PEER) committee. The PEER committee on reading—made up of professors, principals, teachers, curriculum directors, parents, and representatives of community literacy organizations—came to consensus and created "A Balanced Approach to Reading," a report containing recommendations for development of a district-wide reading curriculum, training of all teachers in prekindergarten through fifth grade and secondary reading teachers, creation of a cadre of reading teacher trainers (45 currently), and identification of diagnostic tests and appropriate interventions. Their report has guided our HISD training, curriculum alignment, and development of reading intervention programs. HISD programs are in full agreement with the initiative begun by Governor George W. Bush in Texas and President Bill Clinton and Secretary Richard Riley in Washington, DC.

The report focused attention on six components required in any effective reading program: phonological awareness, print awareness, alphabetic awareness, orthographic awareness, comprehension strategies, and reading practice. During 1997 and 1998, HISD focused on training teachers in Grades K–3 and 4–6 on the six components, providing alphabetic phonics strategies for middle school reading teachers, and codesigning a university course on addressing needs of high school students with reading deficiencies. Schools have written grant proposals to implement effective reading strategies and have used technology solutions provided by the district's technology department to improve reading practice and assessment.

To address the more immediate needs of students already beyond Grades K–3 without grade-level proficiency, the district offered tutoring. The tutorial program is a replication of a University of Texas at Dallas program, Reading One-One, created by Dr. George Farkas. Our participating schools found students eagerly coming back to school at specified times up until 7:00 PM to work with college students trained in the methodology. The college students not only provided tutorial assistance but also served as role models who provided motivation and encouragement for students. Teachers, parents, and students were unanimous in their praise for the program.

In comparisons with students across the state on mandated, criterion-referenced tests, the district has demonstrated higher performance at almost every grade level for each ethnic subgroup. In 1998 TAAS tests, passing rates for African-American students in elementary grades ranged from 76% to 81% passing each grade in reading as opposed to 68% to 72% passing in the state. The same is true for our White students, where passing rates were 94% to 96% versus 89% to 92% for the state.

Mathematics Initiative. Structured district-wide initiatives in mathematics have focused schools on the improvement of instruction in elementary and middle schools, as well as algebra classes in high schools. As the district analyzed middle school mathematics teachers' qualifications in 1995, it determined that nearly 40% of those teachers had fewer than 12 hours of mathematics course work. Student results on TAAS document lower performance on topics beyond arithmetic. Thus, the initiative began with college courses for math teachers taught on school campuses, as well as college-student tutors who could assist middle school students while their teachers learned mathematics concepts. The initiative included summits that brought together teachers of fifth through ninth grades in seminars and workshops. Each summit day ended with the teachers in each feeder pattern working together on plans to clarify the objectives to be taught, improve their mathematics programs, and continue their collaboration.

In recent years, the district has provided curriculum guides that align resources and activities to what is to be taught and what is tested; teacher training; collaborative teacher planning across grades and between schools at elementary, middle, and high school levels; and provision of subject-area experts in district offices to observe, provide information, do demonstration lessons, and share strategies used successfully in other classrooms and schools. Student performance on the state-mandated achievement tests has improved each year since the inception of these programs. Middle school mathematics scores showed the most striking improvements. In addition, a recent study by Dr. Anthony Gary Dworkin and Laurence A. Toenjes (1997) of the Texas Center for University School Partnerships of the Institute for Urban Education at the University of Houston documented that students in the Houston urban district outperformed their peers educated in the suburbs when students were compared by socioeconomic groups.

Curriculum Policies. In September 1997, the board approved an amended curriculum policy that recognized the need to provide district-wide direction for teaching and learning. It stated that the district is committed to providing all students with equal access and opportunities to progress through a curriculum of objectives that set high learning expectations in prekindergarten through Grade 12 and, for students with disabilities, preschool through age 21. It required articulated prekindergarten through Grade 12 curriculum goals and objectives that reflect current research, best practices, and technological advancements to provide students the knowledge and skills they need to make informed and reasoned decisions. It established responsibilities for developing the curriculum, as well as responsibilities for teachers to implement the curriculum goals and objectives through their classroom instruction, and for principals to ensure that the objectives are being effectively taught and assessed.

Within the parameters established by the curriculum, teachers may organize instruction designed to utilize strategies and activities that will best help students master the objectives. This requires teachers to have deep understanding of the content being taught and mastery of many strategies that actively engage students in their learning, while being reflective about their teaching practices.

The district has used a variety of strategies to increase the level of teacher professional development. Of the 187 school days in the teacher contract, up to 10 are used for teacher development designed and provided at the school and district levels in areas identified by each school in its school improvement plan. Specific initiatives in math and reading have each included an additional 5–10 days of training for participating teachers. The district performance incentive pay plan requires the documentation of 45 hours of professional development as a prerequisite for participation.

Texas Essential Knowledge and Skills. The students of HISD are required by state law to have a curriculum that includes Texas Essential Knowledge and Skills (TEKS). The TEKS are standards-driven and provide a framework for a spiraling curriculum that builds knowledge, concepts, and skills within and across grade levels K–12. The TEKS include problem solving, critical thinking, inquiry-based learning, reasoning, decision making, and application in “real-world” situations.

HISD Scope and Sequence. HISD used the TEKS and the Student Expectations, a component of the TEKS that states what the student will know or be able to do, as the foundation for curriculum development. The scope and sequence includes Stanford 9 and Aprenda 2 correlations. These documents assist teachers in planning instruction that aligns the curriculum with the assessment tools used district-wide.

Project CLEAR: Clarifying Learning to Enhance Achievement Results. HISD recognized that many objectives and state student expectations are open to broad interpretation. With such open interpretations possible, all students may not receive the intended, challenging curriculum. Whereas the state has begun online projects to provide sample activities and units that demonstrate the meaning of the Student Expectations (http://www.coe.uh.edu/math/clarifying/index.html), HISD has taken additional steps to ensure that all students have equitable and uniform access to essential learning by initiating an objectives clarification project in mathematics, writing, and science. Implementation started in 1998–1999 with mathematics and writing in Grades K–8 and science in Grades 6–8.

Objectives clarification provides teachers with detailed information about each objective. Critical attributes are specified in detail, keeping jargon to a minimum and using examples to provide additional clarity. Prerequisite knowledge, concepts, and skills are listed when appropriate. The prerequisites often indicate the grade level(s) where the concept was introduced and how it spiraled in previous grade levels. Instructional considerations are included to indicate a variety of strategies and approaches to teach the objective. Because we want to encourage teaching objectives in logical clusters that reinforce and build knowledge, concepts, and skills, each objective clarification includes linkages to other objectives. For example, a computation mathematics objective is linked with process objectives that require students to apply the mathematics in problem-solving situations; communicate mathematical ideas using language, tools, and manipulatives; and validate their conclusions. Finally, critical attributes for assessment of the objective are listed with examples. Examples also are drawn from released state assessments and Stanford 9/Aprenda sample items, when applicable.

Implementation of Project CLEAR. The district established mathematics as a priority to ensure a strong foundation for students to achieve high performance in high school mathematics courses. If teachers are to feel confident to move instruction beyond computation, they need precise understanding of the curriculum to be taught. Recognizing that elementary teachers could not be expected to implement more than two curricular areas at one time, the district focused on the three areas that had received the most emphasis over the previous 4 years: mathematics, reading, and writing. Elementary science was initiated in 1999–2000.

In middle schools, where teachers are responsible for instruction in a single discipline, the focus is on reading and writing, mathematics, and science. Science in Grades 6–8 was selected for 1998–1999 because the new TEKS require teachers to change from a discipline-oriented curriculum (general science, life science, and earth science) to an integrated curriculum, where all three sciences will be taught each year in a spiraling, articulated sequence. This represents a challenge for staff development as well as for curriculum design. The ultimate goal is to have middle school experiences that prepare students to willingly rise to meet the challenges of a rigorous high school curriculum.

One week of summer professional development for lead teachers in every elementary school and middle school was held in August 1998, and the response of the teachers to the new tool was extremely positive. Lead teachers in mathematics and science received four modules to present on their campuses in the fall. If the powerful information in these documents is to have maximum impact in creating a vital, challenging curriculum for all students, additional support is needed for teachers. The objectives clarification initiative will also be expanded to include high school courses to maintain high expectations for all students.

QUALITY OF PERSONNEL

Transition from Probationary to Continuing Contracts

In 1994, the district identified the need to place a greater emphasis on the transition of teachers from probationary to tenured status. In many cases, school principals were automatically moving teachers into continuing contracts without asking the fundamental and critical question: Do I have reasonable evidence that this teacher will make a positive contribution to the learning of children in the classroom in the future? Unless this question could be answered affirmatively, teachers were entering the system who were likely to be problems in the future, and who would be candidates for the teacher termination process at some point. Therefore, the district started an annual process of sending to each principal in February the list of teachers who were completing the third year of probation in the district. Principals were asked to review each teacher's record over the prior 3 years and determine if that teacher had demonstrated the qualities desired in a contract teacher in the district. If not, the principal recommended termination or a fourth year of probation to continue the development, mentoring, and review process. Since that time, there are greater numbers of probationary teachers who are asked to remain on probation for a fourth year or who are denied a contract with the district.

Incentive Pay

Each month, the superintendent of schools meets with an ad hoc advisory committee made up of the teachers of the year from each school in the district. This group provides feedback on programs and processes as they appear from the vantage of the classroom. This enables the district to identify possible areas of improvement as well as areas where program implementation does not measure up to program design. One of the outcomes of this committee's input was the development of incentive pay for teachers in 1995–1996. In a discussion of program implementation, teachers noted that it was unfair that all teachers received the same level of compensation regardless of their level of effort or expertise.

The human resources department, in collaboration with a group of teachers, designed an incentive program that allowed individual schools to customize the incentive plan to address the specific needs and challenges of their campus. Each school received a sum equivalent to 2% of its teachers' salaries. The overall guidelines call for 25% of the funds to be allocated based on the improvement of student learning. Each school then established the other areas it chose to focus on: teacher attendance, service to students, parental involvement, and so on. In addition, everyone at a school is rewarded if the school is *exemplary, recognized* with progress, or *acceptable* with *exemplary* progress on the annual accountability matrix. The program has had positive reactions from teachers surveyed, although some believe it is divisive to recognize the efforts of some people. More than 80% of the teachers have received incentive payments of $250–$4,000 as a result of school rewards.

Dedicated Substitutes

Each day, teachers across the district are absent because of health problems or the need to care for ill family members. Two years ago, the district determined that the academic program at each school would be less disrupted if a cadre of substitutes who knew the school, the students, and the teachers were assigned to replace absent teachers in the building. If no teachers are absent, the school can share the substitute with a neighboring school, if needed, or use the person as a tutor or team teacher. Although the district could not afford to have enough substitutes on the payroll at each school to replace every teacher who might be absent, it could afford to assign, on average, one substitute for one third of the teachers absent. This position has given the substitute the opportunity to earn a steady salary and benefits, which ordinary substitutes do not earn. It has worked well for the substitute and for the school, but the greatest beneficiaries are the students who have a substitute they know and respect as a member of the faculty.

Performance Contracts

As HISD moved to implement decentralization and focus on performance, it became clear that the district needed a new brand of leader: one who could act independently, yet take action consistent with the goals of the district. To be successful, HISD needed to be able to remove those who were still tied to the old ways of doing things and those who were not able to meet the new demands being placed on school leaders. Just as in the private sector, the district wanted to be able to shake hands and wish the administrator well as he or she departs the organization. Because of the term contract that all school administrators had at the time, this became a daunting task. Designed to protect the rights of the administrator and enforced by the Term Contract Nonrenewal Act (TCNA), this contract made it difficult to make management changes without going through protracted legal steps. In fact, it was not unusual for such a case to take 1 to 2 years and cost several hundred thousand dollars. Therefore, if HISD were to make the needed change, it needed a way to streamline this process.

After much research, it was determined that the district could contract with the administrator in such a way that the incumbent administrator voluntarily gives up the protections under the TCNA in return for an increase in his or her salary of $7,500. In essence, the district purchased a waiver of those rights. For any new administrators, the performance contract would not be optional: If they want the position, they must take the contract that goes with it. In return, the district has the ability to remove the administrator during the term of the contract without cause by simply buying out the remainder of the contract (up to a maximum of 1 year's salary and a minimum of 2 months' salary). In addition, the district may simply elect not to renew the contract when it expires. This option does not require board approval, thus simplifying the process even further. A third option is to return the employee to a position at the level of employment prior to the performance contract, such as an assistant principal. However, because this type of contract places the administrator at greater risk, the district had to ensure that a process was in place to keep the administrator advised of how he or she was performing.

In December 1994, performance contracts were approved for direct reports to the superintendent of schools, to include the 12 subordinate district superintendents. In August 1995, performance contracts were established for all administrators at the level of principal and above. When the district first fielded the contract in the fall of 1995, it was done on a voluntary basis. However, the initial conversion rate was approximately 95%. All subsequent assignments to this level position have been done on an involuntary basis. As the district transitioned, it met with the administrators to address their concerns about the new contract—it was important that the district get their buy-in.

The single most-asked question was: "How do I know if I am doing a good job?" The answer was a simple one; the administrator must talk to his or her supervisor. This discussion starts with a goal-setting conference, which the district incorporated into the administrator-appraisal system. In this conference the supervisor is expected to establish goal criteria that include the standards expected. These goals are expected to be directly tied to the School Improvement Plan (SIP) and should, in fact, be a road map to achieving the school's goals. At the end of the appraisal period, the appraisal should then reflect the administrator's ability to achieve the goals and standards established at the outset of the period. It is further expected that throughout the period, the supervisor and the administrator will have periodic discussions about the progress to date. This tie to the appraisal system is critical to the success of the performance contract.

Professional Development

Within the district, professional development is planned both bottom-up and top-down. The bottom-up planning starts with professional development needs identified at the school level. Each school prepares an SIP, which identifies the focus areas for school improvement. Data on student achievement and student enrollment are analyzed to determine the areas of need for teacher/counselor/administrator development and student learning at the school. The school then uses district and regional catalogues to identify the professional development workshops and courses that meet the needs of its staff. Where the needs are widespread among the faculty, the school will arrange the sessions at the school. Where there are only a few staff members who need a particular course, the school will identify the options for taking the course with other schools or districts.

The needs identified in the schools' SIPs are aggregated at the district office level to determine the need for professional development within the administrative district. The district office then offers or arranges for workshops and courses that include teachers, administrators, and counselors from several to all of the schools in that district. District office services support district-wide initiatives as well as projects particular and common to the schools of that administrative district.

The central office uses the district office improvement plans to identify needs that cross districts and require a district-wide approach. Through this kind of analysis, the Algebra Initiative was started in 1997–1998. When it became clear that all high schools were facing similar needs to upgrade the quality of teaching and learning, as well as the level of monitoring of instruction and scheduling students into algebra classes, the central office, in collaboration with the Rice University School Math Project, developed the Algebra Initiative.

Centralized professional development is planned through the achievement institute (curriculum, assessment, and professional development), special education, multilingual, career and technology, instructional technology, and the counseling departments to ensure that all staff working with all groups of students become knowledgeable of the content, pedagogy, and procedures of the initiatives. These services provide opportunities to investigate best practices in content and instruction that may be of interest to individuals in many administrative districts and schools.

Professional development services are provided by the staff members at each of the three levels listed earlier, as well as from the Texas State Systemic Initiative, Regional Education Service Center, Harris County Department of Education, universities, organizations, city departments, and outside consultants and businesses. Again, the focus is on identification of the expertise required to meet the objectives of the organization.

EFFICIENCY AND EFFECTIVENESS OF SERVICE DELIVERY

The district has been engaged in efficiency and cost-effectiveness studies. These studies have reduced the costs of many business areas through efficiency measures and the establishment of partnerships with the private sector to provide best practices management for district departments. Through MEM, the district recognized it needed a system for identifying, controlling, and improving the cross-functional systems in the organization. Although there are administrators in charge of the specific areas in the organization—such as human resources, finance, facilities management, educational administration, and so on—no one but the superintendent is responsible for the systems that cross departments, unless that responsibility is identified and assigned. The district has identified and trained systems managers for those cross-functional systems. In addition, the district has created a cadre of internal consultants who have received extensive training in systems thinking, process analysis, and strategies for improving cross-functional systems in the organization. Their role is to work with systems managers to analyze specific areas and identify recommendations for improvement of the processes and procedures.

Partnerships With Private-Sector Companies. At the current time, the district has contracts for the management of food services and for the management of facility maintenance and operations. These practices make available to the instructional program funds that were previously used to provide goods and support services. These partnerships continue to provide excellent results and the concept is being expanded to broader areas of the business side of the district's enterprise. The district subscribes fully to the philosophy that the administrative areas of the district are no different than those in the private sector and should be operated in accordance with best business practices.

The district recently installed SAP financial systems with the assistance of SAP America and a training company. This is the largest school district installation in the nation, and it came on line in 9 months because of the excellent partnering between the district and SAP. To manage such large-scale business projects, the district has developed a new model that involves a steering committee made up of representatives from each of the major business projects and led by an external consultant. Each project's management team reports weekly to the steering committee to identify issues, resolve conflicts, and maintain communication. A similar process has been used to implement PeopleSoft, a human resources and payroll system that will enable district staff to complete all time and labor reports online in real time.

CONCLUSION

What works in Houston is the result of many factors. It cannot be overstated that the positive organizational climate of Houston has enabled the district to focus on continuous improvement of services to students. The MEM training in management has enabled administrators and support staffs to understand the assumptions, values, and beliefs of the organization. If the organization has a well-understood philosophy and sense of direction, then each employee can elect to stay or leave based on individual agreement with the organization's expectations, values, rewards, and objectives. Those who choose to stay are committed to contributing to its success.

The conceptualization of the district as two entities, business and education, has also played a major role in the improvement of "both sides of the house." The use of business principles and identification of best practices from the corporate sector has improved the quality and efficiency of services available to our schools and departments. At the same time, it is recognized that the district must also search for best practices in education in school districts across the continent. Both sides of the house are dedicated to improving the quality and effectiveness of their services to reach the district's purpose.

The accountability systems created by the state and the district have focused teachers' and administrators' attention on improving achievement for all students. Based on an alignment of curriculum, testing, and reporting, accountability has provided a system for improvement of teaching and learning. Whereas many focus on incentives of recognition and sanctions for nonperformance, it has been Houston's experience that the key to improvement is the ability to identify what needs to be done and provide assistance in doing it. We have found that when teachers know what they are doing well and what needs to be improved, they are willing to do what it takes for their students to be successful. We are truly fortunate in Houston to be able to make that claim for employees in our schools as well as in our district and central offices.

REFERENCES

Collins, J. C., & Porras, J. I. (1994). *Built to last: Successful habits of visionary companies.* New York: Harper Business.

Dworkin, A. G., & Toenjes, L. A. (1997). *Comparative analysis of TAAS performances in the Houston Independent School District.* Houston: Texas Center for University School Partnerships of the Institute for Urban Education.

Appendix for Chapter 8

Percent Passing TAAS Reading and Mathematics Scores for the 1993-94 through 1997-98 Academic Years for Selected Student Subpopulations by Grade Level HISD

Reading

Grade	All Students not in Special Education					Gain
Level	1994	1995	1996	1997	1998	94-98
3	72	74	77	79	85	13
4	70	73	77	82	89	19
5	70	75	82	84	88	18
6	59	67	64	73	75	16
7	58	64	71	74	75	17
8	59	60	63	74	75	16
10	64	63	70	79	81	17

Grade	African American Students					Gain
Level	1994	1995	1996	1997	1998	94-98
3	66	64	73	76	83	17
4	63	66	73	77	86	23
5	64	68	78	81	86	22
6	55	63	65	75	79	24
7	54	61	71	74	75	21
8	55	59	64	74	76	21
10	62	60	71	83	84	22

Mathematics

Grade	All Students not in Special Education					Gain
Level	1994	1995	1996	1997	1998	94-98
3	56	63	74	75	77	21
4	51	61	77	77	84	33
5	56	64	76	84	88	32
6	46	46	64	69	75	29
7	42	40	55	67	71	29
8	39	34	52	62	72	33
10	46	44	52	60	69	23

Grade	African American Students					Gain
Level	1994	1995	1996	1997	1998	94-98
3	49	57	69	70	73	24
4	41	51	70	69	77	36
5	46	53	67	77	84	38
6	37	40	61	65	73	36
7	33	32	49	60	65	32
8	39	27	46	58	68	29
10	38	36	46	57	66	28

Grade	Hispanic Students					Gain
Level	1994	1995	1996	1997	1998	94-98
3	69	70	74	75	82	13
4	68	73	74	81	89	21
5	67	74	80	82	88	21
6	54	63	56	68	67	13
7	52	59	65	70	70	18
8	53	52	55	69	70	17
10	56	53	62	71	75	19

Grade	Hispanic Students					Gain
Level	1994	1995	1996	1997	1998	94-98
3	52	59	72	74	74	22
4	49	61	77	79	86	37
5	53	65	78	85	90	37
6	43	40	59	66	72	29
7	36	34	49	64	70	34
8	33	27	46	57	69	36
10	39	34	45	51	63	24

Grade	White Students					Gain
Level	1994	1995	1996	1997	1998	94-98
3	90	91	93	94	95	5
4	89	92	91	95	98	9
5	91	92	95	96	97	6
6	84	91	91	93	96	12
7	89	93	94	96	95	6
8	87	91	93	95	96	9
10	90	93	94	96	96	6

Grade	White Students					Gain
Level	1994	1995	1996	1997	1998	94-98
3	80	85	90	92	92	12
4	77	86	91	94	96	19
5	82	88	92	95	96	14
6	77	82	90	90	94	17
7	81	79	88	92	93	12
8	76	77	86	90	91	15
10	75	78	82	89	90	15

Source: TEA TAAS Summary Reports (Data do not include Fondren Future Year Round Education.)

Percent Passing TAAS Reading and Mathematics Scores for the 1993-94 through 1997-98 Academic Years for Selected Student Subpopulations by Grade Level HISD

Reading

Grade	Economically Disadvantaged					Gain
Level	1994	1995	1996	1997	1998	94-98
3	65	68	72	75	82	17
4	65	68	72	78	87	22
5	64	70	78	81	86	22
6	52	61	57	68	70	18
7	50	57	65	69	69	19
8	49	51	56	67	70	21
10	52	51	60	68	75	23

Grade	Not Economically Disadvantaged					Gain
Level	1994	1995	1996	1997	1998	94-98
3	83	83	88	87	92	9
4	80	83	87	89	94	14
5	82	83	91	91	94	12
6	67	76	80	83	87	20
7	66	71	81	82	85	19
8	67	67	72	82	85	18
10	69	67	75	83	85	16

Mathematics

Grade	Economically Disadvantaged					Gain
Level	1994	1995	1996	1997	1998	94-98
3	48	57	69	71	72	24
4	44	54	73	73	81	37
5	48	58	72	81	86	38
6	39	38	59	66	72	33
7	33	32	47	62	67	34
8	29	25	45	56	68	39
10	37	35	43	51	65	28

Grade	Not Economically Disadvantaged					Gain
Level	1994	1995	1996	1997	1998	94-98
3	69	74	86	84	87	18
4	64	73	86	84	90	26
5	70	74	85	89	93	23
6	55	57	76	76	84	29
7	50	49	66	73	80	30
8	46	42	61	69	79	33
10	49	47	56	63	72	23

Grade	Title I (Part A) Participants					Gain
Level	1994	1995	1996	1997	1998	94-98
3	65	68	73	76	83	18
4	64	68	75	79	88	24
5	63	69	79	82	88	25
6	60	59	60	70	71	11
7		48	64	70	70	
8	38	40	55	69	72	34
10	60			63	76	16

Grade	Title I (Part A) Participants					Gain
Level	1994	1995	1996	1997	1998	94-98
3	49	56	70	72	74	25
4	44	53	75	74	83	39
5	48	57	73	82	88	40
6	43	38	61	68	73	30
7		22	47	63	67	
8	7	14	43	58	69	62
10	0			56	36	36

Grade	Title I (Part A) Non-Participants					Gain
Level	1994	1995	1996	1997	1998	94-98
3	84	84	88	87	91	7
4	84	84	85	90	93	9
5	85	85	91	90	93	8
6	59	71	74	78	82	23
7	58	68	76	79	83	25
8	59	66	68	80	82	23
10	65	63	71	79	81	16

Grade	Title I (Part A) Non-Participants					Gain
Level	1994	1995	1996	1997	1998	94-98
3	69	76	85	84	87	18
4	67	75	84	85	88	21
5	74	78	85	87	92	18
6	46	50	71	71	80	34
7	42	45	61	70	79	37
8	39	40	58	67	77	38
10	46	44	52	60	69	23

Source: TEA TAAS Summary Reports (Data do not include Fondren Future Year Round Education.)

Percent Passing TAAS Reading and Mathematics Scores for the 1993-94 through 1997-98 Academic Years for Selected Student Subpopulations by Grade Level HISD

Reading

Grade	Limited English Proficient					Gain
Level	1994	1995	1996	1997	1998	94-98
3	67	69	72	76	83	16
4	57	64	67	75	85	28
5	48	58	68	69	76	28
6	31	41	31	42	43	12
7	25	31	38	43	32	7
8	23	24	28	36	37	14
10	21	19	28	36	41	20

Grade	Not Limited English Proficient					Gain
Level	1994	1995	1996	1997	1998	94-98
3	72	74	77	79	85	13
4	72	74	78	82	90	18
5	72	77	84	86	90	18
6	64	72	72	81	83	19
7	63	70	78	81	82	19
8	63	65	70	80	81	18
10	70	69	77	86	88	18

Mathematics

Grade	Limited English Proficient					Gain
Level	1994	1995	1996	1997	1998	94-98
3	56	64	74	76	80	24
4	42	56	75	77	81	39
5	42	57	70	81	84	42
6	27	22	42	48	55	28
7	17	16	29	44	41	24
8	16	12	27	33	47	31
10	23	19	24	31	43	20

Grade	Not Limited English Proficient					Gain
Level	1994	1995	1996	1997	1998	94-98
3	56	63	74	75	76	20
4	52	62	77	77	84	32
5	58	65	77	84	89	31
6	49	51	70	75	81	32
7	45	45	61	71	77	32
8	41	37	57	66	76	35
10	49	47	57	65	73	24

Grade	Bilingual					Gain
Level	1994	1995	1996	1997	1998	94-98
3	64	67	76	85	92	28
4	57	65	62	74	87	30
5	47	62	69	71	74	27
6	33	43	27	45	40	7
7	24	42	50	60	32	8
8	22	50	48	50	80	58
10		92				

Grade	Bilingual					Gain
Level	1994	1995	1996	1997	1998	94-98
3	57	62	80	91	92	35
4	41	59	68	79	86	45
5	47	62	72	82	84	37
6	31	29	46	56	67	36
7	21	24	39	52	41	20
8		29	29	40	70	
10		67				

Grade	Not Bilingual					Gain
Level	1994	1995	1996	1997	1998	94-98
3	72	74	77	79	85	13
4	71	74	77	82	90	19
5	71	75	82	85	89	18
6	59	68	65	74	76	17
7	59	64	71	75	75	16
8	59	60	63	75	76	17
10	65	63	71	79	81	16

Grade	Not Bilingual					Gain
Level	1994	1995	1996	1997	1998	94-98
3	56	63	74	75	76	20
4	52	61	77	77	84	32
5	56	64	76	84	89	33
6	46	47	65	70	76	30
7	42	40	55	67	72	30
8	39	35	52	62	72	33
10	46	44	52	60	69	23

Source: TEA TAAS Summary Reports (Data do not include Fondren Future Year Round Education.)

Percent Passing TAAS Reading and Mathematics Scores for the 1993-94 through 1997-98 Academic Years for Selected Student Subpopulations by Grade Level HISD

Reading

Grade	Migrant					Gain
Level	1994	1995	1996	1997	1998	94-98
3	64	56	64	77	86	22
4	57	78	61	63	96	39
5	45	66	75	71	81	36
6	33	63	40	60	53	20
7	23	41	42	64	64	41
8	41	44	41	52	70	29
10	33	62	50	61	53	20

Grade	Non-Migrant					Gain
Level	1994	1995	1996	1997	1998	94-98
3	72	74	77	79	85	13
4	70	73	77	82	89	19
5	70	75	82	84	89	19
6	59	67	64	74	75	16
7	59	64	71	75	75	16
8	59	60	63	75	76	17
10	65	63	71	80	81	16

Mathematics

Grade	Migrant					Gain
Level	1994	1995	1996	1997	1998	94-98
3	38	44	50	73	86	48
4	33	56	63	78	100	67
5	38	65	77	77	85	47
6	33	38	51	64	60	27
7	24	16	28	57	67	43
8	32	8	38	39	69	37
10	29	47	24	38	49	20

Grade	Non-Migrant					Gain
Level	1994	1995	1996	1997	1998	94-98
3	56	63	74	76	77	21
4	51	61	77	77	84	33
5	56	64	76	84	88	32
6	46	47	64	69	76	30
7	42	40	55	67	71	29
8	39	35	52	63	72	33
10	46	44	52	60	69	23

Grade	English as a Second Language					Gain
Level	1994	1995	1996	1997	1998	94-98
3	65	72	79	85	81	16
4	55	64	69	77	84	29
5	51	57	63	67	78	27
6	29	37	26	37	40	11
7	22	26	32	38	29	7
8	20	19	23	31	32	12
10	18	13	23	30	33	15

Grade	English as a Second Language					Gain
Level	1994	1995	1996	1997	1998	94-98
3	56	68	78	88	79	23
4	41	55	78	80	77	36
5	42	56	68	77	84	42
6	24	19	39	42	52	28
7	15	12	23	40	40	25
8	13	10	23	30	42	29
10	23	18	20	27	39	16

Grade	Not English as a Second Language					Gain
Level	1994	1995	1996	1997	1998	94-98
3	72	74	77	79	85	13
4	71	74	77	82	90	19
5	71	75	83	85	89	18
6	62	70	70	79	82	20
7	62	68	77	80	81	19
8	63	64	69	79	80	17
10	68	68	75	85	87	19

Grade	Not English as a Second Language					Gain
Level	1994	1995	1996	1997	1998	94-98
3	56	63	74	75	77	21
4	52	61	77	77	84	32
5	57	64	76	84	89	32
6	48	49	68	73	80	32
7	45	43	59	70	75	30
8	40	37	56	66	75	35
10	48	46	56	64	72	24

Source: TEA TAAS Summary Reports (Data do not include Fondren Future Year Round Education.)

Achievement Gap Analysis of Percent Passing TAAS Reading and Mathematics for the 1993-94 through 1997-98 Academic Years for Selected Student Subpopulations by Grade Level HISD

Reading

Grade	Gap: White - African American					CHG
Level	1994	1995	1996	1997	1998	94-98
3	24	27	20	18	12	-12
4	26	26	18	18	12	-14
5	27	24	17	15	11	-16
6	29	28	26	18	17	-12
7	35	32	23	22	20	-15
8	32	32	29	21	20	-12
10	28	33	23	13	12	-16

Grade	Gap: White - Hispanic					CHG
Level	1994	1995	1996	1997	1998	94-98
3	21	21	19	19	13	-8
4	21	19	17	14	9	-12
5	24	18	15	14	9	-15
6	30	28	35	25	29	-1
7	37	34	29	26	25	-12
8	34	39	38	26	26	-8
10	34	40	32	25	21	-13

Mathematics

Grade	Gap: White - African American					CHG
Level	1994	1995	1996	1997	1998	94-98
3	31	28	21	22	19	-12
4	36	35	21	25	19	-17
5	36	35	25	18	12	-24
6	40	42	29	25	21	-19
7	48	47	39	32	28	-20
8	37	50	40	32	23	-14
10	37	42	36	32	24	-13

Grade	Gap: White - Hispanic					CHG
Level	1994	1995	1996	1997	1998	94-98
3	28	26	18	18	18	-10
4	28	25	14	15	10	-18
5	29	23	14	10	6	-23
6	34	42	31	24	22	-12
7	45	45	39	28	23	-22
8	43	50	40	33	22	-21
10	36	44	37	38	27	-9

Grade	Gap: Not Econ Disadv - Econ Disadv					CHG
Level	1994	1995	1996	1997	1998	94-98
3	18	15	16	12	10	-8
4	15	15	15	11	7	-8
5	18	13	13	10	8	-10
6	15	15	23	15	17	2
7	16	14	16	13	16	0
8	18	16	16	15	15	-3
10	17	16	15	15	10	-7

Grade	Gap: Not Econ Disadv - Econ Disadv					CHG
Level	1994	1995	1996	1997	1998	94-98
3	21	17	17	13	15	-6
4	20	19	13	11	9	-11
5	22	16	13	8	7	-15
6	16	19	17	10	12	-4
7	17	17	19	11	13	-4
8	17	17	16	13	11	-6
10	12	12	13	12	7	-5

Grade	Gap: Not Title I - Title I					CHG
Level	1994	1995	1996	1997	1998	94-98
3	19	16	15	11	8	-11
4	20	16	10	11	5	-15
5	22	16	12	8	5	-17
6	-1	12	14	8	11	12
7		20	12	9	13	
8	21	26	13	11	10	-11
10	5			16	5	0

Grade	Gap: Not Title I - Title I					CHG
Level	1994	1995	1996	1997	1998	94-98
3	20	20	15	12	13	-7
4	23	22	9	11	5	-18
5	26	21	12	5	4	-22
6	3	12	10	3	7	4
7		23	14	7	12	
8	32	26	15	9	8	-24
10	46			4	33	-13

Source: TEA TAAS Summary Reports (Data do not include Fondren Future Year Round Education.)

Table 2: A Longitudinal Comparison of State and HISD TAAS Passing Rates for Non-Special Education Students for Reading, Math, Writing, Science, and Social Studies: Spring Results 1994–98

		Reading		Math		Writing		Science		Social Studies	
		HISD	State	HISD	State	HISD	State	HISD	State	HISD	State
Grade 3	1998	85	86	77	80						
	1997	79	81	75	81						
	1996	77	80	74	76						
	1995	74	79	63	72						
	1994	72	77	56	62						
Grade 4	1998	89	89	84	86	89	88				
	1997	82	82	77	82	87	87				
	1996	77	78	77	78	88	86				
	1995	73	79	61	70	83	84				
	1994	70	75	51	59	84	85				
Grade 5	1998	88	88	88	89						
	1997	84	84	84	86						
	1996	82	83	76	78						
	1995	75	79	64	72						
	1994	70	77	56	62						

Grade 6	1998	75	85	75	86						
	1997	73	84	69	81						
	1996	64	78	64	77						
	1995	67	78	46	63						
	1994	59	73	46	60						
Grade 7	1998	75	85	71	83						
	1997	74	84	67	79						
	1996	71	82	55	70						
	1995	64	78	40	61						
	1994	58	75	42	59						
Grade 8	1998	75	85	72	83	76	83	74	84	54	69
	1997	74	83	62	76	70	80	74	85	53	67
	1996	63	77	52	68	60	76	63	77	54	69
	1995	60	74	34	56	59	74	61	76	50	65
	1994	59	76	38	57	52	69				
Grade 10	1998	81	88	69	78	82	89				
	1997	79	86	60	72	79	88				
	1996	70	81	52	65	73	85				
	1995	63	76	44	59	75	86				
	1994	64	76	46	57	68	81				

9

Incentive Effects New York's Minimum Competency Exams

John H. Bishop
Cornell University
Ferran Mane
Rovira I Virgili University

Educational reformers and the majority of the American public believe that teachers ask too little of their pupils. African-American and Hispanic parents, in particular, criticize the low expectations and goals that teachers and school administrators often set for their children. These low expectations, they believe, result in watered-down curricula and a tolerance of mediocre teaching and inappropriate student behavior. The result is that the prophecy of low achievement becomes self-fulfilling.

The problem of low expectations is not limited to minority students or lower income communities; it's endemic. High school subjects are taught at vastly different levels, and yet research has shown that learning gains are substantially larger when students take more demanding courses. Controlling for teacher qualifications and student ability and socioeconomic status (SES) does not significantly reduce the positive effects of course rigor on test-score gains (Bishop, 1996b; Kulik & Kulik, 1984; Monk, 1994). Why then do students not flock to more demanding courses? First, these courses are considerably more work and grades tend to be lower. Second, the rigor of these courses is not well signaled to parents, neighbors, employers, and colleges, so the rewards for the extra work are small for most students. Admissions staff of selective colleges learn how to read the transcripts of the high schools they recruit from and evaluate grades in the light of course demands. Historically, however, most colleges have not factored the rigor of high school courses into their admissions decisions.[1] Employers hardly ever consider the rigor of high school courses when they make hiring decisions. Consequently, the bulk of students who do not aspire to attend a selective college quite rationally avoid rigorous courses and demanding teachers.

Many parents support their children's preference for taking easier courses. Even in wealthy communities, they often pressure guidance counselors to let their children switch to easier courses where it is easier to get good grades. As one guidance counselor described the situation prior to the high school's switching to the All-Regents (1997):

> A lot of...parents were in a "feel good" mode. "If my kids are not happy, I'm not happy...." Probably...25 percent...were going for top colleges. They were pushing their kids hard. The rest—75 percent (I'm guessing at the numbers)—said "No, that's too hard, they don't have to do that...." If they [the students] felt it was too tough, they would back off. I had to hold people in classes, hold the parents back. [I would say] "Let the kid get C's. It's OK. Then they'll get C+'s and then B's." [But they would demand,] "No! I want my kid out of that class!"

Further, teachers often supported students switching to easier classes:

> Frankly we couldn't get the staff to agree [to holding struggling or lazy students in more demanding classes] either. They would say, "He's not learning....Get him out....Let the kid drop into an easier class."

This guidance counselor's wish to place students into more challenging courses is unusual. Most counselors see themselves as helping students set "realistic" goals and avoiding courses where they will be "in over their heads." At most schools, parents who want their children in more demanding courses are accommodated, but they are referred to as "pushy." Most parents, however, are not aware that class assignments will be changed if they demand it. Minority parents and parents with limited education are less likely to question class assignments, which contributes to their children's disproportionately assignment to classes that set minimal, low learning goals.

PUBLIC OPINION ABOUT STANDARDS AND MINIMUM COMPETENCY EXAMS

Political and educational leaders at the state level have been concerned for decades about these problems. The traditional policy instruments—budgetary support for schools and school construction, teacher certification rules, and so on—do not address learning standards, so states have sought other instruments. Many states have increased the number of courses required to graduate. This, however, has not assured that students take challenging courses or that students work hard in these courses. Another approach has been to require that schools give students achievement tests and publish the results. The hope is that publicly identifying low-performing schools will spur the local superintendent and school board into taking remedial action. Some states and cities have developed interventions such as reconstitution for poorly performing schools. Other jurisdictions have rewarded schools for year-to-year gains in achievement test scores.

Probably the most common response to the problem of low expectations and low achievement has been to define standards for learning, test students against these standards, and require that students pass exams assessing their achievement of these standards before graduating. Table 9.1 presents data from 1980 and 1992 on the proportion of high school students who are required to pass minimum competency examinations (MCEs) to graduate from high school. School principals provided the information on graduation requirements. In most cases, MCEs have been developed and mandated by the state boards of education. In other cases, local school districts have established the requirement. In 1980, 49% of the nation's high school students faced a MCE requirement. In 1992, 56% faced MCE requirements. The increase appears to have been concentrated in states and school districts with large minority populations. In 1992, for example, 79% of the Hispanic and African-American students faced such requirements.

Surveys of public opinion about MCEs suggest that such policies are supported not only by voters and teachers but apparently by students as well (Table 9.2). In 1997, representative samples of adults, teachers, and students were asked the following question: "Suppose your school required students to learn more and tested them before they were allowed to graduate. Do you think that most kids would pay more

TABLE 9.1
High Schools Requiring Passage of a Minimum Competency Test to Graduate: Proportion of Seniors Who Attend

Socioeconomic Status		Low	Medium	High	
	1980	.560	.503	.487	
	1992	.647	.557	.442	
Reading and Math Scores		Low	Medium	High	
	1980	.547	.515	.466	
	1992	.643	.565	.457	
Ethnicity		White/ Asian	African-American	Hispanic	Total
	1980	.466	.567	.568	.49
	1992	.479	.790	.790	.56

Note. Tabulations of High School and Beyond (HSB) and National Educational Longitudinal Survey: 1988 (NELS-88) principal survey responses weighted by the number of seniors sampled at the high school. The HSB survey sampled schools with large minority populations. The totals in column 5 are averages of the ethnicity specific rates in columns 1–3 using national proportions of high school students from each ethnic group as weights.

attention to their school work and study harder or not?" (Johnson & Farkas, 1997, p. 46). Seventy-one percent of adults, 75% of teachers, 74% of White high school students, 82% of Hispanic students, and 80% of African-American students responded yes. Similar proportions agreed that in addition, "most kids would actually learn more" (p. 46). This survey also asked "Do you think schools should expect inner-city kids to learn as much and achieve at the same standards as kids from middle-class backgrounds? or Should schools make things easier for inner-city kids because they come from poor backgrounds?" (p. 46).

As seen in Table 9.2, 60% of the adults, 73% of the teachers, 86% of the White students, 78% of the Hispanic students, and 84% of the African-American students selected the first option. The students' responses to these questions suggest that students do not perceive themselves as working very hard and that, if more was required of them, they would try harder. Also noteworthy is the opposition of minority students to making "things easier for inner-city kids because they come from poor backgrounds."

Many survey respondents, however, also thought that tougher graduation tests would also have some negative consequences. Slightly more than half of students agreed with the statement that "more kids will

TABLE 9.2
Student Opinion About the Effects of Minimum Competency Tests

	Percent Responding Yes				
	African-American High School Students	Hispanic High School Students	White High School Students	Adults*	Teachers*
Do you think that most kids would pay more attention to their schoolwork and study harder, or not?	80%	82%	74%	71%	75%
Do you think that most kids would actually learn more, or not?	79%	75%	72%	72%	75%
Do you think that more kids will drop out, or not?	55%	53%	54%	45%	49%
Do you think that more kids will dislike education and resist learning, or not?	55%	56%	51%	38%	27%
Do you think schools should expect inner-city kids to learn as much and achieve at the same standards as kids from middle-class backgrounds?	84%	78%	86%	60%	73%
- or -					
Should schools make things easier for inner-city kids because they come from poor backgrounds?	13%	19%	10%	32%	22%

Note. Students were asked to consider the following: "Suppose your school required students to learn more and tested them before they were allowed to graduate." Data for adults and teachers taken from Johnson (1995) survey. From Johnson & Farkas (1997). Copyright 1997 by Public Agenda. Adapted by permission.

*Question wording for adults and teachers: "Suppose public schools set higher academic standards and they also require kids to show they achieve those standards before they graduate."

drop out" and "more kids will dislike education and resist learning." Are they correct? What effects have MCEs had on high school dropout rates, college entrance rates, and college dropout rates? What effects have they had on the quality of the jobs obtained by high school graduates? Are these effects different for students from less advantaged or minority backgrounds? New York State was one of the first states to make graduation contingent on passing a series of MCEs. How are New York State's policies evolving and what impacts are they likely to have? These are the questions that are addressed in this chapter.

The Effects of Minimum Competency Graduation Requirements on Dropout Rates

A number of studies have examined the effect of MCE graduation requirements on enrollment rates and high school graduation rates. Dean Lillard (1997) and Lillard and DeCicca (1997a, 1997b) found that dropout rates were reduced by increases in the number of courses necessary to graduate but not by MCEs. Their analyses of longitudinal data from the National Educational Longitudinal study (1988; NELS-88) found that different specifications produced different estimates of the impact of MCEs on dropout rates. Models that controlled for state-fixed effects and examined the effect of introducing a state MCE tended to find no effect.

In order to study this issue in greater depth, state-level data on enrollment rates and high school graduation rates were analyzed. The dependent variables was the enrollment rate of 17-year-olds (taken from the 1990 Census [Bureau of the Census, 1993] and the National Center for Education Statistics, 1991) and the high school graduation rate (the ratio of the number of high school diplomas and general education diplomas [GEDs] awarded in the state to the number of 17-year-olds).[2] Data on each state's high school graduation requirements—MCEs and the number of Carnegie units required to graduate—were taken from the *Digest of Educational Statistics* (National Center for Educational Statistics, 1992, 1996). The information from the two different sources is not completely consistent so separate regressions were run using indicators of state graduation requirements taken from each source. The control variables characterizing the demographic background of the state's high-school-age youth were as follows:

- A parents' education index equal to the average of the percent of parents with a high school diploma and the percentage of parents with a university degree.
- Incidence of poverty for children under the age of 18.
- Percentage of population foreign born.
- Percentage of African-American public school students.
- Percentage of Hispanic public school students.
- A dummy variable for New York State (testing whether the voluntary Regents exams have any impact on dropout rates).

The results of the regression analysis are presented in Table 9.3. Four of the six coefficients on the state MCE variable are negative, but none come even close to statistical significance at the 10% level. The only significant coefficient on the MCE variable is positive. One has to conclude that there is no evidence in these data that MCEs as they existed in the early 1990s lowered graduation rates. New York State's voluntary Regents exams also appear to have no significant effects on dropout rates or graduation rates. However, the number of Carnegie units required to graduate does have significant negative effects on enrollment rates. For graduation rates, the Carnegie unit requirement variable is negative and similar in magnitude to the enrollment rate regressions, but far from statistically significant.

Many states have increased their graduation requirements by 3 or 4 Carnegie units over the last few decades. The regressions imply that these increases in Carnegie unit graduation requirements should have, *ceteris paribus*, decreased enrollment rates of 17-year-olds by about 1 percentage point. Data on trends in dropout rates by ethnicity are presented in Table 9.4. Despite the policy shifts making high school graduation more difficult, high school completion rates of 19- and 20-year-old African Americans rose from 67.2% in 1972–1973 to 70.6% in 1981–1982 and then to 75.2% in 1990–1992. During the 1970s high school completion rates of White 19- to 29-year-olds fell slightly from 85.3% in 1972–1973 to 84.7% in 1981–1982. Rates then rose during the 1980s to 87.7% in 1990–1992. Hispanic completion rates also increased. Event and status dropout rates also declined during the period in which MCEs were introduced and graduation requirements were increased. Clearly, if tougher graduation standards do tend to increase dropout

TABLE 9.3
Determinants of School Enrollment and High School Graduation Rates

	Percent of 17-Year-Olds Enrolled in High School—1990 Census		Percent of 17-Year-Olds Enrolled in High School—1991 States and Nations		Secondary School Graduates per 100 Persons 17 Years Old	
State Minimum Competency Test[a]	- .76 (1.10)	1.05 (1.41)	- .17 (.37)	.87* (1.81)	-1.19 (.64)	- .08 (.04)
New York State	1.78 (.98)	1.80 (.98)	.33 (.27)	.05 (.04)	-.83 (.17)	-.88 (.18)
Number of Carnegie Units Required to Graduate	-.27** (2.59)	-.34*** (3.22)	-.15** (2.26)	-.19*** (2.88)	-.20 (.73)	-.24 (.82)
No Carnegie Unit Graduation Requirement	-4.79** (2.84)	-5.96*** (2.80)	-3.05** (2.22)	-3.73*** (2.73)	-1.46 (.26)	-1.97 (.34)
Parents Education Index[b]	.29** (3.22)	.34*** (3.19)	.11 (1.55)	.13* (1.97)	.81*** (2.76)	.87*** (3.04)
Percentage in Poverty (People 18 years of age or younger)[c]	.043 (.55)	.063 (.84)	-.02 (.40)	-.014 (.30)	-.04 (.19)	-.01 (.07)
Percentage Foreign Born[d]	-.15* (1.74)	-.22** (2.69)	-.19*** (3.27)	-.22*** (4.18)	-.11 (.44)	-.17 (.77)

Percentage of African-American Public School Students[e]	-.037** (1.40)	-.071** (2.45)	-.040** (2.33)	-.061*** (3.33)	-.215*** (3.04)	-.231*** (2.93)
Percentage of Hispanic School Students[e]	-.036 (.97)	-.046 (1.26)	-.006 (.26)	-.014 (.59)	-.236** (2.40)	-.239** (2.39)
Adj *R* Squared	.4922	.5010	.5405	.5708	.6496	.6460
Root Mean Square Error	1.657	1.642	1.087	1.050	4.463	4.486
Mean of Dependent Variable	88.9	88.9	84.2	84.2	75.8	75.8

*Statistically significant at 10% level
**Statistically significant at 5% level
***Statistically significant at 1 % level

[a]Columns 1, 3, and 5 regressions use a competency test variable based on a 1985 study by the Education Commission of the States in the 1992 *Digest of Educational Statistics* (National Center for Educational Statistics 1992). Columns 2, 4, and 6 regressions use a competency test variable based on the 1996 *Digest of Educational Statistics* (National Center for Educational Statistics, 1996).

[b]Average of the percentage of parents obtaining a secondary high school diploma and the percentage of parents obtaining a university degree (National Center for Education Statistics, 1991, p. 139).

[c]National Center for Education Statistics (1991).

[d]Census Bureau (1990).

[e]National Center for Education Statistics (1993a).

TABLE 9.4
Trends in Dropout Rates by Ethnicity

	Event Dropout Rate—Grades 10–12			Status Dropout Rate—16- to 24-Year-Olds			Completed High School—19- to 20-Year-Olds		
	White	African American	Hispanic	White	African American	Hispanic	White	African American	Hispanic
1972–1973 Avg.	5.4	9.8	10.6	11.9	21.8	33.8	85.3	67.2	55.0
1981–1982 Avg.	4.8	8.7	9.9	11.4	18.5	32.4	84.7	70.6	57.8
1990–1992 Avg.	3.4	5.3	7.9	8.5	14.0	32.3	87.7	75.2	58.1

Note. From National Center for Education Statistics (1993b). The event dropout rate is the percentage of 10th- through 12th-grade students in October of 1 year who are not enrolled in high school or graduated the following October. The status dropout rate is the percentage of 16- to 24-year-olds who have not graduated from high school and are not attending high school currently.

rates, their effects in this case were counterbalanced and indeed overwhelmed by other forces that reduced dropout rates, such as growing incomes and the rising payoff to high school completion and college attendance.

How Important Is It to Improve the Competencies That Minimum Competency Examinations Assess?

Lerner (1990) reported that test sores were raised by the introduction of MCEs in many southern states. Opponents of MCEs sometimes dismiss findings such as Lerner's by arguing that the tests she used to track student performance over time and the MCEs themselves assess low-level literacy skills that are not all that important in the economy. The MCE graduation requirement, some argue, will distort teaching. Teachers will focus on developing low-level literacy skills rather than the "high-order problem-solving skills," writing skills, computer skills, occupation-specific skills, or affective competencies that are presumed "more important." They argue that tests similar to the MCEs used by many states have weak relationships with wages and labor-market success. What is the sense, they argue, of threatening to deny a credential—the high school diploma—that employers reward handsomely in order to induce teachers to teach and students to learn basic reading and math literacy skills that employers do not reward with higher wages?

It is quite true that in the years immediately after high school graduation, tests measuring these basic competencies have very small effects on wage rates and earnings. Effects are small for recent high school graduates because few employers use tests assessing basic literacy skills to help them screen job applicants and most do not ask for information on high school grades. Over time, however, they learn about the competencies of their new employees by observing them on the job. The most competent employees are more likely to get further training, promotions, and good recommendations. Poor performers are encouraged to leave. Because academic achievement in high school is correlated with job performance (Bishop, 1990), the sorting process results in a rising correlation between test scores and labor-market success as the worker ages (Farber & Gibbons 1996). Altonji and Pierret's (1997) analysis of the National Longitudinal Survey of Youth (NLSY) found that, in a model in which schooling and the Armed Forces Qualification Test (AFQT) competed for influence, a 1 standard deviation (*SD*) increase in the AFQT raised the wage rates of those 1 year out of school by only 2.8%. For those 12 years out of school, a 1 *SD* increase in the AFQT raised the wage rates by 16%. By contrast, the percentage impact of a year of schooling decreased with time out of school from 9.2% for those out just 1 year to 3% for those out for 12 years.

When literacy and academic achievement are measured contemporaneously (rather than decades earlier when an individual was in high school), their effects on adults' earnings and unemployment are even larger. When adults are examined, simple tests assessing literacy have at least as strong a relationship with unemployment and earnings as years of schooling. Table 9.5 presents evidence for this assertion from the National Adult Literacy Survey. Males in the top prose literacy group earn three times as much as those in the bottom literacy group and have a one-fifth chance of being unemployed. Male college graduates, by contrast, earn 2.35 times as much as high school dropouts and have a two-fifths chance of being unemployed.

The Effect of Minimum Competency Examination Graduation Requirements on College Attendance and Wages

Proponents of MCEs argue that they force teachers to set higher standards for all students, not just for middle-class White students or for students in honors or college prepatory classes. All students (especially those from lower income backgrounds) will have to take tougher courses and study harder. Students who are at risk of failing the MCE will get

TABLE 9.5
Impact of Literacy and Schooling on the Earnings and Unemployment of Males

Prose Literacy	Earnings	Unemployment Rate—1992	Schooling	Earnings	Unemployment Rate—1992
Level 1	$48,965	2.3%	Bachelors degree or more	$38,115	4.8%
Level 2	$39,941	4.1%	Associates Degree	$31,855	5.5%
Level 3	$29,610	6.4%	13–15 Years	$27,279	7.4%
Level 4	$22,046	11.5%	12 Years	$22,494	8.2%
Level 5	$15,755	14.9%	9–11 Years	$16,194	12.4%

Note. From National Adult Literacy Survey. National Center for Education Statistics (1994).

more attention and tutoring from school staff. They will learn more, which will result in (a) more students entering, staying in, and completing college, and (b) holding completed schooling constant, students getting better jobs.

MCEs are hypothesized to improve job opportunities in two ways. First, by improving student achievement they raise worker productivity (Bishop, 1990). Even when this does not immediately raise workers' earnings, the effect of academic achievement on wages grows with time and eventually becomes large.

The second way MCEs improve job opportunities is by sending a signal to employers that all the graduates of a high school meet or exceed their hiring standards. The fact that students have passed the MCE is proof that they are qualified. In most communities, competencies developed in local high schools are poorly signaled to employers. The lack of signals of achievement in high school tends to make the employers with the best jobs reluctant to risk hiring recent high school graduates. Indeed, they often have negative stereotypes regarding recent high school graduates. A personnel director interviewed for a CBS special on educational reform proudly stated, "We don't hire high school graduates any more, we need skilled workers" (Heller, 1990). Employers prefer to hire workers with many years of work experience because applicants' work records serve as a signal of competence and reliability that helps them identify the most qualified applicants.

Establishing a MCE, therefore, is one way a high school or state education system can try to overcome this signaling problem and help its graduates obtain good jobs. The existence of the MCE graduation requirement is well known to local employers. With the MCE requirement, the school's diploma now signals more than just seat time; it signals meeting or exceeding certain minimum standards in reading, writing, and mathematics. This should make local employers more willing to hire a school's recent graduates. Because of the negative stereotypes that so many employers have regarding minority youth, the MCE graduation requirement should be particularly helpful to this group.

The foregoing logic generates a number of testable predictions regarding the graduates of high schools with a MCE graduation requirement. Holding constant SES, test scores, grades, types of courses taken, working during senior year, current and past college attendance, and a complete set of other individual and school characteristics, graduates of MCE high schools will:

- Be more likely to go to college. This will be particularly true for African-American and Hispanic students, those from low-income backgrounds, and those with low test scores.
- Be less likely to drop out of college.
- Be more likely to complete a bachelor's degree within 5 years.
- Be offered higher paying jobs.
- The tendency of employers to reward graduates of schools with MCEs will be visible in data on wage rates in the first year after high school graduation.

These hypotheses were tested in the two nationally representative longitudinal data sets— High School and Beyond (HSB) seniors of 1980 and the National Educational Longitudinal Study (NELS) students graduating in 1992—that contain information on MCEs mandated by state law or local school boards. The analysis sample are the students in the two longitudinal studies who graduated from high school between January and September of their scheduled year of graduation. The HSB seniors were interviewed 2, 4, and 6 years after graduating from high school about continued schooling, employment, earnings, and changes in family status, so we are able to assess both short and intermediate run effects of school characteristics. NELS 1992 graduates were interviewed 2 years after graduation.

The regression models predicting college attendance and wages included controls for reading and math test scores in the 12th grade, grade point average, courses taken in high school, extracurricular activities, work for pay during senior year, television and homework hours, religion, reading for pleasure, attitudes, an indicator for being handicapped, family demographics, marital and parental status at the end of 12th grade, dummies for region and rural, suburban and urban residence, and six variables describing the quality of the school. The variables describing the quality of the school were a dummy variable for Catholic schools and other private schools, average teacher salary, proportion of teachers with a master's degree or more, average daily pupil attendance rate, and principal reports of school problems.[3] When wage rates or earnings are the dependent variable, months attending college full time and months attending college part time (both current and past) were included as control variables. Otherwise the models predicting wages and the models predicting college attendance were the same. The results of the analysis for graduates categorized by reading and mathematics test scores and by gender are presented in Table 9.6. Results for graduates categorized by SES and race/ethnicity are presented in Table 9.7.

College Attendance. The analysis of HSB data found that MCEs had significant positive effects on the probability of being in college in a majority of subgroups during the 4-year period immediately following high school graduation. Effects were largest for students in the middle and bottom of the test-score distribution and tended to be greater in the second and third year out than in the first, fourth, and subsequent years out. SES also interacts with MCEs in the way hypothesized. MCEs have an immediate and significant impact on the college enrollment of low-SES students. Middle- and high-SES students are affected but not until the second and third year out of high school. For 1992 graduates, the same pattern appears to be developing. Combining full- and part-time enrollment, the point estimates imply that MCEs raise enrollment rates of students from low-SES backgrounds by 4.4 percentage points, middle-SES students by 2.4 percentage points, and high-SES students not at all. Women graduating from MCE high schools are significantly more likely to go to college full time and men are significantly more likely to go part time. When results are broken down by ethnicity, MCEs are found to affect all groups but effects are somewhat larger (though not significantly so) for minority students. Effects were significant in the first year following graduation only for Hispanics and significant for almost all subgroups in the second and third year following graduation.

Wage Rates. MCEs had significant effects on wage rates of 1980 graduates who were in the low and middle test-score groups. They had no effect on wages of high test-score students. Students from low- and moderate-SES backgrounds had significantly higher wage rates when they attended MCE high schools. High-SES students did not. Finally, MCEs appeared to have increased the wage rates of minority youth but not White youth. African-American youth from MCE high schools were paid a significant 4.2% more in the first year after graduating but the effect diminished in later years. Hispanic youth graduating from MCE high schools in 1980 were paid consistently (between 3.7% and 4.6%) more at 1 year, 3 years, and 5 years following graduation.

The wage-rate benefits of graduating from an MCE high school in 1992 were considerably larger than in 1980. MCE graduates in 1992 were paid 4.1% more if they were male and 3.2% more if they were female, as compared to 1.6% to 1.7% more on average for 1980 graduates. The beneficiaries also changed. MCEs appeared to raise wage rates of medium and high test-score students by an astonishing 5.2% to 6.3%, but possibly lowered wage rates of low test-score students by 4.9%. The MCE coefficient for the low test-score group is not significantly less than zero, but it is significantly smaller than the coefficient in the middle test-score group. SES background no longer interacts with MCEs. 1992 graduates who attended high schools with MCEs are paid more without regard to their SES background. White students who did not benefit in the early 1980s are now benefiting. The minority students who in 1980 were the sole beneficiaries of attending a MCE high school no longer benefited in 1992.

Annual Earnings. The earnings regressions capture the effects of variables on time spent working and wage rates. Except for Hispanics, 1980 graduates of MCE high schools did not earn more than graduates of non-MCE high schools in the years immediately following graduation. Earning effects increased over time, however, so that by 1985 annual earnings were $484 higher for Whites, $808 higher for African Americans, and $703 higher for Hispanics. For 1992 graduates, a number of the subgroups appeared to be receiving statistically significant earnings benefits in the first calendar year after graduating from an MCE high school. Low-SES students who graduated from an MCE high school earned $694 more, a greater than 10% increase in earnings. Students

TABLE 9.6
Effects of Requiring Passage of a Minimum Competency Test to Graduate from High School

	Reading & Math Test Scores			Gender	
	Low	Middle	High	Male	Female
Logarithm Average Wage Rate					
Class of 1980 in 1981	.025	.020*	.005	.017	.016
	(1.45)	(1.74)	(.40)	(1.45)	(1.63)
Class of 1980 in 1984	.041*	- .025	- .010	- .012	.007
	(1.85)	(-1.57)	(- .56)	(.75)	(.52)
Class of 1980 in 1986	.021	.029*	.010	.017	.034**
	(1.02)	(1.85)	(.53)	(1.05)	(2.45)
Class of 1992 in 1992–1994	- .049	.052***	.063***	.041**	.032*
	(1.46)	(2.63)	(2.65)	(2.18)	(1.69)
Earnings (1992 $)					
Class of 1980 in 1981	460*	- 207	- 151	- 12	161
	(1.60)	(.99)	(.72)	(.05)	(.96)
Class of 1980 in 1982	- 41	- 89	- 80	- 148	193
	(.11)	(.32)	(.30)	(.53)	(.82)
Class of 1980 in 1983	- 240	40	- 163	- 302	227
	(.63)	(.13)	(.54)	(1.01)	(.95)
Class of 1980 in 1984	77	380	291	473	320
	(.17)	(1.59)	(.77)	(1.40)	(1.16)
Class of 1980 in 1985	474	1077***	368	979**	758**
	(1.01)	(2.89)	(.79)	(2.52)	(2.33)
Class of 1992 in 1993	60	424**	158	269	208
	(.16)	(2.21)	(.93)	(1.28)	(1.40)

College Attendance					
Class of 1980 in 1981–1982	.043*** (3.19)	.011 (.83)	- .009 (- .59)	.017 (1.43)	-.000 (- .07)
Class of 1980 in 1982–1983	.038*** (2.51)	.043*** (2.99)	- .006 (- .33)	.018 (1.39)	.024** (1.88)
Class of 1980 in 1983–1984	.041*** (2.95)	.045*** (3.15)	.007 (.38)	.026** (1.93)	.026** (2.06)
Class of 1980 in 1984	.011 (.857)	.022* (1.62)	.018 (.94)	.021 (1.59)	.008 (.65)
Class of 1980 in 1985	-.001 (.069)	.003 (.21)	.02 (1.16)	-.013 (.92)	.002 (.16)
Class of 1980 in 1986	.015 (.91)	-.017 (-1.09)	- .01 (.85)	-.011 (.97)	-.002 (-.16)
Class of 1992 in 1992–1994 (Full time)	.011 (.52)	.017 (1.04)	- .004 (.24)	- .009 (.57)	.029** (1.99)
Class of 1992 in 1992–1994 (Part time)	- .001 (.06)	.008 (.90)	.005 (.58)	.016** (2.09)	.002 (.26)

Note. Analysis of follow-up data for High School and Beyond-Senior Cohort and National Educational Longitudinal Survey: 1998. Sample is all students who graduated from high school during 1980 or 1992. All models contain a full set of background variables including test scores and grades. In addition, models predicting earnings and wage rates contain controls for the number of months spent attending college full time and months spent attending part time.

*Statistically significant at 10% level on a two-tail test.

**Statistically significant at 5% level on a two-tail test.

***Statistically significant at 1% level on a two-tail test.

Table 9.7
Effects of Requiring Passage of a Minimum Competency Test to Graduate from High School

	Socioeconomic Status			Race/Ethnicity		
	Low	Middle	High	White	African American	Hispanic
Low Wage Rate						
Class of 1980 in 1981	.036** (2.08)	.017* (1.69)	- .012 (.78)	- .005 (.56)	.042** (2.20)	.037** (2.17)
Class of 1980 in 1983	- .017 (.73)	- .006 (.42)	.005 (.25)	- .015 (1.10)	- .014 (- .54)	.045* (1.85)
Class of 1980 in 1985	.019 (.83)	.025* (1.79)	.011 (.52)	.008 (.61)	.031 (1.28)	.046** (1.98)
Class of 1992 in 1992–1994	.039 (1.27)	.037** (2.11)	.049 (1.61)	.047*** (3.09)	- .007 (.22)	- .007 (.22)
Earnings (in current $)						
Class of 1980 in 1981	194 (1.09)	113 (.93)	- 286* (1.74)	- 161 (1.45)	93 (.54)	500** (2.37)
Class of 1980 in 1982	- 86 (.34)	69 (.40)	- 113 (.51)	- 227 (1.46)	111 (.44)	402 (1.42)
Class of 1980 in 1983	- 220 (.83)	64 (.33)	- 149 (.39)	- 208 (1.16)	- 5 (.02)	447 (1.56)
Class of 1980 in 1984	0 (.00)	264 (1.21)	103 (.32)	117 (.56)	470 (1.39)	330 (.91)
Class of 1980 in 1985	377 (1.02)	620*** (2.27)	286 (.72)	484* (1.88)	808** (2.05)	703** (1.67)
Class of 1992 in 1993	694** (2.22)	171 (.94)	107 (.54)	318** (2.31)	59 (.18)	59 (.18)

College Attendance						
Class of 1980 in 1981–1982	.027* (1.72)	.008 (.70)	-.008 (.49)	.000 (.01)	.011 (.59)	.031* (1.77)
Class of 1980 in 1982–1983	.022 (1.26)	.018 (1.37)	.032* (1.66)	.018 (1.41)	.032 (1.56)	.039** (2.04)
Class of 1980 in 1983–1984	.024 (1.42)	.027** (2.12)	.030 (1.52)	.032** (2.49)	.038* (1.89)	.011 (2.04)
Class of 1980 in 1984	.004 (.28)	.013 (1.02)	.029 (1.32)	.022* (1.66)	- .002 (.09)	.002 (.09)
Class of 1980 in 1985	- .009 (.53)	.013 (.98)	.004 (.16)	.009 (.64)	-.014 (.070)	.022 (1.10)
Class of 1980 in 1986	- .012 (.59)	-.011 (.77)	.005 (.24)	- .009 (.64)	-.007 (.32)	.007 (.34)
Class of 1992 in 1992–1994 (Full time)	.032 (1.49)	.011 (.72)	- .003 (.18)	.011 (.93)	.018 (.69)	.018 (.69)
Class of 1992 in 1992–1994 (Part time)	.012 (1.11)	.013 (1.60)	.001 (.07)	.010* (1.71)	.010 (.73)	.010 (.73)

Note. Analysis of follow-up data for High School and Beyond-Senior Cohort and National Educational Longitudinal Survey: 1998. Sample is all students who graduated from high school during 1980 or 1992. All models contain a full set of background variables including test scores and grades. In addition, models predicting earnings and wage rates contain controls for the number of months spent attending college full time and months spent attending part time. The 1992 Hispanic and African-American graduates were merged because of insufficient number of observations for separate analysis.

*Statistically significant at 10% level on a two-tail test.
**Statistically significant at 5% level on a two-tail test.
***Statistically significant at 1% level on a two-tail test.

from the middle of the test-score distribution earned $424 more (a 7.5% increase) when they graduated from an MCE high school.

The reader should be reminded that all of these findings are from regressions that control for the quality of the high school and the individual's academic achievement—test scores, grade point average, participation in extracurricular activities, and an indicator for taking remedial courses in either math or English. Apparently, the existence of the MCE raises achievement in ways not captured by individual test scores and this has long-term effects on students' ability to complete college and get higher paying jobs.

In summary, the MCEs that were in existence in the 1980s and early 1990s did not lower high school completion rates as some feared. Instead, they increased college attendance and college retention rates. Students who graduated from MCE high schools immediately obtained significantly higher paying jobs and kept their pay advantage over the next 5 years. In addition, large earnings benefits appeared 5 years after high school graduation. The immediate wage-rate benefits of graduating from a MCE high school were larger for people graduating in 1992 than in 1980, although there was less egalitarian bias in terms of beneficiaries in 1992 than in the early 1980s.

MCEs are changing. New states and cities such as Chicago, Ohio, and Massachusetts have introduced them. Other states—such as New Jersey and New York—are improving their exams (by adding essays and open-response questions) and raising the standard that must be achieved to graduate. The most dramatic increase in graduation standards has occurred in New York State. The next section of this chapter provides background on New York State's Regents examination system and plans to reform it by requiring all students to take and pass Regents exams in five core subjects. The succeeding section reports on interviews with teachers and administrators in New York State high schools that have eliminated the bottom-track classes and now require all students to take demanding Regents courses in five core subjects. The primary change has been a massive redirection of energy and attention to struggling students.

The New York State Regents Examinations

New York State has been administering curriculum-based Regents examinations to high school students since June 1878. As Sherman Tinkelman, Assistant Commissioner for Examinations and Scholarships, described in a 1966 report:

> The Regents examinations are closely related to the curriculum in New York State. They are, as you can see, inseparably intertwined. One supports and reinforces the other.... These instruments presuppose and define standards.... They are a strong supervisory and instructional tool—and deliberately so. They are effective in stimulating good teaching and good learning practices. (p. 12)

Sponsorship by the state Board of Regents is crucial to the role these examinations have played in setting and maintaining high standards and promoting reform. On occasions examinations have been deliberately revised to induce changes in curriculum and teaching:

> For years our foreign language specialists went up and down the State beating the drums for curriculum reform in modern language teaching, for change in emphasis from formal grammar to conversation skills and reading skills. There was not very great impact until we introduced, after notice and with numerous sample exercises, oral comprehension and reading comprehension into our Regents examinations. Promptly thereafter, most schools adopted the new curricular objectives. (Tinkelman, 1966, p. 12)

The examinations are taken throughout one's high school career. A student taking a full schedule of college preparatory Regents courses would typically take Regents exams in mathematics and earth science at the end of 9th grade; mathematics, biology, and global studies exams at the end of 10th grade; mathematics, chemistry, English, American history, and foreign language exams at the end of 11th grade; and physics exams at the end of 12th grade.

In 1996, the ratio of the number of students taking the Mathematics Course 1 exam to average enrollment in a high school grade was 89% and, of the students in the course, 28% scored below the 65% passing grade. Participation percentages were in the 60s for the global studies, American history, biology, and English exams. Failure rates were 25% in global studies, 19% in American history, 25% in biology, and 20% in English. Those not taking Regents exams were typically in "local" courses that are considerably less challenging than Regents courses. A system of Regents Competency Tests (RCTs) in reading, writing, math, science global studies, and American history and government set a minimum standard for those not taking Regents courses.

For students the stakes attached to Regent exams are not high.[4] Exam grades count for less than one eighth of the final grade in the course and influence only the type of diploma received. College admissions decisions depend primarily on grades and SAT scores, not Regents exam scores. Employers ignore exam results when making hiring decisions. Students are aware that they can avoid Regents courses and still go to college. Indeed some perceive an advantage to avoiding them:

> My counselor wanted me to take Regents history and I did for a while. But it was pretty hard and the teacher moved fast. I switched to the other history and I'm getting better grades. So my average will be better for college. Unless you are going to a college in the state, it doesn't really matter whether you get a Regent's diploma. (Ward, 1994, P. 1)

Indeed, the modest payoff to taking Regents exams may be one of the reasons why so many students have not been taking Regents courses. In 1996–1997, only 42% of graduating seniors got a Regents diploma signifying they took a series of Regents-level (or above) academic courses and passed the associated exams.

The Statewide Shift to All-Regents

This is about to change. The Board of Regents has announced that students graduating in the year 2000 must take a new 6-hour Regents English examination and pass it at the 55% level. The class of 2001 has the additional requirement of passing an examination in algebra and geometry. The class of 2002 must also pass Regents examinations in global studies and American history. The phase-in of all five new required Regents exams will be completed when laboratory science exams are required, with the graduating class of 2003. New Regents examinations are being introduced in a number of subjects. The new exams are, if anything, more demanding than the exams they replace. Once schools have adjusted to the new exams and the requirement that all students take them, the Regents intend to raise the scores necessary to pass from 55% to 60% and then to 65%. New York State is in the process of establishing the first high-stakes curriculum-based external exit examination system in U.S. history.

All-Regents High Schools: How Did They Do It?

What kinds of changes in school policies and resource allocation will be necessary to move to an All-Regents curriculum in the five core subjects? This question was addressed by interviewing teachers, administrators, and school board members at 10 high schools that had already moved to an All-Regents curriculum and have significantly increased the number of students taking and passing Regents exams. The method of drawing the sample and conducting the interview is described in Monk and Hussain (1998) and is not repeated here. The site visitors wrote a short report about each district. In eight of the school districts, interviews were recorded and about 60 hours of tape was generated. The comments that follow are based on listening to the recorded interviews, reviewing the reports, and talking to interviewers.

Generating Support. The districts that increased their participation in Regents exams to high levels did not accomplish the goal quickly or easily. The key to success was not getting a tax-rate increase through the school board or introducing a new teaching system. In most cases, the formal and structural changes were modest. It was the school's culture—both the teacher culture and the student peer culture—that had to and did change.

The initiative generally came from a new district superintendent who recruited or promoted people into key jobs who would support his vision for eliminating the bottom or local track. Staff and community support for the change was carefully cultivated. In many cases the goal of shifting to an All-Regents curriculum was not announced until many years after important initial steps had been taken and some early successes had been achieved. In most cases, the teachers and the community felt that the school was already doing a great job. They took pride in the accomplishments of the honors students. How could they be convinced to end the low-expectation basic or local track into which struggling and lazy students were fleeing? The Regents exams and the report card outlining district-level results provided the benchmark that the superintendent was able to use to shame and inspire teachers to raise the standards for all students. As one superintendent in an All-Regents district said, "External validation of what you're doing and forcing teachers, administrators and the community to look at yourself as reflected in the eyes of people outside of you and matching a standard that exists outside your school district was critical!" The long history and prestige of Regents exams helped sell the reform to parents: "All-Regents was…helpful for us. It was very concrete. It was something the parents could relate to. When parents thought of a Regents program in their own experience, they thought about students who were college bound" (School board president of an All-Regents school district).

Outside recognition was sought and excellence awards were frequently received:

> The whole community is walking around with their chests out. Which really helps out. There is a pride that this is what _____ is today. (School board president of an All-Regents school district)

> [All-Regents] put us up on a new standard. It made a change in the high school and [brought] the recognition of this high school as a place were positive things are happening. (President of the teachers union local in an All-Regents school district)

The outside recognition increased teacher and community support for the initiative. Praise for past accomplishments spurred teachers to raise standards even higher and work harder. The focus on the external standard meant that the professional pride of the teachers became invested in getting marginal students through the Regents. The visibility of each success made the extra work seem worthwhile.

Eliminating the local or basic track and increasing standards persuaded more students to take honors, advanced placement and international baccalaureate classes: "Every level of kid in that classroom is getting a new challenge. Because we are an All-Regents high school, we are offering more AP classes. Kids are ready for that next challenge" (Principal of an All-Regents high school).

A Focus on Struggling Students

All of the districts substantially increased the time and resources devoted to teaching and tutoring struggling students. Because they had initiated the raising of the bar, school administrators felt a moral obligation to do everything in their power to help students succeed:

> You need to...provide the remedial and tutorial support that every individual kid needs. It's a terrible thing to put in a tough program that kids are going to fail. Every one of these kids can do it—they take a different amount of time to do it. (School board president in an All-Regents school district)

The guidance counselor met with incoming freshmen and developed a plan with the goal of obtaining a Regents diploma. The milestones were tracked and if a student started having difficulties, the counselor arranged tutoring. The extra time was obtained in a variety of ways:

- More homework was assigned—especially for students formerly in local courses.
- Struggling students were assigned to Stretch Regents courses, which take 1½ or 2 years to cover material reviewed in 1 year in a standard Regents course.
- Struggling students were assigned to classes with more than five periods a week. A number of the schools that settled on this option had tried 2-year Stretch Regents courses and felt that extra time in a 1-year period worked better.
- Summer school attendance was increased, especially for struggling primary and middle school students.
- The number of study halls was reduced because most students do not use study halls productively and regular tutoring sessions were substituted.
- Extra periods at the beginning or end of the school day were added and used for giving struggling students additional help.
- Students in the National Honors Society and the international baccalaureate program provided peer tutoring.

Teachers Were Inspired to Work Harder

> [Teachers] worked above and beyond the contract. Nobody asks them to do it.... I've never worked in a place like this before! (Principal of an All-Regents high school)

> The [teachers] were willing to give their every effort and time above and beyond the school day. They would stay for hours on end late in the...evening.... She [the principal] presented it so well. She's just a motivator! (School secretary at the same All-Regents high school)

In many schools, teachers were given more time for tutoring by relieving them of hall duties, lunchroom supervision, and study hall supervision. In one school, the position of department chair was eliminated and the time formerly given to department chairs was reallocated to teaching and tutoring. In some schools, teaching assignments were no longer allocated by seniority. The best teachers were reassigned to classes with significant numbers of struggling students. In some schools teaching assistants who were fully qualified teachers were hired to provide tutoring. Nighttime review sessions were offered in the months preceding the Regents exams. Teacher contracts were not renegotiated, but local union leaders sometimes chose not to make an issue of things that in the past might have led to a grievance.

In one district, many teachers could not adapt to the new procedures and decided to leave. Young teachers who believed the All-Regents goal was both desirable and feasible were hired as replacements.

Implications for State Policy

Requiring all students to reach the Regents standard in five core subjects will significantly increase student achievement, college attendance and completion, and the quality of jobs that students get after high school. The biggest beneficiaries of the policy will be the students, often from disadvantaged backgrounds, who have been encouraged or allowed to avoid rigorous courses in the past. In the All-Regents high schools there was a major reallocation of teacher time and resources toward struggling students, whose achievement increased the most. Administrators reported that college enrollment rates increased after they shifted to All-Regents.

It is not always clear, however, that the parents of struggling students will see it that way. When the principal of an All-Regents high school was asked who opposed the elimination of the easier local courses, she said:

> Parents of children...who...felt [their kids] couldn't do it.... [One parent approached her in the school parking lot.] She started yelling at me. She told me she hated the All-Regents high school. Her kids were not as successful. If you sit in a consumer math class you get a 90. If you sit in a sequential math class, you have to struggle to get a 65.... She was very angry about it.... Parents are a big obstacle....

> Your kids don't want to do this. They're going to complain about it. Which means you are going to work harder as a parent.

Once students start failing Regents exams and having to repeat courses in order to graduate, there will be a crescendo of complaints. Claims will be made that schools have not done enough to help students succeed on the new exams. How can the Regents and the state legislature assist local schools to meet their obligation to help students meet the new higher standards? How can the number of dropouts and graduation delays be minimized?

Most important, the amount of time that struggling students spend on the task of learning must be increased. This is the central recommendation of a representative group of teachers, school administrators, and parent representatives that was convened by New York State's Commissioner of Education to recommend to the Board of Regents means of minimizing the number of students failing to meet the new higher learning standards. This group, inelegantly named the Safety Net Study Group, recommended a radical increase in the amount of instruction that struggling and disadvantaged students receive. The following is quoted extensively from their final recommendations:

> The success of this upgrading of standards will depend on a systemic program of prevention and intervention strategies that each district and, in turn, each school must provide. These strategies include, but are not limited to:
>
> - Providing extra learning opportunities through extended time for students in need of this service.
> - Providing clear direction to students and their parents of what is expected of the student, what is the student's current academic status and what the student still needs to do to earn a Regents diploma.
> - Providing a transitional program from elementary to middle school and from middle school to high school.
> - Providing a clearly defined promotional policy so that all students and their parents understand the criteria from grade to grade.
>
> **Recommendation 1—Grade Specific Curriculum:** Each school district and, in turn, each school should be required to have grade specific curriculum consistent with State standards.... If a district does not meet the learning standards, then State intervention procedures will be implemented [the State intervention program is referred to as Schools Under Registration Review].

> **Recommendation 2—Extra Help/Extra Time:** Each school district should have, at every grade level, an assessment system to provide information on student performance and to prepare all students to meet the standards.... Enrichment and remediation programs should be provided as additions to and to reinforce core courses of study as opposed to "pullout" programs. [Pullout programs take struggling students out of their regular class to give them small group instruction by a resource teacher.] The state should revise the commissioner's Regulations on remediation...to require that students receive the extra help/extra time they may need to meet the standards. These students enrichment and remedial activities will be provided within the school year, including after school instruction, evening instruction, Saturday instruction, etc.
>
> **Recommendation 3—Mandatory Summer School:** When a student fails to meet academic expectations, based on grade-level assessments, then that student would be required to attend summer school.... Since the State is responsible for summer school, it would need both to revise the current summer school requirements and procedures to accommodate this expansion and to review and revise the current assessments provided during the summer sessions.... In addition the State would provide the necessary financial assistance to support the extra cost of mandatory summer school.
>
> **Recommendation 4—Professional Development:** ... Each district should provide professional development to all staff, kindergarten through grade 12, to enable them to assist students to meet the new graduation requirements....
>
> **Recommendation 5—Student Promotional Guidelines:** Each school district should have a plan that explains the movement of students from grade to grade (especially when they move between different school buildings) and identifies the ways that schools engage parents, students and other community members to help students understand and achieve higher standards.... (Safety Net Study Group, 1998, pp. 3–5)[5]

Schools with large numbers of struggling students should probably lengthen the school day and school year for all students, not just a targeted minority who are behind the rest. The Edison schools have been successful with this approach and a non-Edison public school in Massachusetts has successfully copied the idea. Why not contract with Edison to take over some urban public schools in New York or implement the idea in a few pilot schools?

The All-Regents schools the authors studied obtained large increases in teacher contact time with students by reorganizing teacher time and getting teachers to work above and beyond their contracted hours. Inspiring leadership that induces teachers to work way beyond the contract for no additional pay will not be available in most districts. Consequently, teachers will have to be paid extra for working longer hours. Costs of tutoring, longer school days, review sessions, and staff development are associated with preparing students for Regents exams and should not be subject to caps in state funding formulas. A special funding formula should be developed for districts that have large numbers of disadvantaged pupils and low first-grade test scores.

One of the most effective forms of professional development is serving on the committees that grade essays, multistep mathematics problems, and extended answer questions. Canadian teachers who have served on grading committees for their provincial exams describe it as "a wonderful professional development activity" (B.H., personal communication, May 18, 1996). Having to agree on what constituted excellent, good, poor, and failing responses to essay questions or open-ended science and math problems resulted in a sharing of perspectives and teaching tips that most found very helpful. Therefore, teachers should grade the Regents exams in centralized regional locations under the guidance of well-trained leaders. Scoring rubrics should be developed centrally to maintain consistent standards across the state.

What Will Happen to Dropout Rates?

Many school districts have already started shifting to an All-Regents curriculum in anticipation of the new requirements and the number of students taking Regents-level courses and passing Regents exams is increasing. Between 1995 and 1997, the proportion of students taking and passing Regents exams at the 65%-correct level rose from 50.3% to 56.3% in English, from 53% to 59% in Sequential Mathematics I, and from 41% to 44% in Biology.

Nevertheless, we predict extremely high failure rates—between 30% and 50% in some subjects—the first time Regents exams are administered to all students. Even if the reforms proposed previously were implemented immediately, they would not have been operating long enough to prevent this from happening. Many students will have to retake examinations after taking additional academic courses or special summer makeup courses. Will this generate a large increase in dropout rates as students despair of ever passing all five exams? We think not.

Our prediction is that New York students will respond the same way that European students respond to tough graduation requirements; they will study harder and stay in high school longer. The tougher graduation requirements will not be fully phased in until the class of 2003. We predict that 4 years later, in 2007, dropout rates will be at or below current levels. We predict that this will be accomplished without making the Regents exams easier than they are right now. We base this forecast on the following:

- When students discover how difficult the standards are, we expect them to react by studying harder. Teachers will gain experience in teaching to the new standards and will improve. Teachers who are unable to teach to the higher standards will leave the profession and be replaced by teachers who can.
- We expect that the firestorm that will result from the high failure rates in the first year will generate a large infusion of state aid directed specifically at helping struggling students and schools serving disadvantaged populations. The impending rise in graduation standards helped convince the legislature to increase school aid in the most recent budget cycle; much of the aid was targeted at expanding after-school programs and summer schools.
- The high-stakes exam will make teacher quality much more critical than in the past. The competition for quality teachers will drive their wages up. Parent support of more school spending will increase.
- We predict that the plan to increase the 55% passing standard on the Regents exams to 60% and then 65% will be indefinitely postponed.
- The Regents examination graduation requirement replaces a Regents Competency Test (RCT) graduation requirement that already sets a relatively high minimum, so the change in failure rates will not be as dramatic as many expect. In 1996, the ratio of the number of students failing a RCT to average enrollment per grade in the state was 21% in mathematics and global studies and 20% in science. In New York City, failure ratios on the RCT were above 40% in these three subjects.

- The Regents exam graduation requirement does not apply to all high school students in the state. The 10% of students who are in private schools are not covered. Special education students with an individual education plan are exempted.
- Many of the students who are unable to pass all five Regents exams at the 55% level will complete high school by transferring to a private high school or a GED program. A transfer to a GED program is considered a switch to another kind of school, not dropping out of school.

Let us imagine, however, that our prediction of stable or rising high school completion rates is wrong. Would a 2% to 4% decline in completion rates imply that increasing graduation requirements was a mistake? No. Focusing solely on graduation rates mistakes symbol for substance. What counts is how much students learn, not what proportion of them have a specific paper credential. It is the competencies developed in high school that enable a student to survive and thrive in college, not the diploma. Many community colleges admit students without diplomas. Higher standards will result in all students learning more on average (Bishop, 1996a). Those who graduate will be more competent and will be able to command a better wage in the labor market. The section on the effect of MCE graduation requirements on college attendance and wages demonstrates that this effect is quite large—MCEs cause a 3% to 4% increase in average wage rates. The average high school dropout will also be more competent and this too will result in higher pay. College attendance rates will be higher, and those affected in this way will be big gainers. There will be losers—the hypothesized 2% to 4% of the age cohort who would have graduated under the old standards but do not under the higher standards. Altonji and Pierret's (1997) regression predicts that dropping out generates approximately an 18% reduction in earnings in the first year out of school and a 6% loss in the twelfth year out (assuming no change in test scores). These losses pale by comparison to the greater than 4% wage-rate gains experienced by the 96% to 98% of young people whose completed years of schooling are not changed by the higher standards.

ENDNOTES

1. Surveys of college admission officers suggest they are increasing the weight they attach to taking rigorous courses in high school and doing well in these courses. The high school grades have always been the first considered. Standardized test scores have now become the second most important consideration, displacing class rank. Class rank is becoming less important because an increasing number of high schools are refusing to calculate class rank.
2. The population of 17-year-olds was used as the base rather than 18-year-olds because the number of 18-year-olds may be inflated by immigration of college students and military personnel.
3. These controls for school characteristics and region may not be sufficient to avoid omitted variable bias. States and school districts with such exams may be different along unmeasured dimensions that have direct effects on wage levels. A positive selection bias is unlikely, however, because most states appear to have adopted MCEs as a response to a perception that the state's schools were failing to teach basic skills. By 1992, MCEs had been adopted by every southern state except Arkansas and Oklahoma. With the exception of New Mexico, none of the mountain, plains, or Midwestern states had established an MCE prior to 1992.
4. The stakes for teachers and school administrators are higher because information on numbers of students taking and passing each exam are published in local newspapers and on the Internet. Though student stakes are low compared to European and Asian curriculum-based examination systems, they appear to be sufficient to substantially improve achievement of New York students. When the socioeconomic characteristics of students are controlled, New York State students outperform comparable students in other states by about one grade-level equivalent (Bishop, Moriarty, & Mane, 1998).
5. This recommendation was intended to induce school districts to consider ending social promotion at transitions between elementary and middle school and between middle and high school. It leaves the decision in the hands of local school boards, teachers, and administrators. State mandates on grade promotion specifying specific competencies that must be achieved are not feasible or desirable. The committee felt that the best way of responding to the needs of struggling students was to provide extra instruction during the school year and during the summer. The threat of retention is, currently, often used to induce students to attend summer school or after-school programs. Because students naturally want to advance to the next grade with their friends, the possibility of being retained (particularly at transitions between buildings) is a powerful incentive to study. This option, however, should be actually employed only as a last resort. Grade retention rates are quite high in ninth grade in New York State. It might make more sense to make graduation from middle school more contingent on student achievement in order to induce middle school students to work harder and their teachers to set higher standards.

REFERENCES

Altonji, J., & Pierret, C. (1997). *Employer learning and statistical discrimination.* Evanston, IL: Northwestern University.

Bishop, J. (1990). The productivity consequences of what is learned in high school. *Journal of Curriculum Studies, 22*(2), 101–126.

Bishop, J. (1996a). The impact of curriculum-based external examinations on school priorities and student learning. *International Journal of Education Research 23* (8), pp. 653–752.

Bishop, J. (1996b). Incentives to study and the organization of secondary instruction. In W. Becker & W. Baumol (Eds.), *Assessing Educational Practices* (pp. 99–160). Cambridge, MA: MIT Press.

Bishop, J. H., Moriarty, J., & Mane, F. (1998). Diplomas for learning: not seat time. *Educational finance to support high learning standards.* Albany, NY: The State University of New York and State Education Department.

Bureau of the Census. (1993). *1990 census of population: Social and economic characteristics.* Washington, DC: Department of Commerce, U.S. Government Printing Office.

Farber, H., & Gibbons, R. (1996). Learning and wage dynamics. *Quarterly Journal of Economics 111*(4), 1007–1047.

Heller, J. (Executive Producer) (1990, September 6). *America's toughest assignments: Solving the education crisis.* New York: CBS Broadcasting System.

Johnson, J. (1995). *Assignment incomplete: The unfinished business of education reform.* New York: Public Agenda.

Johnson, J., & Farkas, S. (1997). *Getting by: What American teenagers think about their schools.* New York: Public Agenda.

Kulik, J. A., & Kulik, C. (1984). Effects of accelerated instruction on students. *Review of Educational Research 54*(3), 409–425.

Lerner, B. (1990). Good news about American education. *Commentary 91*(3), 19–25.

Lillard, D. (1997). *The effects of state mandates and markets on time to completion and high school dropout decisions* (pp.1–32). Ithaca, NY: Cornell University Press.

Lillard, D., & DeCicca, P. (1997a). *The effects of state graduation requirements on high school dropout decisions* (pp. 1–27). Ithaca, NY: Cornell University Press.

Lillard, D., & DeCicca, P. (1997b). *State education policy and dropout behavior: An empirical investigation* (pp. 1–23). Ithaca, NY: Cornell University Press.

Monk, D. (1994). Subject area preparation of secondary mathematics and science teachers and student achievement. *Economics of Education Review 13*(2), 125–145.

Monk, D., & Hussain, S. (1998). Resource allocation implications of increased high school graduation expectations. In J. Wycoff (Ed.), *Educational finance to support high learning standards* (pp. 27–53). Albany, NY: New York State Board of Regents.

National Center for Education Statistics. (1991). *Education in states and nations.* Washington, DC: U.S. Department of Education.

National Center for Education Statistics. (1992). *The digest of education statistics: 1992.* Washington, DC: U.S. Department of Education.

National Center for Education Statistics. (1993a). *The digest of education statistics: 1993.* Washington, DC: U.S. Department of Education.

National Center for Education Statistics. (1993b). *Dropout rates in the United States 1992.* Washington, DC: U.S. Department of Education.

National Center for Education Statistics. (1994). *Literacy in the labor force.* Washington, DC: U.S. Government Printing Office.

National Center for Education Statistics. (1996). *The digest of education statistics: 1996.* Washington, DC: U.S. Department of Education.

Safety Net Study Group. (1998, June). *Providing fairness and maintaining high standards for all students.* Report to the commissioner of education. Albany, NY: New York State Department of Education.

Tinkelman, S. (1966). *Regents examinations in New York State after 100 years.* Albany, NY: The University of the State of New York.

Ward. (1994, January). A day in the life. *N.Y. Teacher*, pp. 1–4.

10

Contracted Solutions to Urban Education Problems

James W. Guthrie
Vanderbilt University

The recent worldwide economic downturn has blunted some of the rationale for American education reform. The American economy now clearly leads the world and the education doomsday message initiated 15 years ago by *A Nation at Risk* appears, at least, to have been premature. However, regardless of the rhetoric about education and our collective economic fate, the American citizenry has maintained its personal interest in school reform, and nowhere is this more accurate than among inhabitants of our big cities. However, city school districts are caught between two contrasting views of what constitutes education reform. One paradigm suggests that higher achievement results from individual schools complying with centrally promulgated regulations. The other strategy places individual schools at the center of reform and argues to construct enabling policies in support of them. This chapter describes those contrasting strategic views of reform and explains their practical consequences.

EDUCATION REFORM MAY HAVE LOST ITS CONVENTIONAL *RAISON D'ÊTRE*

The 1983 *A Nation at Risk* used hyperbole and drumbeat alliteration to drive home the message that low academic achievement was about to economically sink the United States. The education systems of our

European and Asian economic competitors were portrayed as dynamic engines fueling a productive labor force to which we were likely to succumb (Johnson, 1982). The high academic standards of these nations were repeatedly portrayed as models for the United States to emulate (Coy, 1986). Only if we achieved similar levels of academic excellence could we as a nation hope to survive. The entire undertaking was remarkably reminiscent of the rhetoric surrounding the 1957 launching of Sputnik. The only difference with *A Nation at Risk* was that the external threat was economic and commercial, not military and technological.

Release of *A Nation at Risk* triggered the formation of hundreds of state- and local-level task forces, blue ribbon panels, and strategic planning groups empowered to design and redesign the American education system. Legislatures could not enact new statutes fast enough. High school graduation standards were intensified; college admission requirements were elevated. New textbooks were written. Homework assignments were imposed until parents became exhausted. Advanced placement classes were extolled. State testing systems were constructed. School board members, administrators, and teachers were exhorted to work harder and hold higher standards for themselves and their students.

Despite the well-intentioned efforts of states and school districts, matters apparently did not improve. Six years later, President Bush and the nation's governors met in Charlottesville, Virginia, and dedicated the nation to a set of laudable and rigorous national education goals. Even as recently as 1996 and 1999, governors and business officials reconvened at IBM's headquarters in New York and rededicated their commitment to enacting content and performance standards and achieving higher levels of academic excellence.

In some ways, the United States' desperate attempt to reform appeared hopeless. How could an entire nation be elevated educationally in sufficient time to overcome the imminent twin perils of domestic decay and international subjugation? However, by the beginning of the 1990s, a set of counterclaims began to emerge. Authors, analysts, and public school advocates such as Gerald Bracey (1995), the Sandia National Laboratory (Carson, Huelskamp, & Woodall, 1991), David Berliner and Bruce Biddle (1995), and Richard Rothstein (1998) repeatedly reported that despite critics' appraisal of our nation's academic performance, it was no worse than it had ever been.

Others began to look more closely at claims regarding U.S.

international academic default. Whereas it was still clear that most of our 12th-grade students could not stand up to international colleagues in science and mathematics, our 4th- and 8th-graders did much better. Moreover, comparisons of international 12th-grade scores with those of several selected states proved that there were components of the American education system that, contrary to widespread perception, could hold their own against overseas competition.

Once learning of America's apparent economic health, European and Asian self-confidence eroded and performance anxiety set in. The economies of our global competitors disintegrated. The Japanese yen sank. European unemployment soared. Russia raced to the edge of economic oblivion. Once touted second-world tigers such as Malaysia, Thailand, and Indonesia, despite having education systems with high expectations, were on the verge of civic chaos and had to be bailed out economically by the International Monetary Fund. Financial markets shuddered to think what would happen in places with really poor education systems such as Brazil.

As the 20th century has drawn to a close, matters appear to have reversed themselves. Though much beyond our shores appears economically dismal, the U.S. economy, the same economy that only 16 years before was presumed imperiled by a rising tide of educational mediocrity, is about to set a new record for sustained growth. After 4 or 5 years of unemployment rates routinely below 5%, we are redefining theoretical full employment. We have reduced welfare rolls; accepted millions of new immigrant workers into our midst; cut back on federal government employees and armed forces personnel; undergone numerous corporate downsizings; substituted technology for labor in virtually every undertaking; absorbed women, baby boomers, and senior citizens into the workforce; and we are still short of labor. All the while, given this economic growth, inflation has remained at unexpectedly low levels.

A POSSIBLE NEW REFORM DRIVER: INDIVIDUAL ECONOMIC INTERESTS

While policy wonks have been gyrating and debating, the American people have steadfastly kept education a priority. Poll after poll reveals that U.S. citizens want a better education system. This has been true throughout the debate about our possible economic inundation by foreign trading powers. This concern for improving education is particularly evident from polling results of citizens regarding big-city schools and from big-city parents. Eighty-six percent of respondents in the most recent Kappan poll (Rose & Gallup, 1998) indicated that improving inner-city schools is very important. Another 10% said it is fairly important to improve inner-city schools. There was no variation in response among the demographic groups polled.

If our collective well-being is not as clearly connected with national education achievement levels as may have been naively argued by authors of *A Nation at Risk*, then why do citizens continue to care individually about education reform? The answer may reside in a far more micro world.

In a 1994 *Atlantic Monthly* article, Peter Drucker argued that the United States is undergoing a social transformation. He contended that the high-wage jobs available throughout most of the 20th century to low-educated workers are evaporating. A high school dropout can no longer expect to find a manufacturing job paying $50,000 annually, making the link between a higher lifetime income and higher levels of schooling more evident than ever. To drop out of high school now is to place one's self at substantial risk of holding a low-income job (Drucker, 1994).

Also, whatever one can say about U.S. school achievement in general, one cannot say regarding big-city achievement in particular. The academic achievement of urban students is lower than that of surrounding suburban districts and of states in general. Urban children overwhelmingly suffer from poverty. Urban school districts disproportionately serve disabled and limited-English-speaking students. Their teachers tend to be less qualified, their buildings larger and older, their leadership unstable, their management strategies less effective, and their governance mechanisms and political dynamics vulnerable to special interests and those less concerned with academic achievement (see Chubb & Moe, 1990; Consortium on Renewing Education [CORE], 1998).

Thus, citizens and their elected officials, particularly state and urban officials, have been seeking solutions to America's achievement challenge. President Clinton has proposed national examinations, national payments for smaller class sizes, tax relief for parents paying their children's college tuition, and federal dollars for school construction. The Republican Party, nationally, has been less focused on a strategy but generally has advocated voucher plans, charter schools, and state and local initiatives.

A BATTLE FOR THE PERCEPTIONS OF POLICYMAKERS AND REFORMERS

Outside the glare of the media spotlight and electioneering rhetoric, a quieter battle is being waged for the intellectual soul of education reform. This is an academic or conceptual conflict over the paradigm, or fundamental road map, that should undergird education reform efforts. The issue is abstract but the practical consequences are significant.

The description that follows is deliberately overdrawn. The effort here is to crystallize the two sets of strategic ideas in their most oppositional form so that a reader can thereby understand the essence of the difference. In fact, the two paradigms do share several common features, and when the time comes to translate paradigm consequences into policy practice, there are places where the two models overlap in reality. Still, when distilled, here is the difference.

A POLICY-CENTERED PARADIGM

The principal proponent of this point of view is the Consortium for Policy Research in Education (CPRE), the federally funded think tank centered at the University of Pennsylvania.

The CPRE systemic reform paradigm is displayed in Figure 10.1. Here a reader can see that the principal reform dynamic is *policy alignment*. The assumption is made that if important policy levers, controlled by the state and to a lesser degree by local school districts, can be properly specified and aligned then their combined impact on schools will be positive. Student achievement is held to respond to the various regulations and inducements that will result from such coherence and alignment (Fuhrman, 1994).

In this depiction of reform, schools are taken to be nodes in an administrative neural network. Schools will certainly be more effective, the paradigm holds, if teachers, students, and parents know what subject-matter content and learning outcomes are expected, if textbooks and computer programs used in classes are aligned with these content standards, if state and local tests examine a student's grasp of this content, if teachers are trained to instruct in this content, if staff development activities are consistent with these expectations, and so on.

In this depiction of the ideal policy world for education, the

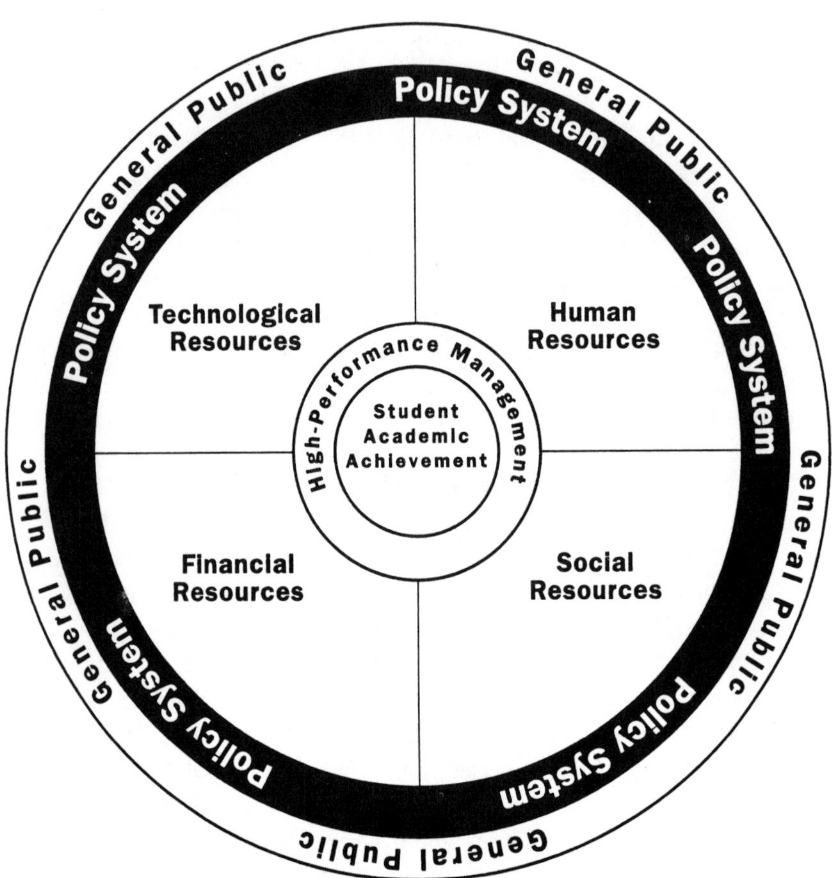

FIG. 10.1. The CPRE Systemic Reform Paradigm

individual school is viewed as an operational recipient of these good policies. If the policies are correct and consistent, then this harmonic convergence of preferences should trigger higher student performance. The important policy lever is compliance. If the policies are correct, then there should be little deviation on the part of a school. Schools should not be seen as empowered agents and free to set their own courses of action. To provide schools with such discretion would be to run the risk that they might take actions that would disalign some element of the policy web.

This has proven to be an attractive strategy. State after state has pursued the construction and adoption of content standards. Efforts have been made to promote testing aligned with such standards. Multiple task forces have operated nationally to persuade states to adopt credentialing standards and to get schools of education to undertake teacher training in a manner consistent with these content standards. The Clinton administration proposals regarding national examinations are in large part based on this model of education reform.

It should be mentioned that this strategy of alignment closely matches what is generally taking place overseas in other developed nations with highly centralized education systems.

A SCHOOL-CENTERED PARADIGM

Figure 10.2 depicts the Consortium on Renewing Education (CORE) paradigm. CORE is a foundation-sponsored association of academic, civic, and business officials interested in education reform.

The CORE paradigm assumes that the school is a unique hybrid organization. Like a corporation, it is composed of fungible resources and specific people with definite skills and knowledge, all tied together by some overall conception of how the people, money, and equipment combine to deliver instruction and help students learn and develop skills, habits, and values. The CORE paradigm views the school as a community in that it requires and develops bonds of trust among the people who work within it, parents, neighbors, and the broader society. The school is productive because it has the incentive and the capacity to adapt its educational program to changing needs, both those of its students and of the society and economy that students will someday enter (Hill & Guthrie, 1999).

The CORE paradigm is almost the converse of the systemic

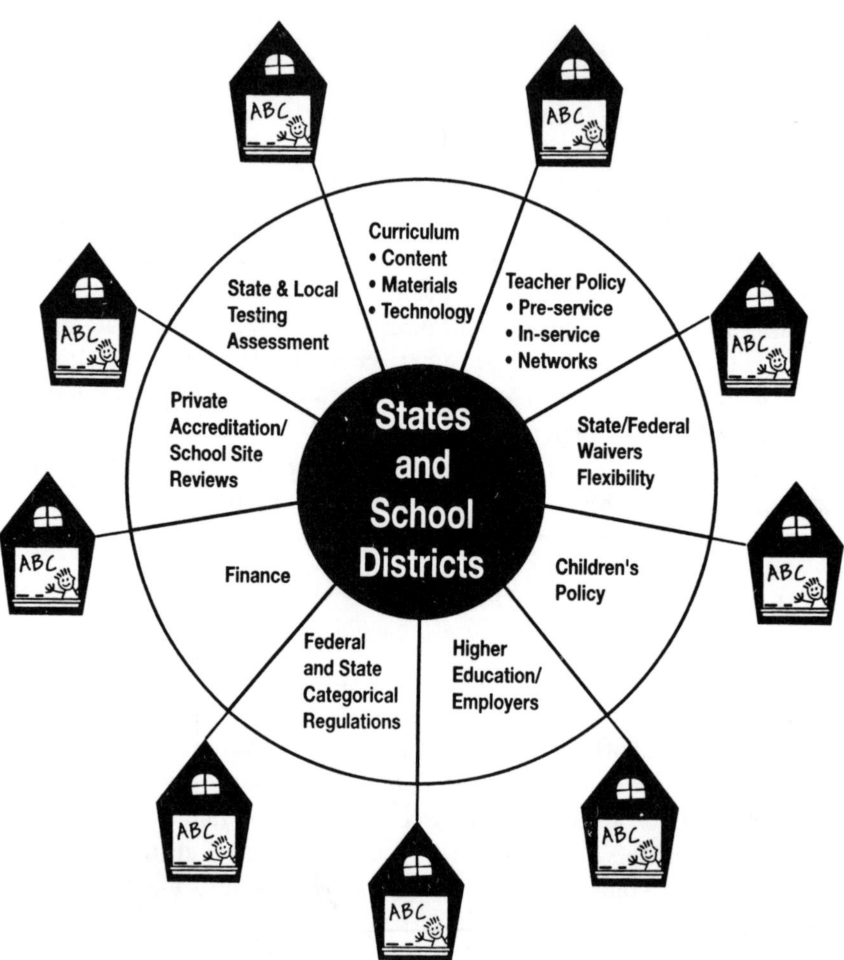

FIG. 10.2. The CORE Paradigm

reform paradigm. CORE places the individual school at the center of action and then searches for means by which the policy environment can facilitate and reinforce the actions of the school. The CORE assumption is that an effective school possesses a difficult-to-capture but nonetheless real trait labeled *integrative capacity*. Integrative capacity is the characteristic that likely distinguishes effective from ineffective schools.

Integrative capacity is the set of organizing principles that suggests the manner in which a school should deploy its resources, namely its human, social, political, and financial capital. All schools have some integrative capacity. Even failing or weak schools have capital resources; they just do not consciously or deliberately array them for purposes of attaining high academic achievement.

The CORE paradigm suggests that policies, no matter how well intended, can in fact disrupt the performance of a school, even when such policies convey added resources. Federal programs intended to benefit low-income youngsters, until recent Title I alterations, often constricted the heart of a school by insisting that youngsters be pulled out of class-rooms and placed with specialized teachers for part of the instructional time. Such actions interrupt effective schooling and poignantly display the dysfunctional effect of policies that focus on regulation rather than individual student achievement.

PARADIGMS COMPARED

The CPRE policy-centered paradigm attempts to take advantage of schools' resource dependency on government. Because schools are agents of states and local districts, they are ill positioned to reject policies issued from such sources. To reject such policies is to risk the continued flow of resources. Regulatory compliance is not only assumed, it is to be desired in the CPRE model. The challenge is to design policies so that they are deserving of being complied with (Hill & Celio, 1998).

The CORE school-centered paradigm takes resource dependency to be the principal weakness in today's large school systems. Here, resource dependency is the evil to be overcome. In the CORE paradigm, it is this very dependency that interferes with and interrupts the efforts of successful schools to design and implement their own management strategy, to effectively construct an integrative capacity that will lead to academic achievement. The CORE paradigm seeks means for attenuating or diluting resource dependency.

Questions raised by the CORE paradigm are significantly different from those derived from the traditional policy research paradigm that starts with policymakers' tools and asks how they can be used to change schools in ways desired by public officials (Hill & Marks, 1982; McDonnell & Elmore, 1987). The conventional policy research framework regards the school as a receiver of assets created elsewhere and as an implementer of decisions made by a central school board.

The CORE paradigm does not eliminate the need for research and policy discussions structured by other paradigms—as long as schools are publicly funded and subject to oversight by public officials, there will be some need for the policy-research paradigm. However, a new framework like the CORE paradigm described previously is required to structure research on how to strengthen schools as active agents and problem solvers, rather than as passive responders to outside forces.

Much current educational policy and research treat the school as a black box: things are done to or for the school, not by it. Assets (staff members, equipment) are added to or subtracted from schools. Constraints in the form of new goals, performance quotas, testing programs, and regulations are imposed on schools by school boards and funding agencies. New curricula and staff training programs are selected for whole districts and then infused into schools. Budget shortfalls are met by mandated districtwide reductions in school staffing or services. Such policies are always intended to make schools better, stronger, or fairer places. But, as decades of research in education and other areas of public service have shown (Berman & McLaughlin, 1979; Bryk, Lee, & Holland, 1993; Darling-Hammond, 1997; Newmann, 1996; Newmann, Rigdon, & King, 1997), productive schools are communities that take their own initiatives and assume responsibility for children's learning; they are not passive material ready to be molded (Table 10.1).

CITY SCHOOLS AS A PARADIGM BATTLEGROUND

Urban schools are the locus of competition between these two strategic paradigms. Rural schools are generally small and the mechanisms by which they are shaped and controlled are frequently tightly linked to local parent preferences and community values. Other than to ensure that they are funded, most states impose few policy imperatives on remote and sparsely populated schools.

Suburban schools may be parts of larger units. However, by virtue of greater socioeconomic homogeneity, their clients and residents are able to maintain greater control over their schools.

Big cities are different because the constituency for achievement in urban settings has been uniquely diluted. Urban parents want better schools and higher achievement for their children. This is made clear in their responses to opinion polls and the intensity with which poll respondents support alternative schooling arrangements when provided with an opportunity. Since 1994, the Kappan poll (Rose & Gallup, 1998) has asked respondents if they favored the idea of allowing parents to send children to the public, private, or parochial school of their choice with part or all of the tuition being paid by the government. In 1998, 51% of respondents favored this idea, while 45% opposed it. Public school parents expressed their support of the idea as well, with 56% approving and 40% disapproving. The 1998 results demonstrate a reversal in margins over the 1996 results, when 43% of respondents supported the idea and 54% opposed it. In terms of demographics, the groups most likely to support the idea in 1998 were non-Whites (68%) and 18-to-29-year-olds (63%), while those most likely to oppose the idea were individuals age 50 to 64 (56%) and those living in rural areas (56%).

The results of the 1998 Kappan poll (Rose & Gallup, 1998) also indicate that Americans generally understand the problems of big-city schools and would like to see these problems addressed. From 1989–1993, support for improving inner-city schools rose from 74% to 81%. Two thirds of respondents in the 1998 poll indicated a willingness to pay more taxes to improve inner-city schools. Non-Whites (79%), Democrats (74%), 50-to-64-year-olds (78%), and manual laborers (73%) comprise the groups most willing to pay taxes to improve inner-city schools; furthermore, no identifiable groups indicated an unwillingness to pay taxes to improve inner-city schools.

However, the voices of parents and the public seem to get lost easily in the cacophony of city politics. Historic alterations in city government and demographic dynamics have provided narrow, nonacademic, political interests with a particularly strong purchase on city schools' governance. Nowhere is the pressure for schools to serve multiple purposes more intense. Nowhere is the political agenda forced on schools so complicated, cross-pressured, discordant, or disruptive. Only state leaders

TABLE 10.1
Different Paradigms Identify Different Questions About How to Improve School Performance*

	Policy Research Paradigm	CORE Paradigm
School purposes and productivity (integrative capital)	How shall public officials define schools' goals and ensure that every school pursues priorities set by public deliberation?	How can a school adopt and implement a clear theory of teaching and learning that meets the needs of its students? What can impede schoolwide integration? What sources of help are available to help schools choose and implement integrating theories of instruction?
Sources and uses of funds (financial capital)	How shall public officials determine the proper amounts and uses of funds for schools, and ensure that schools use funds as intended?	How can schools stabilize income and manage money and risks? How can they make prudent trade-offs between current services and future performance?
Sources, quality, and effectiveness of teachers (human capital)	How shall public officials determine what skills teachers need, ensure that schools have access to properly prepared teachers, and invest in in-service programs to ensure teacher quality?	How can schools define their staff needs, choose between alternatives of hiring new staff and training existing staff, and find qualified people to hire? How can public officials ensure that schools have a wide range of high-quality choices?

Parental and community support (social capital)	What rules should public officials enact to ensure that school staff take parental and community views and aspirations seriously?	How can a school clarify its promises and demands so that teachers and parents know what to expect? How can school leaders balance personalization and responsiveness to parents with the need to keep promises about academic and behavioral standards? How diverse a set of expectations can a school meet?
School's legitimacy as a public institution (political capital)	What rules must all schools follow if they are to be considered public? How should public officials respond to a school's failure to comply with basic rules?	How can schools build and keep the confidence of public officials and voters, while maintaining the freedom of action necessary for self-improvement?

**Note:* From Hill & Guthrie (1999). Copyright 1999 by Jossey-Bass. Adapted by permission.

with the cooperation of mayors and other city government and education officials can overcome this condition and reestablish and sustain a high-priority demand in public schools for academic achievement.

WHAT WENT WRONG IN OUR CITIES?

One hundred years ago, city schools were among the nation's finest educational institutions. Families moved to cities in order to obtain public schooling for the children. What happened? How did such a reversal come about?

Many hypotheses exist. We do not choose here to dispute any particular explanation. However, a piece of history is important. At the beginning of this century, four important reform movements coincided. Each of these had dramatic, negative, and long lasting effects on cities, and the four conditions were mutually reinforcing.

Creating Monster Districts. Near the turn of the last century, with hardly a shred of supportive evidence, a coalition of education professors, business leaders, and civic officials began a national effort to consolidate small school districts and eliminate small schools. They claimed that small was economically and educationally ineffective. They were remarkably successful in promoting this interest. By 1950, the number of school districts had been reduced dramatically, and the reduction continues to this day. In 1929 there were approximately 127,000 local school districts. Today, there are less than 15,000. While this consolidation took place, enrollments grew dramatically. Whereas in 1950 the modal American school held 300 students, today it enrolls more than 600 students. The consequence of consolidation was a legacy of larger and more impersonal organizations for all of American education. However, this condition was intensified in cities where population growth was greatest.

Stifling Public Participation. The outcome of Progressive Era muckraking was an effort to insulate education from partisan politics. Big cities were particular targets. Here reformers eliminated ward-based school boards and centralized governance authority in citywide bodies, often appointed or at least nominated through nonpartisan mechanisms. The long-term effect of depoliticizing urban education has been to pull big-city school systems away from the elected officials who may care most about them, namely, mayors and city council members. Depoliticizing school district governance insulates schools from the concerns of the larger body politic. The result is an ability of specialized interests to dominate city school board politics and impose their narrow agenda over what may well be the preference of the larger population for improved schools and academic achievement.

Reinforcing Bureaucracy. Scientific management proponents and efficiency experts of the "cheaper by the dozen" era argued that schools could be managed like manufacturing plants, a "one best system" of education management. This movement, again intensely directed at big-city schools, reinforced the movement toward centralized bureaucracies.

Diluting Standards. Starting at the turn of the 20th century, professional educators began to argue for a more practical curriculum. They downplayed academic rigor in favor of occupational relevance. They claimed that immigrant children and the children of the poor, those beginning to dominate big-city school enrollments, could not cope with the intensity of a classical academic curriculum. An erosion of standards began and we took a step away from the rigorous courses that are an important basis for the complicated mathematics, science, and critical thinking so necessary in the 21st century.

Subsidizing Suburbia. The previously mentioned four interlocking debilities were exacerbated by the nation's post-World War II policy of subsidizing suburban growth. Federal funding for freeway systems and federally initiated, low-interest home loans put the American dream of home ownership within the grasp of tens of millions of middle-class Americans. These are the families who traditionally benefited from and supported public schools. When they reacted favorably to the incentives to move to suburbs, they took a valuable resource with them, namely, their political sophistication and access to power. Those who had little economic choice but to remain in cities struggled to fill this power vacuum and to protect their schools from special interests. In most cities, they lost, and school quality plummeted.

Suburbanization had another deleterious consequence for urban schools. The departure of large segments of the middle class deprived remaining students of another force for academic achievement, the human capital of middle-class students from whom economically poor students could learn. Middle-class departure also deprived schools of a large constituency to advocate academic achievement.

PARADIGMATIC CONSEQUENCES

Who cares what paradigm prevails? What practical consequence does it make? The differences are not as sharply defined in all instances as the foregoing discussion would imply. In fact, the school-based paradigm does not suggest that schools should be cast adrift from all organizational linkages and rendered completely independent. Even in a system of autonomous schools, there would be a need for a mechanism by which the polity could influence the curriculum and shape a minimum of what is taught. Social cohesion demands some kind of commonality across schools. Also, a set of completely autonomous schools would float free of standards; it would have no quality indicator mechanisms. Hence, the use of some kind of examination system, even one as loosely structured and voluntary as the current National Assessment of Education Progress, would be necessary.

However, there are other differences that may matter more. Under an extreme view of the policy-centered paradigm, permitting the individual school to select its personnel, principal, and teachers is of no consequence. Presumably, all personnel would have met rigorous state-promulgated licensing standards and thus should be considered as interchangeable cogs in a mechanical production process. Giving budgetary discretion to an individual school can be viewed as superfluous because centrally made resource allocation decisions are sufficient and, under this view of the world, no different than what decision makers at a school would make anyway. In a sense, the policy-centered paradigm is a rational, bureaucratic model that assumes it is possible to know what ought to be done and that regulations can be developed that promote production.

The school-based strategy argues for placing as much decision discretion as reasonable at the site of the individual school. Budgetary discretion, personnel decisions, discipline policies, staff-development activities, instructional material, and textbook decisions can all be made by individual schools. Modern inventory and distribution systems can facilitate the operation of individual sites in ways not possible in another era.

In short, the school-centered paradigm argues for charter schools and contract schools. Here are arrangements by which individual schools can operate in the public context, be relatively free of the resources of a central system, and be held accountable for their student performance results and parent satisfaction levels. Such arrangements also dilute the self-serving influence of school district employees on the political process and restore a greater voice for parents and school clients.

WHICH WILL PREVAIL?

The policy-centered, regulatory approach currently has the upper hand. Its advocates, mostly those who would prefer the status quo to a dramatic alteration in authority relationships, hold the balance of power. The transaction costs that must be borne by those who desire to change the paradigm are substantial and the benefits are unclear. Advocates of change are not as well organized as those who benefit from current arrangements. Conversely, the latter are fully aware of the resource risks to them posed by proposals for change and are, therefore, quite willing to undertake the political and organizational efforts necessary to maintain the status quo.

However, an equilibrium point may be reached if it becomes evident to a sufficiently broad political majority that the regulatory approach is incapable of providing the higher levels of results necessary to ensure individual well-being in a knowledge society. In such a context, there may be greater long-run political support for adapting a school-centered paradigm.

REFERENCES

Berliner, D. C., & Biddle, B. J. (1995). *The manufactured crisis: Myths, fraud and the attack on America's public schools*. Reading, MA: Addison-Wesley.

Berman, P., & McLaughlin, M. W. (1979). *Federal programs supporting educational change: Vol. 4: The findings in review*. Santa Monica, CA: RAND.

Bracey, G. W. (1995). *Final exam: A study of the perpetual scrutiny of American public schools.* Bloomington, IN: Agency for Instructional Technology.

Bryk, A. S., Lee, V. E., & Holland, P. B. (1993). *Catholic schools and the common good.* Cambridge, MA: Harvard University Press.

Carson, C. C., Huelskamp, R. M., & Woodall, T. D. (1991). *Perspectives on education in America: Systems studies department*. Albuquerque, NM: Sandia National Laboratory.

Chubb, J. E., & Moe, T. M. (1990). *Politics, markets, and America's schools.* Washington, DC: Brookings Institution.

Consortium on Renewing Education. (1998). *20/20 vision: A blueprint for doubling academic achievement.* Nashville, TN: Peabody Center for Education Policy.

Coy, P. (1986, December 28). U.S. losing its edge in technology. *San Francisco Examiner,* p. 1.

Darling-Hammond, L. (1997). *The right to learn*. San Francisco: Jossey-Bass.

Drucker, P. (1994). The age of social transformation. *Atlantic Monthly, 274*(5), 53–80.

Fuhrman, S. (1994). *Politics and systemic education reform* (Policy brief). New Brunswick, NJ: Consortium for Policy Research in Education.

Hill, P. T., & Celio, M. B. (1998). *Fixing urban schools.* Washington, DC: Brookings Institution.

Hill, P. T., & Guthrie, J. W. (1999). A new research paradigm for understanding (and improving) twenty-first century schooling. In J. T. Murphy & K. S. Louis (Eds.), *Handbook on research in educational administration* (2nd ed., pp. 511–524). San Francisco: Jossey-Bass.

Hill, P. T., & Marks, E. L. (1982). *Federal influence over state and local government: The case of nondiscrimination in education.* Santa Monica, CA: RAND.

Johnson, C. (1982). *MITI and the Japanese miracle.* Stanford, CA: Stanford University Press.

McDonnell, L. M., & Elmore, R. F. (1987). Getting the job done: Alternative policy instruments. *Educational Evaluation and Policy Analysis, 9*(2), 133–152.

Newmann, F. M. (1996). *Authentic achievement.* San Francisco: Jossey-Bass.

Newmann, F. M, Rigdon, M., & King, M. B. (1997). Accountability and school performance: Implications from restructuring schools. *Harvard Educational Review, 67*(1), 41–74.

Rose, L. C., & Gallup, A. M. (1998). *1998 Phi Delta Kappa/Gallup poll of the public's attitudes toward the public schools.* Bloomington, IN: Phi Delta Kappan International.

Rothstein, R. (1998). *The way we were: The myths and realities of American student achievement.* New York: The Century Foundation.

EPILOGUE

Margaret C. Wang
Temple University Center for Research in Human Development and Education

Herbert J. Walberg
University of Illinois at Chicago

Two big and opposing ideas seem likely to continue radicalizing educational policy and practice—decentralization of decision making to citizens and parents, and centralization of decision making to the state and district levels, particularly by aggressive legislatures, state and local boards, and superintendents. Our title exemplifies these two views: The state or district direction of clear goals, best practices, accountability, and strong incentives exemplifies one trend. Representing the other trend are the growing numbers of charter schools, schools with parent governing councils, and private and public scholarships (previously and pejoratively called vouchers), which lodge more authority at the school level and with parents.

These two views, translated into reforms, can be called "bottom-up" and "top-down." The bottom-up reform assumes that parents and professional staff in each school best perceive their distinctive needs and means to achieve their unique goals. In potential or actual opposition is top-down reform that assumes standards, best practices, or best systems of practices that states or large districts more or less uniformly require of schools. Our purpose is to describe rather than endorse these reforms. In the end, however, we conclude that they are reconcilable and, in fact, being reconciled in policy and practice.

Both reforms diminish traditional control in which local boards mediated among state boards, local taxpayers, parents, teachers, and other groups that influence school policy. In business finance, the term *disintermediation* means cutting the layers and costs of middle managers allowing boards and chief executives closer access to customers and managers who serve them directly. Following business, the new trends tend to shrink the role of local boards and central office staff because money is concentrated in schools, and decisions are made by legislators and boards. Before explaining these trends more fully, let us consider why they are occurring.

WHAT CAUSED THE TRENDS?

First, money. To equalize local variations in expenditures and to improve education, state legislatures paid for ever larger shares of the total costs of schools. An old adage says that those who pay the piper call the tune. As the education fraction of the state budgets rose, legislators grew more attentive to school goals, policy, and accountability. They asked if the ever-increasing amounts of money were being spent wisely, efficiently, and well.

In addition, since the publication of *A Nation at Risk* in 1983, legislators and citizens have learned more fully that U.S. students have done poorly on international surveys of achievement. More recent research brought worse news. International achievement surveys in mathematics, science, reading, and other subjects show that the longer U.S. students are in school, the more they fall behind those in other countries. Near the end of secondary school, they score last among economically advanced Asian and European countries (Walberg, 1998). Because they fall behind while in elementary and secondary schools, the problem appeared to be more attributable to schooling than to child rearing and society. To legislators, moreover, money did not seem to be the problem. The per-student costs (adjusted for purchasing power) of schooling are higher in the United States than nearly all other economically advanced countries. Poor practices and lack of accountability seemed to be the problem. For example, after a quarter-century of refinement at a cost of about $120 billion, Chapter I/Title I showed little achievement advantage of children in the program over control groups (Walberg & Greenberg, 1999). Finally, unlike most other public and private enterprises, the productivity of U.S. schooling has declined: Inflation-adjusted costs have risen sharply whereas students have made similar or smaller gains in achievement (Organization for Economic Cooperation and Development, 1998; Walberg, 1998). Such analyses of productivity indicators among nations and across time have provoked much discussion among scholars, legislators, and citizens. All these developments led to the top-down and bottom-up trends displacing local boards and central staff as intermediaries.

Defining the Trends

Table 1 shows the ways in which the new trends differ from the old. A century ago, traditional local control was even more local than today. More than 100,000 local districts, many as small as a hundred students, raised money from local taxes and governed the schools. Some districts had one school; some schools had one classroom; board members knew many of the teachers and students. Today, after much consolidation, only about 15,000 districts survive, and many board members might be hard pressed to name all the schools much less the teachers.

TABLE 1
Means of Organizing K–12 Education

Function	*Traditional*	*New Trends ("Disintermediation")*	
Governance and Direction	Local Control	Increasing State Control	Increasing Citizen Control
	Intermediation	Centralization	Decentralization
	"Middle In"	"Top Down"	"Bottom Up"
Finance	Local District Boards	State Legislatures	Privately Funded Scholarships for Private Schools
Management	Local District Boards	State Legislatures	Publicly Funded Scholarships for Private Schools
Operations	Local District Boards	State Legislatures	School and Parent Leadership
Success Criterion	Local District Boards	State Legislatures	Achievement and Parent Satisfaction

Still, the dominant organizational form is traditional local control, in which the board raises funds and mediates among influence groups. The superintendent and central office staff manage budgets, hire teachers, and provide other central services. They share operational responsibilities with school leaders. Now changing, the traditional goals or criteria for success were often vague, a list to be fought over periodically, then put aside. Few boards could measure progress in outcomes. They looked at class sizes, facilities, and other inputs. As indicated in the table, state legislatures are increasingly specifying achievement goals, setting criteria for proficiency, prescribing management and operational practices, and measuring progress. Such prescription means less latitude for local boards, central office of the school districts, and school leaders and teachers.

Under centralization, the criterion for success is achievement on standardized tests, and increasingly the criterion has teeth. Fail the examinations and you will not graduate from high school. Continued failure, and the school gets put on notice and possibly the seeming humility of “technical assistance.” Without progress, the school closes or the staff is replaced.

The idea of progress or “value-added” achievement also poses a challenge to suburban and middle-class schools. If their socioeconomic composition is taken into consideration, are they gaining as much as comparable schools? Or even without an apples-to-apples comparison, can schools and districts measure up to the new state standards? Thought to be one of the richest and best districts in the United States, Fairfax County, Virginia, had high failure rates on the tough new state examinations.

Even more radical is the second new trend—more direct citizen control. Instead of having their preferences interpreted by local boards and school leaders, parents can increasingly “vote with their feet” by sending their children to competing public schools in their own or another district. Many state legislatures are considering plans to allow such children to go to parochial and independent schools. In Chicago and elsewhere, parents and other citizens also can elect representatives of local school councils that can allocate the budget, hire the principal and teachers, and in other ways exert more control.

Arguably, such citizen control restores an old tradition. For a century, local control was becoming less “local.” In ever larger sized districts, board members represented increasingly larger numbers of citizens and parents. By definition, any individual’s views had less numerical influence. In addition, the states increasingly financed and regulated schools, and acceptance of funds for categorical programs such as bilingual education also meant more regulations. Thus, today's growing direct governance of schools and parent choice represent trends counter to centralization. As indicated in the table, parent satisfaction along with achievement is the success criterion.

National Wingspread Conference on Reform Trends

Given the growing importance, radical nature, and different perspectives of these two trends, we assembled foremost scholars and practitioners on both sides of the centralization/decentralization question. The foregoing chapters are their writings about the research and experiences with programs implemented across the nation. With about two-dozen other scholars, state and federal leaders, superintendents, principals, teachers, union representatives, and parent leaders, they discussed their ideas for 2 intense days at Wingspread Conference Center of the Johnson Foundation, Racine, Wisconsin. The conference was sponsored by the National Center on Education in the Inner Cites (CEIC), the Laboratory for Student Success (LSS) at Temple University Center for Research in Human Development and Education (CRHDE), and the Johnson Foundation. The overall goals were to provide a national forum for examining findings from the latest and most significant research on decentralization and to showcase school systems and programs that appear to be effective in achieving student success.

The participants spent the conference time in small groups analyzing the commissioned papers and their own research and experiences. They discussed what is known from research and practical applications of the various reform strategies and their implications for next-step recommendations to advance schools' capacity for achieving student success. Despite their differing opinions, the conference participants respectfully heard and discussed views sharply different from their own. Finding some common ground, the conferees made constructive suggestions for improved policies and research that would be more definitive with respect to opposing views. Few converted to a contrary view on the major difference, but the conference attained our goals of better defining and analyzing the viewpoints, assembling scholarly research, and identifying effective practices. The rest of this chapter describes the major research findings, conclusions, and recommendations as we viewed them.

Consensual Conclusions

Although conferees with divergent views were not expected to achieve consensus, most agreed with several general conclusions drawn from the deliberations:

1. Even though some bright prospects can be cited, U.S. school systems, especially those in cities, are not performing well; they have not improved substantially since the 1983 publication of *A Nation at Risk.*
2. The continuing lack in progress has induced ever bolder reform strategies—increased parental choice, decentralized governance from states and districts to schools and parents, high standards that many students may not attain in the short run, a focus on core curricula and examinations, and specific accountability and incentives for educators to do better.
3. More research on the identification of ideal choice plans and best systems, policies, and practices is urgently needed. Recent research and experience suggest that some proposed changes are promising if not proven.
4. Both parental choice and best system practices require further trials and careful, rigorous, and independent evaluation and research.

PARENTAL CHOICE AND RECOMMENDATIONS

Parental choice includes both charter schools and scholarships. Charter schools are paid for and are accountable to the public for achievement and other matters, but they are governed by private boards and are, to varying degrees, independent of state regulations, local boards, and teachers' unions. "Weak" charter laws in some states, however, allow unsympathetic local boards to retain considerable operating control over charter school staff.

Much more controversial in educational circles are scholarships or vouchers. Private scholarships, now used in about 50 cities, are funded by both firms and wealthy individuals. They enable children and youth, usually from economically and educationally disadvantaged backgrounds, to attend private, that is, parochial and independent schools. As indicated in Table 1, public scholarships distribute publicly funded grants to parents, who can employ them in independent and parochial schools.

Many choice schools to which scholarship students may go are oversubscribed because parents believe they emphasize discipline and academic content. Contrary to common beliefs, the private schools to which scholarship students go are more racially integrated than public schools; their students have more positive interracial experiences in them, and their students more often endorse and engage in voluntary community causes. Through increased competition, moreover, the presence of choice schools appears to increase the effectiveness, cost-efficiency, and responsiveness of nearby public schools. Those convinced by the evidence on parental choice recommended that it be further expanded. Some recommended substantially expanding the number of more than 1,000 charter schools to accommodate parental preferences. Others believed that private and public scholarships demonstrate that largely freeing decision making from state regulations and local district boards is necessary to accommodate parental preferences. Those preferring choice observed that the poor and minority students in cities may benefit most from choice, but, in principle, choice should be extended to all students.

BEST SYSTEM FINDINGS AND RECOMMENDATIONS

Research and practitioner experience represented at the conference suggest a number of "best system practices" that appear to increase students' achievement. The general recommendations are the following:

- Basing planning on research.
- Identifying systemwide achievement goals.
- Aligning curriculum, teaching, and testing to goals.
- Decentralizing operational authority to the school level.
- Employing central information systems to monitor progress.
- Holding schools accountable for meeting standards.
- Providing alternatives in cases of failure.

This series of steps is not unlike the traditional Tylerian model of curriculum, consisting of goals, procedures, and evaluation, except that it distinguishes central direction and monitoring from decentralized operational responsibility.

The general recommendations are supported by the experiences of leaders of successful systems represented at the conference including the following:

- Decentralize state and district operational control. A state or district board can set achievement goals, allocate funds, and measure progress but delegate operational responsibilities to subordinate units within their purview while holding them accountable for results.
- Provide incentives. State and local boards, for example, may require students to pass examinations to graduate from high school. They may require minimum test scores of students before they are allowed to drop out. They may heavily regulate, replace the staff, or close failing schools. Staff that raise achievement or otherwise perform meritoriously can be financially and otherwise rewarded. Students who pass advanced placement examinations can graduate from high school and college earlier, which saves time and tax funds. The award of federal funds for categorical programs may be made contingent on accomplishment of results. Funds for unproven programs, practices, and policies may be reallocated to those proven effective and efficient.
- Emphasize a solid, balanced academic core curriculum.
- Set standards for teaching practices and measure the degree of implementation.
- Agree on standards of student achievement.
- Implement testing policies to measure attainment of the standards.
- Gather baseline and trend data on achievement and other outcomes of schools to measure progress over time.
- Engage universities, regional educational laboratories, and other research and development and technical assistance provider organizations to assist states, districts, and schools in implementing research-based innovations that work, particularly by providing instruments and procedures to measure classroom practices, achievement results, and parent views.
- Forge partnerships and joint programs among the national and local professional education associations.

- Establish coordination and collaborative partnerships among schools, social service, and health service organizations that are focused on educational improvement and student learning.
- Recruit teachers with broad knowledge of the liberal arts and sciences and a deep mastery of their teaching field; review and revise programs for the preparation of teachers and administrators; employ alternative certification programs to attract better teachers.
- Extend learning time through homework, after-school programs, and summer school; provide special services for students who do not meet new rigorous standards.
- Provide parents and the public with credible and reliable evidence on which they can base decisions about their children's education.
- Establish mechanisms or forums in which parents can voice their criticism of present systems of education.
- Issue a "consumer guide" to school reform models based on independent assessment of the features and results.
- Use public opinion data to measure the satisfaction of parents and the public with their schools.
- Investigate and experiment further with the apparently positive outcome effects of smaller schools and smaller school districts.

What Might Work Best?

The evidence on the two distinct reform strategies identified at the conference, parental choice and best system practices, is less than definitive, and discussions about what works and what doesn't remained divided. Yet, in view of the continuing achievement crisis, especially in big cites, substantial changes seem required. Well-designed, careful trials and evaluation of alternative policies, as in medicine, seem the best course.

In our view, moreover, federal, state, and local policies might be based on what research on both reform strategies to make provisions for parental choice and resulting competition among providers to foster best practices. For example, an integrated funding system might be established for categorical programs such as Title I, special education, and bilingual education (Wang, Reynolds, & Walberg, 1994), or states operating under the Ed-Flex waiver provision, as another example. State or local boards in turn might require potential recipients to submit research-based proposals for practices they would employ. They could be required to submit continuing evidence for the attainment of achievement and other outcomes.

Privately and publicly governed schools including charter and for-profit schools could compete for grants proportional to the number of categorical students attracted to their programs. Most students in such categorical programs could receive the full benefit of their regular school. The categorical grants, however, would give them additional specialized services after school, on Saturdays, and during summers at the same or another public or private school.

To restore the American tradition of local school control, the principle of combing choice and best systems might also be extended to states and local districts. They could, for example, set forth clear achievement standards. As long as schools meet these standards, they would remain free of operational regulation. They could be run as conventional, charter, or scholarship schools.

If, on the other hand, a school failed to attain standards or make acceptable progress, best practices could be externally encouraged or imposed. Visiting teams of successful educators might assist in suggesting best practices and evaluating progress. Schools that continued to fail might be reconstituted with new leaders and staff. Alternatively, they might be closed, in which case their students would be given scholarships to attend nearby public and private schools.

Many variations on the design and details of such systems might be considered. They might best be left to local public and private governing boards that are trying create and maintain schools in which children learn and parents are pleased with their offerings. In any case, we can look forward to seeing the outcomes of the new accountability and creative implementation of both best systems approaches and parental choice.

REFERENCES

Organization for Economic Cooperation and Development. (1998). *Education at a glance: OECD indicators.* Paris: Author.

Walberg, H. J. (1998, July). *Spending more while learning less.* Washington, DC: Thomas B. Fordham Foundation.

Walberg, H. J., & Greenberg, R. C. (1999). Educators should require evidence. *Phi Delta Kappan, 81*(2), 132–135.

Wang, M. C., Reynolds, M. C., & Walberg, H. J. (1994). Serving students at the margins. *Educational Leadership, 52*(4), 12–17.

AUTHOR INDEX

A

B

C

Y

Z

Subject Index

A

B

D

N

O

P

S

W